AMERICA SINCE WORLD WAR II

AMERICA SINCE WORLD WAR II

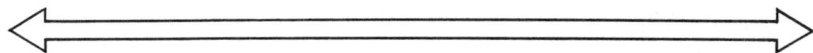

$\Longleftarrow\Longrightarrow$

Historical Interpretations

EDITED BY

Jean Christie

FAIRLEIGH DICKINSON UNIVERSITY

AND

Leonard Dinnerstein

UNIVERSITY OF ARIZONA

PRAEGER PUBLISHERS New York

Published in the United States of America in 1976
by Praeger Publishers, Inc.
111 Fourth Avenue, New York, N.Y. 10003

© 1976 by Praeger Publishers, Inc.

Library of Congress Cataloging in Publication Data
Main entry under title:

America since World War II.

Includes bibliographies.
   1. United States—History—1945-   —Addresses,
essays, lectures. 2. United States—Foreign relations—
1945-   —Addresses, essays, lectures. I. Christie,
Jean Olgilvy. II. Dinnerstein, Leonard.
E742.A65   973.92   74-29357

ISBN 0-275-85280-6

Printed in the United States of America

To
Robert Claus
and
Susan and Paul Yablon

CONTENTS

Preface   ix

I. THE BEGINNINGS OF POSTWAR AMERICA   1

BARTON J. BERNSTEIN, America in War and Peace:
The Test of Liberalism   7
ROBERT LASCH, The Origins of American Postwar
Foreign Policy   34
NORMAN DORSEN AND JOHN G. SIMON, McCarthy and the
Army: A Fight on the Wrong Front   48

II. AMERICAN MINORITIES   63

LEONARD DINNERSTEIN, Southern Jewry and the
Desegregation Crisis, 1954-1970   68
GERDA LERNER, The Feminists: A Second Look   79
BRUCE JACKSON, In the Valley of the Shadows: Kentucky   93
J. H. O'DELL, The Contours of the "Black Revolution" in
the 1970's   115
FRANCIS DONAHUE, The Chicano Story   126

III. RECENT FOREIGN POLICY 137

GABRIEL KOLKO, The United States in Vietnam, 1944-66:
Origins and Objectives 140
BARBARA TUCHMAN, The United States and China 172
J. WILLIAM FULBRIGHT, The Middle East—Myths and
Realities 184
ROGER MORRIS, WITH SHELLEY MUELLER AND WILLIAM JELIN,
The United States, the CIA, and Chile 216

IV. BICENTENNIAL: AN UNCERTAIN CELEBRATION 235

PAUL STARR, Rebels after the Cause: Living with
Contradictions 239
JAMES M. NAUGHTON AND OTHERS, Watergate: The House
Judiciary Committee Decides to Recommend the
Impeachment of President Richard M. Nixon 255
SIDNEY LENS, Running Out of Everything 272

PREFACE

We have gathered in this book a number of essays that bring out certain themes important to the American people during the past thirty years: the struggle for civil rights, the supposed menace of Communism, the appropriate role of the United States in the world, women's liberation, the plight of the poor, the position of minorities, student activism, the responsibilities of the press, the excesses of Presidential power, and the course of the economy. All these topics have been and still are the subjects of bitter debate and therefore have both a current and an historical interest.

The authors in this collection are historians, journalists, lawyers, and politicians. Among our criteria for including their work have been the validity of the insights and analyses expressed and, equally important, the writer's ability to present his or her views in a vivid and clear prose style.

Our selections, we must admit, reflect our own views and concern about the direction American society seems to be taking. We are disturbed by our government's allocation of resources. We believe that too much has been spent for military and defense purposes and that insufficient sums have been devoted to human needs. We are concerned that many people in this country are shunted into dead-end jobs (if any) and are forced to compromise their dignity because of their race, sex, poverty, religion, or age. We believe that the United States must re-examine and reorder national goals and priorities.

The articles in this book, therefore, offer insights and suggest approaches not usually available in conventional texts and readers. For the most part, although not always, we endorse the conclusions reached by the authors of these essays. But history is a complex discipline, and the views of historians are continually subject to re-examination. Interpretations that seem persuasive today may seem dubious in a year, or two, or ten. Nevertheless, the ideas presented in this collection appear to us to be of serious consideration at this time.

The volume is divided into four sections, each with a short general introduction. Brief headnotes for each article provide a transition from one to another, present necessary background information, and somtimes question an author's conclusions or call attention to their implications. We have made no attempt to furnish extensive bibliographies, but in the suggestions for further reading following each article we have listed a few books that interested students may wish to read to explore a subject more thoroughly or deepen their knowledge of different arguments or related fields.

We would like to thank Sandra Buchman for typing the introductory material and Gladys Topkis for providing sage editorial advice.

JEAN CHRISTIE
LEONARD DINNERSTEIN

AMERICA SINCE WORLD WAR II

I

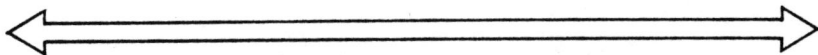

THE BEGINNINGS OF POSTWAR AMERICA

Americans emerged from World War II into a world that Franklin D. Roosevelt had assured them must be and could be based upon "four essential human freedoms"—freedom of speech, freedom of religion, freedom from want, and freedom from fear of aggression anywhere. Alone among the powers, the United States had suffered no bombing of cities, no invasion; it had built a tremendous organization for production and had some 10 million men under arms. Leading citizens believed that America must seize the opportunity —or accept the responsibility—to bring tranquillity and order to ravaged humanity. *Time-Life-Fortune* publisher Henry Luce foresaw an "American century," and New Dealer Henry A. Wallace hailed the "century of the common man." Both, like former Republican Presidential candidate Wendell L. Willkie, perceived that all peoples constitute "one world."

Even before the war was over, a conference of fifty nations, victors over the Axis countries, established the United Nations at a historic meeting in San Francisco. Together they pledged themselves and the new organization to seek peaceful solutions to international quarrels and "to save succeeding generations from the scourge of war . . . to reaffirm faith in fundamental human rights, in the dignity and worth of the human person . . . to promote social progress and better standards or life in larger freedom." To achieve these ends, they promised "to employ international machinery for the promotion of the economic and social advancement of all peoples."

Yet, to judge by their subsequent actions, most of the signers of the U.N. Charter never seriously contemplated adjusting their governments' policies to further the interests of the world's peoples. Major foreign offices carried on as usual their schemes of intrigue and deceit. Only weeks later, President Harry S. Truman ordered that the world's first atomic bomb be dropped on two Japanese cities, in the belief that this would be the most expedient way to end the war in the

2

Pacific. Within two years the Russians and Americans had embarked upon a "cold war," shattering hopes that they would cooperate to build a more peaceful world.

Great Britain, the United States, and the Soviet Union had been the major Allies during World War II in Europe. Supposedly all three worked in unison, but the Soviet Union particularly held deep suspicions of its partners. Since 1917 the United States and Britain had been hostile to the Communist institutions of Russia. Even during their formal alliance, these powers were not so open in their dealings with Moscow as with each other. President Roosevelt and British Prime Minister Winston Churchill communicated frequently without informing Stalin of their views, and the Americans and British developed the atomic bomb together without informing the Russians of the project. Although such secretiveness intensified the Soviets' distrust of the West, wartime exigencies made it necessary for Stalin to remain on good terms with the Western leaders. In a series of conferences, notably at Teheran in 1943 and at Yalta early in 1945, the powers arrived at seemingly amicable agreements on the United Nations, the war against Japan, and the territories soon to be liberated from Nazi occupation.

In truth, however, these meetings left many matters vague and undecided, and as the Russians drove the German invaders westward across Europe, latent conflicts of ideas and interests broke through to the surface. President Roosevelt died in April 1945, leaving many questions unsettled. We cannot know what decisions he would have made, but clearly his successor, Harry S. Truman, who had not been familiarized with the intricacies of American foreign policy during the previous years, relied on advisers who advocated a "tough" stance with Moscow. When, for example, the Russians asked for a multibillion-dollar loan to reconstruct their country, the Americans set preconditions that the Russians decided they could not meet. On top of other irritations, the failure to grant this badly needed assistance aggravated Soviet suspicions of the leading capitalist power. Washington, on the other hand, viewed with dismay the Soviet influence in Eastern Europe and feared that France and Italy, where large and coherent Communist parties had gained prestige through their activity in the Resistance movements, might soon "go Communist." (Actually, Moscow was urging caution on those parties while in China it recognized the anti-Communist regime of Chiang Kai-shek and the Kuomintang.) In Poland, a new government, provided for at Yalta in somewhat ambiguous terms, failed to hold free elections, a fact that reinforced the arguments of Washington hard-liners. Fearful of each other, neither the American nor the Soviet Government dared to take a chance or make any gesture that might smack of "appeasement"; so the wartime partners moved from guarded cooperation to intransigency on both sides.

Mutual recriminations opened a series of moves and countermoves. On the American side, the President set forth, in 1947, the "Truman Doctrine" that "it must be the policy of the United States to support free peoples who are resisting attempted subjugation by armed minorities or by outside pressures." Under this policy, he asked Congress to authorize aid to safeguard Greece and Turkey against Communism. Congress consented and thus kept a conservative government in power in Athens. In Europe the Marshall Plan provided aid for economic reconstruction that would restore popular faith in capitalism. In 1949, through the North Atlantic Treaty Organization, the United States entered into an armed alliance with Great Britain, France, and other Western European nations, again to thwart "Communist aggression." This was the first formal military alliance the United States had made with any European power since the American revolutionaries had obtained help from France in 1778. Subsequently, Washington constructed a network of alliances and informal agreements with other states that permitted it to establish military bases in a "defense perimeter" extending through most of the world except Eastern Europe and China. The distrustful Russians concluded that all their suspicions had been justified. Instead of continuing the relatively flexible policy that they had pursued immediately after the war's end, they adopted, in 1948, an uncompromising course and embarked on a series of counteroffensives, including a coup in Czechoslovakia, the closing of overland routes to Berlin, and a temporary boycott of the United Nations.

Events in 1949 and 1950 shocked Americans already sensitized to the Communist peril. The Russians exploded an atom bomb, to which the United States responded by developing the hydrogen bomb. The Communists in China won a civil war and proceeded to revolutionize their society. Long fed with illusions about the competence and popularity of the Kuomintang regime, bewildered Americans were prepared to believe that the Communists had triumphed only through the assistance of the Russians and possibly of "traitors" in the U.S. State Department. In 1950 war broke out in divided Korea. President Truman immediately decided to send in American forces and, in the absence of the Soviet representative from the Security Council, obtained U.N. support for the defense of South Korea against North Korean Communist aggression.

Politicians of both major parties supported these executive measures, declaring that "politics ends at the water's edge"—that is, that foreign policy should not become a political issue. Many who were known as "liberals" rejoiced that the nation recognized its responsibilities as leader of the "free world." In 1948 a new Progressive Party, led by former Vice-President Henry A. Wallace, did attempt to make the cold war an issue but was decisively beaten in the Presidential election, which retained Truman in office. Probably most Americans did fear the Soviet Union and "international Communism." But the bipartisan approach ensured automatic conformity to decisions made by the executive branch, and it closed off public discussion of fundamental questions of foreign relations.

In 1953 the election of General Dwight D. Eisenhower, a hero of World War II, as President initiated a series of calmer years. The bloody war in Korea had become immensely unpopular, and Eisenhower kept his election promise to end it. Although he continued his predecessor's basic cold-war policies, he tried to cool the rhetoric somewhat. Despite the exhortations of John Foster Dulles, his Secretary of State, who spouted quasi-religious slogans about thwarting the forces of atheistic Communism, Eisenhower decided not to send American troops to fight in Vietnam when, in 1954, the French colonialists were obliged to surrender their last strong position at Dienbienphu.

On the domestic scene, former New Dealers attempted to initiate further social progress. President Harry S. Truman proposed a "Fair Deal" to include the protection of civil rights, river-valley authorities, aid to education and housing, and a national system of universal medical care. But a conservative Congress watered down or rejected these measures, and by the late 1940's the frenzy over Communism and suspected disloyalty had created an atmosphere in which even moderate reformers might well come under suspicion as "pinkos" or "fellow travelers." As the hunt for subversives gained momentum, the civil service, labor unions, and universities conducted spy trials and purges that silenced critics and ensured acceptance of existing institutions and mores. Hysteria about possible Communist influence afflicted America in the 1940's and early 1950's. It promoted to prominence the loudest anti-Communist in the country, Senator Joseph R. McCarthy of Wisconsin. McCarthy's demagogic tactics cowed a generation before he met his comeuppance after he challenged the Secretary of the Army in 1954.

For the rest of the decade, blandness and self-righteousness prevailed. Dwight D. Eisenhower, one of the most popular Presidents in history, radiated equanimity over a people seemingly preoccupied with family life and enjoyment of the Gross National Product. War had ended the Great Depression; Americans, with what they considered their characteristic know-how, utilized capital and technology to convert natural resources into an overwhelming quantity and variety of goods. The birthrate, which had declined since the middle of the 1920's, rose markedly, and the United States became one of the fastest growing industrial nations in the world. On college campuses once boiling with political dispute, a "silent generation" prepared to get on in life, eager to seek favor in corporate hierarchies or to start nest-building in the expanding suburbs. As their standard of living rose, middle-class citizens showed little inclination to worry about continuing racial discrimination or about the constant mergers that created ever larger corporations, nor did they acknowledge the existence of bitter poverty in the midst of a car-borne civilization. Academicians observed that America had solved the problem of democratic government and congratulated their country on shouldering the global burdens of national success.

The articles in this section focus on the crucial years of the late 1940's and early 1950's. Barton J. Bernstein evaluates the lofty aims and meager accomplishments of reformers in the Truman era; Robert Lasch examines the origins of the cold war; and Dorsen and Simon look closely at the Army-McCarthy hearings and consider the principles at stake in the contest.

AMERICA IN WAR AND PEACE:
THE TEST OF LIBERALISM

BARTON J. BERNSTEIN

As World War II was ending, Americans who sought social change turned their attention to peacetime needs and began to gather their energies for agitation and political action. Most of them wanted, not radical revolution, but a series of reforms in the existing capitalist system. The New Deal had dominated and shaped their outlook and their perception of the socially desirable and the politically possible. As they saw it, the New Deal had started the country on the path of promise but, in spite of many accomplishments, had left much yet to be done. War had interrupted, but must not cut short, America's progress toward a more balanced economy and a more humanitarian social order.

In the Great Depression of the 1930's, the Democratic Party had welded together a coalition that included labor, urban ethnic groups, blacks, white Southerners, and most of the country's intellectuals. With this broad support, a Congress dominated by President Franklin D. Roosevelt—magnetic personality and skillful politician—put through a mass of legislation of unprecedented diversity and scope. The federal government attempted, for example, to raise farm prices, to protect labor's right to organize, to provide some income for the aged, to conserve the soil, and to create useful jobs for the unemployed.

Animating these programs and infusing New Deal thought was a set of attitudes and ideas known as "liberalism." Liberals sought a "middle way" between unregulated capitalism and socialism. Accepting capitalism as the base, they believed the people must act through their government (led by a forceful President) to stimulate the

From *Towards a New Past: Dissenting Essays in American History*, edited by Barton J. Bernstein. Copyright © 1968 by Random House, Inc. Reprinted by permission of the publisher Pantheon Books, a Division of Random House, Inc.

economy and aid disadvantaged groups. Political currents (critics said "expediency") shaped the means to these ends. Flexibility was the watchword; liberals gloried in their freedom from dogma. Defending the New Deal against the charge of incoherence, historian Arthur M. Schlesinger, Jr., contends that "in the welter of confusion and ignorance, experiment corrected by compassion was the best answer."

Responding in this spirit of openness to the demands of many groups in society, the New Dealers instituted programs and policies to remedy social ills and relieve immediate distress. Many of these innovations became integrated into American life. Yet the New Dealers did nothing to resolve the urgent problem of medical care, and they offered little aid to the poorest, the most unskilled and despised. The New Dealers "discovered" the Southern sharecroppers, for example, and set up agencies to help them; but the administration shied away from any challenge to the plantation owners, who commanded a powerful wing of the Democratic Party.

So in 1945, as armed conflict subsided, the liberals hoped to take the political initiative again, both in order to combat a new depression, which they greatly feared, and to carry forward the reform movement that had surged ahead in the thirties. Whether they could succeed was an open question, since the conservative elements that had hampered the New Deal had actually gained in prestige and political influence. On their side, however, liberals could count the appeal of the Roosevelt name, progressive tendencies among some labor unionists, and a widespread liberal antifascism that had spurred the war effort and fueled people's hopes for the postwar world.

But their efforts achieved little. Largely because of rising black self-assertion, the cause of civil rights made headway; but no general reform movement dominated the political scene. The New Deal was not to be revived.

Barton J. Bernstein traces the course of events in the Truman era and appraises the strength of the contestants. He notes the power of the conservative forces but finds that the reformers were uncertain and inconsistent. Perhaps, he concludes, "The liberal vision itself is dim."

□　□　□

The domestic events of the war and postwar years have failed to attract as much scholarly effort as have the few years of the New Deal. The reforms of the thirties and the struggle against depression have captured the enthusiasm of many liberal historians and have con-

stituted the major themes shaping their interpretations. Compared
with the excitement of the New Deal years, the events at home during
the next decade seem less interesting, certainly less dramatic.

The issues of these years also seem less clear, perhaps because the
period lacks the restrictive unity imposed upon the New Deal. Despite
the fragmentary scholarship, however, the major issues are definable:
economic policies,[1] civil rights, civil liberties,[2] and social welfare policies.[3] The continued dominance by big business, the consolidation of
other groups within the economy, the challenge of racial inequality—
these are the themes of the wartime Roosevelt administration. Toward
the end of Roosevelt's years, they are joined by another concern, the
quest for social reform, and in Truman's years by such themes as economic readjustment, the renewed struggle against inflation, and the
fear of disloyalty and communism. These problems are largely the
legacy of the New Deal: the extension of its limited achievements, the
response to its shortcomings, the criticism of its liberalism.

It was during the war years that the nation climbed out of depression, that big business regained admiration and increased its power,
and that other interests became effective partners in the political economy of large-scale corporate capitalism. While the major interests
focused on foreign policy and on domestic economic problems—on
mobilization and stabilization, later on reconversion and inflation—
liberal democracy was revealing serious weaknesses. Opposing fascism
abroad as a threat to democratic values, the nation remained generally
insensitive to the plight of its citizens who suffered indignity or injury
because of their color. Violating liberal values in the process of saving
American democracy, Roosevelt's government, swept along by a wave
of racism, victimized Japanese-Americans. Uncommitted to advancing
the Negroes' cause, the war government resisted their demands for full
participation in democracy and prosperity, and grudgingly extended to
them only limited rights.

Though the New Deal had gone intellectually bankrupt long before
Pearl Harbor and reform energies were submerged during most of the
war, they reappeared in the last years of the conflict. Reviving the reform spirit in 1944, Roosevelt called for an "Economic Bill of Rights"
for postwar America. In his last year, however, he was unable to achieve
his goals, and Truman's efforts were usually too weak to overcome the
conservative coalition blocking his expanded reform program. Mobi-
lized by apprehension, liberals wrongly believed that the conservative
bloc wished to destroy unions, to reorganize the corporate economy,
and to leave the nation without protection from depression. But
as unions endured and the economy grew, the fears and energies of
liberals waned. Exaggerating the accomplishments of past reforms and
believing that widespread prosperity had been achieved, they lost much

of their social vision: they came to praise big business, to celebrate pluralism, to ignore poverty. Yet to their surprise they fell under vigorous attack from the right, in a new assault on civil liberties. In viewing McCarthyism as an attack upon the reform tradition, however, liberals failed to understand that they and the Democratic administration, as zealous anticommunists, also shared responsibility for the "red scare."

I

During the war and postwar years, big business regained national admiration and received lavish praise for contributing to victory over fascism. Yet few realized that business had not initially been an enthusiastic participant in the "arsenal of democracy." Such firms as Standard Oil of New Jersey, Dow Chemical, United States Steel, Dupont, General Motors, and the Aluminum Company of America had assisted the growth of Nazi industry and delayed America's preparation for war. Even after most Americans had come to condemn fascism, these corporations had collaborated with German business, sharing patents and often blocking production of defense materials in America.[4] The general ideology of these firms was probably best expressed by Alfred Sloan, Jr., the chairman of the General Motors board, when he replied to a stockholder: ". . . an international business operating throughout the world should conduct its operations in strictly business terms without regard to the political beliefs in its management, or the political beliefs of the country in which it is operating."[5]

In the two years before Pearl Harbor, major industries were also reluctant to prepare for defense. Though the aircraft industry ended its "sit-down" strike after the government had relaxed profit restrictions and improved terms for amortization,[6] other industries continued to resist expansion and production for defense. Sharing the common opinion that American intervention was unlikely, and painfully recalling the glutted markets of the depression decade, the steel industry and the aluminum monopoly (Alcoa) opposed growth, which might endanger profits. Nor were the automobile makers and larger producers of consumer durables willing to take defense contracts which would convert assembly lines from profitable, peacetime goods to preparation for a war that many believed, and President Roosevelt seemed to promise, America would never enter.[7]

Fearful of bad publicity, the leaders of these industries never challenged the administration nor demanded a clear statement of their responsibility. They avoided a dialogue on the basic issues. Still suffering from the opprobrium of the depression, industrialists would not deny corporate responsibility to the nation. Though privately concerned about the welfare of their companies, industrialists never argued that they owed primary responsibility to their stockholders. Fearful of jeopardizing their firms' well-being, company officials did not publicly express their doubts. Yet they could have objected publicly to executive suasion and contended that the issues were so grave that a Congressional mandate was necessary. Instead, they publicly accepted their obligation to risk profits for American defense, but in practice they continued to avoid such risks. Often they made promises they did not fulfill, and when they resisted administration policy, they took refuge in evasion. They restricted the dialogue to matters of feasibility and tactics—that expansion in steel and aluminum was unnecessary, that partial conversion was impossible, and that available tools could not produce defense goods.

The government also avoided opening the dialogue. The prewar mobilization agencies, administered largely by dollar-a-year men, did not seek to embarrass or coerce recalcitrant industries. Protecting business from public censure, the directors of mobilization—such men as William Knudsen of General Motors and Edward Stettinius of United States Steel—resisted the efforts of other government officials to force prompt expansion and conversion. In effect, Knudsen, Stettinius, and their cohorts acted as protectors of "business as usual." Despite the protests of the service secretaries, Roosevelt permitted the businessmen in government to move slowly. Though he encouraged some assistants to prod business, and occasionally spurred the dollar-a-year men, he avoided exerting direct pressure on big business.

The President was following the strategy of caution. Reluctant to encourage public criticism of, or even debate on, his foreign policy, he maneuvered to avoid conflict or challenge. Because the nation respected big businessmen, he chose them to direct mobilization. He too had faith in their ability, and he hoped to win cooperation from the suspicious business community by selecting its leaders as his agents.

While many liberals criticized Roosevelt's reliance upon big business, the most direct, public challenge to business came from Walter Reuther, vice-president of the recently formed United Automobile Workers, and from Philip Murray, president of the CIO and the United Steel Workers.[8] Criticizing "business as usual" policies, they proposed a labor-management council to guide industry during war. The plan shocked industrialists. It was radicalism, an invasion of management's prerogatives, a threat to private enterprise, asserted business leaders.[9] They would not share power or sanction a redefinition of private property. Having grudgingly recognized industrial unions shortly before the war, they remained suspicious of organized labor and were unwilling to invite its leaders into the industrial councils of decision making.[10]

Despite these suspicions, the administration called upon labor leaders and their organizations for cooperation in the war effort. Needing their support, Roosevelt appointed union chiefs to positions in the stabilization and mobilization agencies, and thus bestowed prestige upon organized labor. Calling for a labor-management partnership, he secured a wartime no-strike pledge.[11] As junior partners in the controlled economy, labor leaders generally kept the pledge.[12] Cooperating with business leaders in the defense effort, union representatives, by their actions, convinced many businessmen that organized labor did not threaten large-scale corporate capitalism.[13] By encouraging labor-management cooperation, the war years, then, provided a necessary respite between the industrial violence of the thirties and sustained collective bargaining, and speeded the consolidation of the new organization of the American economy.

It was within a government-controlled economy (dominated by business) that the major interests struggled for economic advantages. Farmers, rescued from the depression by enlarged demand, initially battled price controls but soon acceded to them and tried simply to use political power to increase their benefits. Also reaping the gains of war, workers received higher incomes but bitterly criticized the tight restraints on hourly wage increases. Business, also recovering from the depression, complained about price controls, which indirectly limited profits. Though all interests chafed under the restraints, none disputed in principle the need for government-imposed restraints on wages and prices: all agreed that a free price system during war, when civilian demand greatly outstripped consumer goods, would have created inequity and chaos.[14]

Despite price restrictions and the excess-profits tax, the major corporations prospered, benefitting from cost-plus contracts and the five-year amortization plan (which made the new plants partial gifts from the government).[15] As dollar-a-year men poured into Washington, big firms gained influence and contracts. Smaller businessmen, unable to match the influence and mistrusted by procurement officers, declined in importance. In a nation that prized the large corporation, few had confidence in small business. Even the creation of a government agency to protect small business failed to increase significantly its share in the war economy.[16]

The interests of big business were defended and advanced by the dollar-a-year men, and particularly by those on the War Production Board (WPB), the agency controlling resources. In many wartime Washington agencies, and especially on the WPB, the leaders of big business and the military served together and learned to cooperate. Burying earlier differences about preparation for war, they developed similar views of the national interest and identified it with the goals of their own groups. The reconversion controversy of 1944, which C. Wright Mills views as the beginning of the military-industrial alliance,[17] is the outstanding example of this coalition of interests.

In early 1944, big business was experiencing large military cutbacks and withdrawing subcontracts from smaller firms, often leaving them idle. Temporarily proponents of strong controls, most of the WPB executives from industry and finance would not allow these smaller firms to return to consumer goods. They collaborated with representatives of the military to block the reconversion program. Desiring control of the wartime economy, such military leaders as Robert P. Patterson, Under Secretary of War, James Forrestal, Under Secretary of the Navy, and Major General Lucius Clay, Assistant Chief of Staff for Matériel, feared that reconversion would siphon off scarce labor and disrupt vital production. Joining them were such WPB executives as Charles E. Wilson, president of General Electric, Lemuel Boulware, a Celotex executive and later a General Electric vice-president, and financiers Arthur H. Bunker of Lehman Brothers and Sidney Weinberg of Goldman, Sachs. Sympathetic to military demands, they were also afraid that the earlier return of small producers to consumer markets would injure big business. While some may have acted to protect their own companies, most were simply operating in a value system that could not accept a policy which seemed to threaten big business. Through cunning maneuvering, these military and industrial leaders acted to protect the prewar oligopolistic structure of the American economy.[18]

The war, while creating the limited prosperity that the New Deal had failed to create, did not disrupt the economic distribution of power. Nor did the extension of the wartime income tax significantly reallocate income and wealth, for the Congress even rebuffed Roosevelt's effort to limit the war incomes of the wealthy. Though the wartime measures and not the New Deal increased the tax burden on the upper-income groups, "the major weight," emphasizes Gabriel Kolko, "fell on income groups that had never before been subjected to the income tax." [19]

II

Failing to limit business power or to reallocate wealth, the wartime government was more active in other areas. Yielding to pressures, Roosevelt slightly advanced the welfare of the Negro, but the President also bowed to illiberal pressures and dealt a terrible blow to civil liberties when he authorized the forced evacuation of 110,000 loyal Americans of Japanese descent.

It was the "worst single wholesale violation of civil rights" in American history, judged the American Civil Liberties Union.[20] Succumbing to the anti-Japanese hysteria of Westerners (including the pleas of California Attorney-General Earl Warren and the Pacific coast congressional delegation under Senator Hiram Johnson) and the demands of the military commander on the coast, the President empowered the Army to remove the Japanese-Americans.[21] ("He was never theoretical about things. What must be done to defend the country must be done," Roosevelt believed, later wrote Francis Biddle, his Attorney-General,[22]) "Japanese raids on the west coast seemed not only possible but probable in the first months of war, and it was quite impossible to be sure that the raiders would not receive important help from individuals of Japanese origin," was the explanation later endorsed by Secretary of War Henry Stimson.[23]

Privately Stimson called the episode a "tragedy," but he supported it as War Department policy.[24] Opposing the decision, Biddle could not weaken the resolve of Roosevelt. Though liberals protested the action, the Supreme Court later upheld Roosevelt and the War Department.[25] The meaning of the decision," concludes Arthur Link, "was clear and foreboding: in future emergencies no American citizen would have any rights that the President and the army were bound to respect when, *in their judgment*, the emergency justified drastic denial of civil rights."[26]

Though anti-Japanese feeling was most virulent on the Pacific coast, racism was not restricted to any part of America. In most of America, Negroes had long been the victims of hatred. Frequently lacking effective legal protection in the South, Negroes also encountered prejudice, fear, and hatred in the North. During the war there were racial clashes in Northern cities. New York narrowly averted a major riot. In Los Angeles whites attacked Negroes and Mexicans, and in Detroit whites invaded the Negro sector and pillaged and killed.[27]

Despite the evidence of deep racism, liberal historians have usually avoided focusing upon the hatred in white America and the resort to violence.[28] Curiously, though emphasizing the disorganization of the Negro community, they have also neglected the scattered protests by organized Negroes—boycotts of white-owned stores in Negro areas of Memphis and Houston when they would not hire Negroes, a sit-in in a public library in Alexandria, Virginia, a Harlem boycott of a bus line to compel the hiring of Negro drivers.[29]

Condemned to inferiority in nearly all sectors of American life, Negroes did not share in the benefits of the early defense economy.[30] Denied jobs in many industries, they also met discrimination by the military. The Air Corps barred them, the Navy segregated them to the mess corps, and the Army held them to a small quota, generally restricting them to menial tasks.[31] During the 1940 campaign, Negro leaders attacked the administration for permitting segregation and discrimination, and demanded the broadening of opportunity in the military. It is not "a fight merely to wear a uniform," explained *Crisis* (the NAACP publication). "This is a struggle for status, a struggle to take democracy off a parchment and give it life." [32]

Negroes gained admission to the Air Corps when it yielded under White House pressure, but they failed to gain congressional support for wider participation in the military. At Roosevelt's direction the War Department did raise its quota of Negroes—to their proportion in the population. But the Army remained segregated. Though unwilling to challenge segregation, the administration still courted Negro leaders and the black vote. Rather than bestowing benefits upon the masses, Roosevelt maintained their allegiance by offering symbolic recognition: Colonel Benjamin O. Davis, the Army's highest ranking Negro, was promoted to Brigadier General, and some prominent Negroes were appointed as advisers to the Secretary of War and the Director of Selective Service.[33] ("We asked Mr. Roosevelt to change the rules of the game and he countered by giving us some new uniforms," complained the editors of the *Baltimore Afro-American*. "That is what it amounts to and we have called it appeasement." [34])

As the nation headed toward war, Negroes struggled to wring other concessions from a president who never enlisted in their cause and would not risk antagonizing powerful Southerners. Discriminated against by federal agencies during the depression and denied an equal share of defense prosperity, Negroes were unwilling to acquiesce before continued injustice. In some industrial areas the NAACP and *ad hoc* groups organized local protests. After numerous unsuccessful appeals to the President, Negro leaders planned more dramatic action—a march on Washington.[35]

Demanding "the right to work and fight for our country," the leaders of the March on Washington Movement—A. Philip Randolph, head of the Brotherhood of Sleeping Car Porters, Walter White, executive secretary of the NAACP, and Lester Granger, executive secretary of the Urban League—publicly requested executive orders ending racial discrimination in federal agencies, the military and defense employment.[36] In private correspondence with the President they sought more: the end of segregation in these areas. So bold were their goals that some still have not been enforced by the government, and it is unlikely that Negro leaders expected to secure them.[37]

Refusing to give up the march for the promise of negotiations, Negro leaders escaped the politics of accommodation. Though white liberals urged Randolph and his cohorts to call off the march, they would not yield.[38] Applying pressure on an uncomfortable administration, they ultimately settled for less than they had requested (and perhaps less than they had anticipated [39])—an executive order barring discrimination in defense work and creating a Federal Employment Practices Committee (FEPC). Meager as the order was, it was the greatest achievement in American history for organized Negro action.[40]

FEPC did not contribute significantly to the wartime advancement of the Negro. His gains were less the results of federal efforts than of the labor shortage. Undoubtedly, the committee would have been more effective if Roosevelt had provided it with a larger budget, but the Negro's cause never commanded the President's enthusiasm. Yet he did protect FEPC from its enemies, and by maintaining the agency, stressed its symbolic importance.[41]

It affirmed the rights of Negroes to jobs and focused attention on the power of the federal government to advance the interests of its black citizens. It did not smash the walls of prejudices; it only removed a few bricks. FEPC, concludes Louis Ruchames, "brought hope and a new confidence into their [Negro] lives. It gave them cause to believe in democracy and in America. It made them feel that in answering the call to their country's colors, they were defending, not the oppression and degradation, to which they were accustomed, but democracy, equality of opportunity, and a better world for themselves and their children." [42]

Still relegated to second-class citizenship, Negroes had found new dignity and new opportunity during the war. Loyal followers of Roosevelt, loving him for the few benefits his government had extended, black Americans had become important members of the shifting Democratic coalition. By their presence in Northern cities, they would also become a new political force.[43] For the Democratic party and the nation, their expectations and needs would constitute a moral and political challenge. By its response, white America would test the promise of liberal democracy.

III

When the nation joined the Allies, Roosevelt had explained that "Dr. Win-the-War" was taking over from "Dr. New Deal," and there were few liberal legislative achievements during the war years. Those benefits that disadvantaged groups did receive were usually a direct result of the labor shortage and the flourishing economy, not of liberal politics. By 1944, however, Roosevelt was prepared to revive the reform spirit, and he revealed his liberal vision for the postwar years. Announcing an "Economic Bill of Rights," he outlined "a new basis for security and prosperity": the right to a job, adequate food, clothing, and recreation, a decent home, a good education, adequate medical care, and protection against sickness and unemployment.[44]

Noble as was his vision of the future society Roosevelt was still unprepared to move far beyond rhetoric, and the Congress was unsympathetic to his program.[45] While approving the GI Bill of Rights,[46] including educational benefits and extended unemployment pay, Congress resisted most liberal programs during the war. Asserting its independence of the executive, the war Congress also thwarted Roosevelt in other ways—by rejecting a large tax bill designed to spread the cost of war and to reduce inflationary pressures, [47] and by liquidating the National Resources Planning Board, which had originated the "second bill of rights" and also studied postwar economic planning.[48]

By its opposition to planning and social reform, Congress increased the anxieties of labor and liberals about the postwar years and left the new Truman administration poorly prepared for the difficult transition to a peacetime economy when the war suddenly ended.[49] Fearing the depression that most economists forecast, the administration did, however, propose a tax cut of $5 billion. While removing many low-income recipients from the tax rolls, the law was also of great benefit to large corporations. Charging inequity, organized labor found little support in Congress or the executive, for the government was relying upon business activity, rather than on consumer purchasing power, to soften the economic decline. Significantly, despite the anticipated $30 billion deficit (plus the $5 billion tax), no congressman expressed any fear of an unbalanced budget. Clearly fiscal orthodoxy did not occupy a very high place in the scale of values of congressional conservatives, and they accepted in practice the necessity of an unbalanced budget.[50]

Before the tax bill passed, the wartime harmony of the major interest groups had crumbled: each struggled to consolidate its gains and advance its welfare before the anticipated economic collapse. Chafing under the no-strike pledge and restrictions on wage raises, organized labor compelled the administration to relax its policy and free unions to bargain collectively.[51] Farmers, fearful of depression, demanded the withdrawal of subsidies which artificially depressed prices.[52] Big business, despite anticipated shortages, secured the removal of most controls on the allocation of resources.[53]

As the economic forecasts shifted in late autumn, the administration discovered belatedly that inflation, not depression, was the immediate economic danger. The President acted sporadically to restrain inflationary pressures, but his efforts were too occasional, often misguided, and too weak to resist the demands of interest groups and the actions of his own subordinates.[54]

Beset by factionalism and staffed often by men of limited ability, Truman's early government floundered. By adopting the practice of cabinet responsibility and delegating excessive authority to department chiefs, Truman created a structure that left him uninformed: problems frequently developed unnoticed until they had swelled to crises, and the choice then was often between undesirable alternatives. Operating in a new politics, in the politics of inflation, he confronted problems requiring greater tactical skill than those Roosevelt had confronted. Seeking to maintain economic controls, and compelled to deny the rising expectations of major interest groups, his administration found it difficult to avoid antagonizing the rival groups. In the politics of depression, the Roosevelt administration could frequently maintain political support by bestowing specific advantages on groups, but in the politics of inflation the major interest groups came to seek freedom from restrictive federal controls.[55]

So difficult were the problems facing Truman that even a more experienced and skilled president would have encountered great difficulty. Inheriting the hostile Congress that had resisted occasional wartime attempts at social reform, Truman lacked the skill or leverage to guide a legislature seeking to assert its independence of the executive. Unable to halt fragmentation of the Democratic coalition, and incapable of ending dissension in his government, he also found that conservative subordinates undercut his occasional liberalism. Though he had gone on record early in endorsing a reform program [56] ("a declaration of independence" from congressional conservatives, he called it),[57] he had been unsuccessful in securing most of the legislation—a higher minimum wage, public housing, expanded unemployment benefits, and FEPC. Even the employment act was little more, as one congressman said, than a license to look for a job.[58] The President, through ineptitude or lack of commitment, often chose not to struggle for his program. Unable to dramatize the issues or to command enthusiasm, he was an ineffectual leader.[59]

So unsuccessful was his government that voters began jibing, "To err is Truman." Despairing of a resurgence of liberalism under Truman, New Dealers left the government in droves. By the fall of 1946, none of Roosevelt's associates was left in a prominent position. So disgruntled were many liberals about Truman and his advisers, about his unwillingness to fight for price controls, housing, benefits for labor and civil rights, that some turned briefly to serious consideration of a new party.[60]

IV

Achieving few reforms during his White House years, Truman, with the notable exception of civil rights, never moved significantly beyond Roosevelt. The Fair Deal was largely an extension of earlier Democratic liberalism,[61] but Truman's new vigor and fierce partisanship ultimately made him more attractive to liberals who despairingly watched the GOP-dominated Eightieth Congress and feared a repeal of the New Deal.

Their fears were unwarranted, as was their enthusiasm for the Fair Deal program. In practice it proved very limited—the housing program only provided for 810,000 units in six years of which only 60,000 were constructed; [62] social security benefits were extended to ten million [63] and increased by about 75 percent, and the minimum wage was increased to 75 cents, but coverage was reduced by nearly a million.[64] But even had all of the Fair Deal been enacted, liberal reform would have left many millions beyond the benefits of government. The very poor, the marginal men, those neglected but acknowledged by the New Deal, went ultimately unnoticed by the Fair Deal.[65]

While liberals frequently chafed under Truman's leadership and questioned his commitment, they failed generally to recognize how shallow were his reforms. As the nation escaped a postwar depression, American liberals gained new faith in the American economy. Expressing their enthusiasm, they came to extoll big business for its contributions. Believing firmly in the success of progressive taxation, they exaggerated its effects, and congratulated themselves on the redistribution of income and the virtual abolition of poverty. Praising the economic system, they accepted big agriculture and big labor as evidence of healthy pluralism that protected freedom and guaranteed an equitable distribution of resources.[66]

Despite the haggling over details and the liberals' occasional dismay at Truman's style, he expressed many of their values. Like Roosevelt, Truman never challenged big business, never endangered large-scale capitalism. Indeed, his efforts as well as theirs were directed largely to maintaining and adjusting the powers of the major economic groups.

Fearing that organized labor was threatened with destruction, Truman, along with the liberals, had been sincerely frightened by the postwar rancor toward labor.[67] What they failed to understand was that most Americans had accepted unions as part of the political economy. Certainly most major industrialists had accepted organized labor, though smaller businessmen were often hostile.[68] Despite the overwrought rhetoric of debates, Congress did not actually menace labor. It was not seeking to destroy labor, only to restrict its power.

Many Americans did believe that the Wagner Act had unduly favored labor and was creating unions indifferent to the public welfare and hostile to corporate power. Capitalizing on this exaggerated fear of excessive union power, and the resentment from the postwar strikes, businessmen secured the Taft-Hartley Act.[69] Designed to weaken organized labor, it tried but failed to protect the membership from leaders; it did not effectively challenge the power of established unions. However, labor chiefs, recalling the bitter industrial warfare of the thirties, were still uneasy in their new positions. Condemning the legislation as a "slave-labor" act, they responded with fear, assailed the Congress, and declared that Taft-Hartley was the major political issue.[70]

Within a few years, when unions discovered that they were safe, Taft-Hartley faded as an issue. But in 1948 it served Truman well by establishing the GOP's hostility to labor and casting it back into the Democratic ranks. Both the President and union chiefs conveniently neglected his own kindling of antilabor passions (as when he had tried to draft strikers).[71] Exploiting Taft-Hartley as part of his strategy of patching the tattered Democratic coalition, Truman tied repeal of the "slave-labor" law to price controls, farm benefits, anticommunism, and civil rights in the campaign which won his election in his own right.

V

In courting the Negro the Truman administration in 1948 made greater promises to black citizens than had any previous federal government in American history. Yet, like many Americans, Truman as a senator had regarded the Negro's plight as peripheral to his interests, and with many of his generation he believed that equality was compatible with segregation.[72] As President, however, he found himself slowly prodded by conscience and pushed by politics. He moved cautiously at first and endorsed only measures affirming legal equality and protecting Negroes from violence.

Reluctant to fragment the crumbling Democratic coalition, Truman, in his first year, had seemed to avoid taking positions on civil rights which might upset the delicate balance between Northern and Southern Democrats. While he endorsed legislation for a statutory FEPC that the Congress would not grant, his efforts on behalf of the temporary FEPC (created by Roosevelt's executive order) were weaker. Having already weakened the power of the temporary agency, he also acquiesced in the legislative decision to kill it.[73] Despite the fears of Negro leaders that the death of FEPC would leave Negroes virtually unprotected from discrimination in the postwar job market, Truman would not even issue an order requiring nondiscrimination in the federal service and by government contractors.[74]

Though Truman was unwilling to use the prestige or power of his great office significantly on behalf of Negroes, he did assist their cause. While sidestepping political conflict, he occasionally supported FEPC and abolition of the poll tax. When Negroes were attacked, he did condemn the racial violence.[75] Though generally reluctant to move beyond rhetoric during his early years, Truman, shortly before the 1946 election, found conscience and politics demanding more. So distressed was he by racial violence that when Walter White of the NAACP and a group of white liberals urged him to assist the Negro, he promised to create a committee to study civil rights.[76]

The promise of a committee could have been a device to resist pressures, to delay the matter until after the election. And Truman could have appointed a group of politically safe men of limited reputation—men he could control. But instead, after the election, perhaps in an effort to mobilize the liberals for 1948, he appointed a committee of prominent men sympathetic to civil rights. They were men he could not control and did not seek to control.[77]

The committee's report, undoubtedly far bolder than Truman's expectations,[78] confirmed charges that America treated its Negroes as second-class citizens. It called for FEPC, an antilynching law, an anti-poll tax measure, abolition of segregation in interstate transportation, and the end of discrimination and segregation in federal agencies and the military. By attacking Jim Crow, the committee had moved to a redefinition of equality and interpreted segregation as incompatible with equality.[79]

Forced by the report to take a position, he no longer could easily remain an ally of Southern Democrats and maintain the wary allegiance of Negro leaders and urban liberals. Compelled earlier to yield to demands for advancement of the Negro, pressures which he did not wish fully to resist, Truman had encouraged these forces and they were moving beyond his control. On his decision, his political future might precariously rest. Threatened by Henry Wallace's candidacy on a third-party ticket, Truman had to take a bold position on civil rights or risk losing the important votes of urban Negroes. Though he might antagonize Southern voters, he foresaw no risk of losing Southern Democrats, no possibility of a bolt by dissidents, and the mild Southern response to the Civil Rights Report seemed to confirm this judgment.[80]

On February 2, 1948, Truman asked the Congress to enact most of the recommendations of his Civil Rights Committee (except most of those attacking segregation). Rather than using his executive powers, as the committee had urged, to end segregation in federal employment or to abolish segregation and discrimination in the military, he *promised* only to issue orders ending discrimination (but not specifying segregation) in the military and in federal agencies.[81] Retreating to moderation, the administration did not submit any of the legislation, nor did Truman issue the promised executive orders. "The strategy," an assistant later explained, "was to start with a bold measure and then temporize to pick up the right-wing forces. Simply stated, backtrack after the bang." [82]

Truman sought to ease Southern doubts by inserting in the 1948 platform the party's moderate 1944 plank on civil rights. Most Negro leaders, fearing the taint of Wallace and unwilling to return to the GOP, appeared stuck with Truman and they praised him. Though they desired a stronger plank, they would not abandon him at the convention, for his advocacy of rights for Negroes was unmatched by any twentieth-century president. To turn their backs on him in this time of need, most Negroes feared, would be injuring their own cause. But others were prepared to struggle for a stronger plank. Urban bosses, persuaded that Truman would lose, hoped to save their local tickets, and prominent white liberals sought power and principle. Triumphing at the convention, they secured a stronger plank, but it did not promise social equality. By promising equality when it was still regarded as compatible with segregation, they were offering far less than the "walk forthrightly into the bright sunshine of human rights," which Hubert Humphrey, then mayor of Minneapolis, had pledged in leading the liberal effort.[83]

When some of the Southerners bolted and formed the States Rights party, Truman was freed of any need for tender courtship of the South. He had to capture the Northern vote. Quickly he issued the long-delayed executive orders, which established a federal antidiscrimination board, declared a policy of equal opportunity in the armed forces, and established a committee to end military discrimination and segregation. (In doing so, Truman courted Negro voters and halted the efforts of A. Philip Randolph to lead a Negro revolt against the draft unless the military was integrated.[84]) Playing politics carefully during the campaign, Truman generally stayed away from civil rights and concentrated on inflation, public housing, and Taft-Hartley.

In the new Democratic Congress Truman could not secure the civil rights program, and a coalition of Southern Democrats and Northern Republicans blocked his efforts. Though liberals were unhappy with his leadership, they did not question his proposed legislation. All agreed on the emphasis on social change through legislation and judicial decisions. The liberal way was the legal way, and it seldom acknowledged the depth of American racism or even considered the possibility of bold new tactics. Only occasionally—in the threatened March on Washington in 1941, in some ride-ins in 1947,[85] and in the campaign of civil disobedience against the draft in 1948—had there been bolder means. In each case Negroes had devised and carried out these tactics. But generally they relied upon more traditional means: they expected white America to yield to political pressure and subscribe to the dictates of American democracy. By relying upon legal change, however, and by emphasizing measures to restore a *modicum* of human dignity, Negroes and whites did not confront the deeper problems of race relations which they failed to understand.[86]

Struggling for moderate institutional changes, liberals were disappointed by Truman's frequent unwillingness to use his executive powers in behalf of the cause he claimed to espouse. Only after considerable pressure did he create a FEPC-type agency during the Korean War.[87] His loyalty-and-security program, in its operation, discriminated against Negroes, and federal investigators, despite protests to Truman, apparently continued to inquire into attitudes of interracial sympathy as evidence relevant to a determination of disloyalty.[88] He was also slow to require the Federal Housing Administration to stop issuing mortgages on property with restrictive covenants, and it continued, by its policies, to protect residential segregation.[89]

Yet his government was not without significant achievements in civil rights. His special committee had quietly acted to integrate the armed forces,[90] and even the recalcitrant Army had abolished racial quotas when the President secretly promised their restoration if the racial imbalance became severe.[91] And the Department of Justice, despite Truman's apparent indifference,[92] had been an active warrior in the battle against Jim Crow. Entering cases as an *amicus curiae*, Justice had submitted briefs arguing the unconstitutionality of enforcing restrictive covenants and of requiring separate-but-equal facilities in interstate transportation and in higher education.[93] During the summer of 1952, the Solicitor-General's Office even won the administration's approval for a brief directly challenging segregated primary education.[94]

The accomplishments of the Truman years were moderate, and the shortcomings left the nation with a great burden of unresolved problems. Viewed from the perspective of today, Truman's own views seem unduly mild and his government excessively cautious; viewed even by his own time he was a reluctant liberal, troubled by terror and eager to establish limited equality. He was ahead of public opinion in his legislative requests, but not usually in his actions. By his occasional advocacy, he educated the nation and held high the promise of equality. By kindling hope, he also may have prevented rebellion and restrained or delayed impulses to work outside of the system. But he also unleashed expectations he could not foresee, and forces which future governments would not be able to restrain.

VI

Never as committed to civil rights as he was opposed to communism at home and abroad, Truman ultimately became a victim of his own loyalty-and-security policies. Mildly criticized in 1945 and 1946 for being "soft on communism," the administration belatedly responded after the disastrous election of 1946.[95] Truman appointed a committee to investigate loyalty and security, promptly accepted its standard of judgment ("reasonable grounds of belief in disloyalty"), and created a system of loyalty boards.[96]

Outraging many liberals, his loyalty program provoked vigorous criticisms—for its secret investigations, for the failure to guarantee the accused the right to know the identity of and cross-examine the accuser, for its loose standards of proof, for its attempt to anticipate disloyal behavior by inquiring into attitudes.[97] In seeking to protect the nation, the government seemed to be searching for all who *might* be disloyal —"potential subversives," Truman called them.[98]

Dangerously confusing the problems of loyalty and security, the administration, in what might seem a burst of democratic enthusiasm, decided to apply the same standards to diplomats and gardeners. Disloyalty at any level of government would endanger the nation. "The presence within the government of any disloyal or subversive persons constitutes a threat to democratic processes," asserted Truman in launching the program.[99] Anxious to remove communism in government as a possible issue, Truman had exaggerated the dangers to the nation. And by assuming that disloyalty could be determined and subversives discovered, Truman seemed also to be promising *absolute* internal security.[100]

Shocked by earlier lax security procedures and unwilling to rely exclusively upon counterintelligence to uncover spies, the administration had responded without proper concern for civil liberties. So extreme was the program that it should have removed loyalty and security as a political issue. But by failing to distinguish between radical political activity and disloyalty, the administration endangered dissent and liberal politics: it made present or past membership in organizations on the Attorney-General's list evidence of possible disloyalty. Thus, in justifying investigations of political activity, it also legitimized occasional right-wing attacks on the liberal past and encouraged emphasis on the radicalism of a few New Dealers as evidence of earlier subversion.[101]

In their own activities, many liberals were busy combatting domestic communism. Taking up the cudgels, the liberal Americans for Democratic Action (ADA) came often to define its purpose by its anticommunism. As an enemy of those liberals who would not renounce association with Communists, and, hence, as vigorous foes of the Progressive party, the ADA was prepared to do battle. Following Truman's strategy, ADA members assailed Wallace and his supporters as Communists, dupes of the Communists, and fellow travelers. To publicize its case the ADA even relied upon the tactic of guilt by association and paid for advertisements listing the Progressive party's major donors and the organizations on the Attorney-General's list with which they were or had been affiliated.[102] (Truman himself also red-baited. "I do not want and will not accept the political support of Henry Wallace and his Communists. . . . These are days of high prices for everything, but any price for Wallace and his Communists is too much for me to pay.") [104] In the labor movement liberals like the Reuther brothers led anticommunist crusades, and the CIO ultimately expelled its Communist-led unions. ("Granting the desirability of eliminating Communist influence from the trade union movement," later wrote Irving Howe and Louis Coser, "one might still have argued that mass expulsions were not only a poor way of achieving this end but constituted a threat to democratic values and procedures.") [104]

Expressing the administration's position, Attorney-General J. Howard McGrath proclaimed a "struggle against pagan communist philosophies that seek to enslave the world." "There are today many Communists in America," he warned. "They are everywhere—in factories, offices, butcher stores, on street corners, in private business. And each carries in himself the death of our society." [105] ("I don't think anybody ought to be employed as instructors [sic] for the young people of this country who believes in the destruction of our form of government," declared Truman.) [106]

Calling for a crusade against evil, viewing communism as a virulent poison, the administration continued to emphasize the need for *absolute* protection, for *absolute* security. By creating such high standards and considering their fulfillment easy, by making success evidence of will and resolution, the administration risked assaults if its loyalty-and-security program was proved imperfect. To discredit the administration, all that was needed was the discovery of some red "spies," and after 1948 the evidence seemed abundant—Alger Hiss, William Remington, Judith Coplon, Julius and Ethel Rosenberg.[107]

In foreign policy, too, Truman, though emphasizing the danger of communism, had promised success. Containment could stop the spread of communism: military expansion could be restrained and revolutions prevented. Since revolutions, by liberal definition, were imposed on innocent people by a small minority, a vigilant American government could block them. By his rhetoric, he encouraged American innocence and left many citizens little choice but to believe in their own government's failure when America could not thwart revolution—when the Chinese Communists triumphed. If only resolute will was necessary, as the administration suggested, then what could citizens believe about America's failure? Was it simply bungling? Or treason and betrayal? [108]

By his rhetoric and action, Truman had contributed to the loss of public confidence and set the scene in which Joseph McCarthy could flourish. Rather than resisting the early movement of anticommunism, he had acted energetically to become a leader, and ultimately contributed to its transformation into a crusade which threatened his administration. But the President could never understand his own responsibility, and his failure handicapped him. Because he had a record of vigorous anticommunism, Truman was ill-prepared to respond to McCarthy's charges. At first the President could not foresee any danger and tried to dispense with McCarthy as "the greatest asset the Kremlin has." [109] And later, as the Senator terrorized the government, Truman was so puzzled and pained that he retreated from the conflict and sought to starve McCarthy without publicity. Rather than responding directly to charges, the President tried instead to tighten his program. But he could not understand that such efforts (for example, revising the loyalty standard to "reasonable doubt as to the loyalty of the individual") [110] could not protect the administration from charges of being soft on communism. He only encouraged these charges by seeming to yield to criticism, admitting that the earlier program was unnecessarily lax.

The President was a victim of his own policies and tactics. But bristling anticommunism was not simply Truman's way, but often the liberal way.[111] And the use of guilt by association, the discrediting of dissent, the intemperate rhetoric—these, too, were not simply the tactics of the Truman administration. The rancor and wrath of these years were not new to American politics, nor to liberals.[112] Indeed, the style of passionate charges and impugning opponents' motives may be endemic to American democratic politics. Submerging the issues in passion, using labels as substitutes for thought, questioning motives, these tactics characterized much of the foreign policy debate of the prewar and postwar years as well—a debate in which the liberals frequently triumphed. Developing a more extreme form of this rancorous style, relying upon even wilder charges and more flagrant use of guilt by association, McCarthy and his cohorts flailed the liberals and the Democratic administration.

VII

In looking at the war and postwar years, liberal scholars have emphasized the achievements of democratic reform, the extension of prosperity, the movements to greater economic and social equality. Confident that big business had become socially responsible and that economic security was widespread, they have celebrated the triumph of democratic liberalism. In charting the course of national progress, they frequently neglected or minimized major problems, or they interpreted them as temporary aberrations, or blamed them on conservative forces.[113]

Yet the developments of the sixties—the rediscovery of poverty and racism—suggest that the emphasis has been misplaced in interpreting these earlier years. In the forties and fifties white racism did not greatly yield to the dictates of American democracy, and the failure was not only the South's. The achievements of democratic liberalism were more limited than its advocates believed, and its reforms left many Americans still without adequate assistance. Though many liberal programs were blocked or diluted by conservative opposition, the liberal vision itself was dim. Liberalism in practice was defective, and its defects contributed to the temporary success of McCarthyism. Curiously, though liberalism was scrutinized by some sympathizers [114] who attacked its faith in progress and by others who sought to trace McCarthyism to the reform impulses of earlier generations,[115] most liberals failed to understand their own responsibility for the assault upon civil liberties or to respond to the needs of an "other America" which they but dimly perceived.

NOTES

[1] See Bernstein, "The Economic Policies of the Truman Administration: A Bibliographic Essay," in Richard Kirkendall, ed., *The Truman Period as a Research Field* (Columbia, Mo., 1967).

[2] See William Berman, "Civil Rights and Civil Liberties in the Truman Administration," in *ibid.*

[3] See Richard O. Davies, "Harry S. Truman and the Social Service State," in *ibid.*

[4] Gabriel Kolko, "American Business and Germany, 1930–1941," *Western Political Quarterly*, XV (December 1962), 713–28; cf. Roland Stromberg, "American Business and the Approach of War, 1935–1941," *Journal of Economic History*, XIII (Winter 1953), 58–78.

[5] Quoted in Corwin Edwards, *Economic and Political Aspects of International Cartels*, A Study for the Subcommittee on War Mobilization of the Senate Committee on Military Affairs, 78th Cong., 2nd Sess., pp. 43–44.

[6] House Committee on Ways and Means and Senate Committee on Finance, 76th Cong., 3rd Sess., *Joint Hearings on Excess Profits Taxation*, p. 22; *New York Times*, July 26, August 9, 1940; *Wall Street Journal*, July 15, 1940.

[7] The next four paragraphs draw upon Bernstein, "The Automobile Industry and the Coming of the Second World War," *Southwestern Social Science Quarterly*, XLVII (June 1966), 24–33.

[8] Walter Reuther, *500 Planes a Day* (1940); *CIO News*, December, 1940.

[9] Bruce Catton to Robert Horton, Policy Documentation File 631.0423, War Production Board Records, RG 179, National Archives.

[10] Richard Wilcock, "Industrial Management's Policies Towards Unionism," in Milton Derber and Edwin Young, *Labor and the New Deal* (Madison, Wis., 1957), pp. 305–8.

[11] Joel Seidman, *American Labor from Defense to Reconversion* (Chicago, 1953), pp. 41–87.

[12] *Ibid.*, pp. 131–51. It was in response to the coal strikes led by John Lewis that Congress passed the Smith-Connally Act.

[13] "With few exceptions, throughout the war years labor, not management, made the sacrifices when sacrifices were necessary," concludes Paul A.C. Koistinen, "The Hammer and the Sword: Labor, the Military, and Industrial Mobilization" (unpublished Ph.D. dissertation, University of California at Berkeley, 1965), p. 143.

[14] Bernstein, "The Truman Administration and the Politics of Inflation" (unpublished Ph.D. dissertation, Harvard University, 1963), Ch. 2.

[15] Senate Special Committee to Study Problems of American Small Business, 79th Cong., 2nd Sess., Senate Document 208, *Economic Concentration and World War II*, pp. 42–64. On concentration, see *ibid., passim;* cf. M. A. Adelman, "The Measurement of Industrial Concentration," *Review of Economics and Statistics,* XXXIII (November 1951), 269–96.

[16] *Economic Concentration and World War II*, pp. 22–39.

[17] C. Wright Mills, *The Power Elite* (New York, 1956), p. 273.

[18] This paragraph is based on Bernstein, "Industrial Reconversion: The Protection of Oligopoly and Military Control of the War Economy," *American Journal of Economics and Sociology,* XXVI (April 1967), 159–72. Cf. Jack Peltason, *The Reconversion Controversy* (Washington, 1950).

[19] Gabriel Kolko, *Wealth and Power in America* (New York, 1962), pp. 9–45; quotation from p. 31. Also see U.S. Bureau of the Census, *Income Distribution of the United States* (Washington, 1966), pp. 2–27; and Simon Kuznets, *Shares of Upper Income Groups in Income and Savings* (New York, 1953).

[20] Quoted from Francis Biddle, *In Brief Authority* (Garden City, N.Y., 1962), p. 213.

[21] Stetson Conn *et al., Guarding the United States and Its Outposts,* in *United States Army in World War II: The Western Hemisphere* (Washington, 1964), pp. 115–49. The Canadian government also moved Japanese away from the coast.

[22] Biddle, *In Brief Authority,* p. 219.

[23] Quoted from Henry L. Stimson and McGeorge Bundy, *On Active Service* (New York, 1948), p. 406. The prose is presumably Bundy's, but Stimson apparently endorsed the thought (p. xi). Also see War Department, *Final Report: Japanese Evacuation from the West Coast* (Washington, 1943), pp. 9–10.

[24] Quoted from Biddle, *In Brief Authority,* p. 219.

[25] *Korematsu* v. *U.S.,* 323 US 214, at 219. The Court split and Justice Black wrote the opinion. Justices Roberts, Murphy and Jackson dissented. Also see *Hirabayshi* v. *U.S.,* 320 US 81.

[26] *American Epoch* (New York, 1955), p. 528 (italics in original).

[27] Apparently Roosevelt refused to condemn the riots. Vito Marcantonio to Roosevelt, June 16, 1943, and reply, July 14, 1943, Vito Marcantonio Papers, New York Public Library. Also see Roosevelt's Proclamation No. 2588, in Samuel Rosenman, ed., *The Public Papers of Franklin D. Roosevelt,* (13 vols.; New York, 1938–50), XII, 258–59.

[28] "This was the dark side of an otherwise bright picture," concludes Link, *American Epoch,* p. 529. Also see Frank Freidel, *America in the Twentieth Century* (New York, 1960), p. 405. Oscar Handlin, *The American People in the Twentieth Century* (Cambridge, Mass., 1954), p. 215; Everett C. Hughes, "Race Relations and the Sociological Imagination," *American Sociological Review,* XXVIII (December 1963), 879–90.

[29] *Pittsburgh Courier,* July 15, September 2, 9, November 11, 1939; March 2, 9, 1940; April 26, 1941; cited in Richard Dalfiume, "Desegregation of the United States Armed Forces, 1939–1953" (unpublished Ph.D. dissertation, University of Missouri, 1966), pp. ix–x. For other protests, see *Pittsburgh Courier,* September 16, 30, 1939, November 23, and December 7, 1940.

[30] *Amsterdam News,* May 10, 1940; Louis Ruchames, *Race, Jobs and Politics* (New York, 1953), pp. 11–17.

[31] Ulysses Lee, *The Employment of Negro Troops,* in *United States Army in World War II: Special Studies* (Washington, 1966), pp. 35–52.

[32] Quoted from "For Manhood in National Defense," *Crisis,* XLVII (December 1940), 375. Also see Lee, *Employment of Negro Troops,* pp. 62–65.

[33] Lee, *ibid.,* pp. 69–84.

[34] Dalfiume, "Desegregation of the Armed Forces," p. 57, is the source of this quotation from the *Baltimore Afro-American,* November 2, 1940. Cf. *Pittsburgh Courier,* November 2, 1940.

[35] Herbert Garfinkel, *When Negroes March* (Glencoe, Ill., 1959), pp. 37–38.

[36] Quoted from the *Pittsburgh Courier,* January 25, 1941, and from the *Black Worker,* May 1941.

[37] "Proposals of the Negro March-on-Washington Committee" (undated), OF 391, Roosevelt Library. This was called to my attention by Dalfiume, "Desegregation of the Armed Forces," pp. 172–73.

[38] Edwin Watson to Roosevelt, June 14, 1941; A. Philip Randolph to Roosevelt, June 16, 1941; both in OF 391, Roosevelt Library; Garfinkel, *When Negroes March,* pp. 60–61.

[39] Dalfiume, "Desegregation of the Armed Forces," pp. 173–76, concludes that the Negro leaders may have met defeat. Cf. "The Negro's War," *Fortune,* XXV (April 1942), 76–80ff.; *Amsterdam News,* July 5, 1941; *Chicago Defender,* July 5, 1941; Randolph, "Why and How the March Was Postponed" (mimeo, n.d.), Schomburg Collection, New York Public Library.

[40] For the notion that the events of the war years constitute the beginnings of the civil rights revolution, see Dalfiume, "Desegregation of the Armed Forces," pp. 177–89.

[41] Ruchames, *Race, Jobs & Politics,* pp. 162–64.

[42] *Ibid.,* p. 164.

[43] Samuel Lubell, *The Future of American Politics* (New York, 1952), *passim.*

[44] Message on the State of the Union, January 11, 1944, in Rosenman, ed., *Public Papers of Roosevelt,* XIII, p. 41. For some evidence that Roosevelt was at least talking about a new alignment of politics, see Samuel Rosenman, *Working with Roosevelt* (London, 1952), pp. 423–29. Probably this was a tactical maneuver.

[45] Mary Hinchey, "The Frustration of the New Deal Revival, 1944–1946" (Unpublished Ph.D. dissertation, University of Missouri, 1965), Chs. 1–2.

[46] President's statement on signing the GI Bill of Rights, June 22, 1944, in Rosenman, ed., *Public Papers of Roosevelt,* XIII, 180–82, and Rosenman's notes, pp. 183–84. The GI Bill has generally been neglected as an antidepression measure.

[47] President's veto of the tax bill, February 22, 1944, in Rosenman, ed., *Public Papers of Roosevelt,* XIII, 80–84.

[48] Charles Merriam, "The National Resources Planning Board: A Chapter in American Planning Experience," *American Political Science Review,* XXXVIII (December 1944), 1075–88.

[49] Bernstein, "The Truman Administration and the Politics of Inflation," Chs. 3–4.

[50] Bernstein, "Charting a Course Between Inflation and Deflation: Secretary Fred Vinson and the Truman Administration's Tax Bill," scheduled for *Register of the Kentucky Historical Society.*

[51] Bernstein, "The Truman Administration and Its Reconversion Wage Policy," *Labor History,* VI (Fall 1965), 214–31.

[52] Bernstein, "Clash of Interests: The Postwar Battle Between the Office of

Price Administration and the Department of Agriculture," *Agricultural History*, XL (January 1967), 45–57; Allen J. Matusow, "Food and Farm Policies During the First Truman Administration, 1945–1948" (unpublished Ph.D. dissertation, Harvard University, 1963), Chs. 1–3.

[53] Bernstein, "The Removal of War Production Board Controls on Business, 1944–1946," *Business History Review*, XXXIX (Summer 1965), 243–60.

[54] Bernstein, "The Truman Administration and the Steel Strike of 1946," *Journal of American History*, LII (March 1966), 791–803; "Walter Reuther and the General Motors Strike of 1945–1946." *Michigan History*, IL (September 1965), 260–77; "The Postwar Famine and Price Control, 1946," *Agricultural History*, XXXIX (October 1964), 235–40; and Matusow, "Food and Farm Policies," Chs. 1–3.

[55] Bernstein, "The Presidency Under Truman," IV (Fall 1964), 8ff.

[56] Truman's message to Congress, September 6, 1945, in *Public Papers of the Presidents of the United States* (8 vols.; Washington, 1961–66), pp. 263–309 (1948).

[57] Quoted in Jonathan Daniels, *The Man of Independence* (Philadelphia, 1950), p. 288. For evidence that Truman was trying to head off a bolt by liberals, see *New York Times*, August 12, 1945; Harold Smith Daily Record, August 13, 1945, Bureau of the Budget Library, Washington, D.C.

[58] Harold Stein, "Twenty Years of the Employment Act" (unpublished ms., 1965, copy in my possession), p. 2. Also see Stephen K. Bailey, *Congress Makes a Law: The Story Behind the Employment Act of 1946* (New York, 1950).

[59] Lubell, *The Future of American Politics*, pp. 8–27, while emphasizing the continuation of the prewar executive-legislative stalemate and the strength of conservative forces in the postwar years, has also been critical of Truman. "All his skills and energies . . . were directed to standing still. . . . When he took vigorous action in one direction it was axiomatic that he would contrive soon afterward to move in the conflicting direction" (p. 10). Cf. Richard Neustadt, "Congress and the Fair Deal: A Legislative Balance Sheet," in Carl Friedrich and John Galbraith, eds., *Public Policy*, V, 351–81.

[60] Curtis MacDougall, *Gideon's Army* (3 vols.; New York, 1965–66), I, 102–27. The National Educational Committee for a New Party, which would be explicitly anticommunist, included John Dewey, A. Philip Randolph, Daniel Bell, and Lewis Corey.

[61] On the continuity, see Mario Einaudi, *The Roosevelt Revolution* (New York, 1959), pp. 125, 334; Neustadt, "Congress and the Fair Deal"; Eric Goldman, *Rendezvous with Destiny* (New York, 1952), pp. 314–15; and Goldman, *The Crucial Decade and After, America 1945–1960* (New York, 1960).

[62] Richard O. Davis, *Housing Reform during the Truman Administration* (Columbia, Mo.) p. 136. The original measure aimed for 1,050,000 units in seven years, at a time when the nation needed more than 12,000,000 units to replace inadequate housing. During the Truman years, the government constructed 60,000 units of public housing (pp. 105–38). Rather than creating programs to keep pace with urban needs, the government in these years fell further behind. In contrast, private industry was more active, and it was assisted by noncontroversial federal aid. Under Truman's government, then, the greatest achievement in housing was that private capital, protected by the government, built houses for the higher-income market.

[63] Under the old law, the maximum benefit for families was $85 a month and the minimum was $15, depending on prior earnings. The new minimum was $25 and the maximum $150. (*Social Security Bulletin*, September 1950, p. 3). Unless couples also had other sources of income, even maximum benefits ($1,800 a year) placed them $616 under the BLS "maintenance" standard of living and $109 above the WPA-based "emergency" standard of living—the poverty level. (Calculations

based on Kolko, *Wealth and Power*, pp. 96–98.) Since the payments were based on earnings, lower-income groups would receive even fewer benefits. They were the people generally without substantial savings or significant supplementary sources of income, and therefore they needed even more, not less, assistance.

64 *Congressional Quarterly Almanac*, V (1949), 434–35.

65 Bernstein, "Economic Policies of the Truman Administration." Truman had achieved very little: improved unemployment benefits, some public power and conservation projects, agricultural assistance, and a National Science Foundation. He failed to secure the ill-conceived Brannan Plan and two programs suggested by Roosevelt: federal aid to education and health insurance. For his health insurance programs, see his messages of November 19, 1945, in *Public Papers of Truman* (1945), pp. 485–90, and of May 19, 1947, in *ibid.*, (1947), pp. 250–52. In 1951, when the BLS calculated that a family of four needed $4,166 to reach the "maintenance" level, 55.6 percent of the nation's families had incomes beneath that level (Bureau of the Census, *Income Distribution in the United States*, p. 16.).

66 Brenstein, "Economic Policies of the Truman Administration."

67 Truman to William Green, September 13, 1952, PPF 85, Truman Papers, Truman Library.

68 Wilcock, "Industrial Management's Policies Toward Unionism," pp. 305–11; "Public Opinion on the Case Bill," OF 407B, Truman Papers, Truman Library; Robert Brady, *Business as a System of Power* (New York, 1943) pp. 210–15; Harry Millis and Emily Clark Brown, *From the Wagner Act to Taft-Hartley* (Chicago, 1950), pp. 286–98.

69 R. Alton Lee, *Truman and Taft-Hartley: A Question of Mandate* (Lexington, Ky. 1966), pp. 22–71.

70 Lee, *Truman and Taft-Hartley*, pp. 79–130.

71 Truman's message to Congress, May 25, 1946, in *Public Papers of Truman* (1946), pp. 277–80.

72 Truman's address of July 14, 1940, reprinted in *Congressional Record*, 76th Cong., 3rd Sess., 5367–69.

73 Ruchames, *Race, Jobs & Politics*, pp. 130–36. This section relies upon Bernstein, "The Ambiguous Legacy: The Truman Administration and Civil Rights" (paper given at the AHA, December 1966, copy at the Truman Library).

74 Truman to David Niles, July 22, 1946, and drafts (undated) of an order on nondiscrimination; and Philleo Nash to Niles (undated), Nash Files, Truman Library.

75 Truman to Walter White, June 11, 1946, PPF 393, Truman Papers, Truman Library.

76 Walter White, *A Man Called White* (New York, 1948), pp. 331–32.

77 Robert Carr to Bernstein, August 11, 1966.

78 Interview with Philleo Nash, September 19, 1966.

79 President's Committee on Civil Rights, *To Secure These Rights*. (Washington, 1947), pp. 1–95.

80 Clark Clifford, "Memorandum for the President," November 17, 1947, Clifford Papers (his possession), Washington, D.C.

81 Truman's message to Congress, February 2, 1948, in *Public Papers of Truman* (1948), pp. 117–26.

82 Interview with Nash.

83 On the struggle, see Clifton Brock, *Americans for Democratic Action: Its Role in National Politics* (Washington, 1962), pp. 94–99; quotation at p. 98.

84 Grant Reynolds, "A Triumph for Civil Disobedience," *Nation*, CLXVI (August 28, 1948), pp. 228–29.

85 George Houser and Bayard Rustin, "Journey of Reconciliation" (mimeo, n.d., probably 1947), Core Files, Schomburg Collection New York Public Library.

[86] There was no urging of special programs to assist Negroes left unemployed (at roughly double the white rate) in the mild recession of 1949–1950, nor was there open acknowledgement of race hatred.

[87] National Council of Negro Women to Truman, November 18, 1950, Nash Files, Truman Library; Senator William Benton to Truman, October 21, 1951, OF 526B, Truman Library.

[88] Carl Murphy to Truman, April 10, 1950, OF 93 misc.; Walter White to Truman, November 26, 1948, OF 252K; both in Truman Library.

[89] NAACP press release, February 4, 1949, Schomburg Collection, New York Public Library; Hortense Gabel to Raymond Foley, February 26, 1953, Foley Papers, Truman Library; Housing and Home Finance Agency, *Fifth Annual Report* (Washington, 1952), p. 413.

[90] President's Committee on Equality of Treatment and Opportunity in the Armed Forces, *Freedom to Serve* (Washington 1950); Dalfiume, "Desegregation of the Armed Forces."

[91] Gordon Gray to Truman, March 1, 1950, OF 1285B, Truman Library.

[92] Interview with Philip Elman, December 21, 1966.

[93] *Shelley* v. *Kraemer*, 334 US 1; *Henderson* v. *United States* 339 US 816; *McLaurin* v. *Board of Regents*, 339 US 641.

[94] Interview with Elman; *Brown* v. *Board of Education*, 347 US 483.

[95] "The Report of the President's Temporary Commission on Employee Loyalty," Appendix III, Charles Murphy Papers, Truman Library; Rep. Jennings Bryan to Truman, July 25, 1946, OF 2521, and Stephen Spingarn, "Notes on Meeting of Subcommittee of February 5, 1947," Spingarn Papers, Truman Library.

[96] E.O. 9806, 11 Fed. Reg. 13863; "The Report of the President's Temporary Commission on Employee Loyalty," quotation at 3; E.O. 9835, 12 F.R. 1935. On earlier programs, see Eleanor Bontecou, *The Federal Loyalty-Security Program* (Ithaca, N.Y., 1953), pp. 1–19.

[97] Letter by Zechariah Chafee, Jr., Erwin Griswold, Milton Katz, and Austin Scott, in *New York Times*, April 13, 1947; L. A. Nikoloric, "The Government Loyalty Program," *American Scholar*, XIX (Summer 1950), 285–98; Bontecou, *Federal Loyalty-Security Program*, pp. 30–34.

[98] Quoted from Bontecou, *Federal Loyalty-Security Program*, p. 32, who suggests that Truman may have really meant Communists who might be subject to future orders by the party. Also see Truman's statement of November 14, 1947, in *Public Papers of Truman* (1947), pp. 489–91.

[99] Quoted from E.O. 9835, 12 Fed. Reg. 1935.

[100] Much of the analysis of this program and its contribution to the rise of McCarthyism is indebted to Athan Theoharis, "The Rhetoric of Politics: Foreign Policy, Internal Security and Domestic Politics in the Truman Era, 1945–1950" (paper delivered at the Southern Historical Association, November 1966). Cf. Daniel Bell, ed., *The New American Right* (New York, 1955). On the need for absolute security, see Tom Clark to A. Devitt Vanech, February 14, 1947, OF 2521, Truman Library; "Report of the President's Temporary Commission on Employee Loyalty"; Theoharis, "Rhetoric of Politics," pp. 26–32.

[101] Theoharis, "Rhetoric of Politics," pp. 29–31.

[102] Karl M. Schmidt, *Henry A. Wallace: Quixotic Crusade, 1948* (Syracuse, N.Y., 1960), pp. 159–60, 252–53, 261–62. On the strategy of letting the liberal intellectuals attack Wallace, see Clifford, "Memorandum for the President," November 17, 1947. On the split in liberal ranks on cooperation with Communists, see Curtis MacDougall, *Gideon's Army*, I, 122–25.

[103] Truman's address of March 17, 1948, in *Public Papers of Truman* (1948), p. 189.

[104] Howe and Coser, *The American Communist Party*, 2nd. ed. (New York, 1962), p. 468; see pp. 457–68 for the activity of labor.

[105] McGrath's address of April 8, 1949, McGrath Papers, Truman Library, which was called to my attention by Theoharis. Also see Theoharis, "Rhetoric of Politics," n. 37.

[106] Quoted from transcript of President's News Conference of June 9, 1949, Truman Library. Also see Sidney Hook, "Academic Integrity and Academic Freedom." *Commentary*, VIII (October 1949), cf., Alexander Meiklejohn, *New York Times Magazine*, March 27, 1949, pp. 10ff. In his veto of the McCarran Act, Truman failed to defend civil liberties effectively and instead emphasized that the act would impair the government's anticommunist efforts. Veto message of September 22, 1950, *Public Papers of Truman* (1950), pp. 645–53.

[107] Theoharis, "Rhetoric of Politics," pp. 32–38.

[108] See Truman's addresses of March 17, 1948, in *Public Papers of Truman* (1948), pp. 182–86; and of June 7, 1949, in *ibid.* (1949), pp. 277–80. See Theoharis, "Rhetoric of Politics," pp. 17–27.

[109] Quoted from transcript of President's News Conference, March 30, 1950, Truman Library.

[110] E.O. 10241, 16 Fed. Reg. 9795.

[111] On liberal confusion about this period, see Joseph Rauh, "The Way to Fight Communism," *Future*, January 1962. For the argument that liberal naiveté about Stalinism had led to McCarthyism, see Irving Kristol, "Civil Liberties, 1952 —A Study in Confusion," *Commentary*, XIII (March 1952), 228–36.

[112] For earlier antitotalitarianism, see Freda Kirchwey, "Curb the Fascist Press," *Nation*, CLIV (March 28, 1942), 357–58.

[113] Although there are no thorough, scholarly histories of these years, there are many texts that embody these characteristics. In addition, much of the monographic literature by other social scientists conforms to the pattern described in this paragraph. For a discussion, see Bernstein, "Economic Policies of the Truman Administration."

[114] In particular see the works of Reinhold Niebuhr and the new realism that he has influenced: Niebuhr, *Moral Man and Immoral Society* (New York, 1932); *The Children of Light and the Children of Darkness* (New York, 1944); Arthur Schlesinger, Jr., *The Vital Center* (Cambridge, Mass., 1947). What is needed is a critical study of wartime and postwar liberalism, an explanation for many on "Where We Came Out" (to use the title of Granville Hicks's volume). See Jason Epstein, "The CIA and the Intellectuals," *New York Review of Books*, VII (April 20, 1967), 16–21.

[115] See Bell, ed., *The New American Right*, and the tendency to trace McCarthyism back to earlier reform movements and often to Populism. The volume, interestingly, is dedicated to the managing editor of the *New Leader*. For a former radical's attempt to reappraise the liberal past, see Richard Hofstadter, *The Age of Reform* (New York, 1956).

FOR FURTHER READING

Alonzo L. Hamby. *Beyond the New Deal: Harry S. Truman and American Liberalism.* New York: Columbia University Press, 1973.

Susan M. Hartmann. *Truman and the 80th Congress.* Columbia: University of Missouri Press, 1971.

Donald R. McCoy and Richard T. Ruetten. *Quest and Response.* Lawrence: University of Kansas Press, 1973.

THE ORIGINS OF AMERICAN POSTWAR FOREIGN POLICY

ROBERT LASCH

During the late 1940's and the 1950's, heavy pressures induced most Americans to accept President Truman's version of international politics: that a monolithic Communist force, bent on world domination, had to be "contained." Liberal and labor groups, eager to prove their loyalty to American institutions and values, purged themselves of almost everyone who suggested alternative choices. And almost every organization, from the highest echelons of government to the custodial services in local schools, ferreted out those suspected of less than 100 per cent agreement. Few reputable scholars ventured to challenge the dominant view.

During the past decade, however, new strands of thought have captured American minds. Stimulated in part by the work of William Appleman Williams, a maverick professor who expressed dissent even in the 1950's, a younger generation of historians has questioned the wisdom of Truman's policy, as well as the accuracy of his interpretation of events; a number of them have portrayed the American government as aggressively determined to open the way for capitalist enterprise and to suppress popular social revolutions all over the world. We have all learned, moreover, that Communism is far from monolithic, that the Russian and Chinese versions are far from identical, and that the words of high-level officials in Washington cannot be accepted as gospel.

Robert Lasch, who received a Pulitzer Prize for his editorials on foreign affairs, examines the ideas and motives of American policy-makers of the late 1940's. In his view, these eminent men made errors of judgment, acted on facile and untested assumptions, and opportunistically "established the habit of systematic mendacity which our government has practiced ever since." His account should remind the reader that in studying the past it is important to determine how

Reprinted with permission from Robert Lasch, "How We Got Where We Are," *The Progressive*, July 1971.

many scholarly works have depended for their published conclusions
upon explanations provided by the government. How accurate are such
works in the light of further information and close analysis?

Lasch is severe, but his assessment does not sound extraordinary in
the 1970's. The student might well compare his narrative with Gabriel
Kolko's article in Part III; although both writers express criticism,
a careful reading will bring to light their considerable differences in
emphasis and in basic assumptions about the making of foreign policy.

□ □ □

If the moral bankruptcy of the Vietnam war has convinced Americans
that a foreign policy addressed to the military containment of Communism has reached dead end, it is important to understand the origins
of that policy. As Democrats originated it and liberals in both the
Democratic and Republican parties supported it, a special obligation
rests upon them to re-evaluate the past if they are to improve the future.

With the deepening of national revulsion at the consequences of
attempted containment in Southeast Asia, a comforting rationalization
has developed among liberal Democrats. They argue that in the years
immediately following World War II containment was a necessity
dictated by presumed Soviet expansionism and the frenzies of a megalo-
maniac Stalin, but that changing times and the dispersion of Communist
power have altered the postulates on which American policy should be
based.

The historical record does not bear them out. The plain truth is
that men like Averell Harriman, Clark Clifford, and Dean Acheson, all
of whom supported the Vietnam war so long as there was any prospect
of winning it militarily, founded the containment doctrine twenty years
earlier on their own mistaken judgments, unexamined assumptions, and
a vainglorious aspiration for the worldwide expansion of American
power.

Containment, openly proclaimed, began in 1947 with the Truman
Doctrine of aid to Greece and Turkey, but its roots went back to the
days immediately following Franklin D. Roosevelt's death two years
earlier. Within a month of Harry Truman's accession to the Presidency,
the whole direction of the Roosevelt policy had been reversed. Truman,
who in 1941 had expressed the hope, according to the *New York Times*,

that the Russians and the Nazis would kill each other off, saw no essential difference between Hitler and Stalin. Two weeks after he became President he dressed down Molotov in a famous confrontation, and embarked on a hard-line policy designed to expel Soviet power from Eastern Europe and exclude it from Asia.

Where President Roosevelt had ignored or moderated the anti-Soviet advice of Ambassador Harriman and others in the State Department, Mr. Truman embraced their counsel without reservation. To halt what Harriman called a "barbarian invasion of Europe" he set out, under the plausible pretext of establishing free democratic governments in Poland, Rumania, and Bulgaria, to secure an "open door" for American economic influence, which would mean ultimately political power as well, in the border countries recaptured by Soviet troops from the Nazis.

Because these lands controlled the historic invasion routes to Russia, and before the war had been ruled by fascist and bitterly anti-Soviet forces, Stalin had good reason to suspect the benevolence of a Truman-Churchill move to restore Western hegemony. His suspicions must have been reinforced when Truman resorted to crude economic blackmail, offering and then withholding credits for postwar reconstruction, in an effort to force Soviet compliance. They were further aggravated by Mr. Truman's ostentatious flourishing of the atomic bomb as another instrument of pressure. An increasingly hostile propaganda campaign to enflame American opinion against the Soviets, capped by Churchill's widely exploited Iron Curtain speech at Fulton, Missouri, in 1946, tightened the lines of mutual distrust. By early 1947, the cold war psychology had become deeply entrenched in Washington.

I have always thought it a cruel irony that the late Senator Joseph R. McCarthy should have singled out Dean Acheson as the symbol and apotheosis of softness on Communism. He deserved McCarthy's libels least of all his victims.

Acheson was a principal author of the Truman Doctrine, the engineer of its public acceptance, the theologian of its exegesis. As Undersecretary of State to James Byrnes, he had shrewdly profited from Byrnes's mistake in treating Mr. Truman like an untutored bumpkin. Acheson always cast himself as a respectful adviser presenting the facts for Presidential decision, and never seemed to press his own views. Far from being the evil infiltrator who lost China, he was in fact a founding father of the cold war. When he refused to turn his back on Alger Hiss, and resisted McCarthy's attack on the State Department for allegedly harboring an elastic number of card-carrying Communists, it was not out of softness toward the Communists but because the crudities of McCarthyism offended his sense of decorum.

It is astonishing how little dissent was expressed within the Government, how few critical questions were asked, when such a far-ranging policy as the military containment of Communism was adopted. Joseph Jones, a former *Fortune* editor in the State Department who drafted the Truman message on Greek-Turkish aid in 1947 under Acheson's direction and later wrote a book about it (*The Fifteen Weeks*, Viking, 1955), repeatedly emphasized the Department's total unanimity in dealing with the crisis. "There was only one point of view," he wrote.

A great deal of this unanimity could be traced to Acheson's strong personality and his mastery of the diplomatic apparatus. Once Britain had announced its withdrawal from Greece there was never any question of what the American policy should be; Acheson already knew. At a Sunday staff session to prepare position papers he was asked if they were making a decision or executing one. As he relates in *Present at the Creation* (Norton, 1969), Acheson replied: "The latter; under the circumstances there could be only one decision. At that we drank a martini or two toward the confusion of our enemies."

More broadly, the absence of dissent reflected the fact that by early 1947 the assumptions of the Cold War had been largely accepted throughout the diplomatic establishment and the Truman Administration. Soviet intractability in Eastern Europe and the Middle East had convinced most American leaders not that the Russians were morbidly sensitive about protecting the strategic approaches to their country, but that they had embarked on a career of world conquest.

Americans could generate a sense of horror at the thought that Russia possessed the power to march all the way to the Atlantic, but no reassurance from Russia's failure to do so. The worst apprehensions were confirmed by Moscow's arrogant occupation of northern Iran beyond the agreed date of withdrawal, but oddly not relieved by the withdrawal when it did take place. John Foster Dulles, appointed Republican adviser to the State Department in recognition of his Party's victory in the Congressional elections of 1946, went around the country making truculent speeches for the formation of a Western military bloc against Russia. Acheson, in testimony before a Senate committee, described Soviet foreign policy as "an aggressive and expanding one."

Economic motives also came into play. The Truman Administration was stacked with representatives of big business and finance—men like Harriman, Robert Lovett, James Forrestal, Will Clayton, Dulles—who, having built for war the world's mightiest productive machine, now demanded an expansion of American power to guarantee peacetime markets and investment opportunities. In a speech at Baylor University while his Greek-Turkish aid message was in the final stages of ghostwriting, Mr. Truman expressed the view of these interests. Denouncing socialism and its characteristic practice of state trading as incompatible with American free enterprise, he said our economic system could survive at home "only if it became a world system."

In the summer of 1946, President Truman assigned an able lawyer from St. Louis, Clark Clifford, to prepare a comprehensive report on U.S.-Soviet relations. Clifford, Mr. Truman's special counsel and speech-writer, interviewed the highest officials of the military, diplomatic, and intelligence bureaucracies, and filed an implacably hard-line report, excerpts from which have been published in Arthur Krock's memoirs, *Sixty Years on the Firing Line* (Funk & Wagnalls, 1968). Clifford saw Soviet policy as based on the expectation of a coming war for the world, and counseled the use of military power—"the only language they understand"—to block their expansion. America must be prepared to use atomic and biological weapons if necessary, he argued, and should entertain no proposal for disarmament so long as any possibility of Soviet aggression existed.

With such a world view in his mind, Mr. Truman needed no urging to proclaim his Doctrine. He had wanted to proclaim it, Krock reports, several times during 1946, but had been persuaded to await a better occasion. The occasion was provided by Britain's note of February 21, 1947, announcing that it would terminate military guardianship over Greece at the end of March.

The note was received almost with elation in the State Department. The top desk men, according to Jones, viewed it as a historic delegation to the United States of "world leadership, with all its burdens and its glory." The Department felt called to a high mission. "Tenseness and controlled excitement" filled the room when Acheson expounded the emerging policy at staff meetings. All felt that "a new chapter in world history had opened, and they were the most privileged of men."

Nobody seems to have asked precisely what kind of leadership history had summoned us to. It was taken for granted that the vast expansion of American military and economic power that had already taken place was, like British power, benevolent, freedom-loving, and peaceful, whereas any manifestation of Soviet power must *ipso facto* represent an evil design to capture the world for totalitarian Communism.

The earliest version of the domino theory soon became gospel. If Russia took Greece, then Turkey's position would be untenable; after Turkey, Iran would fall, and then the whole Middle East; at that point Southern Asia and North Africa would lie open, and Western Europe could hardly survive the shock.

Such was the thinking that dominated the Administration to the virtual exclusion of dissent or even discussion. Yet it might have been asked just how an exhausted Russia which had lost 7,500,000 men and seen its own territory laid waste could launch world conquest against an adversary which controlled most of the world's intact industrial plant and *all its nuclear weapons*. The hypothesis might have been advanced that Soviet truculence reflected weakness rather than strength, combined with almost psychotic memories of 1919, when the West had tried to strangle the Soviet Revolution at birth. To all such doubts little attention was paid.

One of the few dissenters, curiously enough, was George F. Kennan, whose memos from Moscow had fed the sources of anti-Communism within the Administration and who was to become the ideologue of containment.

Working under Ambassador Harriman in Moscow, Kennan had burst out of bureaucratic obscurity in early 1946 with a long telegram to the State Department analyzing Soviet policy. The Treasury had sent what he regarded as a foolish and naive message expressing anguish over the Russians' refusal to join the World Bank and Monetary Fund. Convinced that the Kremlin had no intention of cooperating with Western capitalism, but based its policy on the assumption of inevitable conflict, Kennan sat down to instruct Washington in the facts of life as he saw them.

Americans ought to understand, he wrote, that the Soviet leaders were prisoners of a Marxist ideology which preached the impossibility of permanent peaceful coexistence with capitalism. Their neurotic view of the outside world arose, he felt, from a basic insecurity; only by exalting an external menace could they justify their repressive dictatorship and sustain their own leadership of the Russian people. Accordingly, we must expect the Soviets to pursue a policy of expanding their power wherever they could, until met with superior force. "We have here," he wrote, "a political force committed fanatically to the belief that with the United States there can be no permanent *modus vivendi*." The challenge could be met without recourse to a general miliary conflict, Kennan concluded, by blocking Soviet expansion at the critical points.

Reading the shallow and dogmatic long telegram in later years, Kennan was "horrified." It sounded "exactly like one of those primers put out by alarmed Congressional committees or by the D.A.R." But in the agitated Washington atmosphere of 1946 it created a sensation. Even the President read it, so Kennan came to believe. The State Department sent a message of hearty commendation. Secretary of the Navy Forrestal, perhaps the Administration's most passionate Russophobe, circulated hundreds of copies as required reading for the military establishment and Cabinet. Kennan's reputation was made; "my voice now carried."

Having returned to Washington at the end of 1946, Kennan served as part-time member of the special State Department committee set up to discuss Greek-Turkish aid. He saw no alternative, especially in Greece, to a policy of helping the established government subdue insurrection by opening the road to economic revival. But when he saw a draft of the message a few days before Mr. Truman's appearance before Congress, he was disturbed.

Containment as here propounded differed from what he had in mind. He had advocated, so he thought, the exertion of political and economic influence, not to foil a hypothetical world conquest but to sustain a tolerable balance of power. As translated by eager cold warriors like Forrestal, the doctrine became one of worldwide military intervention.

Kennan talked to Acheson to protest Mr. Truman's sweeping generalities and what he suspected to be the Pentagon's infiltration of military expansionism into a program of political and economic aid. He pointed out the dangers of placing aid to Greece "in the framework of a universal policy rather than in that of a specific decision addressed to a specific set of circumstances." He urged less emphasis on military aid to Greece and none at all to Turkey, advised against casting the program in terms of ideological conflict, and warned that the Russians might reply with war.

It is quite possible that Kennan's objections were less vigorous in fact than they were in retrospect—after he had turned against containment. If he sensed a military distortion of his views, nevertheless he was at this very period writing the famous tract "The Sources of Soviet Conduct," published in *Foreign Affairs*, which was to establish him as the philosopher of containment. He signed it "X," but Arthur Krock, a friend of Forrestal's, promptly identified the author in the *New York Times* as Kennan.

Widely reprinted and exhaustively discussed, the "X" article produced the same sensation on the public level as the long telegram had produced in the Washintgon bureaucracy. Again, the timing was perfect. Whipped up by the debate over Greek-Turkish aid, public opinion was peculiarly receptive to a seemingly learned analysis by one who had studied the Russians at first hand.

If Kennan was privately urging a distinction between military and political containment, the distinction did not come through in his published paper. Elaborating on the ideas of the long telegram, he depicted the Soviet leaders as committed by ideology and circumstances to a ruthless policy of expansion, striving to fill "every nook and cranny available . . . in the basin of world power," and stopping only when it meets with some unanswerable force." While he advised against hyteria and blustering toughness, he called for a long-term American commitment to the "adroit and vigilant" application of "unalterable counterforce at every point where they show signs of encroaching upon the interests of a peaceful, stable world." Such a response of "firm and vigilant containment," he wrote, would "increase enormously the strains under which Soviet policy must operate," and promote tendencies within Russia leading to "either the breakup or the gradual mellowing of Soviet power."

Years later, Kennan wrote that the sensation produced by the "X" article made him feel "like one who has inadvertently loosened a large boulder from the top of a cliff and now helplessly witnesses its path of destruction in the valley below." He deplored the deficiencies in his essay that became visible with hindsight—the failure to make clear that he was advocating political rather than military containment, the failure to specify a selective policy addressed to strategically vital areas as opposed to the Truman Doctrine of universal intervention. Even in hindsight he neglected to note his most egregious error—the failure to consider as one source of Soviet conduct the fact that Russia had barely escaped destruction at the hands of a Western anti-Communist power whose aggression the West at Munich had sought to channel in Russia's direction.

Walter Lippmann challenged the Kennan thesis in a brilliant series of newspaper commentaries which he later published as a book. Wounded, Kennan felt Lippmann "mistook me for the author of precisely those features of the Truman Doctrine which I had most vigorously opposed." But Lippmann was analyzing not any misgivings Kennan might have expressed in private, but a published document which undeniably laid the philosophical groundwork for a policy of military adventurism which Kennan only later opposed publicly. He wrote a letter to Lippmann disavowing any attribution to the Russians of aspirations for world conquest. They "don't want to invade anyone—it is not in their tradition," he wrote. But, significantly, he never mailed the letter. As a rising figure in the diplomatic establishment ("my voice now carried") Kennan could not afford to repudiate the "team." He was a captive of his own reputation.

Whatever the scope and vigor of Kennan's objections to the Truman Doctrine as it emerged from the policy-making process, there was no time to heed his misgivings even if anybody had wanted to. Not only had the basic decision for a militant policy been approved at all levels of government, but the ponderous machinery of the public-opinion buildup had already been set in motion.

The public-opinion buildup was vital, and Acheson took charge of it. Six days after Britain's note of February 1947—that it was withdrawing forces from Greece—had been received in Washington, Congressional leaders, with the conspicuous exception of Senator Robert

Taft, were invited to the White House. As Acheson relates in his memoirs, Secretary of State George Marshall, home for a few days between trips, assumed the task of expounding the Administration's decision, and "flubbed" it. The great general found it impossible to lead an ideological charge. His account of events and the policy proposed to deal with them was dry, factual, unemotional. The assembled Congressional leaders sat on their hands.

Acheson, aware that an egg had been laid, asked President Truman's permission to speak. "No time was left," as he later recalled, "for measured appraisal." He roused the meeting from its torpor with a powerful evangelical appeal. He painted the Red menace in lurid tones. He ran through the dominoes until he had his listeners staring at Russian hordes flooding the beaches of the Atlantic Coast. He drew a chilling contract between American freedom and Soviet tyranny, locked in fateful contest at the ancient crossroads of the world. Not since Rome and Carthage, he said, had there been such a polarization of power.

When he had finished, not a single word of dissent was voiced by anybody in the room. Impressed, Senator Arthur Vandenberg, preening his feathers as the new Republican chairman of the Foreign Relations Committee, told Acheson that if the country were given facts like these in strong terms, the Administration could expect support. He advised Mr. Truman to envelop Greek-Turkish aid in a ringing declaration that would "scare hell out of the country."

With what Acheson called "incredible speed," the new policy moved through the various stages of detail work and approval. Five days after the British note, a set of specific recommendations for action had been agreed on by the White House, State Department, and Pentagon. One day later the Congressional leaders were taken in tow, and thirteen days after that, Truman was standing before a joint session of Congress, somberly declaring that totalitarian regimes "imposed on free peoples, by direct or indirect aggression, undermine the foundations of international peace and hence the security of the United States."

In later years, President Truman was to describe this declaration of policy as second in importance only to his decision to drop the atomic bomb. If he believed this, it is incomprehensible that he could have launched the nation on such a fateful course with the casual air of an American Legionnaire swinging a jaunty cane in a patriotic parade. Apparently it never occurred to him to question his facile assumption that the Soviets were just the Nazis all over again, or to make sure that he was presented with alternative courses to the one everybody was recommending. He came to be much admired for his snappy way of making decisions ("The buck stops here," he liked to say), but in this case he and the nation might have benefited from some second thoughts and even a bit of conflicting advice.

Henry Wallace tried to give that kind of advice, but Mr. Truman had ejected Wallace, his Secretary of Commerce, from the Cabinet for publicly disagreeing with Secretary of State Byrnes, and Mr. Truman regarded even Byrnes as too soft on Russia. Out of government and heading for a disastrous campaign for President as a third party candidate, Wallace became the principal spokesman for the opposition. There were other voices of dissent and warning or worried concern, such as Lippmann's and *The Progressive*'s, but in general the country accepted the Administration case.

While Congress considered the policy, the public-opinion buildup proceeded. Acheson met with one group of newsmen after another. Off-the-record interviews were granted to favored correspondents. A Cabinet committee was organized to reach community leaders, especially businessmen, with the word. Senator Vandenberg conducted missionary work among influential Republicans. A growing public information apparatus ground out press releases designed to transmit the Red scare to the remotest corners of the country.

It was of foreboding significance that the public information program to sell the policy to the country was actually drafted before Mr. Truman's message itself. Within a week after receipt of the British note, a coordinating committee of State, War, and Navy press agents started working out a public information (for which read "propaganda"·) outline. They unanimously agreed that "the only way we can sell the public on our new policy is by emphasizing the necessity of holding the line: Communism versus democracy should be the major theme." It was agreed to "relate military aid to the principle of supporting democracy," to assure the nation that "our new policy is not warlike but on the contrary the best way we know of avoiding war," and to proclaim the intention "of this Government to go to the assistance of free governments everywhere."

The paper containing this propaganda prospectus became "the most significant document used in the drafting of the Truman Doctrine," according to Jones of the State Department, who did the drafting. To him, the fusing and interaction of propaganda with policy was a magnificent example of administrative coordination. Others perhaps will be more deeply impressed with the fact that policy had become the reflection of propaganda instead of the other way around.

The Administration bill, providing $300 million for Greece and $100 million for Turkey, passed the Senate by a vote of 67 to 23 and the House by 287 to 107. The country had been assured that aid would be primarily economic and political, but with the arrival of a military mission in Greece these promises went quickly by the board. As with so many other adventures in containment, our intervention rapidly created the conditions to which it was supposed to be a response.

Actually, there had been little guerrilla fighting during the incubation of the Truman Doctrine. In their first bid for control in 1944, the Greek Communists had been smashed by Britain and the Royalists, while Stalin, faithfully adhering to his agreement with Churchill, lifted not a finger to help them. In 1946 and early 1947 the Communists had 10,000 to 12,000 guerrillas in the mountains of the north, but were seeking legal power, or a share of it, through coalition with the Liberal Party under Sofoulis. Once American intervention was assured, Sofoulis broke with the Communists and, in July, 1947, they went underground.

During the first year of the aid program the numbers, morale, and equipment of the guerrilla forces steadily increased. Supplied and encouraged by Communist regimes in Yugoslavia, Albania, and to a lesser degree Bulgaria (Russia confining itself to a proxy role), the guerrillas attacked many towns and controlled substantial territory in the north. For a few weeks in February, 1948, they were operating within twenty miles of Athens. Economic aid, therefore, took second place to winning the civil war which Acheson and Mr. Truman had precipitated. Within two years a modest investment of $300 million expanded fourfold, and most of it went into weapons and training of troops while Greece writhed in poverty. In early 1949 the country was in worse shape than it had been in 1945.

What ended the civil war in Greece was not American power so much as the internal politics of the Soviet bloc. In consequence of Tito's stubborn refusal to subordinate Yugoslav economic interests to those of Moscow, the Cominform on June 28, 1948, publicly denounced him, and thereby revealed to an unbelieving world the yawning fissure in what had been taken for an invincible monolith. The Kremlin's break with Tito shot away the philosophical basis of containment—the assumption that any Communists anywhere must be servants of Russian national interest—but nobody in the U.S. Government was willing to admit it.

Just as they did later when China's break with Moscow disclosed an even greater split, U.S. policy-makers went right on building military barriers to a centrally controlled "Communist imperialism" long after the falsity of central control had been exposed. Meanwhile, however, U.S. officials did not mind profiting from the great fact whose existence they refused to recognize. Tito obligingly closed his borders to the Greek guerrillas, and by late 1949 the civil war was over. Only then could the American mission turn to the economic reconstruction which from the beginning had been Greece's foremost need. By this time the Marshall Plan was in operation, and Greece joined it.

It is to Dean Acheson's credit that he was a principal architect of the Marshall Plan as well as the Truman Doctrine. In common with most officials of the State Department, he regarded the one as a logical development of the other. But in fact, they were contradictory.

The Marshall Plan directed American productive resources to the economic rehabilitation of countries devastated by war. It avoided overt political interference. It worked through a regional organization which enabled the recipients to share policy decisions and allocations collectively. The Truman Doctrine, though decked out in economic aid to make it palatable, was essentially a policy of unilateral military intervention in another nation's internal affairs, and inevitably involved a high degree of political dictation.

There were, of course, anti-Communist motives for the Marshall Plan. When Molotov rejected a half-hearted U.S. offer of participation by the Soviet bloc, the sigh of relief in Washington could be heard 'round the world. As a means of strengthening democracy and weakening Communism, however, the Marshall Plan succeeded and the Truman Doctrine did not.

Military domination of U.S. aid to Greece and Turkey built into the client societies an unavoidable bias in favor of dictatorship. The army seized Turkey's government in 1960 and, though it later permitted elections to be held, has kept a supervisory eye on it ever since. In Greece, the civil government, long subjected to blatant American interference, was overthrown by a colonel's junta in 1967, in part to crush rising public sentiment among the Greeks for withdrawal from NATO and demilitarization of the society.

As containment failed to strengthen the democracy it was professedly intended to save, so also it failed to contain either Communism or Soviet national power. After a total expenditure in Greece and Turkey of $8.8 billion up to 1968—the most intensive dose of aid administered anywhere except in Vietnam—we found the Russians to be embarrassingly close and agonizingly powerful competitors in the Eastern Mediterranean from which we had set out to exclude them. They got there, in force, not by conducting revolutions in Greece and Turkey, but by building a fleet and selling arms—no ideological questions asked —to the Arabs.

One day when Acheson was discussing with his aides how to merchandise the Truman Doctrine, he leaned back in his chair, gazed across the street at the White House, and after some thought said, as

Jones recounts, "If F.D.R. were alive I think I know what he'd do. He would make a statement of global policy but confine his request for money right now to Greece and Turkey."

Measured strictly by expediency, this was probably a sound political judgment. The declaration of global policy would tap the reservoir of anti-Communist emotion; confining the money request to a modest $400 million would conceal the ultimate costs and long-term implications of ideological war. But in so cleverly engineering public acceptance, Acheson set in train far-ranging consequences for which the last bill has yet to be paid.

It is impossible, of course, to know what changes in Soviet policy, if any, might have occurred had our own policy been different. There is no doubt, however, that the cold war snowballed by a process of action and reaction, each side's response to the other's thrust becoming the base for a new round of conflict. One need not assume a kindly benevolence in the Kremlin, or speculate on what might have happened but didn't, to understand our own mistakes.

Whether or not the Soviets were prepared to cooperate in organizing an effective international instrument of collective security, the Truman Doctrine registered our own Government's decision to short-circuit the United Nations except where it might be bent to the service of our national interest. The Doctrine promulgated a double standard of international morality, by which America claimed the right to unlimited national expansion on the pretext of barring Soviet expansion. It accepted and fortified, in popular mythology, the domino theory which regards revolution not as the product of indigenous social forces but as the consequence of "direct or indirect aggression." It committed the United States to defend the status quo everywhere, with a special predilection for army dictatorships. Clothing a program of military intervention in the rhetoric of economic aid and defense of democracy, it established the habit of systematic mendacity which our Government has practiced ever since. And finally the Doctrine sanctioned and exploited a virulent anti-Communist hysteria at a time when responsible leadership called for damping it down.

All these mistakes, in one form or another, became embedded in public attitudes and, as the presuppositions of U.S. foreign policy, set the pattern for increasing military domination of decision and action overseas. From them, in combination with the errors of Soviet policymakers, who have often behaved as if they were members of the same union as ours, flowed a generation of cold war, culminating in the grand calamity of the Indochina war, capped by a "Nixon Doctrine," which under the guise of reducing American forces in Asia reaffirms the intention to stay there in perpetuity.

Kennan's boulder, carelessly dislodged at the top of the cliff, has indeed plunged and crashed a long way, and it still goes rolling destructively along.

FOR FURTHER READING

Robert A. Divine. "The Cold War and the Election of 1948," *Journal of American History*, LIX (June 1972).

* Lloyd C. Gardner. *Architects of Illusion: Men and Ideas in American Foreign Policy, 1941–1949*. Chicago: Quadrangle, 1972, and New York: Franklin Watts.

* Martin F. Herz. *Beginnings of the Cold War*. Bloomington: Indiana University Press, 1966, and New York: McGraw-Hill.

* Walter La Feber. *America, Russia, and the Cold War, 1945–1971*. 2d ed. New York: John Wiley & Sons, 1972.

Thomas Paterson. "The Abortive Loan to Russia and the Origins of the Cold War," *Journal of American History*, LVI (June 1969).

* *Available in paperback.*

McCARTHY AND THE ARMY: A FIGHT ON THE WRONG FRONT

NORMAN DORSEN AND
JOHN G. SIMON

Joseph R. McCarthy, junior senator from Wisconsin from 1947 until his death ten years later, gave his name to a period—the early 1950's—and an attitude. Actually, he took advantage of a wave of emotion that others had summoned up and rode it to the heights, for the campaign against "Communists," "disloyal" elements, and "security risks" with which he is connected had already gotten under way with the dissolution of the wartime U.S.-Soviet alliance and the beginning of the cold war.

From 1945 on, a number of incidents revealed, or seemed to reveal, that Communists had stolen American documents or otherwise engaged in espionage against the United States. In 1947 President Truman issued an order for "loyalty" investigations of government workers. Four years later he changed the order to place the burden on the employees to prove their loyalty. (Later President Eisenhower provided for the firing of those who, though they might be perfectly loyal, had personal weaknesses that might make them targets for blackmail and other pressures and hence "security risks.")

By 1950 politicians of both parties and organizations all over the country were vying to prove their freedom from Communist taint. A Senate committee subpoenaed a number of American employees of the United Nations and convinced the Secretary-General to discharge them. State committees in California and elsewhere conducted hunts for "un-American" people, and countless individuals lost their jobs or their reputations because of alleged associations with leftists and "pinkos."

McCarthy knew a useful issue when he saw one, and he played on anti-Communism in the style of a true demagogue—one who appeals to the baser emotions of the voters. But others had created the atmosphere in which he could do so, and the leaders of his own party in the White House and Congress tolerated his destructive antics. The

Reprinted from *The Columbia Forum*, Fall 1964, Volume VII.

Eisenhower Administration finally balked when he tried to bully the Army, but not, as Norman Dorsen and John G. Simon observe, on grounds of principle. It is worth pointing out, however, that McCarthy's decline dates from his long exposure on television during the hearings, when a large part of the fascinated nationwide audience, even those who did not understand civil liberties in the abstract, on seeing for themselves the senator's methods, were outraged by his contempt for elementary fairness.

□   □   □

The Army-McCarthy affair, which a decade ago left the nation confused and concerned about the men who were guiding its fortunes, returned to the news this year with the release of *Point of Order*, the filmed highlights of the celebrated hearings. The motion picture suggests a re-examination of the case, for it has reinforced ten-year old recollections that the contest was merely a violent and unseemly power struggle between two leviathans. One of them, the junior Senator from Wisconsin, was charged with demanding special favors for a well-connected Army private. The other, the United States Army, was accused of using the youth as a hostage to halt an embarrassing Senate investigation. In the televised spectacular that ensued, Senator McCarthy and his chief counsel, Roy Cohn, vied against Secretary of the Army Robert Stevens, Army General Counsel John Adams, and Army Special Counsel Joseph Welch, with many other colorful supporting players—the Under Secretary of State, F.B.I. agents, several generals, staff assistants accused of phone tapping and photo cropping, and the *casus belli*, Private Gerard David Schine.

The televised extravaganza, however, revealed only one facet of a complex controversy that compassed issues far graver than the saga of Private Schine. One issue was the Army's loyalty-security program and its response to McCarthyism; the other was the right of a Senate committee to obtain Army secrets and question Army witnesses. On the first of these issues, the Army hardly fought at all. On the other, it fought fitfully and in attempted privacy, and it was this sporadic engagement that led, by a winding path, to the televised hearings. Both of these campaigns represented, far more than the case of Private Schine, the nation's involvement with Senator McCarthy.

Throughout this troubled period, the Wisconsin Senator's supporters heard in his anguished cries a klaxon alerting the nation to a Communist "knife held against America's jugular vein"; his detractors heard in them a barbarous assault against the American traditions of fair play and due process. These positions reflected opposing reactions to the major premise underlying the Senator's public acts and utterances—the premise that a man who had any past association with Communists was a threat to the nation and had no claim to civilized treatment at the hands of his government. The premise was not Senator McCarthy's alone. It was shared by many other citizens during the years of the Senator's prominence, for these were the years of the Korean War, of Communist expansion and aggression, and of the conviction of Soviet agents in America and England. To some the premise was particularly attractive because many of the individual targets of McCarthyism came from the ranks of New Deal intellectuals who had complicated life for so long and who now seemed responsible for the latest threat to tranquility posed by Communism.

But what made Senator McCarthy notable among the millions who shared his premise was the sweep and recklessness of his pronouncements. He used larger numbers ("57 Communists . . . in the State Department") and attacked more respectable figures (General-George C. Marshall "serving the world policy of the Kremlin") than anyone else in public life.

Of all the Senator's targets, the one that sustained the heaviest siege was the most respectable—the United States Army. Senator McCarthy began his assault on the Army in the fall of 1953 at Fort Monmouth, New Jersey, the site of the Signal Corps Engineering Laboratories. Many of the engineers and technicians there had had some exposure during the Depression to left-wing groups, some in the penumbra of Communism, and these men had been the subject of loyalty proceedings during the Truman Administration. They had been cleared, but when the Eisenhower Administration took office, an Executive Order was issued substituting a stricter security test for Government employment and requiring reconsideration of all earlier cases in the light of the new standards. These cases were being reviewed when Senator McCarthy, armed with Pentagon intelligence documents that "named names," burst onto the scene.

With a succession of committee hearings and public pronouncements, he swiftly mounted a campaign designed to create the impression that there existed "current espionage" at Fort Monmouth. One technique was to hold an executive session of the Senate Special Subcommittee on Investigations (meaning a session attended by Chairman McCarthy, Counsel Roy Cohn, and one or two staff assistants) and then provide a hungry press with a distorted and often inflammatory version of what had taken place. In one of the Senator's accounts to the press, for example, a witness was said to have testified that he was a close personal friend and an apartment-mate of Julius Rosenberg; in fact, the verbatim transcript (not available to the press) disclosed merely that the man had casually known Rosenberg 10 or 15 years before and that he once had lived in an apartment into which Rosenberg moved *after* the witness had departed.

Another of the Senator's techniques was to use his Congressional immunity to make exaggerated claims on the Senate floor. On one occasion, he asserted that he had received sworn testimony of current espionage at Monmouth. The only evidence he could muster, however, was that two individuals had pleaded the Fifth Amendment before the subcommittee on all subjects, and that one of them had made a large number of unexplained telephone calls to Fort Monmouth. In fact, they had never worked at Monmouth; they were former employees of a private firm that had done some Government contracting.

These techniques yielded headlines—2 IN SIGNAL CORPS STILL SPY, McCARTHY SAYS and SUSPECT FT. MONMOUTH AIDES GAVE REDS A-DATA —but the truth of the matter is that Senator McCarthy came up with exactly nothing in his Fort Monmouth investigation. Not one current or even recent employee was proved to be a past or present member of the Communist party, and not one declined to answer any question put to him by the Government or the subcommittee. If Senator McCarthy had information of "current espionage" at Monmouth, it died with him.

The public was thus deceived, but it was the Monmouth scientists who bore the brunt of the McCarthy siege. The publicity was only part of their torment. Senator McCarthy added a cruel personalized touch by telling at least one scientist that his denial of Communist association was in direct conflict with "other sworn testimony"—a complete misrepresentation, but the scientist did not know it—and then by announcing that the testimony would go to the Justice Department for perjury investigation.

Yet the critical disservice to these employees was rendered not by Senator McCarthy, but by the Army. The Army loyalty-security hearing boards were attempting to judge the strength of current loyalties to the nation in the light of 10- or 20-year-old social relationships or attendance at front-group meetings during the 1930s. Few of the cases involved any allegations more serious or more recent in time. In allowing the men to remain at work while their cases were carefully reappraised under the new Eisenhower criteria, the Army took the view that the existing derogatory information was not serious enough to require precipitate action. Under pressure, the Army abandoned this position.

During the few weeks when Senator McCarthy's investigation was at its height, more than 30 of the Fort Monmouth employees were suddenly suspended—many by the Monmouth Commanding General shortly before they appeared before the McCarthy subcommittee. Most of these men could not be restored to their positions until many months of security hearings had been completed—a period during which they suffered severe financial and personal injury. At the same time, despite efforts by Army Counsel John Adams to halt the process, another group of scientists was denied security clearance and assigned to routine non-sensitive work on the basis of minimal evidence; they labored—or rather, were permitted to vegetate—in what came to be known as the "leper colony" while awaiting issuance of charges or a belated decision that their cases did not warrant prosecution.

Sooner or later, it is true, suspensions and denials of clearance would have been imposed on a few of these men under the new stand-ards even without the stimulus of the McCarthy campaign. But the sudden rush of mass suspensions and assignments to the "leper colony" could only have reflected an acceptance of Senator McCarthy's premise that exposure to Communism meant contamination, and that contami-nated men deserved little or no consideration.

At no point during the Army's controversy with Senator McCarthy, even during the later televised hearings on the Schine case, was the McCarthy premise openly opposed. Instead, the Army sat silent while Senator McCarthy boasted of his contribution to the nation's security. At times the Army acknowledged that he had expedited the suspensions, at times it asserted it was as speedy and vigorous as he, but all the time it maintained that the way it had handled the Monmouth cases had served the national purpose. What was perhaps most revealing was that the Army consistently denied that it had tried to stop the McCarthy investigations. Why *not* try to stop them? The abuse the McCarthy method visited upon the Army's civilian employees was intolerable, unless, of course, one accepted Senator McCarthy's premise and its implied rejection of an American tradition of fairness in the treatment of Government employees.

The Pentagon accepted and applied the McCarthy premise even more strenuously in its treatment of *uniformed* men of the services. Here, as in the Fort Monmouth civilian cases, the Defense Department acted in direct response to a McCarthy campaign—this time, the cam-paign over Major Irving Peress, a dentist brought into the Army under the doctors' and dentists' draft. On his Army loyalty questionnaire and later before the subcommittee, Major Peress pleaded the Fifth Amend-ment on all questions relating to Communism; Senator McCarthy declared he was "part of the Communist conspiracy." Under the routine implementation of an act of Congress requiring grade readjustments for military doctors and dentists in accordance with "professional educa-tion, experience, and ability," Dr. Peress's rank had been readjusted from captain to major, despite his pending security investigation. Thereafter, despite a pending request by Senator McCarthy that Dr. Peress be courtmartialed for alleged subversive activities and for pleading the Fifth Amendment, the Army gave him an early honorable discharge to be rid of him.

The Senator's reaction was ferocious. "Who promoted Peress?" he cried over and over, and what "Commie coddler" gave "this Fifth Amendment Communist" an honorable discharge? The Senator's rage over the Peress case created a fierce and instantaneous clamor at the Pentagon for immediate discharge of all soldier "security risks." As translated by the military personnel machinery in early 1954, this meant removal of soldiers with any derogatory information in their files, no matter how vague, ancient, or indirect. In scores of cases it meant not only speedy discharge, but a damning undesirable discharge, even where the security information pertained solely to civilian life. Because the draft inevitably catches up a heterodox group of young men, the Army's traffic in soldier security cases had always been vastly greater—though considerably less publicized—than the security program of any other agency of the Government. Now, as the Defense Department hastened to act upon Senator McCarthy's premise that an alleged risk deserves rough as well as speedy treatment, this program became not only the most active, but also the most unfair.

In short, during the months that Senator McCarthy was on the attack, the Army and the rest of the military establishment retreated before him, taking his standards as their own and injuring a large number of citizens in the process. This, then, was the front on which the Army never really fought.

Why did the Army not fight? One explanation is that, the national temper being what it was, Administration officials were loath to be thought "soft on Communism." Neither did they want the Republican party damaged by a split; it seemed important to close ranks. Another reason some of these officials did not choose to fight Senator McCarthy was that they could not easily identify with his victims. This inability was perhaps understandable in view of the wide gulf between the executive-suite background of many Administration officials and the less genteel minority-group origins of the average Monmouth scientist or Army draftee in security trouble. Moreover, few of these officials were sufficiently curious about the world of ideas to have any understanding of those who had explored the radical notions of the 'thirties and 'forties. Many of them fit George Kennan's description of young security officers: they were "too virginal intellectually . . . to have known temptation." These were some of the men who translated McCarthyism from angry rhetoric into a program of action for the United States Government.

At length, other voices prevailed within the Army, and where they did not the courts stepped in. On the civilian side, all but a few of the

Monmouth employees eventually were cleared at hearings or by security review boards. On the military side, the Army later provided better procedural protection for accused soldiers and readjudicated the security discharges issued to several hundred men; still other ex-soldiers received improved discharges as the result of a Supreme Court decision holding that the Army could not issue a less-than-honorable discharge on the basis of pre-induction activities.

The fact that most Monmouth employees were ultimately cleared resulted in part from what took place on another Army-McCarthy battleground.

Throughout the investigation of Fort Monmouth, the McCarthy subcommittee repeatedly demanded that the Army make available for questioning the members of the civilian loyalty boards that had "cleared Communists." John Adams resisted these demands, believing that the fair administration of the security program would be jeopardized if security "judges" were forced to account to the Senator. The protection thus afforded Army loyalty board members, and the confidence it stimulated in their ranks, may have made the difference between bold and cowed decision-making and thus affected the eventual outcome of many of the Monmouth cases.

Underlying the loyalty board controversy between the Army and Senator McCarthy was an issue of Constitutional importance; it is one aspect of the doctrine of "separation of powers" between the Executive and Legislative branches of the Government. The question is whether the Congress, when investigating the Executive, is entitled to all the information it wants, or whether the Executive is privileged to reject demands to inspect its papers or interrogate its employees when rejection appears to be in the national interest. This issue—one that was first raised when George Washington prevented Congress from investigating the negotiation of the Jay Treaty—cropped up again and again during Senator McCarthy's probes of the Army. This was the issue that the Administration tried to settle in privacy, and the one that led indirectly to the Army-McCarthy hearings.

Trouble began in September 1953, soon after the Monmouth investigation opened, when Senator McCarthy demanded details from security files. The Army refused to comply, invoking a directive that President Truman had issued in 1948 forbidding dissemination of such information outside the Executive branch in order to protect the reputations of individuals and the independence of security boards. In the face of Senator McCarthy's bitter protests (during which he persisted in referring to the "Truman-Acheson blackout order"), the Army stuck to its guns and continued to do so in later months.

The Executive privilege fight broke out soon again with Senator McCarthy's demand for the appearance before his committee of Army loyalty board members. Because there was little direct precedent to support a refusal, John Adams called upon the Justice Department for guidance and also for reaffirmation of President Truman's 1948 directive. On both points the Justice Department privately supported the Army, but offered nothing in writing and nothing that could be quoted.

Several weeks later, the McCarthy committee suddenly and urgently renewed the demand. On January 18, 1954, while Roy Cohn and David Schine were vacationing together in Florida, John Adams informed Mr. Cohn by telephone that Private Schine's tour of duty at Camp Gordon, Georgia, would last four months or more, instead of eight weeks as Mr. Cohn had hoped. Mr. Cohn terminated his vacation and flew back to Washington that night. The next morning the subcommittee ordered Mr. Adams to produce the members of the loyalty board at 2 P.M. the same day.

The Administration deftly headed off a collision. John Adams attended a strategy meeting with Sherman Adams, Assistant to the President, Attorney General Herbert Brownell, his deputy William Rogers, and Ambassador Henry Cabot Lodge. They decided to explain to the Republican Senators on the subcommittee how the new loyalty board demand had developed directly out of Mr. Cohn's interest in Private Schine's Army tour. Alarmed at the prospect of scandal, the Republican Senators remonstrated with Senator McCarthy. Although Senator McCarthy and Mr. Cohn called this "blackmail," Senator McCarthy called off the subpoenas. Meanwhile, Sherman Adams asked John Adams for a written history of the McCarthy-Cohn efforts to obtain special handling for Private Schine.

A month later, in February 1954, the Executive privilege battle flared up again—this time over the Peress case. Shortly after the dentist's honorable discharge, Senator McCarthy called Dr. Peress's commanding officer, Brigadier General Ralph Zwicker, before the subcommittee and took him to task for not preventing the discharge. He told General Zwicker he was "not fit to wear that uniform" and that he was either dishonest or unintelligent; next he asked for details of the Peress matter, which General Zwicker declined to give on the basis of the 1948 Truman directive. The Senator then angrily demanded that General Zwicker show up at a later hearing ready to "tell us the truth."

Back at the Pentagon, there was outrage over the Senator's abuse of a general—abuse no worse than that earlier tolerated when it was inflicted on the Monmouth employees. Secretary of the Army Stevens stated publicly that he would allow neither General Zwicker nor any other officer to be subjected to further harassment; he would go to the hearing in their place. At last an issue—even if not quite the right issue —would be joined. But suddenly, as the Army was preparing for the great clash, the Associated Press ticker brought news of what came to be known as the "chicken luncheon." The Secretary had attended—alone and in secrecy—a luncheon meeting with the Republican members of the subcommittee. In the resulting Memo of Understanding, Mr. Stevens did an abrupt about-face by promising General Zwicker's appearance and the appearance of all other officers involved in the Peress case. Senator McCarthy capped the story by telling the press that Mr. Stevens had "got down on his knees." The resulting groan was deafening and global. One British paper said that McCarthy had won what Cornwallis never achieved—the surrender of the American Army.

At this point, in the words of President Eisenhower, "the Army moved over to the attack." But the issue on which the Army joined battle was not the fair operation of the loyalty-security program (the Pentagon had already given way on that) or any of the Executive privilege questions. Instead it was the case of G. David Schine. Prodded by Congressmen and newspapermen who had gotten wind of the Schine affair, the Army sent to Capitol Hill a few copies of the Schine case chronology, which Sherman Adams earlier had asked John Adams to prepare. Eight hours later, the full text was in the hands of the public; the next day Senator McCarthy issued countercharges and shortly thereafter 20 million Americans settled down to observe a marathon television spectacular that was stranger than fiction.

The Schine affair had begun almost a year before its appearance on television. In February 1953, David Schine, aged 25, was appointed the unpaid chief consultant to Senator McCarthy's subcommittee on the recommendation of his good friend Roy Cohn, the subcommittee's new chief counsel. Mr. Schine's credentials were sparse. He had written a brief pamphlet entitled "Definition of Communism," which was distributed by his father throughout the Schine hotel chain. His knowledge of internal security had never led to his employment by the Government or anyone else. He did not have legal training or any previous experience in investigation.

In the spring of 1953, Messrs. Schine and Cohn made a fast, well-publicized tour of Europe to investigate the "political reliability" of American information officers overseas. Shortly after their return, Mr. Schine learned that his local draft board had reclassified him 1-A. According to Senator McCarthy, this action was a response to pressure from "extreme left-wing writers," who hated the subcommittee. Whether Mr. Cohn shared this view of the Selective Service System or whether, as the Senator later put it, "[Cohn] thinks Dave should be a general and work from the penthouse of the Waldorf," the fact is that Mr. Schine's bad news precipitated seven months of incessant activity by Mr. Cohn, sometimes assisted (but sometimes secretly sabotaged) by Senator McCarthy. The campaign sought to avoid or at least mitigate the rigors of Mr. Schine's induction by:

(1) Obtaining a direct commission for Mr. Schine in the Army, Navy, or Air Force (July–September 1953)—no success;

(2) Obtaining employment in the Central Intelligence Agency in lieu of Army service (October 1953)—no success;

(3) Excusing him from basic training so he could be a special assistant on Communist problems to the Secretary of the Army (October 1953)—no success;

(4) Excusing him from basic training so he could work for the subcommittee at some post in New York City (October–November 1953)—no success (Senator McCarthy privately opposed it);

(5) Obtaining a two-week delay in the start of basic training (October–November 1953)—success (but curtailed at Senator McCarthy's request);

(6) Obtaining passes from basic training at Fort Dix, New Jersey, and excusing him from duty to confer with the subcommittee staff in person or by phone (November 1953–January 1954)— success (passes on 34 out of 68 training days, 86 long-distance calls placed and dozens received during duty hours);

(7) Obtaining a New York City assignment for Private Schine after basic training so that he could check West Point textbooks for subversive leanings (November 1953–January 1954) —no success;

(8) Canceling his assignment to Camp Gordon, Georgia, on the ground that it was "too far away" (December 1953)—no success;

(9) Attempting to shorten the length of Private Schine's training at Camp Gordon from four or five months to eight weeks (January 1954)—no success;

(10) Obtaining a New York City assignment for Private Schine after his Camp Gordon training (December 1953–January 1954)—no success.

In retrospect, there never was any serious possibility that Mr. Schine would obtain the commission that he so ardently pursued. The C.I.A. and all branches of the armed services that considered the commission question agreed that he had no special training or other qualifications. But the attempts to free him from the duties of an Army draftee were another matter. They could not be repulsed so easily, because the avowed reason for most of these intercessions was "subcommittee business."

What Mr. Schine actually did during his evenings and weekends away from Fort Dix on special pass is a nice question. At the hearings, the McCarthy side asserted he had provided the sub-committee with valuable information, but this was contradicted by earlier statements of the Senator's. On one occasion he said that Mr. Schine was "a good boy, but there is nothing indispensable about him"; on another he described him as "completely useless"; and on still another, the eve of Mr. Schine's induction, he told Secretary Stevens, "I think for Roy's sake, if you can let him come back for weekends or something so his girls won't get too lonesome—maybe if they shave off his hair, he won't want to come back."

Moreover, there was virtually no evidence of Mr. Schine's off-duty efforts. When Mr. Cohn was asked to produce all drafts or notes prepared by Mr. Schine, he came forward with only two and one-half pages, plus a few marginal notes. As the Democratic members of the subcommittee, Senators McClellan, Jackson, and Symington, concluded, "It is hardly credible that such an allegedly prodigious worker could leave such minute traces of his labor."

More important than the question of Mr. Schine's indispensability was whether his Army service was somehow linked to the subcommittee's concentration on Army security. The hearings on alleged espionage at Fort Monmouth opened in August 1953, shortly after the Schine controversy began. That investigation was soon joined by other aggressive probes directed at the Army—into alleged subversion at the Quartermaster Depot in Brooklyn and at a Pentagon cafeteria, into alleged incompetence of the chief of Army Intelligence, into the case of Major Peress and other "Fifth Amendment" doctors and dentists in the Army, and even into the question of whether certain Army files pertaining to soldiers' Communist affiliations had been destroyed during World War II.

There was more than a chronological link between Mr. Schine and these investigations. The Army charged that attempts of subcommittee personnel to obtain favoritism for their colleague were coupled with explicit or veiled promises or threats relating to subcommittee inquiries, and considerable evidence supported the charge. For example, there was the way the subcommittee's demand for the appearance of loyalty board members was peremptorily renewed as soon as Mr. Cohn got the bad news about Private Schine's tour of duty at Camp Gordon. Moreover, the link between the private's fate and the subcommittee's activities was reinforced by the late columnist George Sokolsky, who, playing the role of peacemaker, told the Army that if Private Schine were given a certain assignment, Mr. Sokolsky would "move in and stop this investigation of the Army."

Senator McCarthy and his aides attempted to meet the evidence by saying that the Army had it all backwards; the Army had held Mr. Schine as hostage to force cancellation of the subcommittee's investigation, and the Army had offered to supply "dirt" on the other services in order to turn away the subcommittee. These countercharges were emphatically denied by the Army witnesses and gingerly supported at the hearings by some, but not all, of the McCarthy witnesses.

The major evidence presented in support of the countercharges consisted of 11 memoranda of subcommittee conversations with Secretary Stevens or John Adams in 1953 and early 1954, which, if they actually took place, would bear out the countercharges. The McCarthy side asserted that the memoranda were written and filed immediately after the meetings at which the alleged conversations occurred, but Army cross-examination of McCarthy witnesses pointed up certain bewildering anachronisms in the documents. The Army's further inquiry into the contemporaneity of the memos was wholly frustrated by the McCarthy side. Senator McCarthy's personal secretary testified that she had typed all the memos herself but then declared she could not tell whether a single one of the documents in evidence was an original memo or a later copy; as for her stenographic notebooks, they had all been destroyed. Joseph Welch concluded that the authenticity of the memos was "a riddle . . . wrapped in an enigma that we won't be able to solve."

The hearings lasted from April 22 to June 17, 1954. More than two million words of testimony were recorded, but the undisputed high point occurred about a week before the end. Senator McCarthy, perhaps sensing that his grip on the television audience was slipping, cited a young law associate of Joseph Welch as a former member of "the legal arm of the Communist party." This attack proved to be the Senator's undoing when Mr. Welch, in sorrow and anger, excoriated Senator McCarthy's "cruelty and recklessness" for inflicting needless harm on a respected Boston lawyer. Roy Cohn vainly signaled the Senator to stop the attack. But it was too late—the country had seen McCarthyism at work, and it would not forget.

More testimony and points of order followed this incident, but for practical purposes the hearings were over. Two months later, the special subcommittee that had conducted the hearings released its findings. The Republicans found that Mr. Cohn had been "unduly aggressive and persistent" on behalf of Private Schine but that the Monmouth investigation had not been used as a lever for this purpose; that the Army had tried to "placate" and "appease" Mr. Cohn; that the Army had tried to "terminate or influence" the investigation in unspecified ways; and that no one on either side was guilty of "dishonesty or bad faith." The Democrats came down harder on Mr. Cohn (he had "misrepresented the need of Private Schine's services") and on Senator McCarthy (he had "condoned" Mr. Cohn's actions). They criticized Messrs. Stevens and Adams for "appeasement" of Senator McCarthy and Mr. Cohn, but found "baseless" the McCarthy-Cohn countercharge that the Army had held Private Schine as a hostage.

Neither the press nor the public, however, seemed to pay much attention to the special subcommittee's apportionment of blame, for, in the last analysis, nobody really cared. No matter where the truth lay, the subject in focus was G. David Schine—or, more accurately, improper pressure applied by a Senate committee to achieve personal ends or applied by a military department to achieve bureaucratic ends. It was a subject that involved the personal integrity of certain public servants at a particular moment in history, but, as the special subcommittee must have known, it did not touch upon any of the basic principles of the Republic. As to such matters—the issues of fairness involved in the loyalty-security program, the Constitutional issues involved in the Executive privilege conflict—the Army-McCarthy hearings had nothing to say.

There are those who contend that it all worked out for the best. They argue that if the Army had chosen to battle the Senator publicly on the loyalty-security front or on the Executive privilege front, the contest would only have strengthened McCarthyism in a citizenry nervous about subversives and looking for an uncomplicated approach to problems of national security. By fighting on the Schine front, the argument goes, the Army chose an issue divorced from the Communist question and yet one that would discredit the integrity of Senator McCarthy and his circle.

Certainly the Senator's decline and fall date from the hearings. It may have been coincidental, an early by-product of a nascent thaw, which culminated in the 1955 "Spirit of Geneva." But the hearings no doubt contributed. Unlike the classic demagogue, McCarthy met neither a violent end nor defeat on a momentous issue. Instead, a side affair—indeed a farcical one—brought him to the forefront, and there he perished. Prolonged exposure to the public weakened his position as a man on horseback and sent him a horseless rider down the road to Senate censure and lonely obscurity.

Yet the "all for the best" argument is singularly unappealing. It assumes that the public cannot be trusted on the big issues; that it can be expected to indulge its anxieties as a demagogue fans them; that, in this case, the public would not have respected reason and fair play, even if these concepts had been urged by such an impeccable advocate as the United States Army.

More important, the "all for the best" argument misses a major point about McCarthyism. It was not Senator McCarthy who damaged Monmouth employees and Army draftees so much as their Pentagon superiors. McCarthyism could injure individuals only to the extent that those in power cooperated with it. Thus, destroying Senator McCarthy was not alone what the country needed. It also needed public officials who had the instinct, intelligence, and courage to do the right thing at the time when the issue arose—not two or three years later, when shelving McCarthyism would no longer create a storm. Senator McCarthy did present the ultimate test of the Administration's mettle, and the Administration, by eliminating him, eliminated the challenge. But that should never have been necessary.

FOR FURTHER READING

Norman Dorsen, ed. *The Rights of Americans: What They Are—What They Should Be*. New York: Pantheon, 1971.
* Allen J. Matusow, ed. *Joseph R. McCarthy*. Englewood Cliffs, N.J.: Prentice-Hall, 1970.
* Michael P. Rogin. *The Intellectuals and McCarthy: The Radical Specter*. Cambridge, Mass.: MIT Press, 1969.
* Richard H. Rovere. *Senator Joe McCarthy*. New York: Harcourt Brace Jovanovich, 1959, and World.

II

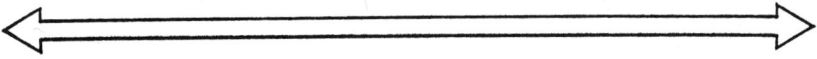

AMERICAN
MINORITIES

Although discontent was muted during the 1950's, from time to time the chorus of celebration was interrupted—perhaps by angry protests against nuclear testing or, more and more insistently, by demands from black citizens for their long-delayed freedom. The historic Supreme Court decision in *Brown* v. *Board of Education of Topeka* startled the country in 1954, but Eisenhower made no comment, and few schools actually desegregated as a result. In 1955 the blacks of Montgomery, Alabama, undertook a boycott of the Jim Crow bus system; in spite of violent attacks, they carried it through to victory more than a year later. A sensational event in 1957 awakened many whites to the logical consequences of the High Court's 1954 decision: When Governor Orville Faubus of Arkansas called out the National Guard to prevent the integration of a Little Rock high school, Eisenhower federalized the Guard; under its protection, nine black children entered the school and attended classes. In 1960 black college students in Greensboro, North Carolina, "sat in" at a white lunch counter and were arrested. Their courageous action set off a wave of similar challenges to the Southern caste system that stirred the conscience and idealism of privileged young whites in leading universities of the country.

In 1960 Democrat John F. Kennedy edged out Republican Vice President Richard Nixon in one of the nation's closest Presidential contests. Wealthy, vigorous, stylish, JFK offered glamour and energy. His inauguration launched a period of innovation and activism. Campaigning on the slogan "Let's get America moving again," the Democrats had struck a note in tune with a mood widespread among the voters.

At first, it is true, the nation experienced the *aura* of action rather than the reality: The new President carried on the established policy of intervention abroad, while at home his energy faltered in face of the conservatives of his party. Yet, after the political complacency of the 1950's, merely to present the concept of action marked some accomplishment. Hesitant, the administration responded to intensifying pressures: Kennedy forced two Southern universities to admit black students, and he consented to a proposal to appoint a Commission on the Status of Women. In Washington a spark of vitality glowed that may have strengthened the resolve of downtrodden groups to improve their lot.

People began to move in directions that Kennedy had never imagined. At the end of the 1950's, a few graduate students and professors had attacked the supposed objectivity of conventional academic research that served to rationalize the current social order. "There is room in scholarship," they insisted, "for the application of reason to the *reconstruction* of society as well as to legalistic interpretation and reform." Subsequently, undergraduates at prestigious universities turned to social criticism and action as they demanded more personal freedom, risked their lives with blacks in the civil rights movement, and defied the House Committee on Un-American Activities. Middle-income citizens learned with discomfort that one-fifth of the American people lived in poverty. Indians, women, homosexuals, welfare mothers, and Mexican Americans—to name only some of the more conspicuous groups—asserted their own worth and organized to obtain an equal place in society.

To make themselves heard and to dramatize their cause, especially determined groups used tactics outside routine electoral politics. Both pacifism and violence marked the decade. Dissidents introduced, on a scale never before seen in the United States, the technique of "nonviolent direct action." Sometimes within the law, sometimes outside it, they sat in, picketed, obstructed naval vessels with canoes, occupied college buildings, burned draft cards and draft-board files, and, when attacked with words or blows, refused to hit back. White supremacists retaliated by burning and bombing black churches and murdering civil rights workers. The wave of violence continued: Assassins killed John and Robert Kennedy and the black leaders Malcolm X and Martin Luther King, Jr.; ghetto residents rioted in Washington, Watts, Newark, and Detroit. With "the whole world watching," Chicago police clubbed demonstrators at the 1968 Democratic Party convention. And, especially toward the end of the decade, some blacks and young radicals turned rather desperately to "trashing," bombing, and arson.

As in the Progressive Era and the Great Depression, widespread public agitation around social issues evoked a measure of response from the holders of political power. In some instances, those who protested against injustices—for example, against subjection of ethnic minorities and discrimination against women in job opportunities and salaries—

obtained federal legislation to protect everyone's civil rights. Lyndon B. Johnson, successor to the murdered John Kennedy, aspired to lead the inchoate excitement: he proclaimed himself one in spirit with the blacks and he outlined a program to aid the poor and to build the "Great Society" in America.

Students and intellectuals of the emerging "New Left," however, put little faith in such promises. They measured exploitation and race hatred, analyzed the corporate economy, inquired into the results of America's leadership of the "free world," and concluded that only transformation of the structure could make the country fit for human beings. Unlike many of their forerunners, these radicals saw little promise in the labor unions, which they viewed as part of the Establishment, and they regarded "liberals" not as people with a concern for human welfare but as sycophants of power who planned to repress the "insurgency" of popular movements throughout the world. Although most were in some sense socialists, few of them joined the "Old Left" Marxist parties, for they were hostile to dogma (or, their critics believed, to orderly thinking), and they viewed centralized government not as a tool for change but as a source of bureaucratic oppression. Rejecting hierarchy and regimentation, they demanded more freedom for personal development and expressiveness. In group deliberations they espoused "participatory democracy," which—at least in theory—allows every individual a voice in collective decisions.

President Johnson, a would-be conciliator, himself wrecked all prospect of harmony as he enlarged the long-standing intervention in Indochina into a war that devastated Vietnam and killed fifty thousand American soldiers. By the mid-1960's, students, professors, writers, and others who advocated peace were holding "teach-ins" and other meetings to inform the public and to awaken sentiment to "get out of Vietnam." The war radicalized some people; others, imbued with traditional values and perhaps already troubled by the rebellious behavior of young men and women, poured out their anger on the protesters as "long-haired," unpatriotic Americans. Nevertheless, as boys were drafted and died in the jungles of Vietnam, increasing multitudes doubted the wisdom of continuing the distant and futile conflict. Noted figures—doctors, actors, college presidents, Catholic priests—engaged in civil disobedience and went to jail. Men of draft age fled abroad or deserted the armed forces, while thousands of ordinary citizens joined in huge street demonstrations against the war.

At last, in 1968, Johnson consented to peace talks and announced his forthcoming retirement from politics. With the Democrats bitterly divided, the Republicans won the Presidency. Shrewdly "Vietnamizing" the war by bringing home most of the American troops, President

Richard M. Nixon pointedly appealed to the fears of whites who were uneasy about the advancement of black people. A contraction in the economy during the early 1970's forced many middle-class people to worry more about bread-and-butter issues than about less immediate problems. And leftist groups, never united on long-term strategy, declined or dissolved because of repression, internal splits, and their own discouragement at what seemed to be the victory of conservative forces. Even the press of the nation, which always celebrates its independence, was inveigled into accepting government pronouncements on military and foreign affairs as fact and failed to alert readers to the chicanery of top officials. Perhaps the Watergate revelations, which showed that White House spokesmen were continually inaccurate, have had a sobering effect on hitherto gullible journalists.

Although organizations weakened, the spirit of the 1960's carried on into the present decade. In life-styles, certainly, "permissiveness" had triumphed among the younger generation. In academic circles, New Left scholars, if not always applauded, had won opportunities to present their "revisionist" views and to challenge accepted opinion with their unorthodox interpretations. In 1972 women, blacks, and poor people forced the Democratic Party regulars to admit them in unprecedented numbers to the national convention that nominated George S. McGovern for President. Although they were badly set back by the subsequent defeat of their candidate, the reformers, it appeared, would manage to keep the party more open than it had been before 1972.

The articles in this chapter touch upon the concerns and the social movements that rose to the surface in the 1950's and 1960's. Leonard Dinnerstein discusses the attitudes of Southern Jews to the movement for desegregation in the South. Bruce Jackson and Gerda Lerner, respectively, explore the war against poverty and the meaning of women's liberation. Francis Donahue introduces the Chicanos, a large ethnic group that only recently has begun to demand rights and recognition from the "Anglo" majority of the nation. Black editor J. H. O'Dell seeks to discern the main currents of the "Black Revolution" in the 1970's after the stirring, heroic, yet often indecisive, events of the preceding decade.

SOUTHERN JEWRY AND THE
DESEGREGATION CRISIS, 1954-1970

LEONARD DINNERSTEIN

During the past decade or so, large numbers of Americans have become increasingly aware of the problems of minority groups in the United States. These groups include blacks, Indians, Mexican-Americans, and Puerto Ricans. On the West Coast, some may focus on Orientals when they think of minorities; in Miami, on Cubans; in the Dakotas or Montana, possibly on the Hutterites, who have set themselves apart in religious communities. Whether these groups are regarded with contempt or with sympathy, members of the majority think of them significantly different from themselves.

Yet that very majority is highly diversified. It includes millions of people whose skin color, income, education, and cultural tastes appear to be comparable to those of the white Protestants, but who find nevertheless that they have still not acquired a solid footing in American society. To some degree these ethnic groups, whose ancestors came to the United States between the 1890's and the 1920's, share in the experience of the acknowledged minorities. Among them are American Jews, people who by any ordinary yardstick of education, occupation, and political and intellectual influence might well consider themselves to be among the nation's elite. History and experience both in this country and in Europe have taught the Jews to feel that, in spite of their achievements or perhaps because of them, they are terribly vulnerable.

The Jews of the United States, like other American minorities, have been victims of social and economic discrimination. They have, however, escaped the greater exploitation and hatred that persons of color have been forced to endure; moreover, despite the discrimination that has existed (and to some extent continues), they have made the most of the opportunities this country has had to offer. Within one to three generations after their forebears had arrived, many Jews were

Reprinted by permission from the *American Jewish Historical Quarterly*, LXII:30 (March, 1973). © 1972 by the American Jewish Historical Society.

entrenched in the middle or upper middle class. In the New York metropolitan area, where more than two million Jews reside, making up about 25 per cent of the population, they have been able to participate energetically in the city's activities. In fact, Jews have exercised an influence in political, business, and cultural life out of proportion to their number. Consequently, they feel as free as they can anywhere to express divergent opinions, and they have not been reticent in presenting their ideas on a variety of subjects. Mindful of the bitter experiences of their people, they have founded a number of national organizations like the American Jewish Committee and the American Jewish Congress, which have been in the forefront of movements to obtain equal rights for all citizens.

In the South, on the other hand, where Jews make up less than 1 per cent of the population, they are wary of stating views publicly that differ from those of the most respectable, or the most vocal, elements in the surrounding community. Southern society historically has not encouraged the expression of nonconformist thought on any subject, and sometimes it has imposed severe economic, social, and even physical, penalties on those who breach its mores. As a result, most Jews who live in the South have kept unpopular opinions to themselves (or have left the region) rather than expose themselves to the possible wrath of their neighbors. For this reason the U. S. Supreme Court's ruling in 1954 in *Brown* v. *Board of Education*, which mandated an end to segregated education, upset them greatly. Certain that the decision would arouse their neighbors, they feared that, as in the past, the crisis would result in an upsurge of anti-Semitism. They also feared that any statements made by American Jews elsewhere would be attributed to Southern Jews. They were therefore alarmed to note that Northern Jews and national Jewish organizations were prominent advocates of speedy enforcement of the Court's decision.

In the following essay, Leonard Dinnerstein elaborates on the dilemma of a minority at a time when social change arouses fear and anxiety among the dominant group.

□   □   □

Conventional opinion has it that Jews are one of the groups that consistently support civil rights causes and promote the welfare of minorities in the United States. To a considerable extent the available evidence supports this thesis. Jews have been prominent in the National Association for the Advancement of Colored People, have participated in marches and protests along with blacks, and have used their legal acumen to help destroy the concept of second-class citizenship. Even a cursory examination of financial contributions, active leadership, and organizational commitment to the civil rights movement finds large numbers of Jewish individuals and groups heavily represented.

Nevertheless, despite the participation of many Jews in the civil rights movement, the level of commitment has differed in various parts of the country. In the South particularly, Jews have been more circumspect in their allegiance to equal rights for all citizens and, except for a few areas like Atlanta and some Hillel groups on college campuses, have been more guarded in their public postures. A significant division, for example, between Northern and Southern Jews occurred in 1954 when the United States Supreme Court, in *Brown* v. *Board of Education of Topeka et al.*, outlawed segregated school facilities. Most Northern Jews applauded the Court's ruling; Southern Jews met it with fear and trepidation.

"The segregation crisis has shaken Southern Jews more severely than any national event since the Civil War," Albert Vorspan, Social Action Director of the Union of American Hebrew Congregations, wrote in 1959. For three centuries Jews had maintained harmonious relations with their Christian neighbors. They had carefully accepted regional customs as their own, and even during the controversy over slavery few Southern Jews publicly condemned the institution. In times of stress, however, Jews had often been singled out and blamed for whatever difficulties society might be undergoing. Hence during the Civil War blatant anti-Semitism arose. The Jews as a group, and Judah P. Benjamin, the best known Jew in the Confederacy, were attacked. As Bertram Korn has noted, "Anti-Jewish prejudice was a characteristic expression of the age, part and parcel of the economic and social upheaval effectuated by the war." During Reconstruction and the Populist eras there were again some examples of hostility to Jews but many fewer than had occurred during the Civil War. The Leo Frank case exacerbated Jewish-Christian relationships before the first World War but as the furor died down, Southern Jews again relapsed into their normally quiet existence. The United States Supreme Court's decision in *Brown* v. *Board of Education*, though, set the stage for renewed tensions.

Jews in the South are, according to sociologist Alfred Hero, Jr., "the most cosmopolitan Southern ethnic group." They are, on the average, better off financially, better educated, concentrated in higher socio-economic groups, and more urban than non-Jews. Nevertheless, they are not entirely secure in their positions and, regardless of where they live, shun controversy. That is because one of the region's cardinal virtues is conformity. As a former rabbi in Norfolk, Virginia, put it, "Probably nowhere [else] in America is the old principle of Jewish history, 'Wie es Christel sich, so Judel sich' (as the Christians do, so do the Jews) so apparent."

The South, however, like every other region in the nation, is composed of different areas and the climate in some communities allows greater opportunities for diversity than in others. In general, though, the activities and thoughts of Jews below the Mason-Dixon line are in direct relationship to the sophistication of the city in which they reside. Where the gentiles are cosmopolitan the Jews are likely to be also. Where the Christians are more conservative, one finds Jews similarly inclined. Atlanta is perhaps the most cosmopolitan of Southern cities and some Jews there have been among the most ardent advocates of integration. In more conservative Alabama few Jews have committed themselves. Norfolk, Virginia Jews backed integration in the schools but Richmond's Jews were considerably more reserved. The small towns in the South are generally conservative. Jews in Shreveport and Charleston, South Carolina, are more cautious publicly than those in New Orleans. In Houston and Dallas the Jewish community divides between liberal and conservative factions, but even one of the more reserved rabbis acknowledges, "The Jews, of course, take their place with those who advocate desegregation. . . ."

Most Southern Jews are merchants, highly dependent on the good will of their neighbors for sustenance. They therefore find it wise to fit in with the accepted customs of the community. This means, especially in the smaller towns, that they hold membership in the local temple, avoid public airing of controversial views, and claim as their own the community's standards of thought. They are particularly anxious to ingratiate themselves with the gentiles in their area and are "extremely sensitive to what non-Jews think about them." The Jew worries if another Jew is "identified with a position that is extremely unpopular" because he feels that all Jews will then be visited with economic reprisals or social ostracism. When one central Virginia Jewish community heard, in 1958, that Arthur B. Spingarn, a New York Jew, was President of the NAACP, it received the news with "grim silence." "The knowledge that a Northern Jew was head of the leading organization for Negro rights," a commentator explained, "had shaken the security of this Virginia Jewish community."

Religion is an important aspect of Southern life. As a result, the minister or rabbi assumes a more esteemed role in the community than his counterpart in other regions. The rabbi of the Reform congregation in a Southern community is well known to his neighbors and is frequently asked to participate at Christian interfaith meetings. To the extent that he does this job well, his own Jewish congregation applauds him. In fact, many Jews judge their rabbi on the basis of the respect and esteem that he has in the Christian community. It is all the more important, therefore, that the rabbi not arouse the ire of those in a position to harm the Jews, like members of the Ku Klux Klan or White Citizens Councils or even ordinary consumers. When Rabbi Seymour Atlas participated in a "Brotherhood Week" program in 1956, *Life* magazine carried the story and included a picture of the rabbi standing next to a black man. The Board of Trustees of his Montgomery, Alabama, congregation, asked Atlas to "demand" a retraction from the national weekly and to have *Life* inform readers in a future issue that "Brotherhood Week" had nothing to do with Negroes, Reverend Ralph Abernathy, the Supreme Court decisions on segregation, or the Montgomery bus strike.

This incident demonstrates how the 1954 Supreme Court decision alarmed Southern Jews. Many of them believed that it would threaten and erode the good relations that they had tried to develop with their Christian neighbors. These Jews thought that only by keeping absolutely quiet, or by saying nothing about integration that would offend any Southerner, would they be able to continue living peacefully in the South.

Those who held such views were mistaken. Bigots, Ku Kluxers, and members of the White Citizens Councils in many Southern communities used the integration crisis as a springboard for the most vicious acts of anti-Semitism. In one year, from November, 1957, through October, 1958, eight Southern Jewish temples were bombed in communities undergoing stress because of attempts at integration. The bombings that occurred took place both in areas where some Jews had taken a stand as well as in those where they had said nothing. Concomitantly there was an increase in the distribution of anti-Semitic literature. Much of this literature propagated the theme that "desegregation is a Zionist-Communist plot to mongrelize the white race so that the Jews can take over."

Southern Jews for the most part, reacted to the hostility displayed, not by castigating the White Citizens Councils or Ku Kluxers whose activities probably fomented the attacks, but by denouncing Northern coreligionists for making public efforts to promote racial equality. The Southern Jews believed that the endeavors of their Northern coreligionists, such as those in the American Jewish Congress and the Anti-Defamation League of B'nai B'rith, to achieve racial equality triggered the reactions of the Southern bigots.

When Northern Jews marched in Southern demonstrations to show their solidarity with the civil rights movement, local Jews often tried to stop them. One Birmingham teenager phoned a visiting rabbi and admitted, "We are glad that you are doing what we would like to do but do not have the courage to do." Then he added, "But please, do not endanger us, do not get our synagogue bombed."

Other Jews reacted more vehemently. "When a rabbi from New Haven, Conn., takes part in such demonstrations," a Macon Jew explained, "you have no idea the position Jewry in our state is placed. . . . A rabbi from out of our area is detrimental to Jews in the South." "For the probable success in organizing an effective Klan in Albany, Ga.," another Jew wrote to this same New Haven rabbi, "you and your colleagues can take full credit." A Memphis attorney shouted in a closed session meeting of the American Jewish Committee, "If only you Yankee Jews would keep your long noses out of our business," while an Alabama Jewish leader told a representative of a national Jewish agency: "You're like Hitler. You stir up anti-Semitism against us."

Because Jews in the South have fears about being different from white Protestants, it is difficult to say how they really feel about segregation and desegregation. They always seem to consider first how the gentiles will react to their activities. Jews probably are more liberal than non-Jews on most issues, and, as Morton Gaba has pointed out,

> Given the slightest evidence of Christian interest, Jewish leadership, both as individuals and as representatives of Jewish groups, would emerge with the necessary manpower and financial backing in support of the Supreme Court decision as they have in a score of other communal endeavors.

But that would not necessarily indicate how most individual Jews felt. Northern-based Jewish groups have been unstinting in their efforts to foster and develop civil rights throughout the nation despite the fact that many individual Jews are not only unconcerned with the issue but would prefer that blacks enjoy their civil rights in their own neighborhoods and not trespass among the Jews.

Allen Krause, who has examined the opinions of Southern Jewish rabbis, believes that the vast majority of Jews below the Mason-Dixon line—he estimates 75 per cent—are "somewhat ambivalent about the whole issue, but tending toward *thoughts* sympathetic to the Negro." Perhaps this is the closest we can get to analyzing Southern Jewish opinion on desegregation at the present time. But if at least their *thoughts* are on the side of civil rights, this differentiates them from most of their Baptist and Methodist neighbors.

One observer, Elijah E. Palnick, has written that "almost every Jewish community" in the South "is quietly working with the good Christians" to promote integration, but "no Southern Jew boasts of it." Bill Kovach, formerly a reporter with *The Nashville Tennessean,* wrote the author that after "following the trail of civil rights workers" he "was personally impressed with the number of Jews who acted as individuals in support of the [black man's] pursuit of equal rights." He then went on to name specific individuals: the owner of a department store in Fayetteville, which he characterized as a "very small, rural town with the traditional Southern prejudice against Jews and Negroes," an attorney in East Tennessee, and a host of individuals in Nashville.

But these observations are a far cry from the remarks of others who claim that there has been a "conspiracy of silence" or a "pronounced and emphatic" silence among Jews in regard to desegregation. Probably both opinions are accurate. Most Jews in Southern communities have done little to promote equal rights openly, but at the same time there have been a few individuals who have worked, overtly or covertly, to see that Negroes are treated justly. Nevertheless, one must not minimize the consequences for many Jews who enter the fray. Only if the Southern Jew "has a strong moral sense of justice combined with a disregard for the physical safety of himself and his family," Daniel Snowman emphasized in 1964, "will he throw in his lot openly with the various civil rights groups."

Participation figures vary from city to city. Rabbi Perry Nussbaum estimated that in Jackson, Mississippi, no more than five of the 150 Jewish families did anything to help the movement, and that those five were only "moderately active." On the other hand, Rabbi Malcolm Stern wrote that "the overwhelming majority of Norfolk Jews have wholeheartedly supported in every feasible way the local attempts by the School Board and others to comply with the Supreme Court decision." Jackson and Norfolk are probably the extremes, with most other Southern Jewish communities falling in between but not necessarily in the middle. In the early 1960's Alfred Hero found that Southern Jews kept their views "so quiet on controversial issues, including race, that Southern Gentiles . . . greatly underestimated their real divergence from Protestant thinking on public and social questions."

Almost all the articles that have been published about the reactions of Southern Jews avoid naming specific communities. Hence one reads of "Southern City," "Deltatown," "Antebellum Town," etc. Individuals are similarly protected. It is therefore difficult to pinpoint what specific individuals have done. There is one group of Southern Jews whose opinions on desegregation have been examined and analyzed—the rabbis. More often than not these men reflected the views of their congregations in their public (and private) utterances.

Most of the rabbis were cautious, shunned the limelight, and followed a moderate approach to desegregation. "I don't see how we can do much," a New Orleans rabbi wrote, "until the Protestant ministry avows a more positive stand. They could change the situation over-night." From South Carolina another acknowledged: "While I have spoken against segregation and in favor of integration from my pulpit from time to time—to the great discomfiture of my members—I have put nothing in writing [because] we have a dangerous powder keg in Florence which might explode at any time." A Tennessean sermonized, "As a Southern congregation, we need not initiate or take an overly conspicuous role in advocating integration." A North Carolinian used a Jewish holiday as an occasion to present his views obliquely: "The festival of Purim teaches us that we must oppose all attempts at stifling man's freedom and his right to enjoy that freedom. The problem of desegregation, with which we of the South are confronted today, takes on another light if we apply the lesson of Purim." And another rabbi, in West Tennessee, advised his followers: "We must move slowly and gradually."

Perhaps six to ten rabbis in the South worked diligently to pro-mote the cause of civil rights. Two or three had the support of a sig-nificant number of their congregants. Others worked quietly, behind the scenes; and even though some Jews in their community knew of their activities their discretion allowed these individuals to continue with their work. The most notable among them include Rabbis Jacob Rothschild of Atlanta, Emmet Frank of Alexandria, Virginia, Perry Nussbaum of Jackson, Mississippi, and Charles Mantinband of Ala-bama, Mississippi, and Texas.

During the height of the civil rights controversy, in the early 1960's, Mantinband ministered to the Jews of Hattiesburg, Mississippi. He engaged in civil rights activities openly despite the fact that most of his congregation frowned on such work. He claimed that too many Jews of his acquaintance both chanted and believed

> Come weal
> Come woe
> My status
> Is quo

His Board of Trustees considered the rabbi "crazy" and "ahead of his times" in the area of civil rights. They told him "in no uncertain terms" that they preferred him to remain silent on the issue, but he ignored their wishes. At home he entertained guests of his own choos-ing, and on one occasion the sight of black people entering his house by the front door so unnerved a neighbor that he later demanded, "Who are those people?" "Some of my Christian friends," the rabbi replied coolly.

Mantinband did curtail some of his activities because of com-munity pressure. His congregants' fears were so great that he avoided some biracial meetings—although he spoke on many occasions at Negro colleges—and shunned press publicity for his efforts. One Christmas the Taconic Foundation of New York sent a check of $2500 to his congregation in honor of Mantinband's "sane approach to the race question." The gift threw the congregation into a panic. A committee investigated for months, and not until it was discovered that others, including Christian groups, had received similar bequests did the congregation finally accept it.

Another Southern rabbi who has been advocating civil rights causes is Jacob Rothschild of Atlanta. Rothschild spoke out for Negro equality long before it became fashionable and almost a decade before the Supreme Court's decision on the subject. During the 1948 presidential campaign, in which the Dixiecrats bolted from the Democratic Party over the civil rights program proposed by Harry S. Truman, he decried the growing race hatred that threatened the South and urged his people to "be among those who are willing to *do* something" to reverse the tide. He invited Negroes to his home and he visited theirs. In his temple he held integrated workshops, forums, and discussion groups. In 1957 he joined with 79 other Atlanta clergymen in issuing the "Atlanta Manifesto," which demonstrated clerical support for the civil rights movement. Unlike Mantinband, Rothschild had considerable support from local Jews. When one member of his congregation resigned from the temple because she was incensed at seeing Rothschild's daughter with a Negro friend in a restaurant, the Board of Trustees wrote her a letter regretting that she had failed to "learn the lesson of Judaism taught by our rabbi in word and deed."

The most dramatic Southern Jewish supporter of the civil rights movement, Rabbi Emmet Frank of Alexandria, Virginia, chose the holiest night of the Jewish year—the eve of the Day of Atonement—to denounce the most powerful political figure in the state in 1958—Senator Harry Byrd. Rabbi Frank, who had spoken on the subject both before and after that September evening, insisted that "the Jew cannot remain silent to injustice." He excoriated those who advocated "massive resistance" to integrated public schools and then continued:

> Let the segregationists froth and foam at their mouth. There is only one word to describe their madness—Godlessness, or to coin a new synonym—Byrdliness. Byrdliness has done more harm to the stability of our country than McCarthyism.

Frank received nationwide publicity for this sermon and his attitudes at that time. Judging from the amount of letters that he received, most of his correspondents, as well as his congregants, supported the stand that he took although a minority did not. "As the years go on," one of his detractors wrote, "you will reflect on the damage you have done those to whom you were supposed to be a religious leader."

The fourth rabbi is Perry Nussbaum of Jackson, Mississippi. Unlike Mantinband, Rothschild, and Frank, Nussbaum tried to be circumspect in his actions. Had he publicized his early activities he probably would never have had an opportunity to engage in later ones from a Mississippi pulpit. Unlike Rothschild and Frank, he could not count on any significant support from his congregation. He made quiet efforts in the 1950's to see what he could do to promote integration, and in 1961 he instituted a chaplaincy program for the arrested freedom riders of all denominations (many were Jewish) who were jailed by Mississippi officials. Fortunately, as he acknowledges,

> the newspaper people understood the sensitive nature of the program, so that nothing was publicized locally. This would have been the last straw for my own people. If it became generally known, for instance, that I conducted worship services regularly at the Penitentiary, the reactions from many of my own people and certainly from the White Citizens Councils would be tremendous!

During the next few years the rabbi's views on desegregation received greater circulation and the retaliations against him began in earnest. A bomb exploded just outside his temple study in September, 1967, and two months later his home was bombed. On both occasions he escaped with his life only through luck.

It is interesting that of the four rabbis about whom we have the most information, three are not native Southerners. Mantinband was born in New York, reared in Norfolk, Virginia, but attended college in the North. Rothschild was born and raised in Pittsburgh and attended college in Cincinnati. Nussbaum comes from Canada. The only native Southerner, Emmet Frank, was born and spent his early years in New Orleans, one of the South's more cosmopolitan cities, and attended college in Houston. Further study might show that the few Southern Jews who tried to promote integration were first or second generation Southerners to whom the Southern heritage meant little.

Within the past two or three years, more Southerners have accepted desegregation and this has eased the strain within the various Jewish communities. School integration is proceeding at a pace that only a few years ago would have been considered impossible, and Jews now feel less uncomfortable about the expressions of coreligionists on the subject. National defense organizations like the American Jewish Committee and the Anti-Defamation League are experiencing a regional revival following more than a decade of resignations and protests about Northern lack of sympathy for the Southern Jew's situation. The

KKK and White Citizens Councils—with their anti-Semitic outbursts —have toned down considerably. And even in Mississippi the unthinkable has come to pass with hardly any notice: Rabbi Nussbaum attended an integrated meeting of the Freedom Democratic Party in a Jackson hotel and sometime later participated in an integrated protest rally against the Vietnamese war on a local college campus. In 1965 or 1966, Nussbaum claims, such activities would have been "unthinkable." But now the "power structure" in Mississippi, he contends, will no longer tolerate the excesses of the past. For the Southern Jew this means that he no longer has to fear obeying the law of the land or acknowledging that perhaps integration and equal rights for all people are not as dreadful as they may have seemed only a decade ago.

FOR FURTHER READING

* Leonard Dinnerstein, ed. *Antisemitism in the United States*. New York: Holt, Rinehart & Winston, 1971.

Leonard Dinnerstein and Mary Dale Palsson, eds. *Jews in the South*. Baton Rouge: Louisiana State University Press, 1973.

Anthony Lewis. *Portrait of a Decade: The Second American Revolution*. New York: Random House, 1964.

THE FEMINISTS: A SECOND LOOK

GERDA LERNER

During World War II America's leaders summoned women
to the factories and shipyards. Suddenly women welded steel and
assembled airplanes, while, on a limited scale, the federal government
provided day-care centers for their children. Yet once the combat
had ended they were told that they belonged at home. Reinforcing
the views of men who feared women as economic rivals, both
the popular media and the most prestigious cultural and intellectual
authorities insisted that only abnormal females would seek fulfillment
outside the circle of "family living." The names of pioneer
feminists, if remembered at all, evoked only ridicule. Women of
the 1950's, in fact, married younger than ever before in the twentieth
century, and with prosperity they produced larger families than
in the 1930's, creating a "baby boom." Yet, once their children
had entered school, increasing members of young married
women found jobs. The rewards were often of dubious value: Psychologists and other "experts" taught them to feel guilty for "neglecting"
their families, the gap between their pay and that of men grew
ever wider, and in most professions their already small numbers
steadily diminished. Out of this paradoxical situation a new force
arose.

During the 1960's many women awoke from passivity to view
themselves as individuals and assert their right to determine their
own place in life. A suburban housewife fulfilling the "many roles of
the American woman"—cook, laundress, maid, children's nurse, chauf-
feur, mistress—might have read Betty Friedan's *The Feminine
Mystique* and identified the source of her own discontent; a young
student devoted to the civil rights movement might have found herself relegated to bed and typewriter and thus perceived that even her
male allies in the cause of black freedom maintained a system of

sexual caste. Hesitantly, for they had been conditioned to accept a secondary role, such women shared their experiences and their half-guilty resentment. Gradually they gained self-respect and recognized, often with rage, the extent of their oppression. A new women's movement arose that challenged some of the fundamental institutions of the social order.

Because women have been taught to denigrate themselves, the first step to liberation has been "consciousness-raising," the development of a sense of identity and self-worth. People who have achieved this awareness of themselves refuse to tolerate the insults and exploitation that pervade society. Our language embodies the assumption that the normal person is a "he," while humans collectively are "man." Business, universities, and government assign women low-paying jobs and block them from positions of authority. Laws and mores circumscribe their physical freedom. Parents, teachers, and psychologists urge young women to conceal their intelligence, cultivate their appearance, and thus try to attract husbands to direct their lives. Although the numerous feminist groups that have sprung up differ in theory, tactics, and the priority of their objectives, even the demands made by the relatively conventional National Organization for Women imply marked change, as one Senator perhaps understood when he opposed the Equal Rights Amendment on the ground that to give equal pay to women would ruin the American economy.

In the following article, Gerda Lerner, biographer of the early feminist abolitionists Sarah and Angelina Grimké, surveys the movement and its theoretical foundations. Surprisingly, she finds the latter a bit shaky. Other activists might disagree with some of her views and statements, but her vigorously critical analysis should provoke sharp thinking on the nature and sources of women's oppression. At the end she assesses proposals for new kinds of family relationships and describes the future as radical feminists see it: a society in which men and women, freed from the tyranny of gender roles, can live fully as human beings.

□　□　□

I ask no favors for my sex. All I ask our brethren is that they take their feet from off our necks and permit us to stand upright on the ground which God designed us to occupy. ANGELINA GRIMKÉ, 1838

Women are the best helpers of one another. Let them
think; let them act; till they know what they need. . . .
But if you ask me what offices they may fill, I reply—
any . . . Let them be sea-captains if you will.
—MARGARET FULLER, 1845

Within the past three years a new feminism has appeared on the
scene as a vigorous, controversial, and somewhat baffling phenomenon. Any attempt to synthesize this diffuse and dynamic movement
is beset with difficulties, but I think it might be useful to view it in historical perspective and to attempt an evaluation of its ideology and tactics on the basis of the literature it has produced.

Feminist groups represent a wide spectrum of political views and
organizational approaches, divided generally into two broad categories:
the reform movement and the more radical Women's Liberation groups.
The first is exemplified by NOW (National Organization of Women),
an activist, civil rights organization, which uses traditional democratic
methods for the winning of legal and economic rights, attacks mass
media stereotypes, and features the slogan "Equal Rights in Partnership
with Men." Reform feminists cooperate with the more radical groups in
coalition activities, accept the radicals' rhetoric, and adopt some of their
confrontation tactics; yet essentially they are an updated version of the
old feminist movement, appealing to a similar constituency of professional women.

Small, proliferating, independent Women's Liberation groups, with
their mostly youthful membership, make up a qualitatively different
movement, which is significant far beyond its size. They support most of
the reform feminist goals with vigor and at times unorthodox means, but
they are essentially dedicated to radical changes in all institutions of
society. They use guerrilla theater, publicity stunts, and confrontation
tactics, as well as the standard political techniques. Within these groups
there is a strong emphasis on the re-education and psychological reorientation of the members and on fostering a supportive spirit of sisterhood.

What all new feminists have in common is a vehement impatience
with the continuance of second-class citizenship and economic handi-
caps for women, a determination to bring our legal and value systems
into line with current sexual mores, an awareness of the psychological
damage to women of their subordinate position, and a conviction that
changes must embrace not only laws and institutions, but also the minds,
emotions, and sexual habits of men and women.

An important parallel exists between the new feminism and its
nineteenth-century counterpart. Both movements resulted not from relative deprivation but from an advance in the actual condition of women.
Both were "revolutions of rising expectations" by groups who felt themselves deprived of status and frustrated in their expectations. Education,

even up to the unequal level permitted women in the 1830s, was a luxury for the advantaged few, who found upon graduation that except for schoolteaching no professions were open to them. At the same time, their inferior status was made even more obvious when the franchise, from which they were excluded, was extended to propertyless males and recent immigrants.

The existence of the early feminist movement depended on a class of educated women with leisure. The women who met in 1848 at Seneca Falls, New York, did not speak for the two truly exploited and oppressed groups of women of their day: factory workers and black women. Mill girls and middle-class women were organizing large women's organizations during the same decade, but there was little contact between them. Their life experiences, their needs and interests, were totally different. The only thing they had in common was that they were equally disfranchised. This fact was of minor concern to working women, whose most urgent needs were economic. The long working day and the burdens of domestic work and motherhood in conditions of poverty gave them not enough leisure for organizing around anything but the most immediate economic issues. Except for a short period during the abolition movement, the interests of black women were ignored by the women's rights movement. Black women had to organize separately and, of necessity, they put their race interests before their interests as women.

Unlike European women's rights organizations, which were from their inception allied to strong socialist-oriented labor movements, the American feminist movement grew in isolation from the most downtrodden and needy groups of women. William O'Neill, in his insightful study *The Woman Movement: Feminism in the United States and England* (Barnes & Noble, 1969), describes the way the absence of such an alliance decisively affected the composition, class orientation, and ideology of the American women's rights movement. Although there were brief, sporadic periods of cooperation between suffragists and working women, the feminists' concentration on the ballot as the cure-all for the ills of society inevitably influenced their tactics. Despite their occasional advocacy of unpopular radical causes, they never departed from a strictly mainstream, Christian, Victorian approach toward marriage and morality. By the turn of the century, feminist leadership, like the male leadership of the Progressives, was nativist, racist, and generally indifferent to the needs of working women. (Aileen Kraditor demonstrates this well in *The Ideas of the Woman Suffrage Movement: 1890–1920*, Columbia University Press, 1965.) Suffrage leaders relied on tactics of expediency. "Give us the vote to double your political power" was their appeal to reformers of every kind. They believed that once enacted, female suffrage would promote the separate class interests since women, as an oppressed group, would surely vote their common good. Opportunist arguments were used to persuade males and hostile females that the new voters would be respectable and generally inoffensive. A 1915 suffrage banner read:

> For the safety of the nation to
> Women give the vote
> For the hand that rocks the cradle
> Will never rock the boat

Not surprisingly, after suffrage was won, the women's rights movement became even more conservative. But the promised bloc-voting of female voters failed to materialize. Class, race, and ethnic, rather than sex, divisions proved to be more decisive in motivating voting behavior. As more lower-class women entered the labor market and participated in trade-union struggles with men, they benefited, though to a lesser extent, where men did. Middle-class women, who now had free access to education at all levels, failed to take significant advantage of it, succumbing to the pressure of societal values that had remained unaffected by the narrow suffrage struggle. Thus, at best, the political and legal gains of feminism amounted to tokenism. Economic advantages proved illusory as well, and consisted for most women in access to low-paid, low-status occupations. The winning of suffrage had to emancipate women.

If the new feminism did not appear on the scene in the 1930s or 1940s, this was because the war economy had created new job opportunities for women. But at the end of World War II, returning veterans quickly reclaimed their "rightful places" in the economy, displacing female workers, and millions of women voluntarily took up domesticity and war-deferred motherhood. The young women of the 1940s and 1950s were living out the social phenomenon that Betty Friedan called the "feminine mystique" and Andrew Sinclair the "new Victorianism." Essentially it amounted to a cultural command to women, which they seemed to accept with enthusiasm, to return to their homes, have large families, lead the cultivated suburban life of status-seeking through domestic attainments, and find self-expression in a variety of avocations. This tendency was bolstered by Freudian psychology as adapted in America and vulgarized through the mass media.

It was left to the college-age daughters born of the World War II generation to furnish the womanpower for the new feminist revolution. Like their forerunners, the new feminists were, with few exceptions, white, middle class, and well educated. Raised in economic security—an experience quite different from that of their Depression-scarred mothers —they had acquired an attitude toward work that demanded more than security from a job. They reacted with dismay to the discovery that their expensive college educations led mostly to the boring, routine jobs reserved for women. They felt personally cheated by the unfulfilled promises of legal and economic equality.

Moreover, they were the first generation of women raised entirely in the era of the sexual revolution. Shifting moral standards (especially among urban professionals), increased personal mobility, and the availability of birth control methods afforded these young women unprecedented sexual freedom. Yet this very freedom led to frustration and a sense of being exploited.

Many of these young women had participated, with high hopes and idealism, in the civil rights and student movements of the 1950s and 1960s. But they discovered that there, also, they were expected to do the dull jobs—typing, filing, housekeeping—while leadership remained a male prerogative. This discovery fueled much of the rage that has become so characteristic of the Women's Liberation stance, and turned many of these young women to active concern with their identity and place in society.

They continued in the nineteenth-century tradition by emphasizing equal rights and accepting the general concept of the oppression of women. The reformists have adopted, also, the earlier conviction that what is good for middle-class women is good for all women. Both branches, reform and radical, learned from the past the pitfalls of casting out the radicals in order to make the movement more respectable. Until now, they have valiantly striven for unity and flexibility. They have jointly campaigned for child-care centers, the equal rights amendment, and the abolition of abortion legislation. They have organized congresses to unite women and a women's strike, and they have shown their desire for unity by accepting homosexual groups into the movement on the basis of full equality. But the radicals in Women's Liberation have gone far beyond their Victorian predecessors.

Radical feminism combines the ideology of classical feminism with the class-oppression concept of Marxism, the rhetoric and tactics of the Black Power movement, and the organizational structure of the radical student movement. Its own contribution to this rich amalgam is to apply class-struggle concepts to sex and family relations, and this they have fashioned into a world view. On the assumption that the traditional reformist demands of the new feminist are eminently justified, long overdue, and possible of fulfillment, the following analysis will focus on the more controversial, innovative aspects of radical theory and practice.

The oppression of women is a central point of faith for all feminists. But the radicals do not use this term simply to describe second-class citizenship and discrimination against women, conditions that can be ameliorated by a variety of reforms. The essence of their concept is that all women are oppressed and have been throughout all history. A typical statement reads:

> Women are an oppressed class. Our oppression is total, affecting every facet of our lives. . . . We identify the agents of our oppression as men. Male supremacy is the oldest, most basic form of domination. All other forms of oppression (racism, capitalism, imperialism, etc.) are extensions of male supremacy: men dominate women, a few men dominate the rest. *All men* receive economic, sexual, and psychological benefits from male supremacy. *All men* have oppressed women. [Redstockings Manifesto, *Notes from the Second Year: Women's Liberation*]

Actually opinions as to the source of the oppression vary. Some blame capitalism and its institutions, and look to a socialist revolution for liberation, while others believe that all women are oppressed by all men. Where socialist governments have failed to alter decisively the status of women, the socialists say, it is because of the absence of strong indigenous Women's Liberation movements.

If what they mean by oppression is the suffering of discrimination, inferior rights, indignities, economic exploitation, then one must agree, undeniably, that all women are oppressed. But this does not mean that they are an oppressed class, since in fact they are dispersed among all classes of the population. And to state that "women have always been oppressed" is unhistorical and politically counterproductive, since it lends the authority of time and tradition to the practice of treating women as inferiors.

In fact, in the American experience, the low status and economic oppression of women developed during the first three decades of the nineteenth century and were functions of industrialization. It was only *after* economic and technological advances made housework an obsolete occupation, only *after* technological and medical advances made all work physically easier and childbearing no longer an inevitable yearly burden on women, that the emancipation of women could begin. The antiquated and obsolete value system under which American women are raised and live today can best be fought by recognizing that it is historically determined. It can therefore be ended by political and economic means.

The argument used by radical feminists that the essential oppression of women occurs in the home and consists in their services as housewives is equally vague and unhistorical. The economic importance of housework and the status accorded the housewife depend on complex social, demographic, and economic factors. The colonial housewife, who could be a property-holding freeholder in her own right and who had access to any occupation she wished to pursue since she lived in a labor-scarce, underdeveloped country with a shortage of women, had a correspondingly high status, considerable freedom, and the knowledge that she was performing essential work. A similar situation prevailed on the Western frontier well into the nineteenth century.

The movement's oversimplified concept of class oppression may hamper its ability to deal with the diverse interests of women of all classes and racial groups. No doubt all women are oppressed in some ways, but some are distinctly more oppressed than others. The slaveholder's wife suffered the "disabilities of her sex" in being denied legal rights and educational opportunities and in her husband's habitual infidelites, but she participated in the oppression of her slaves. To equate her oppression with that of the slave woman is to ignore the real plight of the slave. Similarly, to equate the oppression of the suburban housewife of today with that of the tenant farmer's wife is to ignore the more urgent problems of the latter.

New feminists frequently use the race analogy to explain the nature of the oppression of women. A collectively written pamphlet defines this position:

> For most of us, our race and our sex are unequivocal, objective facts, immediately recognizable to new acquaintances. . . . Self-hatred in both groups derives not from anything intrinsically inferior about us, but from the treatment we are accustomed to. . . . Women and Blacks have been alienated from their own culture; they have no historical sense of themselves because study of their condition has been suppressed. . . . Both women and Blacks are expected to perform our economic function as service workers. Thus members of both groups have been taught to be passive and to please white male masters in order to get what we want. I Am Furious—Female, Radical Education Project, Detroit, n.d.)

This analogy between Blacks and women is valid and useful as long as it is confined to the psychological effect of inferior status, but not when it is extended to a general comparison between the two groups. Black women are discriminated against more severely than any other group in our society: as Blacks, as women, and frequently as low-paid workers. So far, radical feminists have failed to deal adequately with the complex issues concerning black women, and the movement has generally failed to attract them.

There is a segment of the radical feminist movement that sees all men as oppressors of all women and thinks of women as a caste. The minority group or caste analogy was first developed by Helen Hacker in her article "Women as a Minority Group" (Social Forces, 1951), which has greatly influenced Women's Liberation thinking. Hacker posited that women, although numerically a majority, are in effect an oppressed caste in society and show the characteristics of such a caste: ascribed attributes, attitudes of accommodation to their inferior status, internalization of the social values that oppress them, etc.

This analogy has since been augmented by a number of psychological experiments and attitude studies, which seem to confirm that women, like men, are socially and culturally prepared from early childhood for the roles society expects them to play. Social control through indoctrination, rewards, punishments, and social pressure, leads to the internalization of cultural norms by the individual. Women are "brainwashed" to accept their inferior status in society as being in the natural order of things. It is, in fact, what they come to define as their femininity. There is increasing experimental evidence that it is their acceptance of this view of their femininity that causes women to fall behind in achievement during their high school years and to lack the necessary incentives for success in difficult professions. And this acceptance creates conflicts in the women who do succeed in business and the professions. Mass media, literature, academia, and especially Freudian psychology, all contribute to reinforce the stereotype of femininity and to convince women who feel dissatisfied with it that they are neurotic or deviant. It is a process in which women themselves learn to participate.

Radical feminists see this system as being constantly reinforced by all-pervasive male supremacist attitudes. They regard male supremacy, or sexism—a term the movement coined—as the main enemy. They claim that like racism, sexism pervades the consciousness of every man (and many women), and is firmly entrenched in the value system, institutions, and mores of our society. Attitudes toward this adversary vary. Some wish to change *institutionalized* sexism; others believe that all men are primarily sexist and have *personal* vested interests in remaining so; still others see a power struggle against men as inevitable and advocate man-hating as essential for the indoctrination of the revolutionists.

In viewing the oppression of women as caste or minority group oppression, one encounters certain conceptual difficulties. Woman have been at various times and places a majority of the population, yet they have shared in the treatment accorded minorities. Paradoxically, their status is highest when they are actually a minority, as they were in colonial New England. Caste comes closest to defining the position of women, but it fails to take into account their uniqueness, as the only members of a low-ranking group who live in more intimate association with the higher-ranking group than they do with their own. Women take their status and privilege from the males in their family. Their low status is not maintained or bolstered by the threat of force, as is that of other subordinate castes. These facts would seem to limit severely the propaganda appeal of those radical feminists who envision feminine liberation in terms of anti-male power struggles. The ultimate battle of the sexes, which such a view takes for granted, is surely as unattractive a prospect to most women as it is to men. This particular theoretical analysis entraps its advocates in a self-limiting, utopian counterculture, which may at best appeal to a small group of alienated women, but which can do little to alter the basic conditions of the majority of women.

The attack on sexism, however, is inseparable from the aims of Women's Liberation; in it means and ends are perfectly fused. It serves to uncover the myriad injuries casually inflicted on every woman in our culture, and in the process women change themselves, as they are attempting to change others. Male supremacy has had a devastating effect on the self-consciousness of women; it has imbued them with a deep sense of inferiority, which has stunned their development and achievements. In fighting sexism, women fight to gain self-respect.

In attempting to define the nature of the oppression of women, radical feminism reveals little advance over traditional feminist theories. All analogies—class, minority group, caste—approximate the position of women, but fail to define it adequately. Women are a category unto themselves; an adequate analysis of their position in society demands new conceptual tools. It is to be hoped that feminist intellectuals will be able to develop a more adequate theoretical foundation for the new movement. Otherwise there is a danger that the weaknesses and limitations of the earlier feminist movement might be repeated.

Largely under the influence of the Black Power movement, Women's Liberation groups have developed new approaches to the organizing of women that include sex-segregated meetings and consciousness-raising groups. Various forms of separatist tactics are used: all-female meetings in which men are ignored; female caucuses that challenge male domination of organizations; outright anti-male power struggles in which males are eventually excluded from formerly mixed organizations; deliberate casting of men in roles contrary to stereotype, such as having men staff child-care centers while women attend meetings, and refusing to perform the expected female services of cooking, serving food, typing.

These tactics are designed to force men to face their sexist attitudes. More important still is their effect on women: an increase in group solidarity, a lessening of self-depreciation, a feeling of potential strength. In weekly "rap" sessions members engage in consciousness-raising discussions. Great care is taken to allow each woman to participate equally and to see that there are no leaders. Shyness, reticence, and the inability to speak out soon vanish in such a supportive atmosphere. Members freely share their experiences and thoughts with one another, learn to reveal themselves, and develop feelings of trust and love for women. The discovery that what they considered personal problems are in fact social phenomena has a liberating effect. From a growing awareness of how the inferior status has affected them, they explore the meaning of their femininity and, gradually, develop a new definition of womanliness, one they can accept with pride. Women in these groups try to deal with their sense of being weak, and of being manipulated and programmed by others. Being an emancipated woman means being independent, self-confident, strong; no longer mainly a sex object, valued for one's appearance.

The effect of the group is to free the energies of its members and channel them into action. This may largely account for the dynamic of the movement. A significant development is that the group has become a *community*, a substitute family. It provides a noncompetitive, supportive environment of like-minded sisters. Many see in it a model for the good society of the future, which would conceivably include enlightened men. It is interesting that feminists have unwittingly revitalized the mode of cooperation by which American women have traditionally lightened their burdens and improved their lives, from quilting bees to literary societies and cooperative child-care centers.

From this consciousness-raising work have come demands for changes in the content of school and college curricula. Psychology, sociology, history have been developed and taught, it is claimed, from a viewpoint that takes male supremacy for granted. Like Blacks, women grow up without models from the past with whom they can identify. New feminists are demanding a reorientation in the social sciences and history; they are clamoring for a variety of courses and innovations, including departments of feminist studies. They are asking scholars to re-examine their fields of knowledge and find out to what extent women and their viewpoints are included, to sharpen their methods and guard against built-in male supremacist assumptions, and to avoid making generalizations about men and women when in fact they are generalizing about men only. Feminists are confident that once this is done serious scholarly work regarding women will be forthcoming. Although one may expect considerable resistance from educators and administrators, these demands will undoubtedly effect reforms that should ultimately enrich our knowledge. In time, these reforms could be more decisive than legal reforms in affecting societal values. They are a necessary precondition to making the full emancipation of women a reality.

Radical feminists have added new goals to traditional feminist demands: an end to the patriarchal family, new sexual standards, a re-evaluation of male and female sex roles. Their novel views regarding sex and the family are a direct outgrowth of the life experiences and life-styles of the younger, or "pill," generation, the first generation of young women to have control over their reproductive functions, independent of and without the need for cooperation from the male. This has led them to examine with detachment the sexual roles women play. One statement reads:

The role accorded to women in the sexual act is inseparable from the values taught to people about how to treat one another. . . . Woman is the object; man is the subject. . . . Men see sex as conquest; women as surrender. Such a value system in the most personal and potentially meaningful act of communication between men and women cannot but result in the inability of both the one who conquers and the one who surrenders to have genuine love and understanding between them.

The question of sexual liberation for both men and women is fundamental to both the liberation of women and . . . the development of human relationships between people, since the capacity for meaningful sexual experience is both an indication and an actualization of the capacity for love which this society stifles so successfully. [*Sisters, Brothers, Lovers . . . Listen,* Judy Bernstein, *et al.,* New England Free Press]

Female frigidity is challenged as a male-invented myth by at least one feminist author, Anne Koedt, in her article "The Myth of the Vaginal Orgasm" (*Notes from the Second Year: Women's Liberation*). She explains that the woman's role in the sexual act has been defined by men in such a way as to offer *men* the maximum gratification. She exposes the way in which women fake sexual pleasure in order to bolster the male ego. It is a theme frequently confirmed in conscious-raising groups.

Radical feminists speak openly about sex and their "hang-ups" in regard to it. This in itself has a liberating effect. Although they take sexual freedom for granted, they challenge it as illusory and expose the strong elements of exploitation and power struggle inherent in most sexual relationships. They are demanding instead a new morality based on mutual respect and mutual satisfaction. This may seem utopian to some men, threatening to others—it is certainly new as raw material for a revolutionary movement.

In America, femininity is a commodity in the market place. Women's bodies and smiling faces are used to sell anything from deodorants to automobiles. In rejecting this, radical feminists are insisting on self-determination in every aspect of their lives. The concept that a woman has the right to use her own body, without interference and legislative intervention by one man, groups of men, or the state, has already proved its dynamic potential in the campaign to abolish abortion legislation.

But it is in their rejection of the traditional American family that radical women are challenging our institutions most profoundly. They consider the patriarchal family, even in its fairly democratic American form, oppressive of women because it institutionalizes their economic dependence on men in exchange for sexual and housekeeping services. They challenge the concept that children are best raised in small, nuclear families that demand the full- or part-time services of the

THE FEMINISTS ■ 91

mother as housekeeper, cook, and drudge. They point to the kibbutzim of Israel, the institutional child-care facilities of socialist countries, and the extended families of other cultures as alternatives. Some are experimenting with heterosexual communal living: communes of women and children only, "extended families" made up of like-minded couples and their children, and various other innovations. They face with equanimity the prospect of many women deliberately choosing to live without marriage or motherhood. The population explosion, they say, may soon make these choices socially desirable. Some feminists practice voluntary celibacy or homosexuality; many insist that homosexuality should be available to men and women as a realistic choice.

Not all radical feminists are ready to go that far in their sexual revolution. There are those who have strong binding ties to one man, and many are exploring, together with newly formed male discussion groups, the possibilities of a new androgynous way of life. But all challenge the definitions of masculinity and femininity in American culture. Nobody knows, they say, what men and women would be like or what their relations might be in a society that allowed free rein to human potential regardless of sex. The new feminists are convinced that the needed societal changes will benefit men as well as women. Men will be free from the economic and psychic burdens of maintaining dependent and psychologically crippled women. No longer will they be constantly obliged to test and prove their masculinity. Inevitably, relations between the sexes will be richer and more fulfilling for both.

What is the long-range significance of the new feminist movement? Judging from the support the feminists have been able to mobilize for their various campaigns, it is quite likely that significant changes in American society will result from their efforts. In line with the traditional role of American radical movements, their agitation may result in the enactment of a wide range of legal and economic reforms, such as equal rights and job opportunities, vastly expanded child-care facilities, and equal representation in institutions and governing bodies. These reforms will, by their very nature, be of greatest benefit to middle- and upper-class women and will bring women into "the establishment" on a more nearly egalitarian basis.

The revolutionary potential of the movement lies in its attacks on the sexual values and mores of our society and in its impact on the psychology of those women who come within its influence. Changes in sexual expectations and role definitions and an end to "sexual politics," the use of sex as a weapon in a hidden power struggle, could indeed make a decisive difference in interpersonal relations, the functioning of the family, and the values of our society. Most important, the new feminists may be offering us a vision for the future: a truly androgynous society, in which sexual attributes will confer neither power nor stigma upon the individual—one in which both sexes will be free to develop and contribute to their full potential.

FOR FURTHER READING

* Vivian Gornick and Barbara K. Moran, eds. *Woman in Sexist Society: Studies in Power and Powerlessness*. New York: Basic Books, 1971.

Aileen S. Kraditor, ed. *Up from the Pedestal: Selected Documents from the History of American Feminism*. Chicago: Quadrangle, 1968.

Gerda Lerner. *Black Women in White America: A Documentary History*. New York: Pantheon, 1972.

Juliet Mitchell. *Woman's Estate*. New York: Pantheon, 1971.

* Robin Morgan, ed. *Sisterhood Is Powerful: An Anthology of Writings from the Women's Liberation Movement*. New York: Random House, 1970.

Ann F. Scott. *The Southern Lady from Pedestal to Politics*. Chicago: University of Chicago Press, 1970.

IN THE VALLEY OF
THE SHADOWS: KENTUCKY

BRUCE JACKSON

In his first State of the Union Message, President Lyndon B. Johnson called for a "war on poverty." He followed up by asking for and obtaining passage of the Economic Opportunity Act of 1964 and a series of related measures. Thus Congress and the executive branch responded to pressure implicit in the civil rights movement and to the discovery by various economists and journalists of a startling fact: that at least one-fifth of the nation's people received incomes inadequate to provide the essentials of decent shelter and a healthy diet.

Who were the poor? They came from many sections of the population: children, the aged, the employed, unemployed, and unemployable. Blacks (a quarter of the total), Mexican Americans, and women were forced to work for low wages. Indians, hidden from public view on their reservations, suffered contempt and neglect. The mechanization of cotton-growing deprived blacks of even their former miserable security in the Deep South and forced them to starve at home or flee to the Northern ghettos. Their right to organize unprotected by law, migrant farm workers constituted perhaps the most exploited body of labor in the country. Because scarcely any child care was available, women with young children struggled on public assistance—"welfare." Tiny Social Security payments mocked the promise made in 1935 that they would suffice to maintain the aged in comfort and dignity. Economic decay marked entire regions, of which the largest was the mountain land known as Appalachia, where descendents of the early pioneers lived in poverty, sickness, and hopelessness.

Those who designed the war on poverty disregarded the proposals of a number of intellectuals that every citizen should receive from society a "guaranteed minimum income" as a human right; rather, they emphasized that the government was not organizing "handouts" but was making opportunity available. Accordingly, the various programs stressed job development and the education or retraining of poor people to fit these jobs. That sounded like a good idea, but, because more than 70 per cent of the people receiving aid consisted of the aged and of dependent children, who could not benefit from these programs, it was misleading. A notable feature was "community action" in which the poor were to take part. Like democracy itself, participation is an explosive idea. Local politicians and established agencies soon recognized its potentialities and complained that the government was organizing a rebellion. Congress and the administration eventually listened to their cries and de-emphasized participation by the genuine poor.

Bruce Jackson describes the particular variety of poverty that characterizes the Appalachian region. His account suggests comparison with the 1930's, when the TVA and the United Mine Workers union appeared to be major progressive forces, and it shows the difficulties and the dangers that inhere in any effort to eradicate poverty.

□   □   □

Along the roadsides and in backyards are the cannibalized cadavers of old cars: there is no other place to dump them, there are no junkyards that have any reason to haul them away. Streambeds are littered with old tires, cans, pieces of metal and plastic. On a sunny day the streams and creeks glisten with pretty blue spots from the Maxwell House Coffee tins and Royal Crown Cola cans. For some reason the paint used by Maxwell House and Royal Crown doesn't wear off very quickly, and while the paint and paper on other cans are peeling to reveal an undistinctive aluminum color, the accumulating blues of those two brands make for a most peculiar local feature.

Winter in eastern Kentucky is not very pretty. In some places you see the gouged hillsides where the strip and auger mines have ripped away tons of dirt and rock to get at the mineral seams underneath; below the gouges you see the littered valleys where the overburden, the earth they have ripped and scooped away, has been dumped in spoil banks. The streams stink from the augerholes' sulfurous exudations; the hillsides no longer hold water back because the few trees and bushes are small and thin, so there is continual erosion varying the ugliness in color only.

Most of the people around here live outside the town in "hollers" and along the creeks. Things are narrow: the hills rise up closely and flatland is at a premium. A residential area will stretch out for several miles, one or two houses and a road thick, with hills starting up just behind the outhouse. Sometimes, driving along the highway following the Big Sandy river, there is so little flat space that the highway is on one side of the river and the line of houses is on the other, with plank suspension bridges every few miles connecting the two. Everything is crushed together. You may ride five miles without passing a building, then come upon a half-dozen houses, each within ten feet of its neighbor. And churches: the Old Regular Baptist church, the Freewill Baptist church, the Meta Baptist church. On the slopes of the hills are cemeteries, all neatly tended; some are large and old, some have only one or two recent graves in them.

In winter, when the sun never rises very far above the horizon, the valley floors get only about four hours of direct sunlight a day; most of the days are cloudy anyhow. One always moves in shadow, in grayness. Children grow up without ever seeing the sun rise or set.

The day of the company store and company house is gone. So are most of the big companies around here. This is small truck mine country now, and operators of the small mines don't find stores and houses worth their time. The old company houses worth living in have been bought up, either as rental property or for the new owner's personal use; the company houses still standing but not worth living in comprise the county's only public housing for the very poor.

At the end of one of the hollows running off Marrowbone Creek, three miles up a road you couldn't make, even in dry weather, without four-wheeled drive, stands an old cabin. It is a log cabin, but there is about it nothing romantic or frontiersy, only grimness. Scratched in the kitchen window, by some unknown adult or child, are the crude letters of the word victory. Over what or whom we don't know. It is unlikely anyway. There are no victories here, only occasional survivors, and if survival is a victory it is a mean and brutal one.

Inside the cabin a Barbie Doll stands over a nearly opaque mirror in a room lighted by a single bare 60-watt bulb. In the middle of the room a coal stove spews outrageous amounts of heat. When the stove is empty the room is cold and damp. There is no middle area of comfort. The corrugated cardboard lining the walls doesn't stop drafts very well and most of the outside chinking is gone. On one side of the room with the stove is the entrance to the other bedroom, on the other side is the kitchen. There are no doors inside the house. A woman lives here with her nine children.

If all the nine children were given perfectly balanced full meals three times a day from now on, still some of them would never be well. A 15-year-old daughter loses patches of skin because of an irreversible vitamin deficiency, and sometimes, because of the suppuration and congealing, they have to soak her clothing off when she comes home from school. Last month the baby was spitting up blood for a while but that seems to have stopped.

It might be possible to do something for the younger ones, but it is not likely anyone will. The husband went somewhere and didn't come back; that was over a year ago. The welfare inspector came a few months ago and found out that someone had given the family a box of clothes for the winter; the welfare check was cut by $20 a month after that. When the woman has $82 she can get $120 worth of food stamps; if she doesn't have the $82, she gets no food stamps at all. For a year, the entire family had nothing for dinner but one quart of green beans each night. Breakfast was fried flour and coffee. A friend told me the boy said he had had meat at a neighbor's house once.

BONY HILLS

This is Pike County, Kentucky. It juts like a chipped arrowhead into the bony hill country of neighboring West Virginia. Pike County has about seventy thousand residents and, the Chamber of Commerce advertises, it produces more coal than any other county in the world. The county seat, Pikesville, has about six thousand residents; it is the only real town for about 30 miles.

The biggest and bitterest event in Pike County's past was sometime in the 1880s when Tolbert McCoy killed Big Ellison Hatfield: it started a feud that resulted in 65 killed, settled nothing and wasn't won by either side. The biggest and bitterest thing in recent years has been the War on Poverty: it doesn't seem to have killed anyone, but it hasn't settled anything or won any major battles either.

About seventy-five hundred men are employed by Pike County's mines: one hundred drive trucks, five hundred work at the tipples (the docks where coal is loaded into railway cars) and mine offices, and six thousand work inside. Most of the mines are small and it doesn't take very many men to work them: an automated truck mine can be handled by about eight men. Some people work at service activities: they pump gas, sell shoes, negotiate contracts (there are about 40 lawyers in this little town), dispense drugs, direct traffic, embalm—all those things that make an American town go. There are six industrial firms in the area; two of them are beverage companies, one is a lumber company; the total employment of the six firms is 122 men and women.

A union mine pays $28-$38 per day, with various benefits, but few of the mines in Pike County are unionized. The truck mines, where almost all the men work, pay $14 per day, with almost no benefits. The United Mine Workers of America were strong here once, but when times got hard the union let a lot of people down and left a lot of bitterness behind. Not only did the union make deals with the larger companies that resulted in many of its own men being thrown out of work (one of those deals recently resulted in a $7.3 million conspiracy judgment against the UMWA and Consolidation Coal Company), but it made the abandonment complete by lifting the unemployed workers' medical cards and shutting down the union hospitals in the area. For most of the area, those cards and hospitals were the only source of medical treatment. There has been talk of organizing the truck mines and someone told me the UMW local was importing an old-time fire-breathing organizer to get things going, but it doesn't seem likely the men will put their lives on the line another time.

With Frederic J. Fleron, Jr., an old friend then on the faculty of the University of Kentucky in Lexington, I went to visit Robert Holcomb, president of the Independent Coal Operator's Association, president of the Chamber of Commerce, and one of the people in the county most vocally at war with the anti-poverty program. His office door was decorated with several titles: Dixie Mining Co., Roberts Engineering Co., Robert Holcomb and Co., Chloe Gas Co., Big Sandy Coal Co., and Martha Collieries, Inc.

One of the secretaries stared at my beard as if it were a second nose; she soon got control of herself and took us in to see Holcomb. (Someone had said to me the day before, "Man, when Holcomb sees you with that beard on he's gonna be sure you're a communist." "What if I tell him I'm playing Henry the Fifth in a play at the university?" "Then he'll be sure Henry the Fifth is a communist too.") Holcomb took the beard better than the girl had: his expression remained nicely neutral. He offered us coffee and introduced us to his partner, a Mr. Roberts, who sat in a desk directly opposite him. On the wall behind Roberts' head was a large white flying map of the United States with a brownish smear running over Louisiana, Mississippi, and most of Texas; the darkest splotch was directly over New Orleans. The phone rang and Roberts took the call; he tilted back in his chair, his head against New Orleans and Lake Pontchartrain.

Holcomb was happy to talk about his objections to the antipoverty program. "I'm a firm believer that you don't help a man by giving him bread unless you give him hope for the future, and poverty programs have given them bread only." The problem with the Appalachian Volunteers (an anti-poverty organization partially funded by the OEO, now pretty much defunct) was "they got no supervision. They brought a bunch of young people in, turned 'em loose, and said, 'Do your thing'. . . . I think they have created a disservice rather than a service by creating a lot of disillusionment by making people expect things that just can't happen."

EXPANDING AND WRECKING

He told us something about what was happening. The coal industry had been expanding rapidly. "Over the last eight years the truck mining industry has created an average of 500 new jobs a year." He sat back. "We're working to bring the things in here that will relieve the poverty permanently." He talked of bringing other kinds of industry to the area and told us about the incentives they were offering companies that were willing to relocate. "We know a lot of our people are not fitted for mining," he said.

(It is not just a matter of being "fitted" of course. There is the problem of those who are wrecked by silicosis and black lung who can do nothing but hope their doctor bills won't go up so much they'll have to pull one of the teenage kids out of school and send him to work, or be so screwed by welfare or social security or the UMW pension managers or the mine operators' disability insurance company that the meager payments that do come into some homes will be stopped.)

The truck mines play an ironic role in the local economy: half the men working in them, according to Holcomb, cannot work in the large mines because of physical disability. The small mines, in effect, not only get the leftover coal seams that aren't fat enough to interest Consol or U.S. Steel or the other big companies in the area, but they also get the men those firms have used up and discarded.

From Holcomb's point of view things are going pretty well in Pike County. In 1960 there was $18 million in deposits in Pikeville's three banks; that has risen to $65 million. There are 700 small mines in the county, many of them operated by former miners. "This is free enterprise at its finest," he said.

The next morning he took us on a trip through the Johns Creek area. As we passed new houses and large trailers he pointed to them as evidence of progress, which they in fact are. In the "hollers" behind, Fred and I could see the shacks and boxes in which people also live, and those Holcomb passed without a word. I suppose one must select from all the data presenting itself in this world, otherwise living gets awfully complex.

We drove up the hill to a small mine. Holcomb told us that the eight men working there produce 175 tons daily, all of which goes to the DuPont nylon plant in South Carolina.

A man in a shed just outside the mine mouth was switching the heavy industrial batteries on a coal tractor. The miner was coated with coal dust and oil smears. He wore a plastic helmet with a light on it; around his waist was the light's battery pack, like a squashed holster. He moved very fast, whipping the chains off and on and winding the batteries out, pumping the pulley chains up and down. Another mine tractor crashed out of the entrance, its driver inclined at 45 degrees. The tractor is about 24 inches high and the mine roof is only 38 inches high, so the drivers have to tilt all the time or get their heads crushed. Inside, the men work on their knees. The tractor backed the buggy connected to it to the edge of a platform, dumped its load, then clanked back inside.

I went into the mine, lying on my side in the buggy towed by the tractor with the newly charged batteries.

Inside is utter blackness, broken only by the slicing beams of light from the helmets. The beams are neat and pretty, almost like a Lucite tube poking here and there; the prettiness goes away when you realize the reason the beam is so brilliant is because of the coal and rock dust in the air, dust a worker is continually inhaling into his lungs. One sees no bodies, just occasional hands interrupting the moving lightbeams playing on the timbers and working face. Clattering noises and shouts are strangely disembodied and directionless.

Outside, I dust off and we head back toward town in Holcomb's truck.

"The temperature in there is 68 degrees all the time," he says. "You work in air-conditioned comfort all year 'round. Most of these men, after they've been in the mine for a while, wouldn't work above ground." (I find myself thinking of Senator Murphy of California, who in his campaign explained the need for bracero labor: they stoop over better than Anglos do.) The miners, as I said, make $14 a day.

"When you see what's been accomplished here in the last ten years it makes the doings of the AVs and the others seem completely insignificant. And we didn't have outside money." The pitted and gouged road is one-lane, and we find ourselves creeping behind a heavily loaded coal truck heading toward one of the tipples up the road. "We think welfare is fine, but it should be a temporary measure, not a permanent one. And any organization that encourages people to get on welfare is a detriment to the community." The truck up front gets out of our way; Holcomb shifts back to two-wheel drive; we pick up speed. "These poverty program people, what they tried to do is latch on to some mountain customs and try to convince people they have come up with something new."

He believes business will help everybody; he believes the antipoverty program has been bad business. He is enormously sincere. Everyone is enormously sincere down here, or so it seems.

So we drove and looked at the new mines and tipples and Robert Holcomb told us how long each had been there and what its tonnage was and how many people each mine employed and how many mines fed into each tipple. One of his companies, he told us, produced 350,000 tons of coal last year and operated at a profit of 15.7 cents per ton.

Hospital death certificates cite things like pneumonia and heart disease. There is no way of knowing how many of those result from black lung and silicosis. The mine owners say very few; the miners and their families say a great many indeed. A lot of men with coated lungs don't die for a long time, but they may not be good for much else meanwhile. Their lungs won't absorb much oxygen, so they cannot move well or fast or long.

"This is a one-industry area," Holcomb had said, "and if you can't work at that industry you can't work at anything." Right. And most of the residents—men wrinkled or contaminated, widows, children—do not work at anything. Over 50 percent of the families in Pike County have incomes below $3,000 per year. Like land torn by the strip-mining operations, those people simply stay back in the "hollers" out of sight and slowly erode.

We talked with an old man who had worked in the mines for 28 years. He told us how he had consumed his life savings and two years' time getting his disabled social security benefits.

"See, I got third-stage silicosis and I've got prostate and gland trouble, stomach troubles, a ruptured disc. Now they say that at the end of this month they're gonna take the state aid medical card away. And that's all I've got; I've got so much wrong with me I can't get no insurance. I've had the card two years and now they say I draw too much social security because of last year's increase in social security benefits and they're gonna have to take my medical card away from me after this month. I don't know what in the hell I'm gonna do. Die, I reckon."

"Yeah, yeah," his wife said from the sink.

"It don't seem right," he said. "I worked like hell, I made good money, and I doublebacked. Because I worked a lot and draw more social security than lots of people in the mines where they don't make no money, I don't see where it's right for them not to allow me no medical card."

He opened the refrigerator and showed us some of the various chemicals he takes every day. In a neat stack on the table were the month's medical receipts. He said something about his youth, and I was suddenly stunned to realize he was only 51.

"You know," he said, "sand's worse than black lung. Silicosis. It hardens on the lung and there's no way to get it off. In West Virginia

I worked on one of those roof-bolting machines. It's about eight, nine-foot high, sandstone top. Burn the bits up drillin' holes in it. And I'd be there. Dust'd be that thick on your lips. But it's fine stuff in the air; you don't see the stuff that you get in your lungs. It's fine stuff. Then I didn't get no pay for it."

"You got a thousand dollars," his wife said.

"A thousand dollars for the first stage. They paid me first stage and I just didn't want to give up. I kept on workin', and now I got third stage. . . . I just hated to give up, but I wished I had of. One doctor said to me, 'If you keep on you might as well get your shotgun and shoot your brains out, you'd be better off.' I still kept on after he told me that. Then I got so I just couldn't hardly go on. My clothes wouldn't stay on me."

The woman brought coffee to the table. "He draws his disabled social security now," she says, "but if he was to draw for his black lung disease they would cut his social security way down, so he's better off just drawing his social security. There's guys around here they cut below what they was drawing for social security. I don't think that's right."

It is all very neat: the black lung, when a miner can force the company doctors to diagnose it honestly, is paid for by company insurance, but payments are set at a level such that a disabled miner loses most of his social security benefits if he takes the compensation; since the compensation pays less than social security, many miners don't put in their legitimate claims, and the net effect is a government subsidy of the insurance companies and mine owners.

Mary Walton, an Appalachian Volunteer [AV], invited Fred and me to dinner at her place in Pikeville one night during our stay. It turned out Mary and I had been at Harvard at the same time, and we talked about that place for a while, which was very strange there between those darkening hills. Three other people were at Mary's apartment: a girl named Barbara, in tight jeans and a white shirt with two buttons open and zippered boots, and two men, both of them connected with the local college. One was working with the Model Cities project, the other worked in the college president's office; one was astoundingly tall, the other was built like a wrestler; they all looked aggressively healthy. Barbara's husband worked for the Council of the Southern Mountains in Berea.

The fellow who looked like a wrestler told me at great length that what was going on in Pikeville wasn't a social or economic attack on the community structure, but rather an attack on the structure of ideas and only now was everyone learning that. I asked him what he meant. He said that the antipoverty workers had once seen their job as enlightening the masses about how messed up things were. "We were ugly Americans, that's all we were. That's why we weren't effective. But now we've learned that you don't change anything that way, you have to get inside the local community and understand it first and work there."

I thought that was indeed true, but I didn't see what it had to do with the structure of the community's ideas; it had to do only with the arrogance or naivete of the antipoverty workers, and that was awfully solipsistic. He hadn't said anything about his clients—just himself, just the way his ideas were challenged, not theirs.

The apartment was curiously out of that world. On the walls were posters and lithos and prints and pictures of healthy human bodies looking delicious. The record racks contained the Stones and *Tim Hardin No. 3* and a lot of Bach. Many of the recent books we'd all read, and others one had and the others meant to, and Mary and I talked about them, but there was something relative, even in the pleasantness, as if it were an appositive in the bracketing nastiness out there.

When we got back to the car I took from my jacket pocket the heavy and uncomfortable, shiny, chrome-plated .380 automatic pistol someone had once given me in San Antonio. I put it on the seat next to Fred's .357 revolver. They looked silly there; real guns always do. But people kept telling us how someone else was going to shoot us, or they recounted the story of how Hugh O'Connor, a Canadian film producer down in the next county the year before to make a movie, was shot in the heart by a man with no liking for outsiders and less for outsiders with cameras, and it did seem awfully easy to be an outsider here.

We went to see Edith Easterling, a lifelong Marrowbone Creek resident, working at that time for the Appalachian Volunteers as director of the Marrowbone Folk School. "The people in the mountains really lives hard," Edith said. "You can come into Pikeville and go to the Chamber of Commerce and they'll say, "Well there's really no poor people left there. People are faring good." Then you can come out here and go to homes, and you'd just be surprised how poor these people live, how hard that they live. Kids that's grown to 15 or 16 years old that's never had a mess of fresh milk or meats, things that kids really need. They live on canned cream until they get big enough to go to the table and eat beans and potatoes."

She told us about harassment and red-baiting of the AVs by Robert Holcomb, Harry Eastburn (the Big Sandy Community Action Program director, also funded by OEO, a bitter antagonist of any antipoverty program not under his political control), and Thomas Ratliff, the commonwealth's attorney (the equivalent of a county prosecutor).

Some of the AVs came from out of state, especially the higher paid office staff and technical specialists, but most of the 14 field workers were local people, like Edith. Since becoming involved with the antipoverty program Edith has received telephone threats and had some windows shot out. The sheriff refused to send a deputy to investigate. Occasionally she gets anonymous calls; some are threats, some call her "dirty communist." She shrugs those away: "I'm a Republican and who ever seen a communist Republican?"

CHANGING A WAY OF LIFE

The Appalachian Volunteers began in the early 1960s as a group of students from Berea College who busied themselves with needed community Band-Aid work: they made trips to the mountains to patch up dilapidated schoolhouses; they ran tutorial programs; they collected books for needy schools. The ultimate futility of such work soon became apparent, and there was a drift in the AV staff toward projects that might affect the life-style of some of the mountain communities. In 1966 the AVs decided to break away from their parent organization, the conservative Council of the Southern Mountains. The new, independent Appalachian Volunteers had no difficulty finding federal funding. During the summers of 1966 and 1967 the organization received large OEO grants to host hundreds of temporary volunteer workers, many of them VISTA and Peace Corps trainees. According to David Walls, who was acting director of the AVs when I talked with him, the organization's mission was to "create effective, economically self-sufficient poor people's organizations that would concern themselves with local issues, such as welfare rights, bridges and roads, water systems, and strip mining."

It didn't work, of course it didn't work; the only reason it lasted as long as it did was because so much of the AV staff was composed of outsiders, people who had worked in San Francisco and Boston and New York and Washington, and it took a long time before the naivete cracked enough for the failure to show through.

The first consequence of creating an organization of the impoverished and unempowered is not the generation of any new source or residence of power, but rather the gathering in one place of a lot of poverty and powerlessness that previously were spread out. In an urban situation, the poor or a minority group may develop or exercise veto power: they can manage an economic boycott; they can refuse to work for certain firms and encourage others to join with them; they can physically block a store entrance. It is only when such efforts create a kind of negative monopoly (a strike line no one will cross or a boycott others will respect) that power is generated. When that negative monopoly cannot be created, there is no power—this is why workers can successfully strike for higher wages but the poor in cities cannot get the police to respect their civil liberties enough to stop beating

them up; if everyone refuses to work at a factory, the owner must cooperate or close down, but there is nothing anyone can refuse a
policeman that will remove the immediate incentive for illegal police
behavior. The poor in the mountains cannot strike—they are unemployable anyway, or at least enough of them are to make specious that kind
of action. Even if they were to get something going the UMW would
not support them. The poor cannot start an economic boycott: they
don't spend enough to hold back enough to threaten any aspect of the
mountain coal company. (There have been a few instances of industrial
sabotage—I'll mention them later on—that have been dramatic, but
pitifully ineffective.) One of the saddest things about the poor in the
mountains is they have nothing to deny anyone. And they don't even
have the wild hope some city poor entertain that something may turn
up; in the mountains there is nothing to hope for.

Another problem with organizations of the very poor is they do not
have much staying power: the individual participants are just too vulnerable. So long as the members can be scared or bought off easily,
one cannot hope for such groups to develop solidarity. In Kentucky,
where welfare, medical aid, disability pensions, and union benefits all
have a remarkable quality of coming and going with political whims,
that is a real problem. Edith Easterling described the resulting condition:
"These people are scared people; they are scared to death. I can talk to
them and I can say, 'You shouldn't be scared; there's nothing to be
scared about.' But they're still scared."

"What are they scared of," Fred asked her, "losing their jobs?"

"No. Some of 'em don't even have a job. Most of the people don't
have jobs. They live on some kind of pension. They're scared of losing
their pension. If it's not that, they're scared someone will take them to
court for something. 'If I say something, they're going to take me to
court and I don't have a lawyer's fee. I don't have a lawyer so I'd rather
not say nothing.' When you get the people to really start opening up
and talking, that's when the county officials attack us every time with
something."

PUBLICITY AND REVENGE

For someone who brings troublesome publicity to the community,
there are forms of retaliation far crueler than the mere cutting off of
welfare or unemployment benefits. One antipoverty worker told of an
event following a site visit by Robert Kennedy a few years ago: "When
Kennedy was down for his hearings one of his advance men got in
contact with a friend of ours who had a community organization going.
They were very anxious to get some exposure, to get Kennedy involved
in it. They took the advance men around to visit some families that

were on welfare. He made statements about the terrible conditions the children there in two particular homes had to live under. He wasn't indicting the families; he was just talking about conditions in general. These were picked up by the local press and given quite a bit of notoriety—Kennedy Aide Makes the Scene—that sort of thing. After he left, about three days later, the welfare agency came and took away the children from both of those families and put them in homes. . . .This is the control that is over people's lives."

The group with the potential staying power in the mountains is the middle class, the small landowners. They have concrete things to lose, while the poor (save in anomalous atrocities such as the one with the children mentioned above) have nothing to lose, they only have possible access to benefits that someone outside their group may or may not let them get. There is a big difference in the way one fights in the two situations. Something else: it is harder to scare the middle class off, for it has not been conditioned by all those years of humiliating control and dependency.

One Appalachian Volunteer, Joe Mulloy, a 24-year-old Kentuckian, realized this. He and his wife decided to join a fight being waged by a Pike County landowner, Jink Ray, and his neighbors, against a strip-mine operator who was about to remove the surface of Ray's land.

RIGHTS FOR PENNIES

The focus of the fight was the legitimacy of the *broadform* deed, a nineteenth century instrument with which landowners assigned mineral rights to mining companies, usually for small sums of money (50 cents per acre was common). When these deeds were originally signed no landowner had any thought of signing away all rights to his property— just the underground minerals and whatever few holes the mining company might have to make in the hillside to get at the seams. In the twentieth century the coal companies developed the idea of lifting off all the earth and rock above the coal, rather than digging for it, and since the broadform deed said the miner could use whatever means he saw fit to get the coal out, the Kentucky courts held that the miners' land rights had precedence over the surface owners—even though that meant complete destruction of a man's land by a mining process the original signer of the deed could not have imagined. The strip miners are legally entitled, on the basis of a contract that might be 90 years old, to come to a man's home and completely bury it in rubble, leaving the owner nothing but the regular real estate tax bill with which he is stuck even though the "real estate" has since been dumped in the next creek bed. First come the bulldozers to do the initial clearing (a song I heard in West Virginia, to the tune of "Swing Low, Sweet Chariot," went: "Roll on, big D-9 dozer, comin' for to bury my home/I'm getting madder as you're gettin' closer, comin' for to bury my home"), then they roll in the massive shovels, some of which grow as large as 18.5 million pounds and can gobble 200 tons of earth and rock a minute and dump it all a city block away. Such a machine is operated by one man riding five stories above the ground.

On June 29, 1967, Jink Ray and some neighbors in Island Creek, a Pike County community, blocked with their bodies bulldozers that were about to start stripping Ray's land. With them were Joe and Karen Mulloy. The people themselves had organized the resistance; the Mulloys were simply helping.

With the strip-mining fight on the mountain, the AVs were for the first time involved in something significant. It was also dangerous: the members of the Island Creek group were challenging not only the basis of the local economy, but the federal government as well: the big mines' biggest customer is the Tennessee Valley Authority, and the Small Business Administration supports many of the smaller mine operators. The antipoverty program and other federal agencies were moving toward open conflict.

What happened was that the antipoverty program backed down and the local power structure moved in. Eleven days after Governor Edward Breathitt's August 1 suspension of the strip-mining company's Island Creek permit (the first and only such suspension), Pike County officials arrested the Mulloys for sedition (plotting or advocating the violent overthrow of the government). Arrested with them on the same charge were Alan and Margaret McSurely, field workers for the Southern Conference Educational Fund (SCEF), a Louisville-based civil rights organization. McSurely had been hired as training consultant by the AV's during the spring of 1967, but the real reason he had been hired was to restructure the cumbersome organization. One of the first things he did was get the AVs to allow local people on the board of directors; he was fired in a month and went to work for SCEF; they even arrested Carl Braden (SCEF's executive director) and his wife, Anne. Anne Braden had never been in Pike County in her life; the first time Carl Braden had been there was the day he went to Pikeville to post bail for McSurely on the sedition charge.

In Washington, the response to the arrests was immediate; Sargent Shriver's office announced that AV funds would be cut off; no funds previously granted were taken away, but no new money was appropriated after that.

The Pike County grand jury concluded that "A well-organized and well-financed effort is being made to promote and spread the communistic theory of violent and forceful overthrow of the government of Pike County." The grand jury said also that "Communist organizers have attempted, without success thus far, to promote their beliefs among our school children by infiltrating our local schools with teachers who believe in the violent overthrow of the local government." Organizers were "planning to infiltrate local churches and labor unions in order to cause dissension and to promote their purposes." And, finally, "Communist organizers are attempting to form community unions with the eventual purpose of organizing armed groups to be known as 'Red Guards' and through which the forceful overthrow of the local government would be accomplished."

UNTOUCHABLE VOLUNTEERS

The AVs came unglued. The Mulloys became pariahs within the organization. "We spent that whole summer and no AV came to see us at all in Pike County," Joe Mulloy said. "Once they came up to shit on us, but that was the only time. Then the thing of our getting arrested for sedition was what just really flipped everybody. . . . This was a real siuation that you had to deal with; it wasn't something in your mind or some ideological thing. It was real. Another person was under arrest. I think that the feeling of a number of people on the staff was it was my fault that I had been arrested because I had been reckless in my organizing, that I had been on the mountain with the fellas and had risked as much as they were risking and I deserved what I got, and that I should be fired so the program would go on; that was now a detriment."

That fall, a special three judge federal court ruled the Kentucky sedition law unconstitutional, so all charges against the Mulloys, the Bradens, and the McSurelys were wiped out. But the AVs were still nervous. "After the arrests were cleared away," Mulloy said, "things started to happen to me on the staff. I was given another assignment. I was told that I couldn't be a field man any more because I was a public figure identified with sedition and hence people would feel uneasy talking to me, and that I should do research. My truck was taken away and I was given an old car, and I was given a title of research rather than field man. It took away considerable voice that I had in the staff until then."

Karen Mulloy said she and Joe really had no choice. "If we had organized those people up there, with possible death as the end result for some of them—fortunately it was kept nonviolent—and if we weren't with them, they wouldn't have spoken to us. We took as much risk as they did. We said to them, 'We're not going to organize something for you that we won't risk our necks for either.' An organizer can't do that."

"These people have gone through the whole union experience and that has sold them out," Joe said. "And a great number of people have gone through the poverty war experience and that hasn't answered anybody's problems, anybody's questions. Getting together on the strip-mining issue—if there was ever one issue that the poverty war got on that was good, that was it. It all fell through because when we started getting counterattacked by the operators the poverty war backed up because their funds were being jeopardized. The whole strip-mining issue as an organized effort has collapsed right now and the only thing that's going on is individual sabotage. There's a lot of mining equipment being blown up every month or so, about a million dollars at a time. These are individual or small group acts or retaliation, but the organized effort has ceased."

(Later, I talked with Rick Diehl, the AV research director, about the sabotage. He described two recent operations, both of them very sophisticated, involving groups of multiple charges set off simultaneously. The sheriff didn't even look for the dynamiters: he probably wouldn't have caught them, and even if he had he wouldn't have gotten a jury to convict. "And that kind of stuff goes on to some degree all the time," Diehl said. "There's a growing feeling that destroying property is going to shut down the system in Appalachia. The people don't benefit from the coal companies at all, 'cause even the deep mines don't have enough employees. The average number of employees in a deep mine is 16 people. So, you can see, there is nothing to lose. It's that same desperation kind of thing that grips people in Detroit and Watts.")

ORGANIZING OUTRAGE

Even though the sedition charges were dropped, the Mulloys and McSurelys weren't to escape punishment for their organizing outrages.

One Friday the 13th Al McSurely came home late from a two or three day trip out of town, talked with his wife a little while, then went to bed. Margaret went to bed a short time later. "I wasn't asleep at all," she said, "but he was so tired he went right to sleep. I heard this car speed up. Well, I had got into the habit of listening to cars at night, just because we always expected something like this to happen. And sure enough, it did. There was this blast. The car took off, and there was this huge blast, and glass and dirt and grit were in my mouth and eyes and hair, and the baby was screaming. So I put on my bathrobe and ran across the street with the baby."

"The state trooper was pretty good," Alan said. "He gave me a lecture: 'The next time this happens call the city police first so they can seal off the holler. They can get here much faster than I can.' I said, 'I'll try and remember that.'"

Joe Mulloy was the only AV with a Kentucky draft board; he was also the only AV to lose his occupational deferment and have his

2-A changed to 1-A. Mulloy asked the board (in Louisville, the same as Muhammad Ali's) for a rehearing on the grounds of conscientious objection, and he presented as part of his evidence a letter from Thomas Merton saying he was Mulloy's spiritual adviser (the two used to meet for talks in Merton's cabin in the woods) and could testify to the truthfulness of Mulloy's C.O. claim. The board refused to reopen the case because, they said, there was no new evidence of any relevance or value. In April 1968 Mulloy was sentenced to five years in prison and a $10,000 fine for refusing induction.

He was fired immediately by the Appalachian Volunteers. Some wanted him out because they honestly thought his draft case would be a major obstacle to his effectiveness with the oddly patriotic mountain people. (In the mountains you can be against the war, many people are, but if your country calls you, you go. It would be unpatriotic not to go. The government and the country are two quite independent entities. The government might screw up the antipoverty program, run that bad war, work in conjunction with the mine owners and politicians, but it isn't the government that is calling you—it is the country. Only a weirdo would refuse that call. But once you're in you are working for the government, and then it is all right to desert.) Others on the AV staff objected to Mulloy's getting involved in issues that riled up the authorities. The staff vote to get rid of him was 20 to 19.

What the AVs failed to admit was that the changing of Mulloy's draft status was an attack on them as well: the only reason for the change was the strip-mine fight. The draft board had joined the OEO, the TVA, the mine owners, the political structure of the state, and UMW in opposition to effective organization of the poor in the mountains.

I asked Joe how he felt about it all now. "I don't know if I can really talk about this objectively," he said. "I feel in my guts as a Kentuckian a great deal of resentment against a lot of these people. And some of them are my friends that have come in and stirred things up and then have left. The going is really tough right now. I'm still here; all the people that have to make a living out in those counties are still there with their black lung. I don't think anything was accomplished. It's one of those things that's going to go down in history as a cruel joke: the poverty war in the mountains."

The two bad guys of the story, I suppose, should be Robert Holcomb, spokesman for the mine owners in the county, and commonwealth's attorney Thomas Ratliff, the man who handled the prosecution in the sedition [case] and who was (coincidentally, he insists) Republican candidate for lieutenant governor at the time; Ratliff got rich in the mine business, but is now into a lot of other things. Like most bad guy labels, I suspect these are too easy. I'll come back to that.

I rather liked Ratliff even though there were things I knew about him I didn't like at all. It is quite possible he really does believe, as he said he does, that the McSurelys and the Bradens are communist *provocateurs*; there are people in America who believe menaces exist, though not very many of them are as intelligent as Ratliff.

He claims the defendants in the sedition case had "a new angle on revolution—to do it locally and then bring all the local revolutions together and then you got a big revolution. Now whether it would have succeeded or not I don't know. I think it possibly could have, had they been able to continue to get money from the Jolly Green Giant, as they call Uncle Sam. I certainly think with enough money, and knowing the history of this area, it was not impossible."

What seems to have bothered him most was not the politics involved but the bad sportsmanship: "The thing that rankled me in this case, and it still does, this is really what disturbed me more about this thing than anything else, was the fact that . . . they were able to use federal money . . . to promote this thing. Frankly, I would be almost as opposed to either the Republican party or the Democratic party being financed by the federal money to prevail, much less a group who were avowed communists, made no bones about it that I could tell, whose objective was revolution, the forceful and violent overthrow of the local government and hopefully to overthrow the federal government, and it was being financed by federal tax money!"

Once Ratliff got off his communist menace line, I found myself agreeing with him as much as I had with some of the remarks Joe Mulloy had made. Ratliff spoke eloquently on the need for a negative income tax, for massive increases in the taxes on the mine operators, things like that. (Whether he meant the things he said is impossible to tell; one never knows with politicians, or anyone else for that matter.)

"It's the reaction to this sort of situation that really bothers me," he said, "because—there is no question about it—there is some containment of free speech, free expression, when you get a situation like this. People become overexcited and overdisturbed. And the laws of physics play in these things: for every action there's a reaction, and the reaction, unfortunately, is often too much in this kind of situation. You begin seeing a communist behind every tree, or anything like that.

"But I think they've accomplished one thing, not what they thought they would. . . . That's the tragic part of it; I don't think they've uplifted anybody. I think they have left a lot of people disappointed, frustrated. . . . But I think they have scared the so-called affluent society into doing something about it. Maybe. I think there are people more conscious of it because of that."

It is so easy to write off Holcomb and Ratliff as evil men, grasping and groping for whatever they can get and destroying whatever gets in the way; for an antipoverty worker it is probably necessary to think such thoughts, that may be the mental bracing one needs to deal as an opponent.

But I think it is wrong.

Holcomb is an ex-miner who made it; uneducated and not particularly smart, he somehow grooved on the leavings in that weird economy and got rich. He thinks what he did is something anyone ought to be able to do; it is the American dream, after all. His failure is mainly one of vision, a social myopia hardly rare in this country. From Holcomb's point of view, those people stirring up the poor probably are communist agitators—why else would anyone interfere with the "free enterprise system at its best"? If you tried to tell him that a system that leads to great big rich houses on one side of town and squalid, leaky shacks on the other might not be the best thing in this world, he'd think you were crazy or a communist (both, actually) too. And Thomas Ratliff is hardly the simple Machiavelli the usual scenario would demand.

Picking out individuals and saying the evil rests with them are like patching schoolhouses and expecting the cycle of poverty to be broken. Even when you're right you're irrelevant. What is evil in the mountains is the complex of systems, a complex that has no use or place or tolerance for the old, the wrecked, the incompetent, the extra, and consigns them to the same gullies and "hollers" and ditches as the useless cars and empty Maxwell House Coffee tins and Royal Crown Cola cans, with the same lack of hate or love.

The enemies of the antipoverty program, malicious or natural, individual or collective, turn out to be far more successful than they could have hoped or expected. One reason for that success is the cooperation of the victims: groups like the AVs become, as one of their long-time members said, "top-heavy and bureaucratic, a bit central office-bound. We are . . . worried about maintaining the AV structure, and responding to pressures from foundations and OEO, rather than from community people." The federal government, presumably the opponent of poverty here, plays both sides of the fence: it supports activities like the AV's (so long as they are undisturbing), but it also supports the local Community Action Program, which is middleclass-dominated and politically controlled; it created a generation of hustlers among the poor who find out that only by lying and finagling can they get the welfare and social security benefits they legitimately deserve; it strengthens the local courthouse power structures by putting federal job programs in [the] control of the county machines and by putting the Small Business Administration at its disposal; it commissions studies to document the ill effects of strip mining and simultaneously acts, through TVA, as the largest consumer of the product.

The mood is much like the McCarthy days of the early 1950s: actual legal sanctions are applied to very few people, but so many others are smeared that other people are afraid of contagion, of contamination, even though they know there is nothing to catch. They avoid issues that might threaten some agency or person of power, they stop making trouble, stop looking for trouble, they keep busy, or they stay home—and no one ever really says, when faced by the complex, "I'm scared."

Everyone has something to do: busy, busy, busy. I remember a visit to the AV office in Prestonsburg; they had there what must have been one of the largest Xerox machines in the state of Kentucky; it was used for copying newspaper articles; someone on the staff ran it. There was an AV magazine assembled by a staff member who, if some of the foundations grants had come through, would have gotten a full-time assistant. The mining went on; the acting director of the AV's, Dave Walls, went about hustling private-foundation grants and being sociable and vague and disarming to visitors, and not much of anything really happened.

I visited eastern Kentucky again a short time ago. There were some changes. The weather was softer and some leaves were on the trees, so you couldn't see the shacks back in the "hollers" unless you drove up close; you couldn't see the hillside cemeteries and junkyards at all.

I found out that Governor Louis Nunn had blocked any new AV funds and most of the other money had gone, so there were ugly battles over the leavings, mixed with uglier battles over old political differences within the organization itself.

Edith Easterling was fired; she now has a Ford grant to travel about the country and look at organizing projects. Rick Diehl has gone somewhere else. Mary Walton is now a staff reporter for the *Charleston* (W. Va.) *Gazette*. The Prestonsburg AV office is still open—with a small group of lawyers working on welfare rights problems; that is the only AV activity still alive and no one knows how much longer there will be any money for that.

I ran into Dave Walls in a movie house in Charleston. The show was *Wild River* with Montgomery Clift and Lee Remick, and it was about how good TVA is and what a swell guy Montgomery Clift is and how homey and true a mountain girl Lee Remick is. Anyway, I saw Dave there and we talked a moment during intermission. He still draws a subsistence salary from the AVs, still lives in Berea, over in the bluegrass country far and nicely away from it all. He is going to school at the University of Kentucky in Lexington, doing graduate work in something. He looked just the same, no more or less mild. Someone asked him, "What's going on in the mountains now? What happened to everything?" He shrugged and smiled. "I don't know," he said, "I haven't gone to the mountains in a long time."

Well, for the other people, the ones who were there before, things are pretty much the same. The woman and her nine children still live in that shack in Poorbottom. The man who worked the mines for 28 years is still kept marginally alive by the chemical array in his refrigerator he still manages to afford.

A DISTRUST OF STRANGERS

Jink Ray, the man who faced the bulldozers, I met on that recent trip. When we drove up he had just put out some bad honey and the bees were a thick swarm in the front of the house. We went into a sitting room-bedroom where his wife sat before an open coal fire and each wall had one or two Christs upon it. We talked about the strip-mine fight. On one wall was a photo of him with Governor Breathitt the day the governor came up to stop the strippers. We went outside and talked some more, standing by the overripe, browning corn standing next to a patch of corn just about ripe, the hills thickly coated and over-lapping to form a lush box canyon behind him. He pointed to the hillside the other side of the road and told us they'd been augering up there. "You can't see it from down here this time of the year, but it's bad up there." The seepage killed the small streams down below: nothing lives in those streams anymore. "We used to get bait in them streams, nothing now, and fish used to grow there before they went to the river. Not now." Suddenly his face hardened, "Why you fellas asking me these questions?" We told him again that we were writing about what had happened in Pike County. "No," he said, "that ain't what you are. I believe you fellas are here because you want to get stripping going again; you want to know if I'll back off this time." He talked from a place far behind the cold blue eyes that were just so awful. We protested, saying we really were writers, but it didn't work—it's like denying you're an undercover agent or homosexual; there's no way in the world to do it once the assumption gets made, however wrong. He talked in postured and rhetorical bursts awhile, and it seemed a long time until we could leave without seeming to have been run off. Leaving him standing there looking at the yellow Hertz car backing out his driveway, his face still cold and hard, polite to the end, but . . . But what? Not hating, but knowing: he knows about strangers now; he knows they are there to take something away, to betray, to hustle; he knows even the friendly strangers will eventually go back wherever strangers go when they are through doing whatever they have come down to do, and he will be just where he is, trying with whatever meager resources he's got to hold on to the small parcel of land he scuffled so hard to be able to own. He'll not trust anyone again, and for me that was perhaps the most painful symptom of the failure and defeat of the anti-poverty program in the mountains.

The others: Joe Mulloy, after about two years in the courts, finally won the draft appeal he should never have had to make in the first place; Al and Margaret McSurely were sentenced to prison terms for contempt of Congress after they refused to turn over their personal papers to a Senate committee investigating subversion in the rural South. Tom Ratliff is still commonwealth's attorney, there in the county of Pike, in the state of Kentucky. And Robert Holcomb still has his mines, his colleries, his offices, and his fine and unshaken belief in the American Way.

FOR FURTHER READING

* Michael Harrington. *The Other America*. New York: Macmillan, 1962, and Baltimore: Penguin.

Herman Miller. *Rich Man, Poor Man*. New York: T. Y. Crowell, 1970.

* Ben B. Seligman. *Permanent Poverty*. Chicago: Quadrangle Books, 1968, and New York: Franklin Watts.

Philip M. Stern. "Uncle Sam's Welfare Program for the Rich," *New York Times Magazine*, April 16, 1972.

THE CONTOURS OF THE
"BLACK REVOLUTION" IN THE 1970'S

J. H. O'DELL

In 1954, nearly a century after ratification of the Fourteenth Amendment, the Supreme Court at last declared that enforced segregation—even in "separate but equal" facilities—constitutes discrimination against the minority. The decision in *Brown* v. *Board of Education of Topeka* was a response not only to an awakened white conscience but also to long and articulate agitation by blacks themselves, and it encouraged them to move farther toward integration into American society. In spite of vicious opposition, blacks could not be so easily repressed as they had been in the 1870's, for by the 1950's, though poor, they possessed some buying power, they had some education, and to some extent they had developed organizations and communications and a determination to support each other. The Montgomery boycott that defeated Jim Crow on the buses of Alabama also brought forward a national leader, the Reverend Martin Luther King, Jr. In the early 1960's, King's philosophy of "black and white together" and nonviolence inspired the civil rights movement to heroic deeds against the Southern system of caste segregation.

How much would whites really sacrifice for the cause? At the Democratic Party convention of 1964, the Freedom Democrats of Mississippi, organized by Fannie Lou Hamer and other activists, demanded that their delegation be allowed to replace the white-supremacist "regular" delegation. At the moment of choice, the Party powers yielded to the white racists and urged the Freedom Democrats to accept a compromise. The experience taught blacks a bitter lesson: to distrust whites, especially white "liberals," and to insist on self-determination. Blacks must free themselves.

It may seem that blacks have little to lose by tearing down the structure of society. Yet, as J. H. O'Dell observes, the black movement

Reprinted from *Freedomways* magazine, Vol. 10, No. 2, 1970. Published at 799 Broadway, New York City.

has not yet, for the most part, adopted a revolutionary outlook, nor does it aim to overturn capitalism or to construct a socialist commonwealth. Some blacks believe that capitalism can accommodate their full emancipation, others, like O'Dell, believe that subjugation of blacks is essential to the structure and that their insistence on freedom "holds creative revolutionary implications" for the entire population and must eventually challenge the legitimacy of the profit system itself.

□   □   □

> All we are saying is: America, be true to what you said on paper. Somewhere I read of Freedom of Speech; somewhere I read of Freedom of the Press; somewhere I read of Freedom of Assembly; somewhere I read of the Right to Protest for Rights.
> —MARTIN LUTHER KING, JR., Memphis, April 3, 1968

I t is in moments of acute popular unrest that events shed the most light, and fissures in the social structure are seen most clearly. The tidal wave of student campus protests against the Pentagon's expanding war in Southeast Asia and the general context within which this development takes place momentarily illuminate the whole canvas of the American social order. They also enable one to anticipate, at least in outline, the developmental patterns which the major social forces in our country are taking as forces which shape the history of our times.

The mood of popular reawakening, which has produced the wide range of movements demanding the progressive reformation of American life, really began in the 1930's and continued through that decade until the late 1940's. Then it gave way to an era of repression in the early 1950's and finally reasserted itself and found new life at Montgomery, Alabama, and has been building ever since, strengthening its militancy. This American Reformation which today embraces large sections of the student and youth population, women's liberation, the poorest sections of the working class, the colonized nationalities and ethnic groups, as well as certain components of the middle class who express a "hippie" culture—is now unmistakably becoming, in all its variations, a majority expression in the life of society.

During the last 15 years, the motor and generator for this movement of social change have been the Freedom Movement built by the Negro community which has come to be called, by some, the "Black Revolution."

This particular period could be characterized as the modern era of this Movement which has existed and organically developed ever since the founding of the Republic. In this modern era it has been spiritually influenced by the great anti-colonial events in the world. By significant historical coincidence, the Bandung Conference of 1955 signaled the end of a period in our Movement's history of reliance primarily upon court actions and the beginning of a new period in which *mass direct action* became the primary instrument of social emancipation. That transformation took place in the crucible of struggle at Montgomery, Alabama.

In the spectrum of national organizations which comprised the Freedom Movement, the following developmental patterns were evident during the past decade of the 1960's.

The NAACP, the oldest of these organizations, remained in the middle of the road, given the upsurge of activities around civil rights, and continued to emphasize court actions in its work. It experienced some temporary growth because of the general windfall of public interest and involvement with the whole civil rights issue and the mass action emphasis that was developing in other areas of the movement during the period.

The Urban League during the 1960's got caught in a certain squeeze—a squeeze between its mildly conservative middle-class posture and the urban crisis that was developing on an unprecedented scale. This required the Urban League to redefine its role, in a sense, and to improve its posture if for no other reason than that the cities were in flames toward the end of the decade. Consequently, the Urban League was required to revamp its program to become something more than just a program for getting typist's jobs for Negro college graduates.

We saw CORE emerge during this decade from a twenty year history which no one knew very much about into an organization of considerable influence and activity, with a tendency in its program toward finding those gimmicks that would keep it in the headlines. I think it would be correct to say that CORE played an important role during the early part of the decade, attracted many dedicated and talented people, but had become a non-organization for all intents and purposes, particularly after 1967. Unable to adequately identify and respond to the new trend within the movement, CORE succumbed to the Black syndrome—not taking fully into account that it was an organizaiton with a predominantly white membership, based in the urban North.

SNCC, born as the organic continuer of the student sit-in movement against segregated public accommodations in the South, became the cutting edge of our movement in the early part of the decade and was the forerunner of today's massive campus-based movements against the government's war policy. Its activities pioneered in breaking through and organizing rural communities of hard-core segregationist influence. The high water mark of its influence was its significant statement against the war in Vietnam in the early winter of 1966, which set a pace and a frame of reference in matters of foreign policy for our movement, whose leaders, in the main, were still reluctant to extend themselves to this area of concern. SNCC's constituency of supporters across the country undoubtedly numbered among them some of the most politically advanced and socially conscious people in the nation in the arts and professions, on the Northern college campuses, and in many other areas of life. Nevertheless, by the end of the decade, SNCC too, like CORE, had declined in influence to that of a non-organization, in which hardly anything more than the rhetoric of militancy remained. This decline began with the SNCC position on the Middle Eastern conflict in 1967, in which the organization's leaders sided with the Arabic people of the Middle East—a position which the large component of Jewish supporters, who had financially aided SNCC over the years, found not to its liking. The SNCC leadership undoubtedly misread the loyalties which this constituency held for Israel, and the resulting decline in financial contributions certainly contributed to SNCC's demise.

SNCC and CORE stood for and carried out mass actions in the struggle for civil rights, as did SCLC. The collective contribution of these three organizations guaranteed the ascendancy of the *mass direct action* trend in the Freedom Movement during that decade. In addition, they took the responsibility to articulate the opposition of the black community to the U.S. military intervention in Vietnam. Of these, only SCLC survived the developmental changes in the life-style of the movement and its program. SCLC, in addition, gave the nation the pre-eminent leader and charismatic personality of that area in the person of Dr. Martin Luther King, Jr., its first President.

The history of SNCC and CORE was marked by many contributions to the success of our movement during the Civil Rights era. But there is no need for us to engage in fantasy. It is also a history which adds to the already abundant evidence confirming the effects of "infantile leftism" among people involved in protest movements. This narrow, self-defeating political and tactical style takes its toll in the weakening and liquidation of organizations and their consequent inability to make the "long haul," poor utilization of human talent and finally a kind of demoralization among some of its cadre, resulting in their dropping out of society altogether or ending up chasing some utopian scheme.

When the last decade began, the term *racism* was hardly known. By the end of the decade, it had become one of the most sensitive words in the English language. When the last decade began, the word *black* was still used as an epithet and an insult to people of African descent. But it is no longer possible to insult an Afro-American by calling him Black. These are major achievements in our centuries-old struggle to influence the American public mind.

During the past decade, in the South we became acquainted in a limited way with the exercise of community power in the form of boycotts, rent strikes, "selective buying" campaigns, and bloc voting. In the North the outstanding example of community power by the end of the decade was SCLC's Operation Breadbasket in Chicago under the leadership of the Reverend Jesse Jackson. These experiences were the prototypes of the early stages of a national effort aimed at recovering from this economy what now amounts to a $30 billion a year shortage in our purchasing power as a community.*

In sum total, in the decade of the 1960's, we established an Afro-American presence in the everyday life of the people of the United States. We ceased to be the invisible men of this society. We did not achieve much in the way of establishing decision-making power, per se, but decisions are now made with us in mind. To appreciate this success, one must understand that the nature of the present social order in the United States has been to reduce people to things, to elevate the importance of property over that of human rights. This tradition had its origin in America's involvement in the African slave trade, an economic function which reduced Africans to the status of property. That tradition and the resistance to it find expression today in the students' demands on the large university conglomerate campuses, insisting that they are more than just a *number* in a computer—that they are *people*—and in garbage workers in Atlanta or Memphis, boldly asserting the supposedly self-evident proposition "I am a Man."

THE DEMAND IS FOR A CIVILIZED SOCIETY

The Freedom Movement during the past decade has commanded the attention and appealed to the sensitive feelings of millions of white Americans who honestly reject racist practices and don't want America to continue to be guilty of this inhumanity. The Freedom Movement has inspired hope among other ethnic groups, who historically share with the Afro-American community the experience of a domestic colonialism. The Indian, Mexican-American, and Puerto Rican communities are rediscovering a sense of power in themselves as a result of the

---

* At the beginning of the decade of the 1960's the yearly shortage in personal income to the Black community was approximately $22 billion. The leap in gross personal income during this period has left the Afro-American community relatively further behind.

example set by the largest ethnic group. The Freedom Movement has been a vehicle through which thousands of youth received their baptism in the struggle for social change. Out of these experiences, they have begun to fashion in their own way a new life-style, bold and refreshing, whose themes are open honesty, love, personal involvement in the lives of the people, rather than in the accumulation of things and the corollary to this—the rejection of hypocrisy, prudish sexual mores, the white-is-right syndrome, and the "success" mania, all of which have traditionally been deeply rooted features of American life up to this decade. In the wake of this, millions among the population of the United States have broken away from the moorings of apathy and self-deluding national chauvinism to become the material force for ushering in an age of critical re-examination and redefinition. All of the myths are coming up for critical review and some of them are no longer passing the test of acceptance. At a time of greatest material prosperity in their history, millions of the population of the United States have decided that they do not like what America is in the modern world and they are committed to change that reality. This growth in its breadth of the movement for social emancipation (with its periodic nationwide eruptions from the civil rights demonstrations of 1963 and the ghetto rebellions in the summers of 1964–67 to the great anti-war Moratorium demonstrations of last October and the current sweep of student resistance on the campuses of the nation today) announces, in its own way and in no uncertain terms, mass dissatisfaction with the status quo. But these events also mark the crisis of the containment policy, the policy which has been the official style of the Establishment.

It is of course clear that the government is attempting to resolve this crisis by a policy of repression. Whereas it has been its historical role to alternate between making a few concessions and repression, the present period is definitely a period in which the emphasis is on repression. One is able to document a long list of abuses to which the federal government is turning to put down dissent: the government's search-and-destroy missions against members of the Black Panther Party; the announcement of increased surveillance of protest groups it considers "extremist" which takes the form of increased wire tapping, the opening of mails, and so forth; the attempts to muzzle the news media and force them to conform their reporting to what the present administration wishes; and in this connection, the efforts of the Justice Department to subpoena news material from newspaper reporters, information gathered in the course of their professional work. There is also the effort to bring the judicial system into line with this general policy of repression in the attempt to place Southern conservatives on the Supreme Court, as well as efforts to impeach Justice William O. Douglas, who has been associated with key civil liberties decisions by the courts in the past years. And, of course, there is the uniformed military bayonet presence everywhere that dissent has expressed itself in any significant organized way.

These policies of government repression stem from an effort to defend policies which are morally and politically indefensible. By all civilized norms, for a nation to spend three million dollars an hour of public taxes in a war of aggression and genocide against a people ten thousand miles away, who have never offended the American people or threatened their security, is indefensible. For a nation to allow its public taxes to be used to subsidize the profits of oil monopolies, railroad trusts, and big farms, but not the creative work of artists, novelists, poets, or composers, is indefensible. Appeals to an already overtaxed working population to contribute *dimes* to support research in cancer, muscular dystrophy, heart disease, and other crippling human diseases, while the government spends billions on atomic missiles and research in overkill weapons, are indefensible.

The contours of the present situation, therefore, are marked by the growing radicalization of large sections of the American people, their consequent alienation from the government, and in response to this, a growing tendency toward violent repression by the government, a tendency which, to all appearances, includes selective political assassination.

What has surfaced is an antagonism between large sections of the American people and their government. This is not likely to be a mere temporary phenomenon. To the contrary, the struggle to resolve this in a progressive democratic direction is likely to shape and determine the revolutionary process in our country in this new decade of the 1970's.

THE NATURE OF THE "BLACK REVOLUTION"

The Freedom Movement of Afro-Americans is a movement of radical reformation. So far in its history, it has not directed itself against the capitalist system, per se, but against racism—the chief idea and practice used against the Negro community, consistent with the general laws of exploitation and in all of its institutionalized forms. Because the Freedom Movement has addressed itself to the institutionalized practice of racism, its impact is felt in the economic, political, cultural, religious, and educational life of the institutions; in short, throughout the total fabric of American society. This Freedom Movement has sometimes, especially in the more recent period, been referred to as the "Black Revolution."

Throughout our long and arduous history on this continent, it is true that we have undergone certain revolutionary changes in our status in society. Beginning as slave labor in plantation agricultural production of this society, we are now *primarily* a wage-earning urban population, largely concentrated in the low-paid service industries in the cities. This could be considered a revolution in our sociology. After all it was cities like Selma, Montgomery, Birmingham, Watts, Detroit, Newark and other such areas that gave us the most significant freedom efforts in the recent period. One could also quite properly describe as revolutionary the change in our psychology as an ethnic group during the past period: the growth of self-esteem among the masses of Black Americans and the mass rejection of those false standards and values which insult the African personality.

Nevertheless, despite these significant changes in our sociology and psychology as a community, our movement is not yet fully a revolution in the classic meaning of the term, because its program is not yet consciously directed toward a fundamental alteration in the economic and political cornerstone institutions and power relations upon which the whole system of oppression is built. Nor has it as yet defined its relationship to the society and the existing institutional structure in that way. This fact in no way detracts from its significance and weight of importance to the contemporary history of society in the United States. Our Freedom Movement mirrors one of the major contradictions in American life and poses fundamental questions about the institutional structure of American society and the capacity of the present structure to solve certain problems of long-standing existence. As life experience confirms for the movement that the institutional fabric of capitalism in our country is incapable of providing an environment in which we are able to "overcome" the legacy of racism and super-exploitation, the transformation of our movement to one guided by a revolutionary outlook, seeking the abolition of capitalism itself, will inevitably evolve.

The political order called the United States has evolved as a polyglot of ethnic groups and nationalities, developed upon the economic base of capitalism; a society shaped by the laws of capitalist relations. Slavery, segregation, the decimation of the Indians are all a congenital part of the early developmental history of this society just as urban slums, rural poverty, a culture of racism, and the growth of institutionalized militarism are the fabric of its history during the twentieth century. The political order of U.S. capitalism had its origin in the American Revolution of 1776 and its extended phases in the War of 1812 and the Civil War, 1861–65. By the turn of the twentieth century, this three-phase consolidation of the U.S. political order had created an overland empire, provided by the dynamic for the consolidation of corporate wealth, and thrust the United States into the competitive arena of rivalries among the capitalist nations of the world as a colonial power.

The government and social system, which in the last quarter of the nineteenth century murdered Reconstruction and restored to power in the South the counterrevolutionary forces of the Ku Klux Klan in order to sweep its way into the competitive world arena among the Colonial Powers, are in the last quarter of the twentieth century the number one Colonial Power and "the greatest purveyor of violence in the world today."

The structure of internal domestic colonialism was the pivotal condition and the main generator guaranteeing this ascendancy. The grabbing of the Indian lands and of much of the national territory of the Mexican Republic placed this particular means of production (land) in the hands of the colonizers. The expropriation of the total product of the labor power of African slaves, except that amount required for subsistence necessary to reproduce physical strength to work, in the Southern states, and the expropriation of the "normal" surplus value created by European immigrant wage labor in the normal course of work, these are the other two dimensions of capitalist expropriation. The infrastructure of nationality and ethnic group oppression combined with the normal exploitation of wage labor constituted the general pattern of capitalist development in the United States consistent with the general laws of exploitation. All of this, of course, is U.S. history. Efforts have been made, in the past as in the present, to create from this a model called *American* confined to a white Anglo-Saxon Protestant definition. It is a natural law of this political order to clothe itself in this façade in an attempt to give authenticity to its existence. Needless to say, this has met with considerable success, as the racist culture of this society will confirm. Nevertheless, as a matter of historical development, the American Revolution hasn't taken place yet.

Consequently, our Freedom Movement holds creative revolutionary implications for the vast majority of the U.S. population. Once this is really understood by broad sections of the American community seeking fundamental social change, what will emerge is not likely to be a "Black Revolution" in any singular isolated sense, but rather a broadly based revolution of social emancipation and national regeneration drawing into its involvement a cross-section of ethnic groups and socio-economic classes, whose interests are tied to the kind of fundamental changes which our interest requires. To be sure such a development would be "our" revolution as Afro-Americans because of the kind of decisive influence that we must exercise to prevent any unprincipled compromises of the kind which overthrew the first Reconstruction. This is the revolution for our times for this generation of citizens of the U.S. Republic. The American Revolution will mark the maturing and flowering of the American nation in this part of the North American continent which is now called the United States. As such, it will take an honorable place in the range of indigenous popular revolutions which will free the hemisphere of the Americas from the capitalist tradition, a tradition of robbery and racism and their institutional mechanisms.

Standing at the beginning of this new decade of the 1970's, our Freedom Movement, or the "Black Revolution" as it is sometimes called, in its program and perspective, is increasingly being shaped by the class imprint of the poor. The forms of this struggle to abolish the poverty condition are varied. This basic new initiative had its symbolic beginnings in the national mobilization in Washington which established "Resurrection City." Today it continues in such events as hunger marches on the state capitals in Illinois, Mississippi, and Alabama, led by SCLC, and the growing cooperation of this organization with progressive sections of the labor movement in efforts to organize the working poor in hospitals, sanitation work, and other low-wage industries.

Another form of this is efforts by members of the Black Panther Party to provide free breakfast for school children in a number of the urban ghettos, and the creative work of the National Welfare Rights Organization to secure an economic bill of rights for the thousands on relief.

Concern with the issue of abolishing poverty is one of the avenues through which our Freedom Movement evolves, out of its experience, from challenging in word and action the legitimacy of segregation to one of challenging the legitimacy of the very profit system which created segregation and poverty in the first place.

The poorest, most exploited sections of the laboring population represent in microcosm the multi-ethnic composition of the larger population in our country. Consequently, to involve the poor in the struggle for their social emancipation, to encourage their organized efforts to free themselves from the material and cultural deprivations imposed upon them by the existing social order open up significant possibilities for establishing strategic ties with organized workers in the heavy industries. The most politically advanced among these workers are often found in organized group "caucuses" of various types. The longshoremen who closed down the ports on both coasts and auto workers who closed many of the foundries in Detroit when Dr. Martin Luther King was assassinated have the striking power to lift from the nation the repression we now face. That is what the students in their courageous acts are trying to do when they close down the schools, colleges, and universities. The ingredients for achieving success in this effort are present, provided we are willing to recommit ourselves to building a movement which will enable us to overcome.

The enemy is the Military State* whose fascist temperament is

---

* For an elaboration of this concept see "The July Rebellions and the 'Military State,'" *Freedomways*, Fall, 1967.

as clearly revealed in the events at Augusta, Georgia, Kent, Ohio, and Jackson, Mississippi, as in the massacre at My Lai, South Vietnam. Fueled by the ideology of racism, this deformity has surfaced and institutionalized violence on a scale unequalled since the overthrow of Reconstruction a century ago. It is "Exhibit A" confirming the underlying parasitism of the present social order and its value system of inhumanity.

Above all it blocks the Freedom Road in an age when the social and economic emancipation of mankind and womankind is irreversibly on the agenda of human history.

The war in Vietnam can be stopped. The military establishment can be harnessed and disengaged from its present position in the national life of our country. The Nixon repression can be shattered, because millions of Americans are understanding for the first time in their lives the implications *for them* of those words in the Declaration of Independence: "Governments [derive] their just Powers from the Consent of the Governed."

FOR FURTHER READING

* James Baldwin, *The Fire Next Time*. New York: Dell, 1964.
* Stokely Carmichael and Charles V. Hamilton. *Black Power*. New York: Vintage, 1967.
* William H. Grier and Price M. Cobb. *Black Rage*. New York: Bantam, 1968.
Gerda Lerner, ed. *Black Women in White America*. New York: Pantheon, 1972.
* Julius Lester. *Look Out, Whitey! Black Power's Gon' Get Your Mama!* New York: Grove Press, 1968.
* Malcolm X. *The Autobiography of Malcolm X*. New York: Grove Press, 1964.

THE CHICANO STORY

FRANCIS DONAHUE

The Mexican Americans—or Chicanos, as most of the younger militant members of the group prefer to be called—number 6 million people and constitute the second largest minority in the United States today. Eighty per cent of them live in five states, mostly in the Southwest: California, Arizona, New Mexico, Texas, and Colorado. Until the past decade they were often referred to as the "forgotten minority" because the national media paid little attention to them.

Mexicans started migrating to this country in the early years of the twentieth century, in part to fill the labor needs of the Southwest's railroads and agribusiness concerns and in part because of the dislocation caused by the Mexican Revolution of 1910. The Immigration Acts of 1921 and 1924, which severely restricted the immigration of Europeans and Asians, stimulated the movement of Mexicans, who were not blocked by quotas. In the 1920's, almost half a million entered legally along with, according to some estimates, a like number of illegal migrants. Although a few thousand moved on to the Midwest, most remained in the Southwest. The Depression in the 1930's curbed further immigration and resulted in the repatriation of many of those who were already here, but with the outbreak of World War II the United States again welcomed Mexicans and arranged with their government to accept temporary farm workers, known as *braceros*, to meet the need for labor in the Southwest. After the war this policy was abrogated, but demands from growers and canners pressured Washington to make another accord for *braceros*, which lasted from 1951 to 1964. In the orchards, fields, and canneries, more than a million such temporary workers and more than 2 million illegal immigrants ("wetbacks") picked and preserved the great Southwestern harvests.

Reprinted with permission from Francis Donahue, "The Chicano Story," *The Colorado Quarterly*, 21 (Winter, 1973), 307–16.

Ignorant of the English language, accustomed to occupying the lowest rung of society, and fearful of losing their meager wages, the Mexican immigrants for the most part raised no objection to the life they were forced to lead in the United States. But in the 1960's, buoyed by other protests in the society and encouraged by forceful American-born or reared leaders, the Chicanos embarked upon a more militant course of action. Cesar Chavez, who organized the grape workers in California; New Mexico's Reies Lopez Tijerina, who wants the Anglos to give back the lands they "stole" from the Mexicans in the nineteenth century; "Corky" Gonzales and his Denver-based Crusade for Justice; and José Angel Gutierrez's La Raza Unida Party in Texas—all have forced other Americans to become more aware of Mexican-American complaints. In the following essay, Francis Donahue summarizes the plight of this formerly "forgotten" minority and discusses the outlook for their future.

□ □ □

A cross the Southwest and in Chicano enclaves elsewhere in this country, an epic crusade is shaping up as Mexican Americans struggle valiantly to be considered respected and equal members of America's multi-racial society. As the nation's second disadvantaged group (after the blacks), Chicanos formerly constituted an "invisible minority" who meekly accepted their role as a subservient mass of farm-hands and unskilled or blue collar workers.

No longer. In the past seven years Chicanos have been galvanized into joining the major historical current which has swept over the United States in the last twenty-five years, the home-grown revolution of rising expectations—first the Blacks, then Students, Women, the Gays, and now the Chicanos. Sparking their crusade have been *La Huelga*, the Chicano grape strike and subsequent boycott of California grapes and other agricultural products; *La Causa*, a general term related to the overall advancement of Chicanos and *La Raza*, a growing awareness of self-identity as an ethnic group with its own singular culture and life-style.

Six million Chicanos live in the United States, totalling approximately 3 percent of the national population. Three million are in California (16 percent of the state's population), with the rest residing mainly in Texas, New Mexico, Arizona, Colorado, and Utah. Los Angeles, with almost a million, is the third largest "Mexican" city in the world (after Mexico City and Guadalajara). During the 1965–1972 period, sizeable migrations of Chicanós have moved into Illinois, Michigan, Ohio, Indiana, Wisconsin, Missouri, Iowa, and Kansas. Chicago estimates its Spanish-speaking population at 400,000, of which perhaps 300,000 are Chicanos.

For Chicanos, the birth rate is 50 percent higher than that of the general population. Among Chicanos the average life expectancy is 57 years as against 70.8 for the population as a whole; they have a median age of 20. Their median education level is 8.6 years, as compared with the Blacks' 10.5 and the Anglos' 12.2. Chicano youth are seven times less likely than Anglos to enroll in college.

More than 80 percent of the Chicanos reside in cities and towns in the Southwest. They are seven times more likely than Anglos to be in sub-standard housing. Economically, Chicanos are generally mired in the lower echelons of American society. In California 23 percent are unskilled laborers, 46 percent are engaged in blue collar work as skilled or semi-skilled workers, while 22 percent are in white collar, professional, and related occupations.

The farm worker stands as the most newsworthy Chicano of all. Yet he constitutes a small minority of the Chicanos—under 400,000 in California. "Since I joined the farm workers, I've visited farm labor camps all over the state and it's horrible how these people live," explains Margie Coons, a volunteer working out of the Los Angeles office of the United Farm Workers Union. She helps organize workers and, on weekends, accosts shoppers, urging them to boycott the market because it handles non-union grapes or lettuce.

> Whole families crammed into tiny cardboard shacks, sometimes with no plumbing, no lights, no sanitation of any kind. And they work so hard that they look like old men and women while they're still young. The average life span of a Chicano field worker is only forty-nine years. And the average family income is only $2,300 a year.

In 1962 emerged the first charismatic Chicano leader, Cesar Chavez, who, in that year, launched his now-famous campaign to unionize Chicano and other farm workers in California. Born in 1927 near Yuma, Arizona, on an eighty-acre farm, Chavez at an early age came to know the heat-blistered, penny-pinched existence of the migrant field hand. When the family farm failed during the Depression, Cesar's parents loaded their belongings and their children into a beat-up automobile and headed for the Golden State. From the Imperial and Coachella valleys in the south, the family worked its way—hoeing, leafing, and picking apricots, grapes, asparagus, beets, potatoes, and plums—through the San Joaquin Valley and into the northern reaches of the Napa Valley. Cesar had his share of brushes with prejudiced Anglos. Once when he refused to move to the "Mexican section" of a San Jose theater, he was ushered out and subjected to a verbal dressing-down at the police station. Cesar was sixteen.

Chavez's dawning social conscience was honed by experience with the Community Service Organization in San Jose, where he was engaged in welfare work among Chicanos for ten years. Besides reading widely, he followed the course of the Negro Civil Rights Movement and came to acquire his own stable of social saints: Emiliano Zapata, Mexican peasant leader of the 1911 Revolution; Mahatma Gandhi, Jawaharlal Nehru, and Martin Luther King, all noted for their dedication to non-violent social change.

With his $1,200 savings Chavez founded the National Farm Workers Association (now the United Farm Workers Union) and, within two years, had signed up about a thousand members. He created a credit union, issued a newspaper, and soon moved to bring pressure on grape growers in the Delano, California, area for better wages and working conditions for "his men."

Through a spectacular 1965 strike, which grabbed headlines across the country, Chavez dramatized the farm workers' cause. Within a short time, growers came up with an offer to increase wages 120 percent. Chavez had won the first round and was on his way. He trained his sights on other table grape growers, to the tune of marches by workers bearing aloft the banner of the Mexican Virgin of Guadalupe, flanked by a new Chicano symbol, a banner depicting a black Aztec eagle on a red field. *Viva la huelga* ("strike")! *Viva la causa! Viva la union!* Demonstrations staged in focal spots across the California countryside breathed life into a nascent populist movement.

Converging on Delano were newsmen, TV cameras, and interviewers from radio shows. The Chavez story was soon beamed into homes here and abroad. Behind that story, the news media uncovered the sorry specifics of Chicano existence throughout the Southwest, compounded of prejudice, discrimination, inadequate education, poverty, and second-class citizenship. Thanks to Chavez and the news media, the "invisible minority" became visible. It was becoming vocal as well.

Chicanos now had a home-grown hero, as well as a positive *causa* around which they could rally. "With the poetic instinct of *La Raza*, the Delano grape strikers have made it [*huelga*] mean a dozen other things," states Luis Valdez, director of El Teatro Campesino, a Chicano dramatic aggregation based in San Juan Bautista California.

It is a declaration, a challenge, a greeting, a feeling, a movement. We cry *huelga*. It is the most significant word in our entire Mexican American history. Under the name of *huelga* we created a Mexican American *patria* [homeland] and Cesar Chavez was our first *presidente*. We came back with an utterly raw and vibrant Mexican character. We shouted *viva la Huelga* and that word became the word of life for us.

Faced with the need to publicize their cause, Chicanos began to agitate in 1966 for a White House Conference on Mexican American Affairs. Washington deemed such a conference premature. Instead, it offered a Cabinet Committee Hearing on Mexican American Affairs in El Paso, Texas, in October, 1968. During deliberations many Chicano delegates became convinced the hearing was geared to lining up support for the Establishment rather than coming to grips with issues which Chicanos had raised. They walked out of the hearing, which was held in a posh downtown hotel, and moved to a slum *barrio* ("neighborhood") where they held a rump session. After scoring Anglos for downgrading Chicano culture, they pointed to the pressing need to organize the *barrios* in pursuit of economic, political, and educational goals.

Showcasing this rump session was a setting befitting a political convention. Held proudly aloft by brown hands were placards proclaiming *La Huelga*, "Chicano Power," and "Adequate programs and funds for 'Our People' first, then 'Viva Johnson.' " To the still ill-defined organization, the raucous rump session gave the name *La Raza Unida*.

At a subsequent meeting in San Antonio, in January, 1969, the *Raza Unida* party began to define its goals. These included efforts to develop community organizations to work for Chicano civil rights, to plug for better schools and for sanctions against companies known to practice discrimination in hiring or promotion.

For the Chicano Movement, the past seven years are the prologue to a wider struggle for a more rewarding tomorrow. "Change now, not *mañana*, we've waited too long already!" That is the pulsating mood of the militant new minority. In taking their battle to the Establishment, the Movement runs along today on four major monorails, whose destinations may be listed as self-identity, a pluralistic philosophy for subculture, social protest, and unity within the burgeoning Movement itself.

In their struggle for a respectable place in American society, Chicanos are striving for a clearer understanding of their own identity as members of a subculture. The latter, a variation of lower class culture, stands in marked contrast to the predominantly white, Anglo, middle-class culture which prevails throughout the United States.

Pervading that subculture is an emerging ethos, an integrated amalgam of characteristics stemming from Mexican culture, particularly its Indian elements, from American culture, and from the century-old experience of living as an exploited minority in the United States.

Rankled by Anglo attitudes which have undervalued "Mexican culture" as practiced by Chicanos, the latter feel a compelling need to proclaim their life-style as an alternative way of living constructively in this country. They see no need to be assimilated into the Melting Pot in order to be considered loyal citizens.

Basic to the Chicano ethos is marked emphasis on the family. While more equalitarian than its Mexican prototype, the family does not regularly prove to be a stable unit. The father, who is the dominant force, is often absent. The mother remains the one continuing, adhesive element holding the family together. Teenage pregnancies inside and outside of marriage are frequent.

Highly prized is personal pride or dignity. This is closely associated with *machismo* ("the masculinity cult"), which has various outlets: it may be the need to redress vigorously any slight to one's honor or that of the family; it may connote an exaggerated concern for sexual conquests; it may express itself in a haughty squandering of money on friends, or in gambling, usually to the financial detriment of the economically strapped family.

Concern for spiritual values (good friendship, close family ties, politeness in social relationships, reverence for the land) overrides a quest for materialistic values. Not that the Chicano does not want material goods. Still, he does not feel the driving motivation inherent in the Puritan work ethic which spurs Anglos to continue working long after their basic material needs have been provided for.

Influencing the Chicano's approach to life is a brotherhood concept, an inherited *copadrazgo* system of institutionalized social obligations forged between godparents and godchildren and between godparents themselves. It is not enough for one "to make it on his own." Rather, as a member of a brotherhood, the Chicano senses an obligation to stay in the *barrio* and work for the betterment of his fellow *carnales* ("brothers"). Those who rise to professional or administrative positions are expected to continue working on behalf of the Chicano community. If, instead, they integrate with the Establishment and move to the suburbs, they are branded *Vendidos* ("traitors to the cause").

Basic to the ethos is language—Spanish, liberally condimented with English expressions and often with "invented" words with an intonation peculiar to northern and central Mexico. A binary phenomenon characterizes the speech of many Chicanos, that is, a mixture of linguistic symbols of English and Spanish blended into the syntactic structure of one of the two languages: "Looking at his younger son, the *jefito se pone a pensar*. . . . 'I had a dream *la otra noche*.' "

Besides this increased concern for self-identity, a majority of Chicanos espouse a philosophy which holds that subcultures, like the Chicano, should be allowed to maintain and develop their heritage without the need to follow the time-honored custom of "assimilation" into the

WASP (White, Anglo-Saxon Protestant) mold, which has distinguished most immigrant groups. Chicanos do not consider themselves immigrants. They were here first. The Anglos came to join them, and subsequently to control them.

The Chicano aim is to be considered as equal, if unique, members in a democratic corporation of subcultures, known collectively as the United States. "Integration is an empty bag," explains Rodolfo "Corky" Gonzales, leader of the Denver-based Chicano Crusade for Justice. "It's like getting out of the small end of the funnel. One may make it, but the rest of the people stay at the bottom."

To promote this anti–Melting Pot philosophy, the major vehicle is the alternative plan of education which is being implemented at the elementary level in the Southwest. "English as a Second Language," a program pioneered in the early 1960s, channels the Chicano first grader into classes designed to teach him English the entire school day. The purpose is to prepare him for an English-dominated classroom. Yet, when the Chicano has mastered sufficient English, Anglo and Black students of his age group often have a two-year headstart on him in subject matter work. To remedy this, many public schools in California, and elsewhere in the Southwest, began in 1966 to adopt a Bilingual Bicultural Approach. Spanish is the language in which the entering Chicano learns basic subject matter. During certain class hours he is given instruction in English. The outcome of this approach is that the Chicano is now succeeding in moving from grade to grade with his Black and Anglo peers while picking up English, formally and informally, along the way.

The alternative plan has reached the high school level in such areas as Stockton and Berkeley, where Chicanos may opt for voluntary separation. At the college level, Mexican American Studies are widely offered across the Southwest. Courses emphasize Mexican history, *barrio* life and its problems, and aim to instill pride in positive achievements of Mexicans and Chicanos alike.

Clearly, the thrust of these alternative programs is to enhance the Chicano's concept of his personal worth, to equip him with skills acquired partly in his own language, while he gradually acquires a command of English. At age eighteen, or perhaps twenty-one, he will be able to make his own decision whether to remain separate from the dominant Anglo culture or to assimilate.

As its third major goal, the Movement regularly mounts programs and demonstrations of social protest to alert Chicanos to their plight as an exploited minority whose civil rights, economic status, and personal safety are not as secure as those of Anglos. It also strives to sensitize the community outside of the *barrio* to abuses committed against Chicanos. Spearheading the protest was Cesar Chavez's *Huelga* which has now taken the form of a lengthy boycott of many California growers. Added to this are efforts to spotlight injustices in the courts, with police and politicians, in military and business practices, to name a few. Chicanos gave wide coverage to the racist attitude of a San Jose judge who, in hearing a case involving a Chicano teenager, blurted out in anger: "Maybe Hitler was right . . . you and your kind should not be allowed to live."

Tension between police and Chicanos peaked in Los Angeles in August, 1970, when the National Chicano Moratorium Committee sponsored an anti-war rally to protest the disproportionate number of Mexican Americans called for combat service in Vietnam. Some five hundred police were on hand as marchers, estimated from seven thousand to twenty thousand, demonstrated against the military's treatment of their *carnales*. A case of looting ignited already smoldering emotions. A riot followed. Police soon reached for tear gas canisters to rout demonstrators. Fifty Chicanos were injured, two hundred arrested. Dead lay Ruben Salazar, a respected Los Angeles newsman, who was cut down by police gunfire into a cafe where he was talking with friends. Property losses totalled some 170 businesses extensively damaged. Loss in human terms proved much greater. When a sullen calm descended over the *barrio*, Chicanos felt strongly that police had once again grossly overreacted.

A quest for unity in the Movement, the fourth goal, is being noted increasingly in Denver, Los Angeles, San Antonio, Phoenix, and Santa Fe. Fanning out across the Southwest and extending into Middle West enclaves are a plethora of organizations representing special interest groups within the Chicano community. Among groups and committees there is ample evidence of rivalry and inadequate coordination. Chicanos experience marked difficulty in developing viable, large-scale organizations.

After the sharp exchanges at the first conference of *La Raza Unida*, with its rump session in 1967, a second attempt at unity grew out of the Chicano Youth Liberation Conference held in Denver in March, 1970. On behalf of Aztlan, the Indian name for the ancient Aztec nation, delegates drafted a "Spiritual Plan" which reads in part, "Aztlan belongs to those who plant the seeds, water the fields, and gather the crops . . . not to the foreign Europeans. We do not recognize capricious frontiers on the Bronze Continent. . . . With our heart in our hands and our hands in the soil, we declare the independence of our Mestizo Nation." This ambitious statement, while carrying a strong emotional charge, did not produce a fusion of groups in the Movement.

At the First National Chicano Political Caucus, in April, 1972, the issue of unity was again paramount. The purpose of the conclave was to write a platform that Chicano activists could support during the 1972 presidential year, one that would indicate to candidates what Chicanos expect in the way of reforms in exchange for their political support. In attendance at the caucus were Chicanos representing the Democratic, Republican, and *Raza Unida* parties.

Sponsors of the caucus lost control of the meeting when *Raza Unida* delegates were able to get a 2 to 1 vote in favor of Chicanos lining up behind their national separatist political party. *La Raza Unida* forced through a vote to adjourn the session at the fashionable Hyatt House and to move to the Lee Mathson School in San Jose *barrio*, where stormy deliberations were resumed. State presidents of three prestigious Chicano organizations—the Mexican American Political Association, the League of United Latin American Citizens, and the American G.I. Forum—later announced they would not endorse the separatist *Raza Unida* party.

What the caucus revealed is that Chicanos are sharply divided over whether they can best gain concessions and reforms through supporting established parties or through backing their own national party. Manifestly, Chicano long-range political aims do not have a national projection, but a regional one limited to the Southwest and to those states where in the future Chicanos can expect to wield considerable political clout. *La Raza Unida* may conceivably follow the lead of the Liberal Party, which functions as a minority aggregation in New York State, usually nominating candidates already selected by Democrats and Republicans. By maintaining their identity as a party which appears on the ballot, the Liberals are able to prod successful candidates to vote for legislation favored by their party. In like manner, *La Raza Unida* by appearing on the ballot would dramatize the strength of the Chicano vote and gain support for measures of pressing concern to Mexican Americans.

In keeping with their desire for cultural pluralism, Chicanos are moving toward a policy of working for local control of areas in which they are in the majority. Such control would include city hall, the schools, the police and fire departments, and other community services. California, with its massive concentration of Chicanos, is the logical state to kick off a drive for Chicano control of *barrio* areas. While Chicanos serve as mayors and councilmen and on school boards in some Southern California towns, the three million Mexican Americans of California have no state senator out of forty, only two state assemblymen out of eighty, and only one congressman out of thirty-eight. In Los Angeles none of the fifteen city councilmen is a Mexican American. To correct this situation, Chicano activists, with some outside support, launched a campaign in 1971 to establish Chicano districts in the California state reapportionment battle. Although they were unsuccessful—

the state failed to draft a reapportionment plan—the idea proved very attractive to many Chicano leaders.

"Gerrymandering has kept Chicanos politically impotent and has prevented the *barrios* from electing their own people," declares Francisco Sandoval, Professor of Chicano Studies at California State University (Long Beach). "But we can't wait another ten years for Republicans and Democrats to redistrict the areas. We can't wait ten years for crumbs off the table. The Chicano must take his destiny into his own hands."

Despite the lack of unity in the Movement, Chicano power is gradually being forged and wielded in a variegated process designed to assure social justice and an enriched quality of life for a minority group which, as history books will one day chronicle, came of age in the 1965–1972 period.

FOR FURTHER READING

Carey McWilliams. *North from Mexico*. New York: Greenwood, 1968.

* Matthew S. Meier and Feliciano Rivera. *The Chicanos: A History of Mexican Americans*. New York: Hill & Wang, 1972.

* Matthew S. Meier and Feliciano Rivera, eds. *Readings on La Raza*. New York: Hill & Wang, 1974.

* Wayne Moquin, ed. *A Documentary History of the Mexican Americans*. New York: Praeger, 1971.

*Edward Simmen, ed. *Pain and Promise: The Chicano Today*. New York: New American Library, 1972.

III

RECENT
FOREIGN POLICY

S tartling events of the 1950's challenged the policy of containment that the Truman Administration had set forth so confidently. The Vietnamese victory over the French and other related occurrences gave notice to thoughtful observers that the world was in process of rapid change: Europeans could no longer rule the globe, and from their disintegrating empires a "Third World" was emerging, consisting of the poor and underdeveloped countries, for the most part former colonies and protectorates. Nations as large as India and Nigeria and others as small as Malta or Trinidad shook off their bonds, demanded independence, and entered the United Nations as sovereign states. In some of them the movements that won political autonomy called for social revolution as well.

Such revolutionary nationalism disturbed the American government when it manifested itself in China or in Vietnam, and even more so when, in 1959, it came alarmingly close to home in the seemingly secure "protectorate" of Cuba. In that year guerrillas led by Fidel Castro ousted the reactionary Batista regime and began to challenge the dominance both of U. S. emissaries and of the large American corporations that controlled much of the island's business and natural resources. In an earlier age of turmoil, the Austrian Prince Metternich had accused the young United States of "fostering revolutions wherever they show themselves"; by the late twentieth century, however, the nation once denounced as subversive had itself assumed the task of preserving the established order against revolution anywhere.

Although with more dash and style, John F. Kennedy expounded a foreign policy that was based on the same premises as that of the two preceding administrations. With stirring rhetoric, he summoned Americans "to bear the burden of a long twilight struggle . . . a struggle against the common enemies of man: tyranny, poverty, disease and war itself." His own actions included acquiescence in an attempt to overthrow the government of Cuba that had been planned

138

during the Eisenhower Administration; an increase in military spending; and, on the discovery in 1962 of Russian missile bases in Cuba, a response that, though less "firm" than some advisers wanted, brought the world to the brink of nuclear war. A positive accomplishment was the limited ban on atmospheric nuclear testing agreed to in 1963 by Great Britain, the Soviet Union, and the United States. It may be, however, that Kennedy will be remembered chiefly because he dispatched a sizable contingent of American troops to "advise" the government that the previous administration had installed in Saigon, in South Vietnam. Kennedy's successor, Lyndon B. Johnson, continued and expanded the intervention, which became the longest war that the United States had ever fought. A growing resistance to American participation brought foreign policy back into the arena of public controversy and political debate.

Richard Nixon, elected President in 1968, intensified the bombing of Indochina but withdrew most American troops; yet he continued to give financial and material support to the Saigon regime. Amazingly, he entered into closer relations with the Soviet Union and also visited its bitter rival the Communist government in Peking. The original cold war had ended. Monolithic Communism had broken up. In a world of revolutions and uneasy dictatorships, no one could prophesy what the United States would do or what power it would hold. In Chile, in 1973, American agencies were able to help a military junta to take over; in the following year, however, the Greek people ousted a regime that had long been closely bound to the United States; and in Indo-China in the spring of 1975 popular leftist forces at last overthrew the government that Washington had installed and upheld at incalculable cost. At the time of this writing, at least, the American people seemed in no mood to go forth once more to combat revolutions. Perhaps their anxiety focused on the problem of surviving in the midst of inflation and unemployment. One might also consider the suggestion of historian Barbara Tuchman that all nations are "really in the same boat, in danger of being overturned by environmental disaster; . . . the enemy is not so much each other as it is the common enemy of us all: unrestrained growth and pollution. Perhaps the relaxation in international relations, if there is such, is a kind of subconscious preparation to deal with this state of affairs."

In this chapter Gabriel Kolko provides a historical survey of the one issue that by the late 1960's overshadowed all other international concerns of the United States—Vietnam; Barbara Tuchman assails our shortsighted China policies; Senator J. William Fulbright attempts to chart a course through the reefs and riptides of the Middle East; and Roger Morris assays the performance of our information media in the Chilean crisis.

THE UNITED STATES
IN VIETNAM, 1944-66:
ORIGINS AND OBJECTIVES

GABRIEL KOLKO

In August of 1964, President Lyndon B. Johnson reported to
Congress that the North Vietnamese had wantonly attacked American
destroyers in the Gulf of Tonkin. He asked for authorization "to take
all necessary measures to repeal any armed attack against the forces
of the United States and to prevent further aggression." In the entire
Congress only two people—Senators Ernest Gruening of Alaska and
Wayne Morse of Oregon—voted nay. After his re-election the following
November, the President made what one adviser described as "maximum
use of a Gulf of Tonkin rationale" to bomb the Democratic Republic
of Vietnam (North Vietnam) and to dispatch a half-million
American soldiers to South Vietnam. At the time, relatively few
citizens openly doubted the morality or the necessity of the war; what
criticism there was came mainly from liberals of independent mind,
such as Gruening and Morse, from the peace movement, which had
been trying to moderate the arms race, and from the developing
"New Left."

Gabriel Kolko's account of the war was published in 1969.
Kolko had not had access to inside information. Publication of the
"Pentagon Papers" in 1971 made it clear that he had been an accurate
reporter, for the planners of that war confirm his statements in their
own words. The documents, in fact, show even more duplicity than
Kolko's narrative would indicate, for they prove that the United States
was carrying on operations, which included bombings of the inhabitants
of Laos, to such an extent and on such a scale that the conflict must
properly be called the Indochina War. The destroyers in the Gulf of
Tonkin in the summer of 1964 were gathering intelligence for raids

that, with other "destructive undertakings," had been secretly initiated six months before; advisers had composed "scenarios" for further action, which they hoped to justify by such a resolution as Congress handed them in August.

Unlike some critics, Kolko sees the war as no mere "blunder" but as a consequence of a policy followed since the end of World War II, which has led the United States to shore up any dictatorship that professed anti-Communism or, as in Vietnam, to install its own favorites regardless of the popular will. Thus the American government has sought to make over the economy and the polity of other peoples to suit its "national interests."

Obviously, the welfare of the Indochinese played no part in the deliberations of the planners. When, in 1964, Walt Rostow of the State Department urged further "pressure" (that is, land and air attacks) against the Vietnamese, he referred to such action as an "exercise" and insisted that "at this stage of history we are the greatest power in the world—if we behave like it." It is worth remembering that in Washington in the early 1960's journalists frequently praised such attitudes as "hard-nosed." The callousness of these men seems to have been based on an inability to recognize that we owe all people and their values and cultures the same respect we accord to those with whom we are more familiar.

☐ ☐ ☐

The intervention of the United States in Vietnam is the most important single embodiment of the power and purposes of American foreign policy since the Second World War, and no other crisis reveals so much of the basic motivating forces and objectives—and weaknesses—of American global politics. A theory of the origins and meaning of the war also discloses the origins of an American malaise that is global in its reaches, impinging on this nation's conduct everywhere. To understand Vietnam is not just to comprehend the present purposes of American action but also to anticipate its thrust and direction in the future.

Vietnam illustrates, as well, the nature of the American internal political process and decision-making structure when it exceeds the views of a major sector of the people, for no other event of our generation has turned such a large proportion of the nation against its government's policy or so profoundly alienated its youth. And at no time has the government conceded so little to democratic sentiment, pursuing as it has a policy of escalation that reveals that its policy is formulated not with an eye to democratic sanctions and compromises but rather the attainment of specific interests and goals scarcely shared by the vast majority of the nation.

The inability of the United States to apply its vast material and economic power to compensate for the ideological and human superiority of revolutionary and guerrilla movements throughout the world has been the core of its frustration in Vietnam. From a purely economic viewpoint, the United States cannot maintain its existing vital dominating relationship to much of the Third World unless it can keep the poor nations from moving too far toward the Left and the Cuban or Vietnamese path. A widespread leftward movement would critically affect its supply of raw materials and have profound long-term repercussions. It is the American view of the need for relative internal stability within the poorer nations that has resulted in a long list of U.S. interventions since 1946 into the affairs of numerous nations, from Greece to Guatemala, of which Vietnam is only the consummate example—but in principle not different from numerous others. The accuracy of the "domino" theory, with its projection of the eventual loss of whole regions to American direction and access, explains the direct continuity between the larger United States global strategy and Vietnam.

Yet, ironically, while the United States struggles in Vietnam and the Third World to retain its own mastery, or to continue that once held by the former colonial powers, it simultaneously weakens itself in its deepening economic conflict with Europe, revealing the limits of America's power to attain its ambition to define the preconditions and direction of global economic and political developments. Vietnam is essentially an American intervention against a nationalist, revolutionary agrarian movement which embodies social elements in incipient and similar forms of development in numerous other Third World nations. It is no sense a civil war, with the United States supporting one local faction against another, but an effort to preserve a mode of traditional colonialism via a minute, historically opportunistic *comprador* class in Saigon. For the United States to fail in Vietnam would be to make the point that even the massive intervention of the most powerful nation in the history of the world was insufficient to stem profoundly popular social and national revolutions throughout the world. Such a revelation of American weaknesses would be tantamount to a demotion of the United States from its present role as the world's dominant superpower.

Given the scope of U.S. ambitions in relation to the Third World, and the sheer physical limits on the successful implementation of such a policy, Vietnam also reveals the passivity of the American Military

Establishment in formulating global objectives that are intrinsically economic and geopolitical in character. Civilians, above all, have calculated the applications of American power in Vietnam, and' their strategies have prompted each military escalation according to their definitions of American interests. Even in conditions of consistent military impotence and defeat, Vietnam has fully revealed the tractable character of the American military when confronted with civilian authority, and their continuous willingness to obey civilian orders loyally.

It is in this broader framework of the roots of U.S. foreign policy since 1945 that we must comprehend the history and causes of the war in Vietnam and relate it to the larger setting of the goals of America's leaders and the function of United States power in the modern world.

Throughout the Second World War the leaders of the United States scarcely considered the future of Indo-China, but during 1943 President Roosevelt suggested that Indo-China become a four-power trusteeship after the war, proposing that the eventual independence of the Indo-Chinese might follow in twenty to thirty years. No one speculated whether such a policy would require American troops, but it was clear that the removal of French power was motivated by a desire to penalize French collaboration with Germany and Japan, or De Gaulle's annoying independence, rather than a belief in the intrinsic value of freedom for the Vietnamese. Yet what was critical in the very first American position was that ultimate independence would not be something that the Vietnamese might take themselves, but a blessing the other Great Powers might grant at their own convenience. Implicit in this attitude was the seed of opposition to the independence movement that already existed in Vietnam. Indeed, all factors being equal, the policy toward European colonialism would depend on the extent to which the involved European nations accepted American objectives elsewhere, but also the nature of the local opposition. If the Left led the independence movements, as in the Philippines, Korea, or Indo-China, then the United States sustained collaborationist alternatives, if possible, or endorsed colonialism.

Though Roosevelt at Yalta repeated his desire for a trusteeship, during March 1945 he considered the possibility of French restoration in return for their pledge eventually to grant independence. But by May 1945 there was no written, affirmative directive on U.S. political policy in Indo-China. The gap was in part due to the low priority assigned the issue, but also reflected growing apprehension as to what the future of those countries as independent states might hold.

At the Potsdam Conference of July 1945, and again in the General Order Number 1 the United States unilaterally issued several weeks later, the remaining equivocation on Indo-China was resolved by authorizing the British takeover of the nation south of the 16th parallel and Chinese occupation north of it, and this definitely meant the restoration of the French, whom the British had loyally supported since 1943. One cannot exaggerate the importance of these steps, since they made the United States responsible for the French return at a time when Washington might have dictated the independence of that nation. By this time everyone understood what the British were going to do.

Given the alternative, U.S. support for the return of France to Indo-China was logical as a means of stopping the triumph of the Left, a question not only in that nation but throughout the Far East. Moreover, by mid-August French officials were hinting that they would grant the United States and England equal economic access to Indo-China. Both in action and thought the United States Government now chose the reimposition of French colonialism. At the end of August De Gaulle was in Washington, and the President now told the French leader that the United States favored the return of France to Indo-China. The decision would shape the course of world history for decades.

The O.S.S. worked with the Vietminh, a coalition of Left and moderate Resistance forces led by Ho Chi Minh, during the final months of the war to the extent of giving them petty quantities of arms in exchange for information and assistance with downed pilots, and they soon came to know Ho and many of the Vietminh leaders. Despite the almost paranoid belief of the French representatives that the O.S.S. was working against France, the O.S.S. only helped consolidate Washington's support for the French. They and other American military men who arrived in Hanoi during the first heady days of freedom were unanimous in believing that Ho "is an old revolutionist . . . a product of Moscow, a communist." The O.S.S. understood the nationalist ingredient in the Vietnamese revolution, but they emphasized the Communist in their reports to Washington.

During September the first British troops began arriving in the Indo-Chinese zone which the Americans assigned them and imposed their control over half of a nation largely Vietminh controlled with the backing of the vast majority of the people. The British arranged to bring in French troops as quickly as they might be found, and employed Japanese troops in the Saigon region and elsewhere. "[On] the 23rd September," the British commander later reported to his superiors, "Major-General Gracey had agreed with the French that they should carry out a *coup d'état*; and with his permission, they seized control of the administration of Saigon and the French Government was installed." The State Department's representative who visited Hanoi the following month found the references of the Vietnamese to classic democratic rhetoric mawkish, and "Perhaps naively, and without consideration of the conflicting postwar interests of the 'Big' nations themselves, the new government believed that by complying with the conditions of the wartime U.N. conferences it could invoke the benefits of these conferences in favor of its own indepedence." From this viewpoint, even in 1945 the United States regarded Indo-China almost exclusively as the object of Great Power diplomacy and conflict. By the end of the Second World War the Vietnamese were already in violent conflict not only with the representatives of France, but also England and the United States, a conflict in which they could turn the wartime political rhetoric against the governments that had casually written it. But, at no time did the desires of the Vietnamese themselves assume a role in the shaping of U.S. policy.

1946-49: U.S. INACTION AND THE GENESIS OF A FIRM POLICY

It is sufficient to note that by early 1947 the American doctrine of containment of communism obligated the United States to think also of the dangers Ho Chi Minh and the Vietminh posed, a movement the United States analyzed as a monolith directed from Moscow. It is also essential to remain aware of the fact that the global perspective of the United States between 1946 and 1949 stressed the decisive importance of Europe to the future of world power. When the United States looked at Indo-China it saw France, and through it Europe, and a weak France would open the door to communism in Europe. But for no other reason, this meant a tolerant attitude toward the bloody French policy in Vietnam, one the French insisted was essential to the maintenance of their empire and prosperity, and the political stability of the nation. Washington saw Vietnamese nationalism as a tool of the Communists.

In February 1947 Secretary of State George C. Marshall publicly declared he wished "a pacific basis of adjustment of the difficulties could be found," but he offered no means toward that end. Given the greater fear of communism, such mild American criticisms of French policy as were made should not obscure the much more significant backing of basic French policy in Washington. By early 1949 Washington had shown its full commitment to the larger assumptions of French policy and goals, and when Bao Dai, the former head of the Japanese puppet regime, signed an agreement with the French in March 1949 to bring Vietnam into the French Union, the State Department welcomed the new arrangement as the "basis for the progressive realization of the legitimate aspirations of the Vietnamese people." Such words belied the reality, for the course of affairs in Asia worried Washington anew.

The catalysis for a reconsideration of the significance of Vietnam to the United States was the final victory of the Communists in China. In July 1949 the State Department authorized a secret reassessment of American policy in Asia in light of the defeat of the Kuomintang, and appointed Ambassador-at-Large Philip Jessup chairman of a special committee. On July 18th Dean Acheson sent Jessup a memo defining the limits of the inquiry: "You will please take as your assumption that it is a fundamental decision of American policy that the United States does not intend to permit further extension of Communist domination on the continent of Asia or in the southeast Asia area." At the end of 1949 the State Department was still convinced the future of world power remained in Europe, but, as was soon to become evident, this involved the necessity of French victory in Vietnam. Most significant about the Jessup Committee's views was the belief, as one State Department official put it, "In respect to Southeast Asia we are on the fringes of crisis," one that, he added, might involve all of Asia following China. It appears to have been the consensus that Bao Dai, despite American wishes for his success, had only the slimmest chance for creating an effective alternative to Ho in Vietnam. The Committee compared French prospects to those of Chiang Kai-shek two years earlier, and since they acknowledged that the Vietminh captured most of their arms from the French, the likelihood of stemming the tide seemed dismal.

There were two dimensions to the Vietnam problem from the U.S. viewpoint at the end of 1949. First, it was determined to stop the sweep of revolution in Asia along the fringes of China, and by that time Vietnam was the most likely outlet for any U.S. action. Second, it was believed that small colonial wars were draining France, and therefore Europe, of its power. Yet a Western victory had to terminate these struggles in order to fortify Europe, the central arena of the Cold War. "I found all the French troops of any quality were out in Indo-China," Marshall complained to the Jessup Committee, "and the one place they were not was in Western Europe. So it left us in an extraordinarily weak position there." Massive American intervention in Vietnam was now inevitable.

1950–53: AMERICA ESCALATES THE WAR IN INDO-CHINA

The significance of the struggle in Vietnam for the United States always remained a global one, and for this reason Vietnam after 1950 became the most sustained and important single issue confronting Washington. The imminent crisis in Asia that the Jessup Committee had predicted was one John Foster Dulles, even then one of the key architects of U.S. diplomacy, also anticipated. Dulles, however, thought it a mistake to place the main emphasis on American policy in Europe, and he, like everyone else in Washington, was not in the least impressed by the future of the Associated States of Vietnam, Laos, and Cambodia which the United States recognized on February 7, 1950, with a flurry of noble references to independence and democracy. A "series of disasters can be prevented," Dulles advised in May 1950, "if at some doubtful point we quickly take a dramatic and strong stand that shows our confidence and resolution. Probably this series of disasters cannot be prevented in any other way." It would be necessary, he believed, even to "risk war."

The official position of the Truman Administration at this time was to insist on regarding Vietnam as essentially an extension of a European affair. As Charles E. Bohlen of the State Department explained it in a top secret briefing in April:

> As to Indo-China, if the current war there continues for two or three years, we will get very little of sound military development in France. On the other hand, if we can help France to get out of the existing stalemate in Indo-China, France can do something effective in Western Europe. The need in Indo-China is to develop a local force which can maintain order in the areas theoretically pacified. . . .
>
> It is important, in order to maintain the French effort in Indo-China, that any assistance we give be presented as defense of the French Union, as the French soldiers there would have little enthusiasm for sacrificing themselves to fight for a completely free Indo-China in which France would have no part.

Suffice it to say, the French were hard-pressed economically, and they needed U.S. aid on any terms, and in May 1950 direct U.S. economic aid was begun to Cambodia, Laos, and Vietnam. Immediately after the Korean affair Truman pledged greater support to the French and the Bao Dai regime.

During mid-October 1950, shortly after some serious military reverses, Jules Moch, the French Minister of National Defense, arrived in Washington to attempt to obtain even greater U.S. military aid. By this time, despite earlier reticence, the French had come to realize that the key to their colonial war was in Washington.

The aggregate military aid the United States contributed to the French effort in Vietnam is a difficult matter of bookkeeping, but total direct military aid to France in 1950–1953 was $2.956 million, plus $684 million in 1954. United States claims suggest that $1.54 billion in aid was given to Indo-China before the Geneva Accords, and in fact Truman's statement in January 1953 that the United States paid for as much as half of the war seems accurate enough, and aid rose every year to 1954. The manner in which this aid was disbursed is more significant.

The United States paid but did not appreciate French political direction, though no serious political pressure was put on the French until 1954. Dulles, for one, was aware of Bao Dai's political unreliability and inability to create an alternative to the Vietminh, and he regretted it. "It seems," he wrote a friend in October 1950, "as is often the case, it is necessary as a practical matter to choose the lesser of two evils because the theoretically ideal solution is not possible for many reasons

—the French policy being only one. As a matter of fact, the French policy has considerably changed for the better." It was Dulles, in the middle of 1951, who discovered in Bao Dai's former premier under the Japanese, Ngo Dinh Diem, the political solution for Indo-China. At the end of 1950 he was willing to content himself with the belief that the expansion of communism in Asia must be stopped. The French might serve that purpose at least for a time.

In developing a rationale for U.S. aid three major arguments were advanced, only one of which was later to disappear as a major source of the conduct of U.S. policy in Vietnam. First of all, the United States wished to bring France back to Europe via victory in Vietnam: "The sooner they bring it to a successful conclusion," Henry Cabot Lodge explained in early 1951, "the better it would be for NATO because they could move their forces here and increase their building of their army in Europe." The French insistence until 1954 on blocking German rearmament and the European Defense Community until they could exist on the continent with military superiority over the Germans, a condition that was impossible until the war in Vietnam ended, gave this even more persuasive consideration special urgency. From this viewpoint, Vietnam was the indirect key to Germany. In the meantime, as Ambassador to France David Bruce explained it, "I think it would be a disaster if the French did not continue their effort in Indo-China."

Victory rather than a political settlement was necessary because of the two other basic and more permanent factors in guiding U.S. policy. The United States was always convinced that the "domino" theory would operate should Vietnam remain with the Vietnamese people. "There is no question," Bruce told a Senate committee, "that if Indo-China went, the fall of Burma and the fall of Thailand would be absolutely inevitable. No one can convince me, for what it is worth, that Malaya wouldn't follow shortly thereafter, and India . . . would . . . also find the Communists making infiltrations." The political character of the regime in Vietnam was less consequential than the larger U.S. design for the area, and the seeds of future U.S. policy were already forecast when Bruce suggested that "the Indo-Chinese—and I am speaking now of the . . . anti-Communist group—will have to show a far greater ability to live up to the obligations of nationhood before it will be safe to withdraw, whether it be French Union forces or any other foreign forces, from that country." If the French left, someone would have to replace them.

Should Vietnam, and through it Asia, fall to the Vietminh, then the last major American fear would be realized. "[Of] all the prizes Russia could bite off in the east," Bruce also suggested,

the possession of Indo-China would be the most valuable and in the long run would be the most crucial one from the standpoint of the west in the east. That would be true not because of the flow of rice, rubber, and so forth . . . but because it is the only place where any war is now being conducted to try to suppress the overtaking of the whole area of southeast Asia by the Communists.

Eisenhower and Nixon put this assumption rather differently, with greater emphasis on the value of raw materials, but it has been a constant basis of U.S. policy in Vietnam since 1951. "Why is the United States spending hundreds of millions of dollars supporting the forces of the French Union in the fight against communism?" Vice President Richard Nixon asked in December 1953.

If Indo-China falls, Thailand is put in an almost impossible position. The same is true of Malaya with its rubber and tin. The same is true of Indo-nesia. If this whole part of Southeast Asia goes under Communist domin-ation or Communist influence, Japan, who trades and must trade with this area in order to exist, must inevitably be oriented towards the Communist regime.

"The loss of all Vietnam," Eisenhower wrote in his memoirs,

together with Laos on the west and Cambodia on the southwest, would have meant the surrender to Communist enslavement of millions. On the material side, it would have spelled the loss of valuable deposits of tin and prodigious supplies of rubber and rice. It would have meant that Thailand, enjoying buffer territory between itself and Red China, would be exposed on its entire eastern border to infiltration or attack. And if Indo-China fell, not only Thailand but Burma and Malaya would be threatened, with added risks to East Pakistan and South Asia as well as to all Indonesia.

Given this larger American conception of the importance of the Vietnam war to its self-interest, which impelled the United States to support it financially, the future of the war no longer depended largely on whether the French would fight or meet the demands of the Viet-namese for independence. Already in early 1952 Secretary of State Dean Acheson told Foreign Minister Anthony Eden, as recorded in the latter's memoirs,

. . . of the United States' determination to do everything possible to strengthen the French hand in Indo-China. On the wider question of the possibility of a Chinese invasion, the United States Government con-sidered that it would be disastrous to the position of the Western powers if South-East Asia were lost without a struggle.

If Acheson promised prudence by merely greatly increasing arms aid to the French, he also talked of blockading China. The war, even by 1952, was being internationalized with America assuming ever greater initiative for its control. When Eisenhower came to the Presidency in January 1953, Acheson presented Vietnam to him as "an urgent matter on which the new administration must be prepared to act." Given Dulles' experience and views on the question, Acheson's words were not to be wasted.

By spring 1953, the U.S. Government was fully aware of the largely tangential role of the French in its larger global strategy, and it was widely believed in Congress that if the French pulled out the United States would not permit Vietnam to fall. The United States was increasingly irritated with the French direction of affairs. The economic aid sent to Vietnam resulted merely in the creation of a speculative market for piastres and dollars which helped the local *compradors* enrich themselves while debilitating the economy. "Failure of important elements of the local population to give a full measure of support to the war effort remained one of the chief negative factors," the State Department confided to Eisenhower. [It] was almost impossible," Eisenhower later wrote, "to make the average Vietnamese peasant realize that the French, under whose rule his people had lived for some eighty years, were really fighting in the cause of freedom, while the Vietminh, people of their own ethnic origins, were fighting on the side of slavery." Bao Dai, whom the United States had always mistrusted, now disturbed the Americans because, as Eisenhower recalls, he "chose to spend the bulk of his time in the spas of Europe."

The French, for their part, were now divided on the proper response the massive American intervention into the war demanded. But during July 1953 Bidault and Dulles conferred and Dulles promised all the French desired, also admonishing them not to seek a negotiated end to the war. In September the United States agreed to give the French a special grant of $385 million to implement the Navarre Plan, a scheme to build French and puppet troops to a level permitting them to destroy the regular Vietminh forces by the end of 1955. By this time the essential strategy of the war supplanted a strict concern for bringing France back to NATO, and the Americans increasingly determined to make Vietnam a testing ground for a larger global strategy of which the French would be the instrument. Critical to that strategy was military victory.

The difficulty for the U.S. undertaking was that, as General LeClerc had suggested several years earlier, there was "no military solution for Vietnam." The major foreign policy crisis of late 1953 and early 1954, involving Dulles' confusing "massive retaliation" speech on January 12, 1954, was the first immediate consequence of the failure of the Navarre Plan and the obvious French march toward defeat. The vital problem for the United States was how it might apply its vast military power in a manner that avoided a land war in the jungles, one which Dulles always opposed in Asia and which the Americans too might lose. At the end of December 1953 Dulles publicly alluded to the possibility that in the event of a Chinese invasion of Vietnam the Americans might respond by attacking China, which several weeks later was expressed again in the ambiguous threat of the American need "to be willing and able to respond vigorously at places and with means of its own choosing." Every critical assumption on which the United States based its foreign and military policy it was now testing in Vietnam.

1954: THE GENEVA CONFERENCE

Given the larger regional, even global, context of the question of Vietnam for the United States, a peaceful settlement would have undermined the vital premise of Washington since 1947 that one could not negotiate with communism but only contain it via military expenditures, bases, and power. In February 1954, as Eden records, "our Ambassador was told at the State Department that the United States Government were perturbed by the fact that the French were aiming not to win the war, but to get into a position from which they could negotiate." The United States was hostile to any political concessions and to an end to the war. To the French, many of whom still wished to fight, the essential question was whether the U.S. Government would share the burden of combat as well as the expense. The French would make this the test of their ultimate policy.

At the end of March the French sought to obtain some hint of the direction of U.S. commitments, and posed the hypothetical question of what U.S. policy would be if the Chinese used their aircraft to attack French positions. Dulles refused to answer the question, but he did state that if the United States entered the war with its own manpower, it would demand a much greater share of the political and executive direction of the future of the area.

It is probable the U.S. Government in the weeks before Geneva had yet to define a firm policy for itself save on one issue: the desire not to lose any part of Vietnam by negotiations and to treat the existing military realities of the war as the final determining reality. Eden's memory was correct when he noted that in April the Undersecretary of State, Walter Bedell Smith, informed the English Government "that the United States had carefully studied the partition solution, but had decided that it would only be a temporary palliative and would lead to Communist domination of South-East Asia."

During these tense days words from the United States were extremely belligerent, but it ultimately avoided equivalent actions, and laid the basis for later intervention. On March 29th Dulles excoriated Ho and the Vietminh and all who "whip up the spirit of nationalism so that it becomes violent." He again reiterated the critical value of Vietnam as a source of raw materials and its strategic value in the area, and now blamed China for the continuation of the war. After detailing the alleged history of broken Soviet treaties, Dulles made it clear that the

United States would go to Geneva so that "any Indo-China discussion will serve to bring the Chinese Communists to see the danger of their apparent design for the conquest of Southeast Asia, so that they will cease and desist." Vice President Richard Nixon on April 16th was rather more blunt in a press conference: Geneva would become an instrument of action and not a forum for a settlement.

[The] United States must go to Geneva and take a positive stand for united action by the free world. Otherwise it will have to take on the problem alone and try to sell it to others. . . . This country is the only nation politically strong enough at home to take a position that will save Asia. . . . Negotiations with the Communists to divide the territory would result in Communist domination of a vital new area."

The fact the United States focused on Chinese "responsibility" for a war of liberation from the French that began in 1945, years before the Chinese Communists were near the south, was not only poor propaganda but totally irrelevant as a basis of military action. There was at this time no effective means for U.S. entry into the war, and such power as the Americans had would not be useful in what ultimately had to be a land war if they could hope for victory. War hawks aside, the Pentagon maintained a realistic assessment of the problem of joining the war at this time from a weak and fast-crumbling base, and for this reason the United States never implemented the much publicized schemes for entering the war via air power. The U.S. Government was, willy-nilly, grasping at a new course, one that had no place for Geneva and its very partial recognition of realities in Vietnam.

On April 4th Eisenhower proposed to Churchill that the three major NATO allies, the Associated States, the ANZUS countries, Thailand, and the Philippines form a coalition to take a firm stand on Indo-China, by using naval and air power against the Chinese coast and intervening in Vietnam itself. The British were instantly cool to the amorphous notion, and they were to insist that first the diplomats do their best at Geneva to save the French from their disastrous position. Only the idea of a regional military alliance appealed to them. Despite much scurrying and bluster, Dulles could not keep the British and French from going to Geneva open to offers, concessions, and a *détente*.

On May 7th, the day before the Geneva Conference turned to the question of Vietnam, Laos, and Cambodia, Dien Bien Phu fell to the victorious Vietnamese. Psychologically, though not militarily, the United States saw this as a major defeat in Vietnam. Militarily, about three-quarters of Vietnam belonged to the Vietnamese, and imminent French defeat promised to liberate the remainder. That same evening Dulles went on the radio to denounce Ho as a "Communist . . . trained in Moscow" who would "deprive Japan of important foreign markets and sources of food and raw materials." Vietnam, Dulles went on, could not fall "into hostile hands," for then "the Communists could move into all of Southeast Asia." Nevertheless, "The present conditions there do not provide a suitable basis for the United States to participate with its armed forces," and so the hard-pressed French might wish an armistice. "But we would be gravely concerned if an armistice or cease-fire were reached at Geneva which would provide a road to a Communist take-over and further aggression."

The U.S. position meant an explicit denial of the logic of the military realities, for negotiations to deprive the Vietminh of all of their triumphs was, in effect, a request for surrender. Even before the Conference turned to the subject, the United States rejected—on behalf of a larger global view which was to make Vietnam bear the brunt of future interventions—the implications of a negotiated settlement.

THE GENEVA AGREEMENT

Others have authoritatively documented the U.S. role during the Geneva Conference discussion of May 8—July 21—the indecision, vacillation, and American refusal to acknowledge the military and political realities of the time. The British, for their part, hoped for partition, the Russians and the Chinese for peace—increasingly at any price—and the Vietnamese for Vietnam and the political rewards of their near-military triumph over a powerful nation. The American position, as the *New York Times* described it during these weeks, was "driving the U.S. deeper into diplomatic isolation on Southeast Asian questions," and "Though the U.S. opposes . . . these agreements, there appears to be little the U.S. can do to stop them."

To the Vietnamese delegates led by Pham Van Dong, the question was how to avoid being deprived of the political concomitant of their military triumph, and they were the first to quickly insist on national elections in Vietnam at an early date—elections they were certain to win. As the Conference proceeded, and the Russians and then the Chinese applied pressure for Vietnamese concessions on a wide spectrum of issues—the most important being the provisional zonal demarcation along the 17th parallel—the importance of this election provision became ever greater to the Vietminh.

To both the Vietnamese and the United States partition as a permanent solution was out of the question, and Pham Van Dong made it perfectly explicit that zonal regroupments were only a temporary measure to enforce a cease-fire. Had the Vietminh felt it was to be permanent they unquestionably would not have agreed to the Accords. When Mendès-France conceded a specific date for an election, the world correctly interpreted it as a major concession to Vietnamese independence.

By the end of June, the Vietnamese were ready to grant much in the hope that an election would be held. During these very same days, Eden finally convinced the United States that a partition of Vietnam was all they might hope for, and on June 29th Eden and Dulles issued a statement which agreed to respect an armistice that "Does not contain political provisions which would risk loss of the retained area to Communist control." Since that loss was now inevitable, it ambiguously suggested that the United States might look askance at elections, or the entire Accord itself. When the time came formally to join the other nations at Geneva in endorsing the Conference resolutions, the United States would not consent to do so.

The final terms of the Accords are too well known for more than a contextual résumé here. The "Agreement on Cessation of Hostilities" that the French and Vietnamese signed on July 20th explicitly described as "provisional" the demarcation line at the 17th parallel. Until general elections, the Vietnamese and French, respectively, were to exercise civil authority above and below the demarcation line, and it was France alone that had responsibility for assuring conformity to its terms on a political level. Militarily, an International Control Commission was to enforce the terms. Arms could not be increased beyond existing levels. Article 18 stipulated that "the establishment of new military bases is prohibited throughout Vietnam territory," and Article 19 that "the two parties shall ensure that the zones assigned to them do not adhere to any military alliance," which meant that Vietnam could not join the Southeast Asia Treaty Organization the United States was beginning to organize. The Final Declaration issued on July 21st "takes note" of these military agreements, and "that the essential purpose of the agreement relating to Viet-Nam is to settle military questions with a view to ending hostilities and that the military demarcation line is provisional and should not in any way be interpreted as constituting a political or territorial boundary." Vietnam was one nation in this view, and at no place did the documents refer to "North" or "South." To achieve political unity, "general elections shall be held in July 1956, under the supervision of an international control commission," and "Consultations will be held on this subject between the competent representative authorities of the two zones from 20 July 1955 onwards."

To the United States it was inconceivable that the French and their Vietnamese allies could implement the election proviso without risk of total disaster. It is worth quoting Eisenhower's two references to this assumption in his memoirs: "It was generally conceded that had an election been held, Ho Chi Minh would have been elected Premier." "I have never talked or corresponded with a person knowledgeable in Indo-Chinese affairs who did not agree that had elections been held as of the time of the fighting, possibly 80 percent of the population would have voted for the Communist Ho Chi Minh as their leader rather than Chief of State Bao Dai."

The United States therefore could not join in voting for the Conference resolution of July 21st, and a careful reading of the two U.S. statements issued unilaterally the same day indicates it is quite erroneous to suggest that the United States was ready to recognize the outcome of a conference and negotiated settlement which it had bitterly opposed at every phase. Eisenhower's statement begrudgingly welcomed an end to the fighting, but then made it quite plain that

> ... the United States has not itself been a party to or bound by the decisions taken by the Conference, but it is our hope that it will lead to the establishment of peace consistent with the rights and needs of the countries concerned. The agreement contains features which we do not like, but a great deal depends on how they work in practice.

The "United States will not use force to disturb the settlement. We also say that any renewal of Communist aggression would be viewed by us as a matter of grave concern." Walter Bedell Smith's formal statement at Geneva made the same points, but explicitly refused to endorse the 13th article of the Agreement, requiring consultation by the members of the Conference to consider questions submitted to them by the International Control Commission, "to ensure that the agreements" on the cessation of hostilities in Cambodia, Laos and Viet-Nam are respected."

THE AFTERMATH OF GENEVA:
THE U.S. ENTRENCHMENT, 1955–59

The United States attached such grave reservations because it never had any intention of implementing the Geneva Accords, and this was clear from all the initial public statements. The *Wall Street Journal* was entirely correct when on July 23rd it reported that "The U.S. is in no hurry for elections to unite Viet Nam; we fear Red leader Ho Chi Minh would win. So Dulles plans first to make the southern half a showplace —with American aid."

While various U.S. missions began moving into the area Diem controlled, Dulles addressed himself to the task of creating a SEATO organization which, as Eisenhower informed the Senate, was "for defense against both open armed attack and internal subversion." To Dulles from this time onward, the SEATO treaty would cover Vietnam, Cambodia, and Laos, even though they failed to sign the treaty and in fact the Geneva Agreement forbade them to do so. Article IV of the SEATO treaty extended beyond the signatories and threatened intervention by the organization in case of aggression "against any State or territory" in the region, or if there was a threat to the "political independence . . . of any other State or territory." Under such an umbrella the United States might rationalize almost any intervention for any reason.

The general pattern of U.S. economic and military aid to the Diem regime between 1955 and 1959, which totaled $2.92 billion in that period, indicates the magnitude of the American commitment, $1.71 billion of which was advanced under military programs, including well over a half-billion dollars before the final Geneva-scheduled election date.

That elections would never be held was a foregone conclusion, despite the efforts of the North Vietnamese, who on January 1st 1955 reminded the French of their obligations to see the provision respected. Given the internecine condition of the local opposition and its own vast strength among the people, the Democratic Republic of Vietnam had every reason to comply with the Geneva provisos on elections. During February 1955 Hanoi proposed establishing normal relations between the two zones preparatory to elections, and Pham Van Dong in April issued a joint statement with Nehru urging steps to hold elections to reunify the country. By this time Diem was busy repressing and liquidating internal opposition of every political hue, and when it received no positive answer to its June 6th pleas for elections, the D.R.V. again formally reiterated its opposition to the partition of one nation and the need to hold elections on schedule. During June the world turned its attention to Diem's and Dulles' response prior to the July 20th deadline for consultations. Diem's response was painfully vague, and the first real statement came from Dulles on June 28th when he stated neither the United States nor the regime in the south had signed the agreement at Geneva or was bound to it, a point that Washington often repeated and that was, in the case of the south, patently false. Nevertheless, Dulles admitted that in principle the United States favored "the unification of countries which have a historic unity," the myth of two Vietnams and two nations not yet being a part of the American case. "The Communists have never yet won any free election. I don't think they ever will. Therefore, we are not afraid at all of elections, provided they are held under conditions of genuine freedom which the Geneva armistice agreement calls for." But the United States, it was clear from this statement, was not bound to call for the implementation of the agreement via prior consultations which Diem and Washington had refused until that time, nor did Dulles say he would now urge Diem to take such a course.

Diem at the end of April 1955 announced he would hold a "national referendum" in the south to convoke a new national assembly, and on July 16th he categorically rejected truly national elections under the terms of Geneva until "proof is . . . given that they put the superior interests of the national community above those of Communism." "We certainly agree," Dulles stated shortly thereafter, "that conditions are not ripe for free elections." The response of the D.R.V. was as it had always been: Geneva obligated the Conference members to assume responsibility for its implementation, including consultations preparatory to actual elections, and in this regard Diem was by no means the responsible party. But the English favored partition, and the French were not about to thwart the U.S. Government. The fraudulent referendum of October 23rd which Diem organized in the south gave Diem 98 percent of the votes for the Presidency of the new "Government of Vietnam." Three days later Washington replied to the news by recognizing the legitimacy of the regime.

In reality, using a regime almost entirely financed with its funds, and incapable of surviving without its aid, the United States partitioned Vietnam.

To the D.R.V., the U.S. and Diem administrations' refusal to conform to the Geneva Accords was a question for the members of the Geneva Conference and the I.C.C. [International Control Commission] to confront, and while it had often made such demands—during June and again November 1955, and directly to Diem on July 19th—in September and again on November 17th, 1955, Pham and Ho publicly elaborated their ideas on the structure of an election along entirely democratic lines. All citizens above eighteen could vote and all above twenty-one could run for office. They proposed free campaigning in both zones and secret and direct balloting. The I.C.C. could supervise. On February 25th, 1956, Ho again reiterated this position.

On February 14th, 1956, Pham Van Dong directed a letter to the Geneva co-chairmen pointing to the repression in the south, its de facto involvement in an alliance with the United States, and the French responsibility for rectifying the situation. He now proposed that the Geneva Conference reconvene to settle peacefully the problem of Vietnam. The British refused, and again on April 6th the Diem government announced that "it does not consider itself bound by their provisions." On May 8th the Geneva co-chairmen sent to the north and south, as well as to the French, a demand to open consultations on elections with a view to unifying the country under the Geneva Accords. Three days later the D.R.V. expressed readiness to begin direct talks in early June at a time set by the Diem authorities. Diem refused. The D.R.V. continued to demand consultations to organize elections, submitting notes to this effect to the Geneva co-chairmen and the Diem government in June and July 1957, March and December 1958, July 1959, and July 1960, and later, for arms reduction, resumption of trade, and other steps necessary to end the artificial partition of Vietnam. These proposals failed, for neither Diem nor the United States could [tolerate] their successful implementation.

Washington's policy during this period was clear and publicly stated. On June 1st, 1956, after visiting Diem with Dulles the prior March, Walter S. Robertson, Assistant Secretary of State, attacked the Geneva Accords, which "partitioned [Vietnam] by fiat of the great powers against the will of the Vietnamese people." He lauded Diem's rigged "free election of last March" and stated the American determination.

> ... to support a friendly non-Communist government in Viet-Nam and to help it diminish and eventually eradicate Communist subversion and influence. . . . Our efforts are directed first of all toward helping to sustain the internal security forces consisting of a regular army of about 150,000 men, a mobile civil guard of some 45,000, and local defense units. . . . We are also helping to organize, train, and equip the Vietnamese police force.

Such policies were, of course, in violation of the Geneva Accords forbidding military expansion.

The term "eradicate" was an apt description of the policy which the United States urged upon the more-than-willing Diem, who persecuted former Vietminh supporters, dissident religious sects, and others. An estimated 40,000 Vietnamese were in jail for political reasons by the end of 1958, almost four times that number by the end of 1961. Such policies were possible because the United States financed over 70 percent of Diem's budget, and the main U.S. emphasis was on the use of force and repression. There were an estimated minimum of 16,600 political liquidations between 1955 and 1959, perhaps much more. Suffice it to say, every objective observer has accepted *Life* magazine's description in May 1957 as a fair estimate:

> Behind a façade of photographs, flags and slogans there is a grim structure of decrees, "re-education centers," secret police. Presidential "Ordinance No. 6" signed and issued by Diem in January, 1956, provides that "individuals considered dangerous to national defense and common security may be confined on executive order" in a "concentration camp." . . . Only known or suspected Communists . . . are supposed to be arrested and "re-educated" under these decrees. But many non-Communists have also been detained. . . . The whole machinery of security has been used to discourage active opposition of any kind from any source.

The International Control Commission's teams complained of these violations in the south, and in the north they claimed that the only significant group to have its civil liberties infringed was the Catholic minority, approximately one-tenth of the nation. The cooperation of the D.R.V. with the I.C.C. was a critical index of its intentions, and an example of its naïve persistence in the belief Geneva had not in reality deprived them of its hard-fought victory. The vast military build-up in the south made real cooperation with the I.C.C. impossible, and its complaints, especially in regard to the airfields and reprisals against civilians, were very common. In certain cases the Diem regime permitted I.C.C. teams to move in the south, but it imposed time limits, especially after 1959. Although there is no precise way of making a count of what figures both Diem and the United States were attempting to hide, by July 1958 the D.R.V.'s estimate that Diem had 450,000 men under arms was probably correct in light of Robertson's earlier estimate of U.S. plans and the $1.7 billion in military expenditures for Diem through 1959.

Although the large bulk of American aid to Diem went to military purposes, the section devoted to economic ends further rooted an entirely dependent regime to the United States. That economic aid was a total disaster, exacerbated a moribund economy, ripped apart the urban society already tottering from the first decade of war, and enriched Diem, his family, and clique. Yet certain germane aspects of the condition of the southern economy are essential to understand the next phase of the revolution in Vietnam and further American intervention, a revolution the Americans had frozen for a time but could not stop.

The Vietminh controlled well over one-half the land south of the 18th parallel prior to the Geneva Conference, and since 1941 they had managed to introduce far-reaching land reform into an agrarian economy of grossly inequitable holdings. When Diem took over this area, with the advice of U.S. experts he introduced a "land reform" program which in fact was a regressive "modernization" of the concentrated land control system that had already been wiped out in many regions. Saigon reduced rents by as much as 50 percent from pre-Vietminh times, but in fact it represented a reimposition of tolls that had ceased to exist in wide areas. In cases of outright expropriation, landlords received compensation for property that they had already lost. In brief, the Diem regime's return to power meant a reimposition of a new form of the prewar 1940 land distribution system in which 72 percent of the population owned 13 percent of the land and two-thirds of the agricultural population consisted of tenants ground down by high rents and exorbitant interest rates. For this reason, it was the landlords rather than the peasantry who supported "agrarian reform."

Various plans for resettling peasants in former Vietminh strongholds, abortive steps which finally culminated in the strategic hamlet movement of 1962, simply helped to keep the countryside in seething discontent. These *agrovilles* uprooted traditional villages and became famous as sources of discontent against the regime, one which was ripping apart the existing social structure. In brief, Diem and the United States never established control over the larger part of South Vietnam and the Vietminh's impregnable peasant base, and given the decentralization and the corruption of Diem's authority, there was no effective basis for their doing so. The repression Diem exercised only rekindled resistance.

In the cities the dislocations in the urban population, constantly augmented by a flow of Catholic refugees from the north, led to a conservative estimate in 1956 of 413,000 unemployed out of the Saigon population of 2 million. The $1.2 billion in nonmilitary aid given to the Diem regime during 1955–59 went in large part to pay for its vast import deficit, which permitted vast quantities of American-made luxury goods to be brought into the country's inflationary economy for the use of the new *comprador* class and Diem's bureaucracy.

The United States endorsed and encouraged the military build-up and repression, but it did not like the strange mélange of mandarin anticapitalism and Catholic feudalism which Diem jumbled together in his philosophy of personalism. Diem was a puppet, but a not perfectly tractable one. The United States did not appreciate the high margin of personal graft, nor did it like Diem's hostility toward accelerated economic development, nor his belief in state-owned companies. Ngo Dinh Nhu, his brother, regarded economic aid as a cynical means of dumping American surpluses, and the United States had to fight, though successfully, for the relaxation of restrictions on foreign investments and protection against the threat of nationalization. Ultimately Diem was content to complain and to hoard aid funds for purposes the United States thought dubious.

The United States thought of Vietnam as a capitalist state in Southeast Asia. This course condemned it to failure, but in April 1959, when Eisenhower publicly discussed Vietnam, "a country divided into two parts," and not two distinct nations, he stressed Vietnam's need to develop economically, and the way "to get the necessary capital is through private investments from the outside and through government loans," the latter, insofar as the United States was concerned, going to local capitalists.

1959–64: THE RESISTANCE IS REKINDLED

Every credible historical account of the origins of the armed struggle south of the 17th parallel treats it as if it were on a continuum from the war with the French of 1945–54, and as the effect rather than the cause of the Diem regime's frightful repression and accumulated internal economic and social problems. The resistance to Diem's officials had begun among the peasantry in a spontaneous manner, by growing numbers of persecuted political figures of every persuasion, augmented by Buddhists and Vietminh who returned to the villages to escape, and, like every successful guerrilla movement, it was based on the support of the peasantry for its erratic but ultimately irresistible momentum. On May 6th, 1959, Diem passed his famous Law 10/59, which applied the sentence of death to anyone committing murder, destroying to any extent houses, farms, or buildings of any kind, or means of transport, and a whole list of similar offenses. "Whoever belongs to an organization designed to help to prepare or perpetuate crimes . . . or takes pledges to do so, will be subject to the sentences provided." The regime especially persecuted former members of the Vietminh, but all opposition came under the sweeping authority of Diem's new law, and the number of political prisoners quadrupled between 1958 and the end of 1961. The resistance that spread did not originate from the north, and former Vietminh members joined the spontaneous local resistance groups well before the D.R.V. indicated any support for them. Only in 1960 did significant fighting spread throughout the country.

At the end of 1960 the United States claimed to have only 773 troops stationed there. By December 1965 there were at least fourteen major U.S. airbases in Vietnam, 166,000 troops, and the manpower was to more than double over the following year. This build-up violated the Geneva Accords, but that infraction is a fine point in light of the fact that the United States always had utter contempt for that agreement. In reality, the United States was now compelled to save what little it controlled of the south of Vietnam from the inevitable failure of its own policies.

It is largely pointless to deal with the subsequent events in the same detail, for they were merely a logical extension of the global policies of the United States before 1960. One has merely to juxtapose the newspaper accounts in the U.S. press against the official rationalizations cited in Washington to realize how very distant from the truth Washington was willing to wander to seek justification for a barbaric war against a small nation quite unprecedented in the history of modern times. To understand this war one must always place it in its contextual relationship and recall that the issues in Vietnam were really those of the future of U.S. power not only in Southeast Asia but throughout the entire developing world. In Vietnam the U.S. Government has vainly attempted to make vast power relevant to international social and political realities that had bypassed the functional conservatism of a nation seeking to save an old order with liberal rhetoric and, above all, with every form of military power available in its nonnuclear arsenal.

By 1960 it was apparent that Diem would not survive very long, a point that an abortive palace revolt of his own paratroop battalions emphasized on November 11th. When Kennedy came to office amidst great debates over military credibility and the need to build a limited-war capability, Vietnam inevitably became the central challenge to the intellectual strategists he brought to Washington. In May 1961, Kennedy and Dean Rusk denounced what they called D.R.V. responsibility for the growth of guerrilla activity in the south, a decision Rusk claimed the Communist Party of the D.R.V. made in May 1959 and reaffirmed in September of the following year. This tendentious reasoning, of course, ignored the fact that the prior September, Pham Van Dong again urged negotiations on the basis of reciprocal concessions in order to achieve unity without recourse to "war and force." By the fall two missions headed by Eugene Staley and the leading limited-war theorist, General Maxwell Taylor, went to Vietnam to study the situation. On October 18th Diem declared a state of emergency, and on November 16th Kennedy pledged a sharp increase in aid to the regime, which newspapers predicted would also involve large U.S. troop increases. During November the *Wall Street Journal*, for example, admitted that aid would be going to a regime characterized by "corruption and favoritism," and described the "authoritarian nature of the country" which allowed the National Liberation Front, formed at the end of December 1960, to build up a mass base among "the farmers who welcome an alternative to corrupt and ineffective appointees of the regime."

The U.S. Government could hardly admit that the problem in southern Vietnam was the people's revolt against the corruption of an oppressive regime that survived only with American guns and dollars, and not very well at that, and so it was necessary, while once again violating the Geneva Accords, to build up the myth of intervention from the D.R.V. At this time the U.S. Government effected a curious shift in its attitude toward the Geneva Accords, from denouncing or ignoring it to insisting that it bound the other side and, implicitly, that the United States had endorsed it. When asked about how a vast increase in U.S. military aid affected the agreement, Washington from this time on insisted, in Rusk's words, that "the primary question about the Geneva Accords is not how those Accords relate to, say, our military assistance program to south Vietnam. They relate to the specific, persistent, substantial, and openly proclaimed violations of those accords by the north Vietnamese. . . . The first question is, what does the north do about those accords?" "If the North Vietnamese bring themselves into full compliance with the Geneva Accords," Rusk stated on December 8th as he released the so-called White Paper, "there will be no problem on the part of South Vietnam or any one supporting South Vietnam." Only the prior month Ho publicly called for the peaceful reunification of the country via the terms of Geneva. Not surprisingly, Rusk never referred to the question of elections.

The U.S. White Paper of December 1961 was inept, and an excellent source of information for disproving nearly all the American claims of the time. It consisted of a mélange of data, case histories, and quotes from D.R.V. statements, most obviously out of context. As for China or

Russia supplying the N.L.F. with arms, the White Paper admitted "The weapons of the VC are largely French- or U.S.-made, or handmade on primitive forges in the jungle." Evidence ranged from South Vietnamese interrogation records to reproductions of human anatomy from a Chinese textbook to photos of medical equipment made in China and the cover of a private diary. The White Paper exhibited no military equipment and the long extracts from various D.R.V. congresses and publications revealed merely that the D.R.V. was officially committed to "struggle tenaciously for the implementation of the Geneva agreements" and "peaceful reunification of the fatherland." The State Department's incompetent case was less consequential than the renewed and frank exposition of the "domino" theory: if all of Vietnam chose the leadership of Ho and his party, the rest of Asia would "fall." Above all, as the American press acknowledged, if the United States did not intervene the shabby Diem regime would collapse without anything acceptable replacing it.

During early 1962 the United States announced and began the Staley Plan—Operation Sunrise—for razing existing villages and regrouping entire populations against their will; and in February created a formal command in Vietnam. Officially, to meet I.C.C. complaints, the United States reported 685 American soldiers were in Vietnam, but in fact reporters described the truth more accurately, and Washington intensified a long pattern of official deception of the American public. Yet the U.S. position was unenviable, for on February 27th Diem's own planes bombed his palace. This phase of the story need not be surveyed here—more pliable and equally corrupt men were to replace Diem. As one American officer in April 1962 reported of growing N.L.F. power, "When I arrived last September, the Vietcong were rarely encountered in groups exceeding four or five. Now they are frequently met in bands of forty to sixty."

On March 1st, while alleging D.R.V. responsibility for the war, Rusk declared it "all in gross violation of the Geneva Accords." The problem, he argued over the following years, came from the north. As for the D.R.V.'s appeal that the Geneva Conference be reconvened, he suggested, "There is no problem in South Vietnam if the other side would stay its hand. . . . I don't at the moment envisage any particular form of discussion." No later than March, American forces in Vietnam were actively locked in combat.

Despite propaganda of the lowest calibre which the State Department and White House issued, more authoritative statements from various Government agencies indicated reluctance to base planning on the fiction that the D.R.V. started the war in Vietnam. The Senate Committee on Foreign Relations report of January 1963 admitted that the N.L.F. "is equipped largely with primitive, antiquated and captured weapons." Despite the weakness of the N.L.F. in this regard against a regular army of well over 150,000, plus police, etc., "By 1961 it was apparent that the prospects for a total collapse in south Vietnam had begun to come dangerously close." American intervention had stayed that event. Speaking to the Senate Armed Services Committee in early March, General David Shoup, Commandant of the Marine Corps, freely admitted there was no correlation between the size of the N.L.F. and the alleged infiltrators from the north: "I don't agree that they come in there in the numbers that are down there." Not until July 1963 did the United States publicly and unequivocally claim that, for the first time, it had captured N.L.F. arms manufactured in Communist countries after 1954.

By the summer of 1963 it was obvious that the American Government and its ally Diem were headed toward military defeat in Vietnam and new and unprecedented political resistance at home. Diem's oppression of all political elements, his active persecution of the Buddhists, the failure of the strategic hamlet program, the utter incompetence of his drafted troops against far weaker N.L.F. forces the American press described in detail. At the beginning of September Washington was apparently bent on pressuring Diem but preserving him against mounting Buddhist protests, but as Kennedy admitted on September 9th as audible stirrings from senators were heard for the first time, "What I am concerned about is that Americans will get impatient and say, because they don't like events in Southeast Asia or they don't like the Government in Saigon, that we should withdraw." Quite simply, he stated four days later, "If it helps to win the war, we support it. What interferes with the war effort we oppose." The Americans would not sink with Diem.

On October 21st, after some weeks of similar actions on forms of economic aid, the U.S. Embassy in Saigon announced that it would terminate the pay for Diem's own special political army unless they went into the field. On October 30th this private guard was sent out of Saigon. The next day a military coup brought Diem's long rule to an end.

The United States recognized the new Minh coup on November 4th, amid disturbing reports of continued squabbling within its ranks. On the 8th Rusk confirmed that the mood in Washington was now tending toward winning military victory by rejecting a neutralist solution for Vietnam south of the 17th parallel, linking it to "far-reaching changes in North Vietnam," again insisting that the north was responsible for aggression. "The other side was fully committed—fully committed—in the original Geneva settlement of 1954 to the arrangements which provided for South Vietnam as an independent entity, and we see no reason to modify those in the direction of a larger influence of

North Vietnam or Hanoi in South Vietnam." The creation of this deliberate fiction of two Vietnams—North and South—as being the result of the Geneva Accords now indicated that the U.S. Government would seek military victory.

The new regimes were as unsatisfactory as the old one, and by mid-December the American press reported dissatisfaction in Washington over the dismal drift of the war. In his important dispatches in the *New York Times* at the end of 1963, David Halberstam described the failure of the strategic hamlet program, the corruption of Diem, the paralysis of Minh in these terms: "The outlook is that the situation will deteriorate unless the Government can wrest the initiative from the guerrillas. Unless it can, there appear to be only two likely alternatives. One is a neutralist settlement. The other is the use of United States combat troops to prop up the Government."

The drift toward a neutralist solution at the beginning of 1964 was so great that Washington sought to nip it in the bud. In his New Year's Message to the Minh regime, President Johnson made it clear that "neutralization of South Vietnam would only be another name for a Communist takeover. Peace will return to your country just as soon as the authorities in Hanoi cease and desist from their terrorist aggression." Peace would be acceptable to the Americans after total victory. To alter their losing course, they would escalate.

At the end of January, as the Khanh coup took over, one of the new ruler's grievances against his former allies was that some had surreptitiously used the French Government to seek a neutral political solution. During February, the *New York Times* reported that Washington was planning an attack on the north, with divided counsels on its extent or even its relevance to internal political-economic problems. The United States preferred air bombing and/or a blockade, because as Hanson Baldwin wrote on March 6th, "The waging of guerrilla war by the South Vietnamese in North Vietnam has, in fact, been tried on a small scale, but so far it has been completely ineffective."

On March 15th Johnson again endorsed the "domino" theory and avowed his resolution not to tolerate defeat. On March 26th McNamara in a major address stressed the "great strategic significance" of the issue, and Vietnam as "a major test case of communism's new strategy" of local revolution, one that might extend to all the world unless foiled in Vietnam. Behind the D.R.V., the Secretary of Defense alleged, stood China. The Americans rejected neutralism for Vietnam, reaffirmed aid to the Khanh regime, and darkly hinted at escalation toward the north. During these same days, for the first time in two decades key members of the Senate voiced significant opposition to a major foreign policy. It had become a tradition in the Cold War for Presidents to marshal support from Congress by creating crises, thereby defining the tone of

American foreign policy via a sequence of sudden challenges which, at least to some, vindicated their diabolical explanations. A "crisis" was in the making.

All of the dangers of the Vietnamese internal situation persisted throughout spring 1964. On July 24th the *New York Times* reported that Khanh was exerting tremendous pressures on the United States to take the war to the north, even by "liberating" it. During these same days the French, Soviet, and N.L.F. leaders joined U Thant in a new diplomatic drive to seek an end to the war by negotiations. Washington, for its part, resisted these pacific solutions.

On August 4th Johnson announced that North Vietnamese torpedo boats had wantonly attacked the U.S. destroyer *Maddox* in the Bay of Tonkin and in international waters, and as a result of repeated skirmishes since the 2nd he had ordered the bombardment of North Vietnamese installations supporting the boats. The following day he asked Congress to pass a resolution authorizing him to take all action necessary "to protect our Armed Forces." It was maudlin, fictional, and successful.

It was known—and immediately documented in *Le Monde*—that the United States had been sending espionage missions to the north since 1957—as Baldwin alluded the prior February—and that on July 30th South Vietnamese and U.S. ships raided and bombarded D.R.V. islands. It was too farfetched that D.R.V. torpedo boats would have searched out on the high seas the ships of the most powerful fleet in the world, without scoring any hits which the United States might show the skeptical world. On August 5th the press asked McNamara for his explanation of the events. "I can't explain them. They were unprovoked. . . . our vessels were clearly in international waters. . . . roughly 60 miles off the North Vietnamese coast." When asked whether reports of South Vietnamese attacks in the area during the prior days were relevant, McNamara demurred! "No, to the best of my knowledge, there were no operations during the period." In testimony before the Senate during the same days it emerged that U.S. warships were not sixty miles but three to eleven miles off D.R.V. territory, even though, like many states, the D.R.V. claimed a twelve-mile territorial limit. Over subsequent days more and more information leaked out so that the essential points of the D.R.V. case were confirmed, the long history of raids on the north revealed. By the end of September the entire fantasy was so implausible that the *New York Times* reported that the Defense Department was sending a team to Vietnam to deal with what were euphemistically described as "contradictory reports." They did not subsequently provide further details, for "contributing to the Defense Department's reticence was the secret mission of the two destroyers," a mission the *New York Times* described as espionage of various sorts.

The United States escalated in the hope that it could mobilize a Congress at home and sustain the Khanh regime in Vietnam, which nevertheless fell the following month. During these days the U.S. Government admitted that the war was now grinding to a total halt as the Vietnamese politicians in the south devoted all their energy to byzantine intrigues. With or without war against the D.R.V., the United States was even further from victory. In assessing the condition in the south a year after the downfall of Diem, the *New York Times* reported from Saigon that three years after the massive increase of the American commitment, and a year after Diem's demise, "the weakness of the Government [has] once again brought the country to the brink of collapse. . . . Once again many American and Vietnamese officials are thinking of new, enlarged commitments—this time to carry the conflict beyond the frontier of South Vietnam."

THE BOMBING OF THE D.R.V.

On December 20th, 1964, there was yet another coup in Saigon, and during the subsequent weeks the difficulties for the United States resulting from the court maneuvers among generals who refused to fight were compounded by the growing militancy of the Buddhist forces. By January of 1965 the desertion rate within the South Vietnamese Army reached 30 percent among draftees within six weeks of induction, and a very large proportion of the remainder would not fight. It was perfectly apparent that if anyone was to continue the war the United States would not only have to supply money, arms, and 23,000 supporting troops as of the end of 1964, but fight the entire war itself. During January, as well, a Soviet-led effort to end the war through negotiations was gathering momentum, and at the beginning of February Soviet Premier Kosygin, amidst American press reports that Washington in its pessimism was planning decisive new military moves, arrived in Hanoi.

On the morning of February 7th, while Kosygin was in Hanoi, American aircraft bombed the D.R.V., allegedly in response to an N.L.F. mortar attack on the Pleiku base in the south which cost eight American lives. There was nothing unusual in the N.L.F. attack, and every serious observer immediately rejected the official U.S. explanation, for the Government refused to state that the D.R.V. ordered the Pleiku action, but only claimed the D.R.V. was generally responsible for the war. The U.S. attack had been prepared in advance, Arthur Krock revealed on February 10th, and the *New York Times* reported that Washington had told several governments of the planned escalation before the 7th. The action was political, not military in purpose, a response to growing dissatisfaction at home and pressures abroad. It was already known that De Gaulle was contemplating a move to reconvene the Geneva Conference—which he attempted on the 10th, after D.R.V. urgings—and during·the subsequent weeks, as the United States threatened additional air strikes against the D.R.V., both Kosygin and U Thant vainly attempted to drag the U.S. Government to the peace table. In response, the Americans now prepared for vast new troop commitments.

On February 26th, the day before the State Department released its second White Paper, Rusk indicated willingness to consider negotiations only if the D.R.V. agreed to stop the war in the south for which he held it responsible. Hence there was no possibility of negotiating on premises which so cynically distorted the facts, and which even Washington understood to be false. "They doubt that Hanoi would be able to call off the guerrilla war," the *New York Times* reported of dominant opinion in Washington barely a week before the Rusk statement. The D.R.V. could not negotiate a war it did not start nor was in a position to end. The United States determined to intervene to save a condition in the south on the verge of utter collapse.

In its own perverse manner, the new White Paper made precisely these points. It ascribed the origins of the war, the "hard core" of the N.L.F., "many" of the weapons to the D.R.V. The actual evidence the Paper gave showed that 179 weapons, or less than 3 percent of the total captured from the N.L.F. in three years, were not definitely French, American, or homemade in origin and modification. Of the small number of actual case studies of captured N.L.F. members offered, the large majority were born south of the 17th parallel and had gone to the north after Geneva, a point that was readily admitted, and which disproved even a case based on the fiction—by now a permanent American premise —that Vietnam was two countries and that those north of an arbitrarily imposed line had no right to define the destiny of one nation. The tendentious case only proved total American responsibility for the vast new increase in the aggression.

Despite the growing pressure for negotiations from many sources, and because of them, by March the United States decided to implement the so-called McNamara-Bundy Plan to bring about an "honorable" peace by increasing the war. On March 2nd air strikes against the D.R.V. were initiated once more, but this time they were sustained down to this very day. There were incredulously received rumors of vast increases in troop commitments to as high as 350,000. Washington made an accurate assessment in March 1965 when it realized it could not expect to save Vietnam for its sphere of influence, and that peace was incompatible with its larger global objectives of stopping guerrilla and revolutionary upheavals everywhere in the world. Both McNamara and Taylor during March harked back to the constant theme that the United States was fighting in Vietnam "to halt Communist expansion in Asia." Peace would come, Johnson stated on March 13th, when "Hanoi is prepared

or willing or ready to stop doing what it is doing to its neighbors."
Twelve days later the President expressed willingness to grant a vast
development plan to the region—which soon turned out to be Eugene
Black's formula for increasingly specialized raw-materials output for the
use of the industrialized world—should the Vietnamese be ready to
accept the fiction of D.R.V. responsibility for the war.

It made no difference to the U.S. Government that on March 22nd
the N.L.F., and on April 8th the D.R.V., again called for negotiations
on terms which in fact were within the spirit of Geneva Accords the
United States had always rejected. It was less consequential that on
April 6th the official Japanese Matsumoto Mission mustered sufficient
courage to reject formally the thesis of D.R.V. responsibility for the war
in the south and its ability, therefore, to stop the Vietnamese there from
resisting the United States and its intriguing puppets. More significant
was the fact that, as it announced April 2nd, the Administration had
finally decided to send as many as 350,000 troops to Vietnam to attain
for the United States what the armies of Diem, Khanh, and others
could not—victory. The official position called for "peace," but in his
famous Johns Hopkins speech on April 7th Johnson made it clear that
"We will not withdraw, either openly or under the cloak of a meaning-
less agreement." Though he agreed to "unconditional discussions," he
made it explicit that these would exclude the N.L.F. and would be with
an end to securing "an independent South Vietnam," which is to say
permanent partition and a violation of the Geneva Accords. From this
time onward the United States persisted in distorting the negotiating
position of the D.R.V.'s four-point declaration and effectively ignored
the demand of the N.L.F. for "an independent state, democratic, peaceful and neutral." It refused, and has to this day, a voice for the N.L.F.
in any negotiations and insisted that the N.L.F. and D.R.V. had attached certain preconditions to negotiations which in fact did not exist
and which on August 3rd the N.L.F. again attempted to clarify—to
no avail.

Experience over subsequent years has shown again and again that
the words "peace" and "negotiations" from official U.S. sources were
from 1964 onward always preludes to new and more intensive military
escalation.

To the U.S. Government the point of Vietnam is not peace but
victory, not just in Vietnam but for a global strategy which it has expressed first of all in Vietnam but at various times on every other
continent as well. Johnson's own words in July 1965 stressed this global
perspective while attributing the origins of the war to the D.R.V. and,
ultimately China.

> Its goal is to conquer the south, to defeat American power and to extend
> the Asiatic dominion of Communism.

And there are great stakes in the balance. . . .

Our power, therefore, is a very vital shield. If we are driven from the field in Vietnam, then no nation can ever again have the same confidence in American promises or American protection. . . . We did not choose to be the guardians at the gate, but there is no one else.

One does not have to approve of this vision to accept it as an accurate explanation of why the U.S. Government is willing to violate every norm of civilized behavior to sustain the successive corrupt puppet governments in the south. But any careful reading of the declarations of Rusk and McNamara in the months preceding and following this statement reveals that it was not the Geneva Accords but rather SEATO and, more critically, the survival of U.S. power in a world it can less and less control that have defined the basis of U.S. policy in Vietnam. This official policy, as Rusk expounded it again in March 1966, is that Vietnam is "the testing ground" for wars of liberation that, if successful in one place, can spread throughout the world. When, as in January 1966, Undersecretary of State George Ball explained Vietnam "is part of a continuing struggle to prevent the Communists from upsetting the fragile balance of power through force or the threat of force," in effect he meant the ability of the United States to contain revolutionary nationalist movements, Communist and non-Communist alike, unwilling to accept U.S. hegemony and dedicated to writing their own history for their own people.

Any objective and carefully prepared account of the history of Vietnam must conclude with the fact that the United States must bear the responsibility for the torture of an entire nation since the end of the Second World War. The return of France to Vietnam, and its ability to fight for the restoration of a colony, was due to critical political decisions made in Washinton in 1945, and the later repression depended on financial and military aid given to France by the United States. First as a passive senior partner, and then as the primary party, the United States made Vietnam an international arena for the Cold War, and it is a serious error to regard the war in Vietnam as a civil conflict, or even secondarily as a by-product of one—for in that form it would hardly have lasted very long against a national and radical movement that the vast majority of the Vietnamese people always have sustained.

The U.S. Government responded to its chronic inability to find a viable internal alternative to the Vietminh and the N.L.F. by escalating the war against virtually the entire nation. To escape certain defeat time and time again, it violated formal and customary international law by increasing the scale of military activity. The United States met each overture to negotiate, whether it came from the Vietnamese, the French, or the Russians, by accelerated warfare in the hope of attaining its unique ends through military means rather than diplomacy.

Ultimately, the United States has fought in Vietnam with increasing intensity to extend its hegemony over the world community and to stop every form of revolutionary movement which refuses to accept the predominant role of the United States in the direction of the affairs of its nation or region. Repeatedly defeated in Vietnam in the attainment of its impossible objective, the U.S. Government, having alienated most of its European allies and a growing sector of its own nation, is attempt- to prove to itself and the world that it remains indeed strong enough to define the course of global politics despite the opposition of a small, poor nation of peasants. On the outcome of this epic contest rests the future of peace and social progress in the world for the remainder of the twentieth century, not just for those who struggle to overcome the legacy of colonialism and oppression to build new lives, but for the people of the United States themselves.

FOR FURTHER READING

* J. William Fulbright. *The Arrogance of Power*. New York: Random House, 1966.
* George McTurnan Kahin and John W. Lewis. *The United States in Vietnam*. Rev. ed. New York: Dell, 1969.
* Gabriel Kolko. *The Roots of American Foreign Policy*. Boston: Beacon Press, 1969.
John T. McAllister, Jr., and Paul Mus. *Vietnam*. New York: Harper & Row, 1970.
* *The Pentagon Papers*. One-volume ed., New York: Bantam, 1971; five-volume ed., Boston: Beacon Press, 1971–72.

THE UNITED STATES AND CHINA

BARBARA TUCHMAN

As Robert Lasch and Gabriel Kolko have pointed out, American foreign policy has little to do with democratic principles or ideology, despite Woodrow Wilson's 1917 pledge to "make the world safe for democracy." Since that time the United States has almost consistently supported governments that would maintain the *status quo* for American interests and has undermined proposals for social reform and political change that threatened to establish true democracy. In China American intervention prolonged a civil war but could not stem the force of revolution.

In the following essay, first published in 1972, a year after President Richard M. Nixon visited China, Barbara Tuchman underscores the illusions and failures that led to the rupture of American-Chinese relations in 1949. Throughout the 1930's and 1940's America had supported the corrupt and fascistic Chiang Kai-shek regime despite clear indications that Chiang lacked the support of the Chinese people. Insensitivity and a misconceived policy of self-interest would not allow the United States to work with Mao Tse-tung and the Communists, who in 1949 finally ousted Chiang and took control of mainland China. In the 1940's most Americans still believed in a monolithic Communism, dictated and controlled by Moscow and strictly followed by all Communists the world over. We have at last learned that no ideology is totally inflexible when actually put into practice. Efforts have recently been made by the United States to relate officially to the mainland government of China—which it ignored from 1949 until President Nixon's visit in 1971. We may hope that greater understanding on the part of an educated American public will pave the way for a more enlightened foreign policy in the future.

Barbara Tuchman, "The United States and China," *The Colorado Quarterly*, 21 (Summer, 1972), 5–17.

□ □ □

Whenone proposes to talk about the United States and China, everyone immediately wants to know what one thinks of the President's trip. I will come to that later, but first I think that what a historian can more usefully do is to tell you something of the past that led to the twenty-five years of broken relations and profound mutual hostility through which we have just passed. In 1954—to remind you of the attitude of those years—*Life* magazine described Chou En-lai, Mr. Nixon's recent host, as "a political thug, a ruthless intriguer, a conscienceless liar, a saber-toothed political assassin." At the same time the Chinese were regularly denouncing us as vicious imperialists and aggressors, brutal oppressors, and of course paper tigers. All this name calling was not funny, but a tragic testimony to the failure of our China policy. Considering that the failure led to two wars—in Korea and Vietnam—the damage done, as much morally to this country as physically to Asia, will leave a long-enduring mark.

Our century and a half of relationship with China was broken off in 1949, four years after the end of World War II, with the crash of Chiang Kai-shek's government and his replacement by the Communists. The break marked a wasted effort and the utter defeat of our wartime objective in Asia. That objective was a stable, united democratic China, strong enough to be able to fill the vacuum that would be left by the defeat of Japan, a China that, as the fourth pillar of the United Nations structure, would keep the peace of Asia in the postwar world. This was Roosevelt's constant aim. Stilwell was less deceived about possibilities, but both he and FDR, for all that they so miserably misunderstood each other, kept one fundamental goal in mind: that China's vast population, the famous 500 million of that day, between a fifth and a quarter of the world's people, must be on our side in the difficult future. That future is now the present, and the Chinese cannot be said to be on our side in any sense of underlying alliance or common aim. There has been reopening of dialogue, to be sure, which is certainly welcome and long overdue, but let us not suppose that it will blossom into friendship overnight or that it is based on anything but a very precariously balanced concept of mutual expediency.

In World War II we had technically won a victory in Asia insofar as we defeated the enemy Japan, but we lost the goal that would have made sense of the victory—a China on our side. The reason for the failure was that we overlooked, or failed to take into consideration, the Chinese revolution. As a result, in the last twenty-two years we have fought two more wars in Asia, one of them the longest, wrongest, least successful belligerent action in our history.

An American foreign policy that brought us to this predicament, dislike abroad and alienation at home, must have something wrong with it. As a historian I believe three main factors can be discerned as responsible: first, the illusion not only that we should, but that we can, shape the destiny of other peoples in conformity with our own; second, the corruption of power, and the greater corruption of becoming a Great Power, which has transformed the United States from a progressive into a reactionary nation in world affairs; third, the persistent failure to form policy on the basis of available knowledge and information.

The first factor is a product of the Christian, especially Protestant, missionary urge to confer our ways, our values, and our methods upon those we choose to regard as heathen, ignoring the fact that they have social and cultural values of their own as valid as ours and older, which may well entitle them to regard *us* as heathen. The Chinese, in fact, have always regarded all foreigners as barbarians and themselves as superior, in token of which no foreigner could approach the Emperor during the last dynasty without performing the kowtow, prostrate on the floor. Their tragedy during their humiliating century of foreign penetration from about 1840 to 1940 was that somehow, inexplicably, superior values could not be made to prevail over barbarian force.

The American missionary impulse that was an essential part of this penetration was based on the twin illusion, as regards Asia, (a) that our ways were applicable and (b) that they were wanted. The motive is beneficent but the attitude is arrogant, and the beneficence is never unmixed. It was intended to work both ways, as much to the benefit of the donor as the recipient. Originally China's vastness excited the missionary impulse; it appeared as the land of the future whose masses, when converted, offered promise of Christian and even English-speaking dominion of the world. Disregarding the social and ethical structure which the Chinese found suitable, the missionaries wanted them to change to one in which the individual was sacred and the democratic principle dominant, whether or not these concepts were relevant to China's way of life. Inevitably the missionary, witnessing China's decay in the nineteenth century, took this as evidence that China could not rule herself and that her problems could only be solved by foreign help.

Along with this went the alluring prospect of 400 million (as they were then reckoned) customers; if each added a half inch to the length of his shirt-tail and a half ounce of oil to the lamps of China, our commerce would reap grand and illimitable profits. This too provided an illusion, now laid to rest in the textbooks as the "Myth of the China Market."

While that myth was vanishing, another myth was replacing it:

that China, following the Revolution of 1911 that overthrew the Manchus, was a developing democracy just like ours. Because Dr. Sun Yat-sen and many of his associates in the new Chinese republic were Christian and Westernized, in many cases American-educated, Americans at once assumed that 1911 was China's Bunker Hill and Valley Forge, so to speak. The American public on the whole wanted to believe what the missionaries were always promising, that China of the 400 million was about to transform itself into that desirable and familiar thing, a democracy. When a rebel leader in Hankow, out of Oriental politeness, which believes in telling people what presumably they want to hear, said to reporters that "the object of our revolt is to make the government of China like that of America," nothing could have seemed more natural to American readers. We habitually forget that Thomas Jefferson did not operate in Asia. Americans tend to think of all people in the Near and Far East and Africa as so many young birds waiting with mouths open for democracy to be dropped in. This is a dangerous misconception.

It was crowned by the advent of Chiang Kai-shek. When, as the successor to Sun Yat-sen, he finally established a national government in 1928, the event was hailed by China's well-wishers as the completion of the democratic process. But Chiang Kai-shek's rise to national power was accomplished at the cost of a profound split between right and left within his party, the Kuomintang.

The left, under the controlling influence of the Communists who were then members of the Kuomintang, was dedicated to carrying out the social revolution delayed since the great Taiping Rebellion of the 1850s, China's failed French Revolution. In 1927 Mao Tse-tung and his comrades were busy organizing rent strikes and antilandlord demonstrations among the peasants, and Mao was promising that soon, all over China, "several hundred million peasants will rise like a tornado and rush forward along the road to revolution." This was hardly calculated to win the support of landlord and capitalist families, whose adherence Chiang Kai-shek needed. To achieve power he had to have the revenue and loans he could only obtain in alliance with capitalism. The Communists, however, besides organizing the peasants were equally active among the proletariat and labor unions of Shanghai. Chiang was determined that that great metropolis of commerce, banking, and foreign trade should not fall under left-wing control as Hankow already had. Shanghai was where the break had to be made.

On the night of April 12–13, 1927, Chiang's forces carried out a bloody purge of the left, disarming and hunting down all who could be found and killing more than three hundred. The Shanghai purge and the choice it represented were as portentous an event as any in modern history. The Kuomintang Revolution was turned from Red to Right. Chiang's coup was both turning point and point of no return. He was now on the way to unity, but he had fixed the terms of an underlying disunity that would become his nemesis.

Foreigners were reassured. The missionaries and educators and advisers, eager to believe that their ideas were taking root, persuaded themselves that the Kuomintang, with its source in the Christian Sun Yat-sen, was the sincerely progressive force that would at last end civil strife and bring good government to China. They, and under their influence the American public, saw in the Chinese a people rightly struggling to be free and assumed that because they were struggling for sovereignty, they were also struggling for democracy.

That the formal unity Chiang had achieved was superficial, that his government rested insecurely on power deals and pay-offs, that for the sake of alliance with landlords and capitalists it had turned against its origins and taken the road of repression and reaction, including a White Terror that claimed an estimated one million victims—all this was given little attention, the more so as Chiang Kai-shek was a Christian, one of the most important and overlooked factors in the American delusion about China.

Chiang was converted to Christianity in order to marry into the wealth, influence, and connections of the Soong family, which had been Christian for several generations. His wife was the attractive, sophisticated, thoroughly Westernized, American-educated Mei-Ling Soong, a graduate of Wellesley. She was to have immeasurable effect on the image of China that came through to Americans. Once when Stilwell, at the height of his frustration, was trying to analyze what Chiang had working for him vis-à-vis the Americans, he wrote a list of factors and put down as number one, "Mme. Chiang's Wellesley diploma." This was not because Wellesley was anything so special (I speak as a graduate of another place), but because Madame with her American schooling and perfect English made China seem more familiar, more comprehensible to us than in fact it was.

The missionaries and the church groups in America rallied to the Chiangs in self-interested loyalty because the Chiangs' Christianity at the helm of China provided such gratifying proof of the validity of the missionary effort. They overpraised Chiang and once committed to his perfection regarded any suggestion of blemish as inadmissible. "China now has the most enlightened, patriotic, and able rulers in her history," stated the *Missionary Review of the World*. If the leaders of the new China were products of Western influence, surely this indicated that the West could indeed shape the destiny of the East. It was a powerful and flattering idea.

By now were present in force the two chief illusions about China: one that pictured her as our ward, and the second that pictured the Chinese as just like us only a little behind, but coming along nicely toward political democracy and the Bill of Rights. These illusions were given classic expression by two great American presidents, Woodrow Wilson and Franklin Roosevelt. In 1921 in the course of a great famine relief program for China organized in the United States under missionary influence, Wilson told the public, "To an unusual degree the Chinese people look to us for counsel and for effective leadership." As an expression of American self-delusion, this has never been surpassed. The Chinese themselves never confused material aid, which was what they looked to America for, with either counsel or leadership.

Roosevelt's statement was made in 1943 in the midst of World War II. At the time Stilwell was urging that Chiang Kai-shek must be told, not asked [to deliver] military performance in return for Lend-Lease. In reproof, Roosevelt wrote to General Marshall, his Chief of Staff, to say that the head of a great state could not be treated like that. "Chiang Kai-shek has come up the hard way," he wrote, "to become undisputed leader of 400 million people and to create in a very short time throughout China what it took us a couple of centuries to attain."

Now it is true that the Chinese people had a cultural unity older and stronger than anything in the United States and a tremendous cohesion that enabled them to withstand bad government. But the idea that Chiang's leadership was undisputed or that in only fifteen harassed and embattled years he had obtained the same degree of national consent and representative government as in the United States was a fantasy. Nor was it a harmless one, for it allowed America to rest policy on an already collapsing base.

The war, of course, confirmed the image of China as one of us. Since China was resisting Japan, a fascist aggressor, and since fascism was opposed to democracy, China must therefore be a democracy. This syllogism became dogma when we entered the war as China's ally. It was the version presented to the American public and endlessly and effectively proclaimed by China's propagandists from Mme. Chiang down. Yet even before the war it had been clear enough to a sober historian, Whitney Griswold, future president of Yale, that Chiang's regime, as he wrote in 1938, was a "fascist dictatorship." It was exasperatingly clear to every American who worked in China under the conditions of a police state during the war. Stilwell used to mutter in his diary about the strange incompatibility of the American effort to support a government that was just like the government we were fighting in Germany. He called Chiang Kai-shek "Peanut" and referred to his hilltop residence as "Peanut's Berchtesgaden."

Throughout the war our endeavor was to supply, sustain, and support China and so energize her war effort as to enable her to contain and ultimately defeat the Japanese, a huge occupation force of over a million men, on the mainland. This was Stilwell's mission. The purpose was not of course eleemosynary. The object was to utilize Chinese, instead of American, manpower for the war on the mainland. In those unsophisticated days it was a fixed principle of our policy not to fight a war on the mainland of Asia. In the end the attempt to mobilize China was in vain. The Chinese concept of war was not ours; the impulse to reform and energize the army was not China's. The enormous effort that Stilwell commanded, the wealth of arms, supplies, and money poured into China through Lend-Lease, the valiant airlift flown for three years over the Hump through the worst flight conditions in the world, all were wasted. Stilwell himself recognized that to remake an army without remaking the political system from which it sprang was impossible. To reform such a system, he wrote, it must first be torn to pieces.

That unpleasant risk the American Government was unwilling to contemplate, although the likelihood of collapse was becoming more and more obvious in China. We had saddled ourselves with support of Chiang and, fearing the alternatives, could not summon the resolution to enlarge our options. Repeatedly our foreign service officers, who made up the best-informed foreign service in China, advised against unqualified support of an already outworn regime which in any free election would have been repudiated by 80 percent of the voters. For America to remain tied to such a regime, as one of the Embassy staff wrote, was a policy of "indolent short term expediency."

The terrible dilemma was that the only alternative appeared to be the Communists. If Chaing had long ago stolen their program, and introduced reforms, lowered taxes and land rents, loosened his repressive measures, opened the one-party government to other groups, widened his base of support, or made any real progress toward the original Three Principles of the Revolution, results might have been different. But the Kuomintang had failed its mandate, and by now the Communists, entrenched in the north, were the only effectively organized rival.

This was the situation that faced us when the Cold War succeeded World War II, and communism replaced fascism as the menace. To detach ourselves from Chiang under the circumstances now appeared more risky than ever, besides [being] certain to raise [a] domestic outcry. All the evidence showed that his government was a losing proposition—powerless, corrupt, and engaged in a prolonged suicide in which the only sign of life was preparation to fight the Communists. We clung to him, however, partly from old illusions and a lethargic refusal to rethink, partly under the very effective pressure of the China Lobby and the Red-scaremongers at home, but mostly from fear of disturbing the status quo and *because* he was anti-Communist. The attachment would have made sense if our client, which was after all the legal government, had also been an *effective* government rooted in national consent. But there is little virtue in a client being anti-Communist if he is at the same time rotting from within.

Nevertheless we did our best to sustain him. We ferried his troops in their race with the Communists to retain control of North China and Manchuria from the Japanese. We continued to send Chiang Kai-shek arms, money, military advisers, and other forms of support. Since at the same time we were endeavoring to mediate between Nationalists and Communists in the hope of preserving our goal of a firm united China after the war, these measures on behalf of one side in China's civil conflict profoundly antagonized the other side, who were soon to be the new rulers of China. It was at this time that our decisions on "the wrong side of history"—to use George Kennan's phrase—were made. As the Communists saw it, our aid to a discredited, failing regime was prolonging the civil war in a country desperately weary of wars and misgovernment. America became in their eyes the guardian of reaction, the associate of landlords and aggressors, and the chief representative of all the old evils of foreign penetration. Our position was transformed from friend to enemy.

We had in fact chosen counterrevolution and made ourselves the ally of the *ancien régime*. We were locked into this position by the second factor of our foreign policy, the fact that since reaching world power in the early years of this century we have joined the Bourbons of history. This once brave young republic, the nation Lincoln called the "last best hope of earth," founded in the New World in conscious rejection of the past, had become a status quo power. Our only policy was to preserve the status quo everywhere as a fancied guarantee of safety. Fearful of political change, afraid to move with history, we clutched in desperate attachment to decrepit and outworn regimes which, lacking roots in popular consent, could not stand on their own feet without our support. This was as true of the Nationalist Government under Chiang Kai-shek as of the ally in Saigon in whom we now place our support.

In China in 1949 the Nationalist Government finally collapsed, and Chiang Kai-shek decamped for Formosa, leaving the mainland to the reign of a new revolution. Our long support of Chiang was now left an empty mockery. Worse than wrong, it had been unsuccessful. It certainly had not succeeded in containing communism.

Meanwhile, Mao had become more doctrinaire, hardened in his view of the world as divided into two opposing camps—socialism and capitalist-imperialism—destined by nature for conflict. That, as Mao insisted, was Marxist law from which there was no escape. The United States, no longer the running dog of the imperialist, but now the arch-imperialist itself, was the prime source of evil, the kind of figure whom the Middle Ages (also doctrinaire) would have called Anti-Christ. As such we could only be regarded by the Chinese as a foe dedicated to their destruction whose every move must arouse the most profound suspicion.

The Chinese appeared to us in exactly the same light. Our policy was in the hands of John Foster Dulles, every bit as doctrinaire as Mao, who regarded communism as a monstrous octopus whose grasping tentacles must be instantly chopped off the minute one appeared. He was abetted by the hot air of McCarthyism, whipped up by a mountebank as cynical as Dulles was priestly, who simply discovered anticommunism to be a good ploy. The American public allowed itself to be gulled, blackmailed, and terrorized into a hysteria of denunciation and witch-hunts, informing on colleagues and wrecking careers. Communist subversion and Communist plots were made the convenient answer to all of the vague fears generated by the Bomb.

For total victory had brought us not self-confidence but anxiety. In the nuclear age Americans felt for the first time what Europeans had always lived with—the possibility of attack. This was the first great shock. Then in 1949, the most populous country in the world, the neighbor of Soviet Russia in Asia, our one-time protégé, our favorite ally in World War II, was taken over by the Communists. That was the second shock. Someone had to be blamed, and so followed the hysteria of McCarthyism in the fifties.

Out of these attitudes on the part of both China and the United States came the Korean War and the Quemoy-Matsu crisis and Dulles brinkmanship and the Taiwan treaty committing the United States, in one of the greatest absurdities of foreign policy ever self-inflicted by a great power, to the defense of a discredited, impotent government in exile—and from there, following the same track, to Vietnam with all its consequences.

I come now to the third factor. We do not choose the Francos and Greek colonels and Chiang Kai-sheks and Diems and Kys out of ignorance of their real nature or misjudgment of their strength. Our information is excellent; our foreign service is, or was, knowledgeable and careful, our intelligence reasonably accurate, at least when the agents confine themselves to intelligence and stay out of operations. Our policy-makers could be well informed if they read and digested the reports and, more important, thought about what they had read. Evidently they do not. Between informants in the field and policy-makers in the capital lies a gulf whitened by the bones of failed and futile policies of the past.

The pile accumulates by repetition. After the Russian Revolution we waited sixteen years before recognizing the Soviet Government, a lapse without discernible benefit to anyone. It certainly did not contain the communism of that time. Learning nothing from the experience, we have now allowed twenty-three years to go by before being pushed by history—and power politics—to open relations with Communist China. This second lapse, of which the war in Vietnam has been part, cannot be said to have accomplished anything but damage to everyone—to the Vietnamese, a people who have never done us any harm, and to ourselves. Their country has been wrecked and ours afflicted by a widespread and increasing mistrust of government, all in the name of anticommunism. Now, suddenly, we have decided to deal with Chinese communism although it is the same communism whose potential for expansion we have fought for eight years in Vietnam to arrest. It would appear, then, that the purpose of the war was invalid, or the danger overrated, which is not much comfort for those who died. If we can work with Chinese communism today, why not eight, ten, or twenty year ago?

Fear of communism, which is essentially the fear of the property-owner for the property-taker, has been the key to the trouble in our foreign policy. If we are so genuinely confident of our own system, why do we need to fear communism so? Despite Mr. Khrushchev, the Communists are not going to bury us, nor we them. In the meantime, why can we not allow a different system to others, whose needs are different, whose position in history is different? As China's is, for one, at least in the physical needs of the people. A reporter in Canton recently quoted a Mrs. Wang, now living in the most meager circumstances in two rooms with her family of five, but on *shore* not on a river boat like generations of her ancestors. "Life in the old days was simply impossible," she said. "My father and older brother died of starvation and so did all of my brother's family.

Surely China had a right to its revolution, as no doubt did Hanoi, which does not mean that it would be right for *us*. But why must we always think of these things in absolute terms, as wrong *per se* if wrong for us? What is unacceptable to us might be necessary for them. If there is anything I have learned through my work, it is that there are few absolutes in history.

I have not personally seen the changes in China since 1949, but I think it is safe to take it from the reports of visitors that the mass of Chinese are better off than they were, in terms of material welfare if not political liberty. For those who for generations have been undernourished, overworked, and overtaxed, enough to eat may well be more important than political liberty and civil rights. Judging from all the documentaries and live news pictures of Chinese life we have seen in recent weeks, there is a regimentation and Big Brother thought control over there which none of us could stand for one week, least of all the Radical Left, who are so given to screaming their heads off about oppression in American society. But we have different traditions, different backgrounds, and are accustomed to different liberties than the Chinese, especially in the area of individual rights. We cannot decide for them what values they should live by.

Personally, I think it unlikely that they will succeed in developing a new "Maoist man," in whom personal desires and ambitions have been replaced by dedication to the communal good. Mao may imagine he is doing it, but if he were to come back ten years after he dies, I imagine he would find a few surprises. I doubt that Maoism will prove to be a fixed condition for China. A nation that has undergone in the last decade the "let a hundred flowers bloom" experiment and then its repression, then the explosion of the Cultural Revolution and then its reversal, cannot be said to be in a state of perfect equilibrium.

I would not venture to predict how China will develop in the next quarter century any more than I would for ourselves. Something is always waiting in the wings to give history a twist in an unexpected direction. I have learned not to predict, because human behavior, in states as in individuals, does not follow the signposts of logic.

As for the trend initiated by the Peking visit, I think it is to the good: first, because it is a recognition of realities, which is always better than make-believe; second, because it expands two sets of dual confrontation, the United States versus Russia and China versus Russia, into a triangle, which makes more room for maneuver.

I am not impressed by all the wailing on the Right about losing the trust of our good friends in Taiwan, Saigon, and Tokyo—I believe they also throw in the Philippines, Thailand, South Korea, and a few others. This is nonsense. The relations of these nations or regimes with us are not based on trust and confidence but on necessity and self-interest. If they do not like our making contact with China, if it has implications that make them nervous, they have very little choice of another protector. But if they are moved toward making deals of their own and toward less dependence on the United States, that, I think, can only be beneficial to them and to us. The idea that the policy of the United States must be tied forever to the tail of Taiwan is hardly sensible. It is an alliance with Rip Van Winkle. Saigon is an alliance with the grave.

Undeniably we are moving away from the spirit of our commitment to Taiwan, but since history is dynamite, not static, that obviously could not last forever—and the Nationalist Chinese would have been foolish if they supposed it could. The treaty has a clause providing for cancellation by either party on one year's notice. Until then it is unlikely that the clause requiring us to defend them militarily will be called upon, because I doubt if the mainland Chinese will attempt to retrieve Taiwan by force. That would upset all kinds of apple carts, and they would hardly have invited the president of the United States to China if a military adventure—and challenge—of that kind was what they had in mind.

As for our friends in Japan, those worthy people who gave us Pearl Harbor, with whom not so long ago we were locked in a death struggle, the idea that they are necessarily our natural partner, whose tender trust in us we must under no account disturb by recognizing the existence of China, seems to me even more peculiar. The relationship we created with Japan, using them as a kind of advance buffer while they relied on our arms, may have worked so long as we were fixed in a position of rigid hostility to Communist China. But lacking a genuine bond of common roots and language and democratic tradition, as we had for instance with Great Britain, it was opportunist and artificial and could not have remained static. We may as well recognize that the future of Asia will be determined by China as well as, if not more than, by Japan, and it would be the most simple-minded stupidity on our part to choose permanent sides and commit ourselves to either one to the exclusion of the other.

The interesting thing that has been happening lately in international affairs, it seems to me—and I may be imagining it, or sensing something that is not yet at the conscious level, certainly not yet formulated—is a kind of approaching recognition that we are all really in the same boat, in danger of being overturned by environmental disaster; that the enemy is not so much each other as it is the common enemy of all: unrestrained growth and pollution. Perhaps the relaxation in international relations, if there is such, is a kind of subconscious preparation to deal with this state of affairs.

FOR FURTHER READING

Warren I. Cohen. *America's Response to China.* New York: John Wiley & Sons, 1971.

David Mozingo. *China's Foreign Policy and the Cultural Revolution.* IREA Project Interim Report No. 1 (March 1970). Ithaca, N.Y.

Tang Tsou. *America's Failure in China, 1941–1950.* Chicago: University of Chicago Press, 1963.

THE MIDDLE EAST— MYTHS AND REALITIES

J. WILLIAM FULBRIGHT

In the Middle East today, material interests and dynamic ideologies clash: the desire for oil and oil profits, Great Power rivalries, Arab nationalism, the demands of desperate refugees, the passion of Jews for their national home. Conflict has centered on the small strip of land once known as Palestine, the ancient home of the Jews, (from which most of them were expelled by the Romans in 70 A.D. Palestine, although briefly conquered by Christian European crusaders, was held for more than a thousand years by Moslem Arabs and Turks. In our day it has become the territory of a new Jewish state, Israel. Since World War II Israel and its Arab neighbors have fought four wars. Bombings, raids, and counterraids have become a part of everyday life, and no solution is in sight. Jews and Arabs are making demands upon each other that simply cannot be met. The interests and aspirations of both are legitimate, but they are incompatible.

The decline of the Ottoman Empire set the conditions for the present controversy. Since the sixteenth century the Ottoman Turks had ruled Palestine as part of a multinational empire, which at its height ranged across northern Africa, east through Arabia, and northwest through Europe almost to Vienna. By the early nineteenth century, however, the Turks were losing control. Diverse elements asserted themselves and demanded national autonomy or independence, while the Great Powers of Europe competed for dominion over sections of the disintegrating empire. World War I completed the process of fragmentation. The Turks, who had been on the losing side, reorganized themselves into a modern nation-state; the

Arabs (with British encouragement) set up their own states; and
the French and the British took over Syria and Palestine, respectively,
as "mandates" under the League of Nations.

Many Jews, like Theodor Herzl, had discovered that "in countries
where we have lived for centuries we are still cried down as strangers."
In the late nineteenth century, a number of European Jews, faced
with rising anti-Semitism and pogroms in Tsarist Russia, founded the
movement called Zionism. Spurred as well by idealism and hope,
they began to "return" to Palestine, where they purchased land from
the Arab inhabitants and settled in cooperative communities to
cultivate the soil. The settlements expanded, and Zionism attracted
influential supporters in Europe and the United States. In 1917,
in the midst of World War I, the British Foreign Secretary, Arthur
Balfour, announced that his government viewed "with favour the
establishment in Palestine of a national home for the Jewish people."
Though vague as to details (the British were aiding Arab movements
as well), the Balfour Declaration marked a step toward the
achievement of Zionist goals.

But the Arab inhabitants could not share the Zionist dream,
nor could they willingly subscribe to the Balfour Declaration; rather,
they saw the Jewish entry into Palestine as an incursion upon their
territory. As the Jewish population grew, so did the hostility of the
Arabs who dreaded becoming a minority in their own country. During
the period of British rule between the two world wars, friction
between Jews and Arabs broke forth in sporadic violence.

After World War II and the Nazi slaughter of six million Jews,
the United Nations sought to bring about an equitable settlement
and, in a moment of agreement between the United States and the
Soviet Union, decided to partition Palestine into a Jewish and an
Arab state, Israel and Jordan. The Arabs refused to acquiesce and
resisted by arms what they believed to be a wrongful attempt to carve
up their territory. They lost the war and, for reasons that are still
subject to controversy, almost a million of them fled from Palestine
to the neighboring countries, where they and their children have
remained ever since. This initial Israeli victory was followed by other
wars, notably in 1956, 1957, and 1973, while border and guerrilla
skirmishes have been continuous.

Israel, which came into existence in 1948, stands today as the
national homeland of the Jews, the only state in the world that has a
policy of unlimited Jewish immigration, no matter what the source.
Zionists and many sympathizers believe that Israel must live in
full territorial integrity, that there must be a place in the world
where Jews *belong*.

But Arabs and Jews live uneasily with each other. Arabs, who have never recognized the legitimacy of Israel in principle, also present specific grievances. In the Six-Day War of 1967, Israel captured and later incorporated a good deal of Arab territory, including the Jordanian sections of Jerusalem, and it insists that, whatever future arrangements are made, Jerusalem is the holy city of the Jews and must remain in Jewish hands. The Arabs want all the lands returned before they will consider recognition of Israel, but (apart from Jerusalem) the Israelis will not return the lands until they obtain recognition. Another grievance is that of the Arab refugees of 1948 who still live in camps in other countries: The Israelis contend that Arab nations must take care of "their own" people, but the Arabs demand that Israel readmit the wanderers; and for their part the refugees have developed an increasingly nationalist consciousness of themselves as "Palestinians." Finally, Israel's policy of unlimited Jewish immigration seems to threaten all the Arabs, who fear that eventually Israel's population will grow too large for its territory (about the size of Vermont) and that the Jews will of necessity seek additional lands from their neighbors. Arab extremists demand that Israel curtail immigration, give up its unique character, and allow itself to be incorporated into a multinational Palestine. Some Arabs have vowed to fight until all the Jews have been tossed into the sea.

Cooler heads look upon such threats as mere bombast, and more responsible spokesmen, like Anwar Sadat of Egypt, have suggested that Israel would be recognized if it would return Egyptian territory acquired in 1967. The Israelis, however, though they would like to live in harmony with their neighbors, still have vivid memories of the holocaust of the 1940's, and they dare not surrender land without a guarantee that the Arabs will allow them to live in peace. The activities of such guerrilla bands as Al Fatah and the Popular Front for the Liberation of Palestine, which have included the hijacking of planes and terrorist raids on Israeli citizens and territory, have undermined the efforts of the moderates. Israeli leaders will not allow themselves to be blackmailed into any political settlement; they are, moreover, suspicious of so-called moderate Arabs and believe that the guerrillas and extremists represent the true sentiments of the Arab world.

Complicating the problems of the Jews and Arabs are the positions of the United States and Russia, which have involved themselves in Middle Eastern politics. The Russians traditionally have sought some influence in the Middle East and entry into the Mediterranean. The Americans, have become involved chiefly as a result of the influence of U.S. oil companies and American citizens of Jewish heritage. During the past few years Secretary of State Henry Kissinger has made numerous attempts to help negotiate an agreement, but at this writing has not yet succeeded. War between the Israelis and Arabs could break out again at any time.

In the following selection, J. William Fulbright, former U.S. Senator from Arkansas and Chairman of the Senate Foreign Relations Committee, analyzes the Middle Eastern problem from the unique vantage point of a man who was intimately involved in the workings of American foreign policy for more than twenty years. His proposed solutions may seem rational to some Americans but have not proved satisfactory to the reigning powers of Russia, the United States, Israel, or the Arab lands.

Since Senator Fulbright wrote this piece, there have been a number of new twists in the Middle Eastern maze. The Egyptians and Syrians attacked the Israelis in October, 1973, on the holiest day of the Jewish year—*Yom Kippur*—and in the ensuing weeks won back some of the territory Israel had obtained in 1967. The war ended inconclusively, but both sides agreed to allow United Nations forces to supervise the cease fire and to occupy buffer territory between Israel and Egypt in the Sinai Peninsula. The war also raised Arab hopes that some negotiated settlement might be in reach.

Another major development during the past few years has been the emergence of Yasir Arafat, an Arab leader who, in the words of one reporter, has the "chameleonlike ability to change with the environment." Arafat, once leader of the guerrilla terrorist unit Al Fatah, now heads the Palestinian Liberation Organization, a group that includes a number of Arab factions. He is now speaking of negotiating with the Israelis and reclaiming the western part of Jordan —which Israel incorporated in 1967—as the new homeland for the Palestinians. Arafat's apparently moderate stance, combined with the world's weariness with conflict in the Middle East, has won a kind of respect for both him and the Palestine Liberation Organization. It remains to be seen, however, whether the Israeli government can be coaxed into a retreat by an Arab chameleon.

□ □ □

The journalist I. F. Stone, who has been concerned long and sympathetically with the aspiration of the Jewish people for a secure national home, has written:

The Arab-Jewish struggle is a tragedy. The essence of tragedy is a struggle of right against right. Its catharsis is the cleansing pity of seeing how good men do evil despite themselves out of unavoidable circumstance and irresistible compulsion. When evil men do evil, their deeds belong to the realm of pathology. But when good men do evil, we confront the essence of human tragedy. In a tragic struggle, the victors become the guilty and must make amends to the defeated. For me the Arab problem is also the Number One Jewish problem. How we act toward the Arabs will determine what kind of people we become: either oppressors and racists in our turn like those from whom we have suffered, or a nobler race able to transcend the tribal xenophobias that afflict mankind.[1]

In the Middle East there is a chance—though only a small one—for Arabs and Jews, Russians, Americans, and others to "transcend the tribal xenophobias that afflict mankind" by attempting something unprecedented in international affairs: the settlement of a major international controversy through the procedures of the United Nations. It need not—and preferably would not—be an "imposed" solution, although we should not shrink from applying certain sanctions as a last resort for the removal of a chronic threat to the peace. The United Nations Charter, to which every nation involved in the Middle East has voluntarily subscribed, spells out a graduated series of sanctions, from economic to military, for the enforcement of peace. It makes no sense at all for us to shrink in horror at the very notion of an "imposed" solution, not only because we are legally bound by the Charter to accept certain kinds of "imposed" solutions, but because the absolute sovereignty of nations is an outmoded principle; it is indeed a principle of international anarchy. No community can function without some capacity for coercion; as President Wilson said of the Covenant of the League of Nations, "Armed force is in the background . . . if the moral force of the world will not suffice, the physical force of the world shall." [2] The crucial distinction is not between coercion and voluntarism, but between duly constituted force, applied through law and as a last resort, and the arbitrary coercion of the weak by the strong.

Far from foreseeing a settlement of this kind, I think the chances for it, as of mid-1972, quite remote. At that time the Israelis were pressing ahead with the settlement and consolidation of their hold on the occupied Arab territories—pursuing the policy, as they call it, of "creating facts"—while President Sadat, frustrated by the cautious policy of the Soviet Union, expelled Soviet military personnel from Egypt and declared that Egypt would "stand alone on the battlefield if need be." "I would rather see our blood shed than live in the present no-war, no-peace deadlock," President Sadat declared.[3] The cease-fire of August 7, 1970, still held, but the prospect was for a continuing arms race, periodic crises, and little if any progress in the desultory United Nations mediation effort.

Despite these unpromising prospects, there remains one basis of hope: the fact that no one of the great powers—which is to say, the permanent, veto-wielding members of the United Nations Security Council—has a direct, valid national interest in the perpetuation of the conflict in the Middle East. The Russians have allowed themselves to be caught up in a sterile, costly bid for "influence" in the Arab world; the Americans, for their part, have allowed themselves to be drawn to the Israeli side by bonds of sympathy and by the impact of the most powerful and efficient foreign-policy lobby in American politics. Such hope as may be held for a United Nations settlement in the Middle East derives from the chance that the Russians and Americans may eventually decide to act upon their own valid interests, which are neither geopolitical nor sentimental. Their real interests are in a settlement which gives security to Israel, restores lost territories to the Arabs, removes the Middle East as an issue of contention between themselves, and breathes life into the United Nations.

THE MYTHS

The myths that shape events in the Middle East are the oldest myths of all.

Some derive from religion. The contested land is a "holy" land; more than a place for raising crops and building cities, it is "sacred soil" for three great religions. Jerusalem contains the Wall of the Temple, which is sacred to Jews, the Dome of the Rock, which is sacred to Muslims, and the Church of the Holy Sepulcher, which is sacred to Christians. Neither Jews nor Arabs can hold exclusive title to the city without also owning the other faith's shrine. Now, as in the days of the Crusades, religion exacerbates the issue, because, now as then, the behavior of the belligerents is more affected by the zeal with which they hold their beliefs than by the humane ethics taught by their respective religions. Now as in the past it is hard to strike a bargain over sacred soil.

Then there are the myths of mutual victimization. Perhaps one should say the half-myths, because both Jews and Arabs *have* victimized each other, though surely not with the deliberate and malign intent that each attributes to the other.

The Jews are obsessed with the fear of a repetition of the Nazi holocaust, and the Arabs do nothing to allay this fear with extravagant talk about "holy wars" and about throwing the Jews into the sea. These threats have understandably alarmed the Israelis in much the same way that Khrushchev's talk of "burying" us agitated Americans a decade ago. Presidents Nasser and Sadat of Egypt and King Hussein of Jordan have repudiated such draconian threats, but the Israelis seem not to have noticed the disavowals. As survivors of genocide, they can hardly be expected to distinguish with perfect clarity between Nazi crimes and Arab rhetoric. All they know is that they came to Palestine in peace, settlers in an underpopulated land, but have been allowed no peace; they have fought three wars they never wished to fight and still their enemies remain implacable, refusing even to talk to them, contesting—until recently—their right to survive as a state. Nonetheless, the Arab-Nazi analogy is a faulty one; it clouds the distinction between the myth and reality of Arab intent—whatever these may be.

The Arabs, for their part, perceive Zionism as a new form of Western imperialism. Having lived on the land of Palestine for thousands of years, they can have little sympathy for the historic sentiments of the Jewish diaspora. It is all but impossible for them to put themselves in the place of the Jews, whose cultural attachment to their ancient homeland sustained them through centuries of dispersal and persecution. The Arabs are on a different wavelength: while the Jews prayed for Palestine—"next year in Jerusalem," they said in their prayer —the Arabs inhabited the land. They could not see the Jews as the Jews saw themselves: as refugees from genocide seeking safe haven. What did this have to do with the Arabs? They had done the Jews no harm and could see no reason why they should compensate the Jews for the crimes of Europeans. In fact, to Arab eyes, the Jews were Europeans, armed with European skills and technology, coming on the heels of other Europeans to drive them from their homes and steal away their lands.

In its way Zionism has seemed to the Arabs even more threatening than the old European imperialism. The British and French after all were only establishing colonies and, bad as that was, colonies come and go. But the Jews were establishing a homeland, and homelands do not come and go. On the contrary, once established, they are likely to expand. The Jewish state actively encourages immigration from all over the world, especially from the Soviet Union, creating for Arabs the specter of a Jewish drive for *Lebensraum*, which could only mean the annexation of even more Arab lands. Some elements within Israel and the world Zionist movement openly proclaim the need of a policy of expansion, which must give rise to a fear among Arabs not unlike that felt by the Jews when the Arabs talk of throwing them into the sea. To the Arabs, in short, Zionism is not a program of deliverance for a persecuted race but a foreign conquest bolstered by strong ties between the conquering people and the most powerful government of the West.

As if the Arab-Israeli problem were not enough, the great powers have made their own special contribution to the mythology of the

Middle East by infusing the crisis with the hocus-pocus of geopolitics. The Middle East, in geopolitical terms, is something far more abstract than an oil-rich desert contested by feuding Semitic peoples. Beyond that, it is the "gateway to the East," the "hinge of NATO," and the crucial cockpit of the historic Russian drive toward warm water. By sending planes and missiles to Egypt the Russians are not merely bolstering a shaky client; to the X-ray eye of the geopolitician, they are embarked upon a drive to convert the Mediterranean into a "Soviet lake." The concept is admittedly vague: would the Russians close the Mediterranean to foreign shipping? prohibit fishing? use it as a vacation resort? No one really knows what a Russian *mare nostrum* would be like, but the concept serves the purpose of its users: it scares people; it imputes the "vital interests" of the great powers to a regional conflict, converting it into a battleground of the cold war. In this frame of reference one even suspects the Russians of an insidious design in wishing to reopen the Suez Canal—something which used to be considered a good thing, before the geopoliticians came along.

The "vital interests" of the great powers are, in fact, involved in the Middle East—primarily because those powers have chosen to become involved. The ultimate danger is that the Arab-Israeli conflict could draw the super powers and the world into a nuclear war—and that certainly is a matter of "vital interest"—but the danger is not inherent in the local situation, nor is it predestined by fate. It has arisen because the great powers have surrendered much of their own freedom of action to the bellicose whims of their respective clients. There is of course one way in which the great powers are *obligated* to intervene: as members of the United Nations Security Council, charged by the Charter with the responsibility to "decide what measures shall be taken" in response to a "threat to the peace, breach of the peace or act of aggression." Instead, the Soviet Union and the United States have played the role of cobelligerents to their respective clients, arming and financing them, committing their own prestige to the issue and, in so doing, converting a local conflict into a potential world conflict. All that can be said in mitigation is that both great powers—the Soviet Union more than the United States—have shown a certain prudence by holding back at times on the arms supplied to the quarreling parties.

Finally there is the myth of militarism, and that affects all of the parties. Each flirts from time to time with the notion that another round may settle things—although three wars have failed to end the conflict—or that some new weapons systems will stabilize the balance of power—as if either side would accept the other's notion of what it takes to establish a proper balance. Since the June war of 1967 the Egyptians have acquired vast arsenals of Soviet weapons, including air support and advanced ground-to-air missiles; from August 1968 until

August 1970 they waged a "war of attrition" along the Suez Canal. What did it get them? The Israelis were compelled to stop their deep-penetration air raids into Egypt but they still hold the Sinai; they still receive a steady flow of military equipment from the United States; and they have every prospect of acquiring additional Phantom and Skyhawk jets, electronic devices and other modern weapons from the United States whenever they judge these necessary to reestablish *their* version of the balance of power. Nor has the Soviet-supplied Egyptian hardware wrung any political concessions from the Israelis: Prime Minister Meir explicitly rejects the borders of 1967 and, instead of offering concessions, Foreign Minister Eban contributes pithy ironies about recognizing the right of the United Arab Republic to exist.[4]

The Israelis, for their part, have hardly profited from their military successes. They have gained territory and they have established their military superiority, but they have failed to gain what they most want: security. In 1967 they felt desperately insecure along the Gaza Strip frontier; today they feel desperately insecure along the Suez Canal, so much so that they and their friends abroad seem almost to have forgotten that it is not their own but Egyptian territory that they are defending so tenaciously. One begins to understand the spheres-of-influence psychology, which causes a nation to believe that it can have no security at all until it has robbed its neighbors of all semblance of security. Surrounded by hostile neighbors, holding down occupied lands inhabited by a million Arabs, plagued from time to time by *fedayeen* attacks, and oppressed by the costs of armaments, Israel is a desperately insecure nation. That is clear, but it is anything but clear that her present policy of relying on military superiority is ever going to alter the situation. Even if the United States provides all the Phantom jets the Israelis want and electronic jamming gear to neutralize the Egyptian SAM-2 and SAM-3 missiles, it is unlikely that Israel will gain more than a respite; the Russians—or perhaps some other foreign arms supplier—will soon enough come up with something else.

A leading Egyptian journalist told a visiting member of the Senate Foreign Relations Committee staff in late 1970 that only generations could bring peace in the full sense, but that a political settlement could be obtained—indeed, must be obtained—because, in his view, neither Egypt nor Israel could win a military victory. If the Israelis should capture Cairo, they would still not have won the war; they could only extend their occupation of Egypt until they exhausted themselves. Similarly, if the Egyptians should occupy Tel Aviv, what would they do with two and one-half million Jews? Somehow they would have to be lived with. (He made no reference to throwing them into the sea.) If the Israelis should destroy the Egyptian army again, the Russians would reequip it with tanks and guns. Or if the Egyptians should destroy Israel's armed forces, the United States would reequip them. This conflict was not, therefore, a traditional European kind of war which could be won or lost. For that reason a political settlement had to be reached, although the journalist was far from optimistic about reaching one easily or soon.

After the First World War the French tried to gain security in somewhat the same way that Israel seeks it today. They too were confronted with a potentially powerful but momentarily weakened antagonist, and they tried to perpetuate that situation by occupying the German Rhineland, temporarily detaching the Saar, and compelling Germany to pay reparations. The effort to make France secure by keeping Germany weak was a failure. Now, almost three decades after the Second World War, France has nothing to fear from Germany although Germany is strong and in possession of all the western territories France once wished to detach. France is secure now not because Germany has lost the power to threaten her but because she has lost the wish to do so.

The analogy is imperfect and simplified but it holds: Israel will be secure when and if the Arabs lose the wish to threaten her. Eliminating that wish should be an object worth pursuing from Israel's point of view. As victors the Israelis are in a position to be magnanimous without being suspected of "weakness"—which is something nations worry about whenever they are thinking about behaving sensibly. But thus far they have shown little inclination to trade their conquests for peace. Instead, they cling to the advantages won by their military victory of 1967, which is a wasting asset. One insecure frontier has been traded for another and all that the future seems to hold is continuing hostility and recurrent conflict, as threatening to the outside world as it is to the Arabs and Israelis.

Because the conflict is a threat to the outside world, it cannot be left solely to the humors of the belligerents. Under the United Nations Charter the Security Council has full authority—possibly even the obligation—to *impose* a settlement upon warring parties who fail to make peace on their own. The very premise of the Charter is that warring nations can no longer be permitted immunity from a world police power. As far as the United States is concerned, it is worth recalling now and then that the United Nations Charter is a valid and binding obligation upon us, ratified as a treaty with the advice and consent of the Senate. As to the Arabs and Israelis, they too are signatories to the Charter and no one can say they have been denied a fair opportunity to settle their differences peacefully and on their own. They might now be reminded of their commitment under Article 25 of the Charter, which states that "The Members of the United Nations agree to accept and carry out the decisions of the Security Council in accordance with the present Charter."

I think it would be a fine thing—a useful step forward for civilization—if, in the absence of a voluntary settlement by the parties, the United Nations were to "impose" a peaceful settlement in the Middle East. It would be an equally fine thing if the United Nations could "impose" a settlement in Southeast Asia. Unfortunately, there is no such prospect for Indochina, but I would not pass up the opportunity in the Middle East for the sake of a baneful consistency.

PERSPECTIVES

There are four major perspectives on the Middle East conflict and need of a fifth. The needed one, as I have suggested, is that of the world community through its duly constituted organ, the United Nations. The development of such a perspective and its translation into action will require changes and adjustments in the long-frozen perspectives of Arabs and Israelis, Russians and Americans. It may be well to review the prevailing perspectives of those involved in the Middle East, with a view to detecting misconceptions, desirable directions of change, and opportunities for future agreement.

Starting with Israel, it is less than adequate to say that the Jewish state is preoccupied with its survival. Surrounded and outnumbered by seemingly implacable foes, the Israelis are obsessed with the fear of being destroyed. This fear is based on salient facts but it is reinforced by fear itself, and by a two thousand years' history which planted the fear of extermination deeply in Jewish minds. The result is a tendency on the part of the Israelis to exaggerate their own vulnerability, to credit their adversaries with more relentless hostility than in fact they may harbor, and to dismiss tentative gestures of conciliation as hypocritical tricks. A visitor who had never been to Israel wrote soon after he arrived. " *'Our existence'*—that is the theme here—at least with all but a very few of the people one talks to. The suspicion of Arab intentions —the certainty, or near certainty, that the Arabs will *never* give up on their hope of destroying Israel—permeates the thinking of both officials and non-officials, along with the menace, as one official put it, of the 'presence of the Russian bear.' "

Chronic suspicion and fear are ultimately unrewarding; they give rise to an outlook which causes myths to displace realities in the minds of statesmen who pride themselves on realism and hardheadedness. It has distorted American perceptions of China and the Soviet Union, and it has distorted the Israeli view of Arab intentions and capacities. When suspicion governs policy, it becomes impossible for adversaries to communicate or negotiate because neither side is receptive to even the bare possibility that the other may be telling the truth when he makes a conciliatory gesture, or that he may be amenable to compromise.

The Israeli conviction of Arab hostility is by no means invention, but there is a touch of paranoia about it—just as there is in the American attitude toward communism—and the worst of it is that the prophecy is self-fulfilling. It is a truism of modern psychology that we influence the behavior of others by our own expectations of how they are going to behave. The critical question for Israel is whether it is willing to risk taking the Arabs at their word when they offer to live in peace—as they have done in effect by accepting the Security Council resolution of November 1967, which calls, among other things, for Israeli withdrawal from occupied territories, the termination of belligerency, the right of Israel and Arab states to "live in peace within secure and recognized boundaries," and a just settlement of the refugee problem. This is not to say that Israel can or should gamble her survival on the hope of Arab good will; Israel has the unchallengeable right to survive as a state and, as I shall indicate later, I would be willing to support a significant new conmitment by the United States to assure Israel's survival. Nonetheless, I think it is incumbent upon Israel to credit her Arab neighbors with good faith when they say—as they have said repeatedly—that they are willing to live in peace. Hitherto, the Israelis have had a tendency to demand specific reassurances of one kind and another from the Arabs and then, when these assurances have been forthcoming, to dismiss them as insincere.

A promising opportunity was lost in the spring of 1970 when the Israeli government refused to authorize the President of the World Jewish Congress, Dr. Nahum Goldmann, to hold talks in Cairo with President Nasser. The "torpedoing" of the Goldmann mission was surprising as well as unfortunate because, as *The New York Times* pointed out at the time, a meeting between a veteran Zionist leader and the Egyptian President would have represented a "significant breakthrough toward the direct contacts on which the Israeli Government has always insisted." [5]

In Dr. Goldmann's view the Zionist movement has suffered since its inception from a failure to grasp Arab psychology. Instead of seeking to minimize the injustices done the Arabs by the establishment of the Jewish homeland in Palestine, Israel, Dr. Goldmann has written, "counted on military force or the intervention of foreign powers to attain its goals." As a result, in Goldmann's view, Israel "has ceased to project the image of a small country threatened with destruction" and has become "an occupying power," which "exercises control over peoples who reject it and whom it has subjected." The result of Israeli policy since the Six-Day War of 1967, Dr. Goldmann believes, is a dangerous impasse which does not work to Israel's advantage, because time is not on Israel's side. Israel's present advantage, Dr. Goldmann pointed out, derives from the virtues, character and technological ability of its citizens, but the Arabs too have demonstrated energy and talent in the past and they greatly outnumber the Israelis. "No one," wrote Dr. Goldmann, "can predict how long it will take them to catch up with Israel technologically, especially in the field of weaponry. But sooner or later the balance of power will shift in their favor." Maintenance of the status quo, Dr. Goldmann concluded, "will lead to new wars, new Arab defeats and growing hatred of the Israelis"—a situation which "could have disastrous consequences for the Jewish state in the long run." [6]

I had a conversation in the summer of 1970 with a prominent Israeli journalist who had played a leading role in the struggle against British rule before 1948. Concerned that Israel has become a garrison state, he expressed fear for his country's survival as a democratic society. I said that I had the same fear for America, because we too have been chronically at war for over two decades. We agreed that both Israel and the United States would do well to recall Alexis de Tocqueville's warning of a century and a half ago, that war is the "surest and shortest means" to the destruction of democracy.[7] The Israeli journalist concluded by expressing the hope that Americans of moderate persuasion would speak out on the Middle East. If they did, he thought, Israeli moderates too would be encouraged to speak in favor of a policy of conciliation.

Israeli policy since the Six-Day War has been characterized by a lack of flexibility and foresight. The establishment of Israeli settlements on the occupied west bank of the Jordan River and in the Sinai can only be interpreted as steps toward foreclosing the return of these territories to their previous Arab owners. The insistence upon the "non-negotiability" of the status of Jerusalem and upon the retention of certain other occupied territories—notably the Golan Heights, the Gaza Strip and Sharm el Sheikh—lends unfortunate credence to the late President Nasser's pessimistic prediction, in accepting Secretary Rogers' peace proposal of 1970, that "While we inform the United States that we have accepted its proposals, we also tell them that our real belief is that whatever is taken by force cannot be returned except by force." [8] President Sadat has reiterated this prognosis in the wake of the failure of the United Nations mediation effort of Ambassador Jarring. Premier Meir's contemptuous rejection of King Hussein's proposal in early 1972 for a federation of the east and west banks of the Jordan River under his leadership provides further evidence of the extreme unlikelihood of a voluntary settlement among the parties; to the Israelis as to the Arabs the rule of force still holds sway. Premier Meir commented on King Hussein's proposed federation that "The King is treating as his own property territories which are not his and are not under his control. He crowns himself king of Jerusalem and envisions himself as the ruler of larger territories than were under his control prior to the rout of June, 1967." [9] Equally distressing although not entirely unprovoked is the Israeli view of the United Nations as what Foreign Minister Eban has called a "packed court" whose recommendations may be ignored. The insistence upon the "non-negotiability" of Israel's annexation of Arab East Jerusalem is in open contempt of the United Nations General Assembly, which censured that unilateral act by a vote of 99 to 0.

I write critically of Israeli policy in part because of my belief that Israel, as the momentary victor, has both an obligation and an interest in a policy of magnanimity. The obligation arises from general considerations of world peace and from the specific injustice which has been done to the Palestinian Arabs, who, as Arnold Toynbee has written, "have been made to pay for the genocide of Jews in Europe, which was committed by Germans, not by Arabs." [10] Israel's self-interest in magnanimity is a matter of the only kind of security which really is security. In the words of a member of the Law Faculty of Hebrew University: "A border is secure when those living on the other side do not have sufficient motivation to infringe on it. . . . We have to remind ourselves that the roots of security are in the minds of men. . . ." [11]

For reasons which may warrant our sympathy, but not our support, Israel pursues a policy of antiquated—and to a great degree delusional—self-reliance. As Foreign Minister Eban expressed it, "a nation must be capable of tenacious solitude." [12] In fact, neither Israel nor any other nation is capable of so profound an isolationism in our time. Israel is heavily dependent on the United States for both arms and economic assistance. Since 1948 private American citizens have provided several billion dollars in tax-deductible contributions and regularly purchase between $300 million and $400 million a year in Israeli bonds. Included in the massive American military aid, which has increased greatly since the 1967 war, have been aircraft, missiles and electronic systems more advanced than those provided to the countries with whom we are allied in NATO or SEATO. I do not see how this can be reconciled with a policy on Israel's part of "tenacious solitude."

A different view is taken by Israel's elder statesman and first Prime Minister, David Ben-Gurion. "Peace," he has said, "real peace, is now the great necessity for us. It is worth almost any sacrifice. To get it, we must return to the borders before 1967." "As for security," Mr. Ben-Gurion continued, "militarily defensible borders, while desirable, cannot by themselves guarantee our future. Real peace with our Arab neighbors—mutual trust and friendship—that is the only true security." [13]

The Arabs too must face up to certain realities: that Israel has come to stay; that it is demagogic nonsense to talk—as some of the

Palestinian guerrillas still do—of driving the Jews into the sea; that in any case the Arab states can have no realistic hope of doing that because they themselves cannot defeat Israel, the Russians are not likely to do it for them, and the United States would almost certainly intervene to save Israel from destruction. Once these facts are recognized—as in large measure they have been recognized by the governments of Egypt and Jordan—the Arab countries will be able to free themselves from their morbid preoccupation with past defeats, from futile dreams of revenge, and from the oppressive burden of armaments which slows their development and makes them dependent upon foreign powers.

Although Egypt and Jordan are still credited with the desire to destroy Israel, both in fact have repudiated any such ambition and have done so explicitly and repeatedly. They did it in the first instance by accepting the United Nations Security Council Resolution of November 22, 1967, which required them to give up positions to which they had held tenaciously for twenty years. By accepting that Resolution, Egypt and Jordan, as already noted, committed themselves to terminate their belligerency against Israel; to acknowledge Israel's sovereignty, territorial integrity and right "to live in peace within secure and recognized boundaries"; and to respect Israel's right to freedom of navigation through the Suez Canal and the Strait of Tiran. Having accepted these provisions of the Resolution—which in fact meet *all* Israel's stated and legitimate aspirations—the Egyptians and Jordanians now emphasize the *other* provisions of the Resolution of 1967: the withdrawal of Israel from occupied territories; a just settlement of the refugee problem; and "the inadmissibility of the acquisition of territory by war." The last is a general principle which goes beyond the special interest of the Arab states. Its vindication—even in one instance—would represent a long step forward toward the establishment of the rule of law in international relations. That would serve everybody's interests—everybody, that is, who wishes to survive in the nuclear age and who still has some hope that the United Nations can be developed into an effective peace-keeping organization. It is natural enough for Israel to resist the honor of being the first modern military victor to be obliged to abide by the principles and specifications of the United Nations Charter, especially when the great powers who dominate the Security Council have set such a wretched example. Be that as it may, the principle involved is too important to be cast away because of the hypocrisy or self-interest of its proponents.

Returning to the Arab perspective, I think there has been insufficient recognition of the distance the Egyptian and Jordanian governments have come toward accommodating themselves to some form of coexistence with Israel. Presidents Nasser and Sadat and King

Hussein have repudiated the contention that they will be satisfied with nothing less than "driving Israel into the sea" not only by subscribing to the Security Council's Resolution of November 1967, but through repeated and explicit public statements. As early as 1969, in a speech in Washington, King Hussein reiterated his own and President Nasser's willingness to abide by each of the provisions of the 1967 Resolution, and he then added: "In return for these considerations, our sole demand upon Israel is the withdrawal of its armed forces from all territories occupied in the June, 1967, war, and the implementation of all the other provisions of the Security Council Resolution." [14]

To take another example: in an American television interview on June 14, 1970, President Nasser stated unequivocally his willingness to accept the boundaries of Israel as they existed before the 1967 war as final boundaries. Asked whether Egypt would promise that its territory would not be used for attacks on Israel once the Israelis withdrew from the occupied territories, President Nasser replied—several times—"Yes." [15]

Unless one is prepared to contend—and back the proposition—that President Sadat and King Hussein have simply not been telling the truth, it seems to me irresponsible to continue accusing either Egypt or Jordan of a policy aimed at "driving Israel into the sea." The Jordanians have long been known to be willing to come to terms with Israel—to end the state of war and recognize Israel's existence as a state in return for the restoration of occupied territory. The United Arab Republic, in its reply of February 16, 1971, to questions put by the United Nations mediator, Ambassador Jarring, stated unequivocally that if Israel would withdraw from occupied Egyptian territory, Egypt would be prepared to end the state of belligerency, ensure freedom of navigation through the Suez Canal and the Strait of Tiran, establish demilitarized zones, agree to the establishment of a United Nations peace-keeping force, and "enter into a peace agreement with Israel. . . ."

The Egyptian reply concedes to Israel all that she once desired, all that she claimed to be struggling for in three wars. Nonetheless, in its own reply to Ambassador Jarring of February 26, 1971, the Israeli government stated bluntly that "Israel will not withdraw to the pre-June 5, 1967 lines." Israel, Mrs. Meir subsequently explained, insists upon the retention of Sharm el Sheikh; the Gaza Strip; the Golan Heights—because, as the Premier explained, "We paid for it"; Jerusalem—considered not even negotiable; and certain undefined parts of the west bank of the Jordan River. In addition, said the Premier, Sinai must be demilitarized, and the demilitarization must be guaranteed by a mixed force including Israelis. The Egyptians too might participate in this force on their own territory. All this, Mrs. Meir conceded, would be painful for President Sadat of Egypt, but people must pay for their deeds.[16]

Withdrawal from the occupied territories is one of two concerns which dominate the Arab perspective; the other is the question of the Palestinian refugees. Whatever the political considerations which have led Israel to evade responsibility and the Arab states to exploit their plight, the unhappy Palestinian refugees remain preoccupied with the indisputable facts that, after almost twenty-five years in exile, they are not permitted to return to their homes and they have been denied compensation for their lost properties. Although, according to United Nations estimates, some 60 percent of the refugees have found new homes and jobs, many thousands—made up mostly of the elderly, the very poor, the sick and the least educated—are still interned in miserable camps, living hopeless lives as wards of the United Nations. Since the 1967 war approximately half of the two and one-half million Palestinian Arabs have been living under Israeli occupation. Despite annual United Nations resolutions recognizing their right to choose between returning to their homes and resettling elsewhere with compensation for lost properties, the refugees remain neglected and embittered pawns in the continuing Middle East conflict, the original 750,000 refugees of 1948 having increased to well over a million. In the words of a study prepared by a working party on the Middle East of the American Friends Service Committee, "the Arabs of Palestine see themselves as a people in diaspora, just at the time when the Jews have won their struggle for a national home." [17]

A member of the staff of the Senate Foreign Relations Committee visited a Palestinian refugee camp near Beirut in November 1970 and reported on the human meaning of the refugee problem:

Accompanied by an UNWRA official, an Embassy control officer and two uniformed, rifle-carrying soldiers of the "Armed Struggle Command," I visited this morning one of the stinking, festering Palestinian refugee camps on the outskirts of Beirut. It was as hateful and ugly, squalid and degraded a place as the worst "favelas" in Brazil or even the slums of Calcutta. The houses were wretched shacks, the stores makeshift huts, the streets—if they can be called that—filthy alleyways lined with open sewers. The population is dense, especially with ragged children. One sees how the 750,000 refugees of 1948 have become 1,400,000. There are differences from the shanty towns of Lima and Recife. First of all there is law and order, enforced by the indigenous soldiery which calls itself the "Armed Struggle Command." Second, there is a semblance of social cohesion: we visited a school within the camp and the children seemed well-tended and were neatly uniformed, although the schoolhouse was makeshift. There also appears to be no hunger—at least not starvation—thanks in part to the pittance—about ten cents per person a day—provided by UNWRA, which also runs the schools and hires and pays the teachers. The most important difference between the refugee camp and the slums I have seen in Asia and Latin America is that these people are not submissive, hollow-eyed sub-revolutionaries. They are political and angry and sometimes violent: they are refugees and their anger and hatred flourish in the fetid soil of the camp. It is not judged wise for visitors—American visitors at any rate—to enter the camp unescorted by the armed guard. They accompanied us everywhere—they were friendly enough themselves—and I would not have wanted them to leave us. As we left the refugee camp, a Palestinian employee of UNWRA called me aside. "Tell the people in Washington," he said, "that we are disappointed with the United States."

Since the June war of 1967 the Palestinians have emerged as active, although militarily ineffective, participants in the Middle East conflict. The largest of the guerrilla organizations, Al Fatah, demands the dissolution of the present state of Israel and the creation of a secular multireligious state. They reject partition but they also deny any wish to "throw the Jews into the sea." Other Palestinian Arabs, more moderate, more realistic and—prudently, under present circumstances —more silent, acknowledge that Israel is here to stay and say that they are prepared to make peace—provided that Israel withdraws from the territories occupied in 1967.

The status of the Palestinians and the question of the occupied territories are the critical issues for peace in the Middle East. The two issues are closely related because many Palestinian Arabs are haunted by the fear that there are no bounds to Israel's territorial aspirations— a fear which feeds upon classic Zionist ideology as well as upon the declarations of military-minded Israelis who press the claim for "strategic" frontiers. A declaration by the Israeli government of willingness to restore the occupied territories as part of a general peace settlement would go far to alleviate Arab fears of Zionist expansionism. Such a statement would meet the Egyptian-Jordanian condition for peace and would also improve the chances for a settlement in Palestine.

In the Arab perspective the central issues are the occupied territories and the Palestinians. In the Israeli perspective the issue is the survival and security of the Jewish state. The United Nations Resolution of 1967 recognizes the legitimacy of both parties' concerns. The question now is whether the two sides, and their great-power mentors, are ready to proceed, either through the renewed mediation of Dr. Jarring or by some other means, toward the translation of general principles into specific agreements.

More perhaps than either would care to acknowledge, the two super powers have played similar roles in the Middle East, both characterized by a certain ambivalence. On the one hand, they have played the traditional great-power role, arming their respective clients, committing their own prestige, building spheres of influence, fretting over geopolitical abstractions—all serving to elevate a regional conflict into a global one. On the other hand, both the Soviet Union and the United States have shown an appreciation of the dangers in the Middle East, and that appreciation has caused them to restrain the two sides at critical moments and to encourage some form of accommodation. It was through Soviet and American mediation, in which the American Secretary of State, William Rogers, played a leading role, that the "war of attrition" along the Suez Canal was stopped in the summer of 1970. The indirect negotiations through Ambassador Jarring which ensued have, however, proven sterile; two years after the indirect negotiations began, the two sides had still failed to achieve even a limited agreement for the reopening of the Suez Canal. The great powers, accordingly, still must determine the kind of role they are to play in the Middle East, whether they are to play power politics or undertake to advance and, if need be, enforce a compromise peace through the United Nations. Heretofore the super powers have vacillated between the temptation to turn the Middle East into a cold war battleground and a caution induced by the well-founded fear of an uncontrollable conflict. The outcome in the Middle East will be determined as much by the great powers' conception of their own interests and of their own proper roles as by the attitudes of the Arabs and Israelis.

Like their czarist predecessors, the Soviet leaders have pursued a foreign policy aimed at the acquisition of "influence" in the Near East and the Mediterranean. What, if anything, they have hoped to gain in concrete terms is unclear—probably even to themselves. The Russians do not appear much inclined to try to communize the region—even if they could; they have overlooked the imprisonment of local Communists and the suppression of Communist parties in Egypt, Syria and Iraq, eagerly providing armaments to all three countries, both before and since the June war of 1967.

The Russians appear to be interested in the Middle East for reasons of security and trade as well as "influence." They would like to see American military power removed from the region, although it is hard to see how that would benefit Soviet security, since American bases would remain in Greece and Turkey. That, however, is the sort of thing big countries worry about, and I for one am inclined to take it at face value. The Russians would of course benefit commercially from the reopening of the Suez Canal, as would other countries, but that could be accomplished through a compromise peace and hardly requires a Soviet "drive for power" in the Middle East. Basically, one suspects, the Russians are motivated by the same vague geopolitical impulses that all great powers are susceptible to: they enjoy sailing their warships around the Mediterranean and would enjoy it even more if we felt constrained to keep our ships out; they would like in general to be "Number One" in the Middle East and would be delighted to see American "influence" reduced or eliminated. It appears to be in large part a matter of ego gratification, or of what the psychologists call "self-maximization," and it is by no means a unique Soviet susceptibility. It is in fact normal behavior for a great power— quite similar to our own. We too keep a fleet in the Mediterranean, which is a good deal farther from our shores than it is from the Soviet Union; and our main objection to Soviet "influence" in the Arab countries is that it detracts from our own.

For the advancement of its vague geopolitical ambitions, Israel is indispensable to the Soviet Union. Israel, in the view of "Kremlinologists," is the Soviet Union's admission ticket to the Middle East. If it did not exist, the Arab states would have little need of Soviet military and political support, and the Russians would have nothing with which to charm the Arabs except their communism, which does not seem to charm them at all. The Russians have had no more success in buying ideological converts with their aid and support than has the United States. Since the mid-fifties the United Arab Republic has received more Soviet aid than any other country, but the Egyptian government has suppressed internal Communists—more indeed than has the Israeli government—and the Russians have been warned repeatedly against meddling in internal Arab affairs. In July 1971 the Russians asked the Egyptian government to apply pressure in Khartoum against a crackdown on Communists in the Sudan, and President Sadat responded with an angry speech before the Arab Socialist Union in which he declared that Egypt would never become Communist or recognize an Arab Communist government.[18] When he ordered the expulsion of Soviet military personnel from Egypt in July 1972, President Sadat said, "Egyptian nationalism and Arab nationalism must stand alone." [19] Without Israel the dream of paramount Russian "influence" in the Middle East and of the Mediterranean as a "Soviet lake" would go aglimmering. If Israel did not exist, say the "Kremlinologists," the Russians would have to invent it.

Israelis can be forgiven for an unwillingness to base their security on Soviet national egoism, but at least they—and their supporters in the United States—ought to take solace in the available evidence that the Russians have a stake in their survival. The Israeli leaders are not known for simple-mindedness or a lack of diplomatic skill, and that causes one to suspect that they may be somewhat less terrified of the Russians than they care to let on. After twenty-five years of the cold war the word has pretty well gotten around that invoking the Communist menace is a fairly reliable way of keeping the Americans in line. Picturing herself as the bastion of democracy in the Middle East, Israel professes to be defending American interests by holding the line against a surging tide of Communist imperialism. Recent visitors to the Middle East assure me that the Israelis are quite sincere in their fear of being "thrown into the sea" and in their conception of the Soviet Union as an insatiable imperialist power, bent, presumably, upon the conquest and communization of the Middle East. Nonetheless, I perceive in this some of the same old Communist-baiting humbuggery that certain other small countries have used to manipulate the United States for their own purposes. When it comes to anti-communism, as we have noted in Vietnam and elsewhere, the United States is highly susceptible, rather like a drug addict, and the world is full of ideological "pushers." It is a fine thing to respect a small country's independence and to abstain from interference in its internal affairs. It is quite another matter when, in the name of these worthy principles—but really because of our surviving obsession with communism—we permit client states to manipulate American policy toward purposes contrary to our interests, and probably to their own as well.

Although the Nixon Administration tended increasingly between 1969 and 1972 to comply with most of Israel's demands for arms, some of its officials, including Secretary of State Rogers, have made a cooler assessment of Soviet intentions in the Middle East. They have recognized that although the Soviet Union has made harsh verbal attacks on Israel, it has been consistent in its advocacy of a political settlement based on the Security Council Resolution of November 1967. It also seems evident that the introduction of Soviet pilots and of SAM-2 and SAM-3 missiles into Egypt in 1970 was something less than a bid for Soviet domination of the Middle East. The Israelis had been flying "deep penetration" raids over Egypt and had even bombed the suburbs of Cairo. The Egyptians at that time seemed unable to counter Israeli air power, and there was even talk that this situation might result in the fall of President Nasser. The steps taken by the Russians since then have been cautious measures designed to bolster a faltering client. From the Egyptian point of view Soviet support has been exceedingly cautious: the Russians have consistently refused to provide the Egyptians with offensive weapons such as long-range bombers and ground-to-ground missiles. Compared with the things we have done to shore up both Israel and our faltering client states in Asia, Soviet support of Egypt has been prudent indeed.

The weight of evidence indicates that the Russians do indeed want a compromise settlement in the Middle East. It seems probable that they would welcome the reopening of the Suez Canal, relief from the heavy costs of arming Egypt, and a reduction of great-power tensions. A solution acceptable to the Arabs, moreover, would earn gratitude for the Russians in the Arab world, would enhance Soviet prestige all over the world, and appease the Jewish population of the Soviet Union.[20] And, most enticing of all, in the Soviet perspective, would be the ego-gratifying prospect of a region-full of neutralist states more amenable to Soviet than to American "influence"—whatever that might mean in concrete terms.

When ideological and moral pronouncements are set aside—as every now and then honesty commends—the American perspective on the Middle East is in a number of important respects the mirror image of that of the Russians. We too attach great importance to our fleet plying Mediterranean waters; we too have an economic stake in the region—American oil companies have large and profitable investments, although the United States is not heavily dependent on Middle Eastern oil, as are some of our allies; we too derive ego-gratification from wielding "influence"—although, like the Russians, we prefer to dress up our egoism in unctuous pieties; and, like our Soviet rival, we are a pushover for geopolitical grandiosities, the Middle East being, in President Nixon's phrase, the "hinge of NATO." [21]

Only in one respect is our interest in the Middle East fundamentally different from that of other outside powers: we are tied to Israel by bonds of culture and sentiment and by the special attachment of our American Jewish population. These bonds represent a perfectly valid basis for the definition of a "national interest" and for the making of a valid commitment based on that interest—provided that the commitment is made in an appropriately constitutional manner, and provided too that it does not infringe upon or derogate from other valid interests. As matters now stand, our commitment to Israel is de facto and undefined: we do not really know the extent of our own obligation, which could be very great, while Israel does not know what in the way of American support she can rely on. This uncertainty in turn appears to have driven Israel to greater militancy and inflexibility in her attitude toward the Arabs. For our part, the lack of a constitutionally legitimate commitment, candidly based on the sentimental and cultural bonds which are the real source of our interest in Israel, drives us to rationalize our involvement in terms of geopolitical metaphors.

The assumption appears to be that there is something illegitimate about sentiment as the basis of a national interest and that we must therefore disguise it behind a facade of tough-sounding realpolitik. I cannot help suspecting that the authors of all that stuff we keep hearing about the Russians testing the "intentions of the free world" in the Middle East and challenging the "national will of the United States" do not really believe it any more than I do. The authors of these statements feel a cultural and religious attachment to Israel but apparently do not feel they can persuade the United States government to pursue a policy designed to serve that attachment unless it can also be justified in terms of the grand strategy of the cold war. I regret this attitude very much because the introduction of cold-war rationalizations has the dangerous effect of expanding a local issue into a global one.

Both President Nixon and Mr. Kissinger have tended at times to speak in those terms. In a televised interview on July 1, 1970, for example, President Nixon spoke of the Middle East as being "terribly dangerous, like the Balkans before World War I, where the two super powers, the United States and the Soviet Union, could be drawn into a confrontation that neither of them wants. . . ." Five days earlier, Mr. Kissinger had said exactly the same thing: ". . . what makes the situation in the Middle East so potentially dangerous is the fact that it has many similarities with the Balkans before World War I." Pressing the analogy, Mr. Kissinger contended that "no one caused World War I"; that it came about as an accident; and that the situation in the Middle East is roughly analogous, Israel and the Arab states each being allied to a super power ". . . each of them to some extent not fully under the control of the major country concerned." [22]

This tough talk, it has been explained, was designed to scare the Russians, not to be taken literally. Whatever effect it had on the Russians, I must say that it scared me, because it reveals a dangerously outmoded way of thinking about international politics. The catastrophe of war is conceived as something fated, controlled by quarrelsome client states if not by the iron "laws" of power politics. Implicit in this outlook is the supposition that the coming of a great war is beyond the control of statesmen—even beyond the control of the Pentagon computers, or of Mr. Kissinger's staff of experts in the White House basement.

The outlook is faulty, and so is the analogy. World War I was not primarily an accident, and it was certainly not predestined. It came about, as recent German historians have shown, because Germany was willing for it to come about and aided and abetted the events which led to the explosion. It was within Germany's power at any time to restrain her Austrian client and, in so doing, to prevent war. The German leaders knew they had this power but consciously chose not to exercise it because they thought they could win a general European war and judged that it would derogate from German pride and grandeur if the great German Empire shrank from war. That is why general war came in 1914, and it is for that kind of reason that it will come again, if it does come again. It will be, as it was in 1914, the result of human choice, human pride and human folly on the part of the leaders of the great powers. Left to their own resources, the Arabs and Israelis have the power to bring on a local war but not a world war. Only the super powers have that option and—whatever the political usefulness of historical misanalogies—they had better not forget it.

Mr. Kissinger has referred to the American interest in the Middle East as deriving from our allies' dependence on Middle Eastern oil. The Japanese, Mr. Kissinger pointed out in 1970, get 90 percent, and the Western Europeans 75 percent, of their oil from the Middle East—"which again is one reason why *we* * can have an overwhelming interest in preventing this area from being dominated by the Soviet Union." [23] For those who are worried about "neo-isolationism" Mr. Kissinger's words should provide ample reassurance that the policeman-of-the-world spirit has survived as a living force in American foreign policy. Without explanation or elaboration it is taken for granted that because Japan and Western Europe need Middle Eastern oil, the United States has to protect the oil supplies from "the Soviets and their radical clients." What about the Japanese and the Europeans? Why do they not send their fleets to keep the Mediterranean from becoming a "Soviet lake"? And why do we not expect them to? The answer appears to derive from the "laws" of geopolitics. The "responsibilities of power" have imposed upon us the duty of serving as the Hessians of the "free world," with the lesser "free world" countries at liberty to provide a regiment or two, if they wish, to put a nice face on things.

What in the world is meant by the notion of a "Soviet lake" anyway? Does anyone really think that the Russians are going to employ their fleet—in the manner of the British in the nineteenth century—to blockade ports or intercept the flow of oil to Europe and Japan on the high seas? In the nuclear age that kind of naval diplomacy is not only obsolete but insane. If the Russians should ever undertake to interfere with Europe's oil supply, it is far more likely that they would try to buy it up or somehow bribe or induce the oil-producing countries to shut it off. This being the likelihood, the rational way for the Western countries to protect their sources of oil in the Arab world is not by practicing an irrelevant, antiquated naval diplomacy but by cultivating and maintaining friendly relations with the Arab countries.

I do not care much for this geopolitical hocus-pocus. Whatever the reasons of strategy or preference that have induced the Nixon Administration to employ it from time to time, there is far more to be said for the sensible, conciliatory approach which brought about the cease-fire along the Suez Canal and the Jarring peace mission, unsuccessful though it has been. The geopolitical formulations of America's inter-

* Italics supplied.

est in the Middle East are basically romantic, historically unsound and dangerous. There is no relevance in the Balkan analogy of 1914, which purports to show that we are helpless. Nor do we have an automatic, unilateral vital interest deriving from the oil requirements of Europe and Japan. There are, to be sure, important American political and economic stakes in the Middle East, but our major specific interest is a cultural and sentimental attachment to Israel, rooted in the strong preference of a great many of the American people and their elected representatives.

We also have a crucial stake in the avoidance of conflict with the Soviet Union. It takes no great feat of imagination to conjure up some new Arab-Israeli crisis in which the two sides manage to draw their respective patrons into a head-on conflict. Premier Meir has said that the United States ought not to press for Israeli withdrawal from the conquered Arab territories because as she put it, "This is not the border of the USA. . . ." [24] If indeed that were the whole of the matter, if Israel, as the Premier has said, really were prepared to "stand up for itself" without involving others, it might make sense to let the Arabs and Israelis work out their differences, or fight them out, and come to their own solution. We all know, however, that that is not the case, that although American economic and security interests are not directly involved in the Arab-Israeli conflict, the gratuitous intrusion of the great powers has created the possibility that another war in the Middle East might set us against the Russians. This being the case, we have not only the right but a positive responsibility to bring an influence to bear.

The Soviet Union and the United States by and large have recognized that they have a surpassing interest in the avoidance of a major confrontation with each other. The Russians, for their part, have consistently counseled their Arab associates against reckless action; they are reported, for instance, to have warned the Egyptians that they would not support a military operation across the Suez Canal. Nor have the Russians ever indicated any expectation of, or desire for, the destruction of Israel; they were indeed among the first to recognize the state of Israel when it came into existence in 1948. The Soviet position is that Israel should return to the borders of 1967; that is substantially the American position as well—at least officially—and it is consistent with the Security Council Resolution of November 1967, which calls among other things for the "termination of all claims or states of belligerency and respect for and acknowledgment of the sovereignty, territorial integrity and political independence of every state in the area."

We also have a nonspecific interest in the Middle East, which we share with the Arabs, the Israelis, the Soviet Union, and the rest of the world. That interest is in the vindication of the United Nations as an instrument for the maintenance of peace. The Security Council Resolution of November 22, 1967, which Secretary Rogers has said "will be the bedrock of our policy," [25] emphasizes "the inadmissibility of the acquisition of territory by war," and it reminds the Middle Eastern parties of their obligations under Article 2 of the United Nations Charter, of which paragraph 3 states that "All members shall settle their international disputes by peaceful means in such a manner that international peace and security, and justice, are not endangered."

This is where a fifth perspective comes in, over and above that of Arabs, Israelis, Russians and Americans. If a United Nations perspective could be developed and brought to bear, we might come out of the Middle East crisis with something better than a peaceful settlement. We might come out with a precedent too, with processes to draw upon in the future.

TOWARD PEACE

For most of the life span of both entities, the United Nations and the state of Israel have been intimately, if not always cordially, involved with each other. Israel was legally initiated by the United Nations; since then its status, borders and policies have been the subject of a series of United Nations resolutions. The United Nations Relief and Works Agency still has primary responsibility for the Arab refugees; a United Nations peace force was placed between Egyptian and Israeli forces after the 1956 war; and United Nations observers have been stationed along the Suez Canal since the June war of 1967. The Security Council Resolution of November 22, 1967, is still the most complete, impartial and generally accepted policy statement for a Middle East settlement, and is still the best hope for a viable peace. If there has ever been an issue which is ripe and appropriate for peaceful settlement under United Nations auspices, it is the conflict between Israel and the Arabs.

First and foremost, a just settlement must vindicate the principle, as spelled out in the Security Council Resolution, of "the inadmissibility of the acquisition of territory by war." This principle goes to the heart of the Charter; Article 2, paragraph 4, states that "All Members shall refrain in their international relations from the threat or use of force against the territorial integrity or political independence of any state. . . ." The return of the conquered territories is the major single requirement for peace as stated by both President Sadat and King Hussein. As King Hussein put it, ". . . Israel may have either peace or territory—but she can never have both." [26]

Restoration of the occupied territories is also official American policy. In his notable speech of December 9, 1969, Secretary Rogers said:

> We believe that while recognized political boundaries must be established and agreed upon by the parties, any changes in the preexisting lines should not reflect the weight of conquest and should be confined to insubstantial alterations required for mutual security. We do not support expansionism. We believe troops must be withdrawn as the resolution provides. . . .

In return for withdrawal from virtually all of the territories occupied in 1967, Israel should be entitled to firm and specific guarantees of her security. One such guarantee might be the stationing of sizable United Nations forces in militarily neutralized zones on *both* sides of the borders at all of the points which are critical to Israel's security. United Nations forces might also be stationed on what is now the occupied west bank of the Jordan River; in and around the Gaza Strip and the old border between Israel and Egyptian Sinai; and at Sharm el Sheikh to guarantee Israel's egress through the Strait of Tiran. In all cases, it should be specified that the United Nations force could be removed only by consent of both Israel and the Arab government concerned. Perhaps too the consent of a majority of the United Nations Security Council might be required, either to remove the United Nations forces or to terminate the neutralized status of the zones in question.

Israel has a right to security, but not to territorial and military arrangements which would rob her Arab neighbors of security. In keeping with the Rogers plan, which would allow of "insubstantial" territorial changes, Israel has a reasonable security claim with respect to the Golan Heights. It would be unreasonable to expect the Israelis to withdraw to the Jordan valley from these highlands from which the Syrians used to fire down on civilian communities—all the more so since the Syrians have refused to accept the Security Council Resolution of November 1967, and have refused to participate in the Jarring peace talks. At the same time, the Israelis have no good claim to the permanent occupation of the entire Syrian territory they now hold. A defensible frontier might be drawn along the high ridge line immediately east of the Jordan valley, giving Israel a small, uninhabited but militarily significant strip of previously Syrian territory.

In the case of the west bank there is everything to be said for the principle of self-determination. Israel might be permitted to retain the "Latrun salient," the narrow finger of land astride the main highway from Jerusalem to Tel Aviv which was part of Jordan before the 1967 war and from which Israeli traffic between the two cities was harassed, but preferably in return for an equivalent cession of territory. There is no justification for claims of land north and south of the west bank which would enable Israel to mount a "pincers" attack in the event of an Arab threat to Israel's narrow coastal strip. This would effectively rob the west bank, whether independent or federated with Jordan, of any semblance of security, and would place still more unwilling Arabs under Israeli rule.

Another necessary provision of an Arab-Israeli peace settlement would be a mutual disavowal of any further efforts by either side to alter the adjusted frontiers of 1967. The Security Council Resolution of November 1967 specifies the right of *every* state in the area to "live in peace within secure and recognized boundaries free from threats or acts of force." The Arabs, it must be remembered, are as frightened of the Zionist doctrine of unlimited Jewish immigration leading to a drive for *Lebensraum* as the Israelis are of an Arab "holy war" to destroy Israel. Both sides are entitled to explicit guarantees against these deeply rooted fears. This could be accomplished by writing into a peace treaty a more explicit and detailed version of that provision of the Security Council Resolution which would require "termination of all claims or states of belligerency and respect for and acknowledgment of the sovereignty, territorial integrity and political independence of every state in the area. . . ."

Israel is entitled to free access through the Suez Canal as well as the Gulf of Aqaba and the Strait of Tiran. That too is called for in the Security Council Resolution and should be guaranteed in the definitive instrument of peace.

As to Jerusalem, I have no specific recommendation. Israel's annexation of the old city is one of those "new facts" with which the world has been confronted. I think it well, nonetheless, to recall that the United Nations General Assembly unanimously condemned Israel's unilateral annexation of the city * and that its status cannot be considered "non-negotiable." Some form of international status would seem to be the appropriate solution. The Friends' study suggests the desirability of "some sort of federal condominium to govern an undivided and demilitarized Jerusalem" and makes the further contention, in which I concur, that Jerusalem "cannot peacefully become the sole possession of one religion or one national state." [27] There may also be merit in Dr. Nahum Goldmann's suggestion that the old Arab section of Jerusalem be constituted "an autonomous enclave with an international status administered by its inhabitants." Such an internationalized city, Dr. Goldmann has suggested, might become a "center for world organizations" as well as a center for three great religions.[28]

Probably the most difficult and intractable of the issues to be re-

* On July 4, 1967, by vote of 99 to 0, the United States abstaining.

solved is that of "achieving a just settlement of the refugee problem" as called for in the Security Council Resolution of 1967. In justice and law—the latter in the form of numerous United Nations resolutions— the Palestinian Arab refugees are entitled to one of two forms of restitution: either repatriation or compensation. As a practical solution it should be feasible to work out an agreement under which Israel would take back within its 1967 borders an agreed number of refugees who would be accepted as Israeli citizens and whose former properties would either be restored or compensated for. For the majority of refugees, repatriation would probably be neither feasible nor desired. A commitment by the Arab states to accept them and assist in their resettlement—as in part they have already done—should be accompanied by generous Israeli financial support, both to compensate these refugees for their losses and to facilitate their resettlement. With contributions from friends abroad, and with the relief from military costs which peace would make possible, Israel should have no great difficulty in meeting these costs, which in any case ought to be accepted as an elementary moral obligation.

In due course the Palestinian Arabs will find it necessary to accept the existence of the state of Israel and to recognize that further efforts to destroy the Jewish state will be futile and will only compound their own suffering. The Palestinians have been done a great historical injustice, but it cannot now be undone in the way they would have it undone. Israel has existed as an independent state since 1948, and it would now be as great an injustice to disrupt that society as it was for the Jews to drive the Arabs from their land in the first place. A certain rough justice accrues to any existing state of affairs, insofar as it affects people's lives and homes, once people are established and living in a place—regardless of how they got there—it becomes an injustice, even if it were a practical possibility, to disrupt and expel them.

This must be a bitter pill for the Palestinian Arabs to swallow, but they are going to have to do it if they want an end to futile guerrilla warfare. In any case, the Palestinians are entitled to some form of self-determination on the non-Israeli territory of Palestine. Whether they will wish to form an independent Palestinian state, or federate with the Kingdom of Jordan as proposed by King Hussein, is beyond the reach of a foreigner's judgment.

Central and indispensable to a peace settlement based on the Security Council Resolution of November 1967 would be the guarantee of the entire settlement by the United Nations. Such a guarantee would properly take the form of a specific commitment by the United Nations Security Council to enforce the peace and all of its specifications, including the "secure and recognized boundaries" of both

Israel and her Arab neighbors and the neutralized status of designated border zones. The agreement should also specify strict limitations on the sale or provision of arms to Middle Eastern states by outside powers. As permanent members of the Security Council, the United States, the Soviet Union, the United Kingdom, France and China would have major responsibility for enforcement of the peace terms, but that obligation would fall upon them not in their capacity as "great powers" but as members of the Security Council, which is entrusted by Article 24 of the Charter with "primary responsibility for the maintenance of international peace and security."

It might also be appropriate and desirable for the Security Council's guarantee to be ratified formally by the legislative bodies of the signatory states. Such action would represent a mark of the seriousness attached to this new commitment by members of the Security Council, although it might not be regarded as juridically essential since, by ratifying the Charter in the first place, every member of the United Nations is already committed, under Article 25, to "accept and carry out the decisions of the Security Council." It would do no harm, however, to remind the members, by formal parliamentary act, of this frequently forgotten obligation. For reasons of varying merit Israel has indicated on numerous occasions a lack of confidence in the United Nations. In order to accommodate this attitude and provide Israel with an added assurance of security, I for one would be willing to supplement a United Nations guarantee with a bilateral treaty—not an executive agreement but a treaty consented to by the Senate—under which the United States would guarantee the territory and independence of Israel within the adjusted borders of 1967. This guarantee should neither add to, nor detract from, nor in any way alter the multilateral guarantee of the United Nations—which would obligate us, as a member of the Security Council, to defend the "secure and recognized boundaries" of both Israel *and* her Arab neighbors. The supplementary, bilateral arrangement with Israel would obligate the United States to use force if necessary, in accordance with its constitutional processes, to assist Israel against any violation of its 1967 borders, as adjusted, which it could not repel itself, but the agreement would also obligate Israel, firmly and unequivocally, never to violate those borders herself.

I conceive of an American treaty of guarantee of Israel as an instrument which would come into effect after—and only after—the multilateral guarantee of the United Nations had been agreed upon and ratified by all parties. The bilateral treaty with Israel would represent no more than a repetition of, and an additional assurance of, our intent to honor the multilateral guarantee of the United Nations. It would reiterate a commitment which every member of the Security

Council, including the Soviet Union, would also have made through their multilateral guarantee of the borders of *all* of the states concerned.

The situation in the Middle East presents the world community with an important, indeed an unprecedented, opportunity. At its present juncture the conflict between Israel and the Arabs is the most significant issue since the end of World War II in which the Soviet Union and the United States have identified enough in the way of common interests to allow even of the possibility of a peaceful settlement mediated and guaranteed by the United Nations Security Council. Hitherto the insuperable obstacle to effective Security Council action has been the paralysis of the Security Council by the great-power veto. China, newly admitted to the United Nations, is an unknown quantity as far as the Middle East is concerned, but if the Russians and Americans meant what they have said about a Middle East settlement, and if they were prepared to back it up by the application of sanctions as provided for in the United Nations Charter, they might not find it impossible to bring about a settlement implementing the Security Council Resolution of November 1967. The importance of the opportunity can hardly be exaggerated. A settlement mediated by the great powers in their capacity as great powers quite possibly could be a fair and durable one, but a settlement mediated by the United Nations could serve as a precedent for the settlement of other conflicts through the procedures of international organization. Perhaps, if the precedents accumulated, and with further advances in civilization, it might even be found possible to apply these procedures in conflicts involving the great powers themselves. That, after all, was why we created the United Nations in the first place—"to save succeeding generations from the scourge of war. . . ."

NOTES

[1] I. F. Stone, "Holy War," in *The Israel-Arab Reader* (Walter Laqueur, ed., New York: Bantam Books, 1969), p. 324.

[2] Quoted in Seth P. Tillman, *Anglo-American Relations at the Paris Peace Conference of 1919* (Princeton University Press, 1961), p. 132.

[3] Speech to the Central Committee of the Arab Socialist Union, July 24, 1972, quoted in Henry Tanner, "Egyptian Asserts Moscow Caution Caused Ousters," *The New York Times*, July 25, 1972, p. 1.

[4] Interview on *The Advocates*, a public television network presentation of KCET, Los Angeles, and WGBH, Boston, June 21, 1970, "The Middle East: Where Do We Go From Here? Part II: The Case for U.S. Support for Israel."

[5] "Sorry Wrong Number," editorial in *The New York Times*, April 10, 1970, p. 38.

[6] Nahum Goldmann, "Israel and the Arabs—an 'Unrepresentative' View," *Le Monde*, Weekly Selection, May 27, 1970, p. 4.

[7] Alexis de Tocqueville, *Democracy in America* (New York: Harper and Row, Publishers, 1966), Vol. II, ch. 22, p. 625.

[8] "Nasser Accepts U.S. Plan, but Asks Aid to Israel End," *The New York Times*, July 24, 1970, p. 1.

[9] "Mrs. Meir Asserts Hussein's Plans Skirt Peace Issue," *The New York Times*, March 17, 1972, p. 1.

[10] "The Argument Between Arabs and Jews," in *The Israel-Arab Reader*, p. 262.

[11] Quoted in *Search for Peace in the Middle East* (Philadelphia: American Friends Service Committee, 1970), p. 43.

[12] Quoted by Peter Grose in "Israel and U.S. in a Game of 'Diplomatic Chicken,'" *The New York Times*, March 21, 1971, p. 4E.

[13] Interview with John McCook Roots, quoted in "Ben-Gurion Quoted in Article as Favoring Major Pullback." *The Evening Star*, Washington, D.C., March 25, 1971, p. A-3.

[14] Speech to the National Press Club, Washington, D.C., April 10, 1969.

[15] *The Advocates*, June 14, 1970.

[16] Interview with a correspondent of *The London Times*, quoted in "Mrs. Meir Cites Border Changes Sought by Israel," *The New York Times*, March 13, 1971, pp. 1, 6.

[17] *Search for Peace in the Middle East*, p. 36.

[18] Hess, John L., "Sadat Said to Warn Soviet He'll Resist Reds in Middle East," *The New York Times*, August 6, 1971, p. 2.

[19] Speech to the Central Committee of the Arab Socialist Union, July 24, 1972, quoted in Henry Tanner, "Egyptian Asserts Moscow Caution Caused Ousters," *The New York Times*, July 25, 1972, p. 1.

[20] Bernard Gwertzman, "Soviet Role in Mideast," *The New York Times*, August 3, 1970, p. 2.

[21] Televised interview of July 1, 1970.

[22] Background Briefing, San Clemente, California, June 26, 1970, unpublished, p. 20.

[23] Background Briefing, San Clemente, California, June 30, 1970, p. 9; June 26, 1970, p. 23.

[24] Interview with a correspondent of *The London Times*, in "Mrs. Meir Cites Border Changes Sought by Israel," *The New York Times*, March 13, 1971, pp. 1, 6.

[25] Briefing by Secretary of State William P. Rogers, *Hearings Held Before the Committee on Foreign Relations, U.S. Senate*, March 27, 1969 (Washington: U.S. Government Printing Office, 1969), p. 3.

[26] Speech to the National Press Club, Washington, D.C., April 10, 1969.

[27] *Search for Peace in the Middle East*, p. 56.

[28] "Israel and the Arabs—An 'Unrepresentative' View," *Le Monde*, Weekly Selection, May 27, 1970, p. 4.

FOR FURTHER READING

Theodore Draper. *Israel and World Politics*. New York: Viking, 1968.

* Irene L. Gendzier, ed. *A Middle East Reader*. New York: Pegasus, 1970.

* Walter Laqueur. *Road to War: The Origin and Aftermath of the Arab-Israeli Conflict, 1967–68*. Baltimore: Penguin, 1969.

* Walter Laqueur. *Struggle for the Middle East*. Baltimore: Penguin, 1972.

THE UNITED STATES, THE CIA, AND CHILE

*ROGER MORRIS, WITH
SHELLEY MUELLER AND
WILLIAM JELIN*

By the First Amendment to the Constitution of the United States, the press is protected from governmental interference and, in principle, is free to provide citizens with the information and analysis they must have in order to make intelligent decisions on public questions. Regarding with contempt the controlled press of many other countries, Americans have generally assumed that their own news-papers, broadcasters, and news magazines, untrammeled by censor-ship, search out and present the truth of events. As a result, the people have therefore tended to accept uncritically reports that the media bring to them.

And yet, in the 1970's, as Americans reappraise their past policies, especially in foreign relations, they need also to re-examine the per-formance of the press. Before 1965, although the United States intervened in countries throughout the world and sent Americans as volunteer teachers to Africa or as drafted soldiers to Indo-China, the mass media seldom questioned official actions or examined the basis for the policy of "containment." Some doubters, it is true, were able to express their views on the air or in slimly financed periodicals; but Pacifica radio stations and publications like *The Nation, The Progressive,* and *I. F. Stone's Weekly* could reach only a few listeners and readers. Along with most of the Congress, the majority of the agencies of information were proud to defer to the White House, the Department of Defense, and the Central Intelligence Agency. An official whisper of "national security" stopped respected publishers from exploring leads or featuring stories that might imply executive

Reprinted from the *Columbia Journalism Review*, November/December 1974.

error or wrongdoing. Only a few mavericks found flaws in President Lyndon B. Johnson's account of the incidents in the Bay of Tonkin; an outstanding newspaper played down a report on plans for the Bay of Pigs invasion of Cuba; and only an incurious press could have allowed the government to keep secret for years its unauthorized war in Laos.

In 1895, Secretary of State Richard Olney blusteringly informed the British: "Today the United States is practically sovereign on this continent, and its fiat is law upon the subjects to which it confines its interposition." Subsequently the United States in fact achieved in Latin America a hegemony that European nations no longer cared to contest. North American banks and corporations invested in utilities, copper, bananas, oil, and sugar, and in the 1950's the administration in Washington could count on the support of a solid bloc of Latin American votes in the United Nations. Yet within the countries of South and Central America, socialist and nationalist movements gathered force to challenge both domestic and foreign domination. The revolution that convulsed Mexico for more than a decade after 1910 and the Cuban revolution that triumphed in 1959 especially shocked the American government and threatened American "interests." U.S. efforts to counter such movements have taken various forms: "Good Neighbor" diplomacy, the Alliance for Progress, and military action. In 1954 the CIA assisted a rightist group in successful efforts to overthrow the Guatemalan government, and in 1961 it trained exiles to make a similar attempt in Cuba; in 1965 President Johnson dispatched U.S. Marines to protect conservatives in the Dominican Republic. By 1975 there was no longer any doubt that the United States had played a role in overthrowing the Allende government in Chile in 1973 and replacing it with a military junta.

In the late 1960's and 1970's Americans may have lost some of their faith in authority. The débâcle in Indo-China, the deception revealed by the "Pentagon Papers," the Watergate crimes, and the exposure of certain CIA activities may have dispelled some of the glamour that formerly surrounded high executives. In some of these disclosures the press has played an important role. And yet, as Roger Morris mountains, the media still tend to offer shallow reports of major events and to disseminate uncritically the word from the White House. Morris tackles some common misconceptions of the situation in Chile at the time of the coup and disquietingly suggests that, although the American press is legally free, it may censor itself voluntarily when so-called national interests are at stake.

□　　□　　□

> *"The question is," said Alice, "whether you can make*
> *words mean so many different things."*
> *"The question is," said Humpty Dumpty, "which is*
> *to be master—that's all."* LEWIS CARROLL

In a sense, it was a caricature. Elected President by a narrow plurality, plagued by economic problems, within three years overthrown and killed in a bloody *coup d'état* by a military junta, Salvador Allende Gossens, and with him Chilean democracy, went the way of so many casualties of the chronic instability in Latin America.

If one looks beyond that familiar picture, however, Allende's rule in Chile from 1970 to 1973 appears in some respects as an extraordinary episode. The first popularly elected socialist-communist coalition government in the hemisphere, it was seen—by supporters and opponents, U.S. policy makers and Chileans—as the most formidable force for change in Latin America in a decade. It was also the object, we now know, of a sustained covert intervention in Chile by the U.S. Central Intelligence Agency, which reportedly spent at least $8 million during 1970-73 for purposes including bribery of the Chilean Congress to block Allende's election and instigation of strikes to help overthrow the government.

As this article is written, the story of the CIA in Chile is still evolving. Both journalists and the Congress have called for an investigation of the Chilean interlude and beyond to the larger issue of covert operations as an instrument of policy. But the CIA disclosures are not the only history worth recalling. The Allende regime was a remarkable looking glass in which to see American journalism as well as Washington's *realpolitik*.

We have surveyed news coverage and commentary by U.S. television networks and several major newspapers between 1970 and 1973.* It is a great mass of material. Some of the coverage of Chile under Allende stands as accurate, searching, and disinterested. But more often, it appeared to be a journalism stunted by cliche and banal-

---

* The survey included both news reports and editorial comment. It is recognized that commentary is not subject to the same standards as reportorial journalism. Yet the aim of this analysis is an assessment of the overall thrust of U.S. journalism regarding Chile—judgments and interpretations as well as news coverage.

There is no pretense here of having seen every item on Chile over three years, or of having measured coverage by some quantifiable content analysis. And there may well be isolated exceptions to the points that follow. But this article draws on a great and representative quantity of reports from and about Chile, and the examples cited reflect trends that can be documented with numbing frequency.

ity, notable for the important stories never reported. Despite the presence of correspondents with long experience in Latin America, there was a consistent lack of analysis and perspective on complex events. And in much of the coverage there was a one-sided characterization of Allende and his government that obscured both developments in Chile and the reality of U.S. policy toward that country. The reporting of Allende's Chile leaves disturbing questions about the depth and range of foreign news coverage, about the working relationship of correspondents to the U.S. government, and, not least, about the impact of culture and ideology on the efforts of a free press to report international affairs.

For most of the American public, the election of Allende in the autumn of 1970 came as an obscure and largely unheralded event, although in Chile, the three-way race for the presidency had been heated for months. (The CIA reportedly made a $400,000 campaign contribution to Allende's opposition.) During this period there were scarcely more than scattered news accounts from Chile, with little background on the candidates and parties, on Allende's platform or support. Though all three major television networks were to report regularly on Allende's regime, none offered comparable attention to Chile in the nine eventful months before his election.

Why did Chile suddenly seem important to journalists? The news accounts of Allende's election give a clue. CBS reported that Allende had "promised a strong socialist government," adding that "Chile's democracy has also won a victory." NBC noted that Allende was "a long-time Castroite and confirmed Marxist. It was, apparently, the victory of a Marxist that transformed Chile, in the minds of many U.S. journalists, from an ignored land of sombreros into a news story. "A story had merit," said one reporter who filed frequently from Chile, "if there was a relationship to the red menace." "Castro made Latin America newsworthy," said another correspondent, recalling that his organization had no reporters on the continent at all before 1961. "If you didn't hit the Castro theme," he continued, "you had a hard time selling your story." One wince-producing example of the "red menace" theme would later be seen on the CBS Evening News. Walter Cronkite reported that Chileans had rejected an effort by the "Marxist regime" to replace Santa Claus figures with "jovial representatives of the workers" distributing presents to the poor. As Cronkite spoke, the picture behind him was of a hammer and sickle flashing on and then off a smiling Santa Claus.

Did the interest in news that could be hooked to a "red menace" mean that U.S. journalists, like U.S. policy-makers, were opposed to Castro and to "Marxism" in Latin America? There are many Chileans and some U.S. academics who would answer "yes" to this question. Most journalists would say "no"; political preferences are not the same as news judgment, and socialism in Latin America was news because it was unusual, dramatic, destined to affect U.S. interests—it was, in other words, both good copy and an important story. Such non-ideological considerations obviously do affect U.S. foreign reporting. Canada's Premier Pierre Trudeau, covered generously because he was perceived as a "swinger," is a case in point. Yet, as Allende governed, events that painted him as a "Castroite" and facts that portrayed him and his administration in a negative light, were the usual occasions for U.S. news stories; omitted more frequently were facts that would cause sympathy for Allende, facts that would indicate the successes or democratic aspects of his policies. The issue is not whether Allende was a statesman or tyrant—there is evidence that he was a little of both. But, as one reviews the news coverage (and commentary), one is ultimately forced to wonder whether ideology has as little to do with foreign news coverage as U.S. journalists usually assume.

MARXISM AND CONSTITUTIONALISM

An early and persistent theme in the coverage of Allende was the "ominous" political character of the regime. This new "Marxist" government had "outright Communist internal policies," commented ABC's Howard K. Smith soon after Allende's election in the autumn of 1970. There were now "totalitarian inclinations" in Chile, the Los Angeles *Times* editorialized, wondering less than six month after the election if the new regime would "allow itself to be voted out as freely as it was voted in." Almost without exception, news reports emphasized that Allende was a "minority" president, that "Communists" were in his government, that his purposes were "revolutionary." The prevailing point of reference for Chile became Cuba ten years earlier ("another Communist beachhead," predicted several observers), and for Allende, Castro (the "other Marxist leader" in the hemisphere, ABC said, with literal accuracy, when Castro visited Chile in 1971). Both the New York *Times* and the Washington *Post* pondered whether Chile's "free institutions" could survive" what the *Times* called the country's "sharp turn to the left."

But there would also be much evidence that Chile in 1970-73 was *not* Cuba. Behind Allende's self-proclaimed radicalism and the presence of an ambitious Communist party in his coalition were formidable yet seldom reported restraints on the sinister trends seen by American journalism. Correspondents rarely led, for example, with the equally clear declarations by Allende that his regime would also work through the constitutional system. This "Chilean way" was a major and continuing theme in Allende's campaign throughout 1970, and on into the new regime. ". . . . There will be legality," Allende pledged in a key congressional message as president. "We accept the political liberties of the opposition," he went on, "and continue our political activities within the boundaries of our institutions." And if Allende's rhetoric—like all rhetoric—was deserving of suspicion, there remained tangible limits on the "totalitarian" urges of the new government. Though reports from Chile scarcely paused to mention Chilean political history, it was relevant that the governing coalition was made up not only of Communists, but also of several other mutually suspicious parties and organizations, including Allende's own democratic socialists. That coalition took office with a history of bitter, often violent divisions —among the Communists, within the non-Communist left, and between Socialists and Communists. In the opposition-controlled Congress that confirmed Allende's popular election, Communists held only six of 50 seats in the Senate, and only 22 of 150 in the Chamber of Deputies. Moreover, Chilean politics also had its ambitious Right, well organized and generously financed elements who matched their leftist counterparts in barely disguised impatience with the democratic system. It was not Fidel Castro riding into Havana on the ruins of Batista's dictatorship, and rather more complicated than a hammer and sickle on Santa.

MINORITY AND PLURALITY

Allende, as journalists tirelessly reminded the U.S. audience, was clearly a "minority" president, winning by about 37 percent in a race determined by a few thousand votes. But so too was Jorge Alessandri, the Conservative elected in 1958, as Allende would be in 1970, in a three-way race. The phrase "minority president" suggests an impropriety to a U.S. audience, but Allende's minority (plurality) was not an aberration in Chilean or Latin American politics, where clear majority victories are rare. Nor should Allende's constitutional legitimacy have been alien to a country that, in three-way races, had elected by pluralities Woodrow Wilson, Harry Truman and most recently Richard Nixon. But such details were given scant attention in reporting that reiterated Allende's precarious "minority" position.

Support for the Allende coalition candidates in the municipal elections of April, 1971, was over 50 percent, a fact not widely reported in the U.S. at a time when stories and columns on Chile were already reporting the new regime's waning popularity. On the other hand, in reporting the January, 1972, congressional by-election losses for Allende, ABC's evening TV news program, like many others, did not explain that the two elections were in traditionally conservative districts. Al-

lende was unquestionably a controversial figure with heavy and growing opposition. But American journalism tended to obscure at the same
time his enduring and in some cases increasing support from many
Chileans—support that helps to explain not only Allende's actions, but
also the later wide-ranging repression by the junta that replaced him.

Perhaps the most obvious measure of Allende's politics, however,
would be the daily record of his government's actions toward the opposition. A press which worried from the outset about the regime's "inclinations" did not report as readily or consistently the conflicting facts
on the evolution of political freedom under Allende. As the New York
Times and others reported, the Allende regime in 1971 fixed the price
of newspaper advertising rates and ended a policy of regular government advertising in the press; both actions were a blow to opposition
news media. But few U.S. reports also noted that the opposition-controlled Congress had earlier passed legislation prohibiting government
advertising.

Similarly, *El Mercurio*, the chief anti-Allende conservative paper,
was closed down briefly after publishing an editorial suggesting the
ouster of the regime. Another right-wing paper was harassed by the
government. The regime refused to license a new radio station for the
Catholic University in Concepcion known to be opposed to Allende.
Meanwhile, government-owned or subsidized papers and publishers, as
well as two of the three Santiago television stations, conveyed Allende's
propaganda. These events, often accompanied by opposition criticism,
were reported.

Less visible in the American coverage of Allende were signs of
Chile's continuing political vitality. Two-thirds of the country's radio
stations were controlled by the opposition; private schools and universities, many with anti-Allende administrations, received regular government subsidies. Most notably, opposition parties, the Congress and
courts functioned throughout 1970-73. Only weeks before Allende was
overthrown, reported Princeton Professor Paul Sigmund in *World View*
magazine, there were papers for sale on the streets of Santiago openly
calling for insurrection against the government. Apart from the "intentions" of Allende and his Communist colleagues, the reality in Chile
was complex and paradoxical, defying simplistic imagery.

Allende himself was apparently aware of how the American media
portrayed his government in this respect. The facile vocabulary of repression and "totalitarianism" in the press must have seemed bitterly
ironic to the head of a beleaguered regime in a country where the opposition so persistently and openly demanded his removal. One of his last
interviews, given to John P. Wallach in June, 1973 and published in
the Washington *Post* a week after the coup in September, contained a
plea against simplistic labels. "I want to insist," he said to Wallach as
he had to other newsmen,

that Chile is not a socialist country. This is a capitalist country, and my government is not a socialist government. Neither, as the press likes to say, is it a Marxist government. I am a Marxist. That's something else. But the government is made up of Marxists, laymen and Christians.

But then, Allende had made almost the same appeal against such loaded journalism, word for word, years earlier on *Meet The Press*, and to little avail. According to the transcript of the program, the next interviewer, Jeremiah O'Leary of the Washington *Star*, prefaced his question to Allende, with the phrase, "Comrade President . . ."

Probably the most familiar refrain in U.S. journalism on Chile was the reporting of economic mismanagement and ultimately breakdown. "Hardly a better example of the barren results of radical politics could be found than Chile," said the *Wall Street Journal* in a post-coup editorial that seemed to summarize a media view of Allende's economic policies. The regime had been toppled, the *Journal* concluded, largely because it had "been willing to destroy much of the Chilean economy." It was a view that had echoed through the reporting from Santiago. There was "uncertainty and mistrust" in the Chilean economy, cabled Juan de Onis to the New York *Times* in a dispatch that would reflect the pattern. As early as 1971, de Onis found investment at a "standstill" and businessmen and farmers "going under." Reporters and editorial writers apparently saw vividly the disruption of production, the scarcities of food and manufactured goods in the cities, the high prices, and the mounting public unrest in the wake of these developments. From the countryside came reports of confiscations and seizures. In Santiago the government was nationalizing large sections of industry, freezing prices and raising wages among laborers. Correspondents found depleted shops and reported them. In short, the connection between radical economic policies and "chaos" was repeatedly drawn.

There seems little doubt that the Allende regime often mismanaged both the design and pace of its economic efforts. Its policies were anathema to a large number of Chileans. Its rhetoric and style, radical from the outset, hardened almost in proportion to its blunders and opposition. But beyond these generalities, there was also evident an equally revealing variety and ambiguity in the economy under Allende.

INCOME AND PRODUCTION

First, amid the gathering portents of economic ruin, there were also measures of economic progress, statistics that often belied empty shops yet were little reported. Writing in *The Nation* in January, 1973, for example, Rutgers scholar on Latin American John Pollock cited public Chilean figures marking a doubling of agricultural production in 1971, a 9 percent rise in the construction industry, a decline in unemployment from over 8 percent in 1970 to less than 5 percent in 1971, the lowest in Chile in a decade. Consumer prices under Allende, argued Pollock and other scholars, rose in 1971 at one-half the rate they had risen under the previous regime.* In some respects most interesting, American and British academic researchers found that Allende's redistributive economic policies were apparently working. Beef and bread consumption were up some 15 percent in 1971-72, a sign, along with the shortages in Santiago, of greater purchasing by the working poor in cities and the countryside. Another index of that development: the salary and wage percentage of Chile's national income went from 51 percent in 1970 to nearly 60 percent in 1971. And in part as a result of all this, Chile's growth in GNP for Allende's first year was 8.5 percent, the second highest in Latin America. But such available figures, if considered at all, apparently made less interesting copy than scenes of collapse.

Similarly, there were dramatic stories about as many as 2,000 "seizures" of farms under Allende, stories that may well have led Americans to imagine barn burnings and yeoman farmers driven from their land. Few readers of those descriptions were also told that Chile was a country where 5 percent of the families owned some 35 percent of the land, mostly in huge 2,500 acre estates, while 250,000 rural families were landless; that the Allende government ran its land reform under a statute passed previously by a conservative Congress; that the moderate regime preceding Allende's had already redistributed land to 30,000 peasant families; that violence was rare in the "seizures"; or that Allende himself had clashed with the left wing of his own party in opposing, as he said in the same Congressional message that pledged legality, "indiscriminate occupations of estates and farms." Allende was elected to power in a constitutional government that already provided 70 percent of the country's investment, employed large numbers of the population and was already interfering extensively in the private economy. But such history was apparently not "news."

---

* Statistics on Allende's Chile are difficult to come by, have been abused by all sides, and are often impossible to check. The junta, for example, has claimed there was a 100 percent "rate of inflation" in the last two years of the Allende regime. Authoritative explanation of this figure—consumer prices, wholesale prices, etc.—was not available from scholarly sources consulted, nor was it provided after two requests made to the Chilean embassy in Washington. Consequently, the 100 percent figure, true or false, does not appear in the text.

While all figures cited are drawn from reputable U.S. and British scholars, and seem duly documented, no additional claim is made for their validity. Chile—and press coverage of Chile—have received substantial academic attention. The Library of Congress lists eighteen recent studies, including seven dissertations. Most of this research has been openly sympathetic to Allende. Whatever the eventual perspective of history, the important point is that such academic studies draw on data that was also available to reporters, that conflict with the impression given by most coverage, and that therefore deserved also to be reported.

COPPER: SEIZURE AND NATIONALIZATION

The lack of perspective was especially apparent in the accounts of Allende's nationalization of the U.S. owned mining interests of Anaconda and Kennecott Corporations. Every major U.S. news organization reported the move, most in the conventional terminology of "seizure," as in "President Salvador Allende of Chile today seized. . . ." In the wake of previous depiction of Allende's "Castroite" and "revolutionary" character, the nationalization might have seemed on the surface the hostile, selfish, and predictable act of one man. Yet the "seizure" had added dimensions, only occasionally reported. *Both* Allende and the Christian Democratic opponent he narrowly defeated had campaigned for nationalization of copper. Together they received more than 60 percent of the presidential vote. The nationalization was approved in 1971 by a unanimous vote of the opposition-controlled congress. The nationalization was a law, wrote a British scholar, "against which no Chilean politician would go on public record any more than he would publicly vote for polygamy." In taking over the copper, Chile followed several other Latin American countries of various political stripes, from elected nationalists to right-wing juntas, in similarly "seizing," buying out, or otherwise expelling U.S. interests—including, since 1968, Peru, Ecuador, Bolivia, Columbia, Argentina, and Venezuela.

Copper accounted for about 75 percent of Chile's foreign earnings, providing exchange that would be crucial to support or even increase Chile's traditionally high food imports as Allende tried to increase consumption among the poor. So when copper production fell drastically in 1972-73, the effects on the economy were disastrous, in part the result of faulty management of the mines and an exodus of skilled personnel who preferred the corporate ownership. The *Wall Street Journal* went beyond this cause and effect, however, to report that the copper companies had deliberately left the mines in disrepair and later even attempted to organize boycotts of Chilean copper in international markets.

THE MIDDLE CLASS AND OTHER CLASSES

Probably no single event illustrated more clearly the gaps in the Chile coverage than the widely reported "march of the pots," a demonstration against Allende's economic policies in December, 1971, by several thousand women banging empty pots in Santiago. The protest involved street violence—the worst such outbreak yet under Allende. Reports from Santiago of the march varied in the color and detail, but most emphasized that the women were protesting food shortages, that the demonstrators were attacked by "leftists," and that the event was "ominous" for the Allende regime. "Supporters of Marxist President Allende set upon the marchers hurling bricks and rocks and swinging clubs," reported Cronkite on CBS before a film of police shooting tear gas and a close-up of a woman with blood running down her head. Allende now faced, said a New York *Times* editorial, "the worst political crisis of his thirteen months in power . . . a trap that he himself helped to prepare." According to the *Christian Science Monitor* the march had "polarized" a now "volatile" Chile, and Allende was on the "hot seat."

The protest did symbolize an authentic food scarcity. But few accounts—a thorough report in the *Christian Science Monitor* was a conspicuous exception—brought home the equally important point that the protesting women were generally well-fed and well-dressed, that the din of the banging pots was loudest in the relatively affluent section of Santiago, or that the march was organized by the more conservative Christian Democratic party. "Their pots were not all that empty," commented a U.S. diplomat who served in Chile at the time. Again, the reality of Allende's Chile was more complex than the broadly reported image of a "Marxist" starving his people in economic mismanagement. The regime was engaged in radical redistributive economics, unique in Latin America. Some elements were squeezed, in this case middle income housewives, and they reacted with highly visible opposition. The same reforms also benefited others whose response was less visible. Both effects deserved investigation.

The most misleading label in the Chile coverage was the ubiquitous "middle class." Now "fleeing" the country, now "facing destruction" (said broadcasters), the Chilean "middle class," according to the New York *Times*, made up "half of the population" of Chile's nine million people. Usually the exact size of the middle class was not given.

Polls tell us that almost 80 percent of the people in the U.S. see themselves as "middle Americans." "Middle class" has a different meaning in Latin America. One of the standard books on Latin American politics, *Political Change in Latin America*, by former State Department analyst John J. Johnson, put the "middle sectors" in Chile at no more than 30 percent of the nation. Another study by Penn State Professor James Petras indicated that only 23 percent of Chile's population took almost 80 percent of Chile's national income. Some experts argue that the Chilean economy and social structure were so lopsided in this respect that only about 300,000 out of the nine million were effective consumers for sophisticated industry, meaning that the vast majority of Chileans would be unaffected by the empty shops in Santiago seemingly so conspicuous to U.S. reporters. In any event, the apparent similarities between Chile's "middle class" and inflation-plagued U.S. families were profoundly misleading without added context. In 1970,

Chile's GNP per capita, a standard index of comparative wealth used by international institutions such as the World Bank, was scarcely one-seventh of that of the U.S., and Chile's growth rate from 1960 to 1970 one of the lowest in the world at 1.6 percent. In short, most of Chile's people belonged to an impoverished mass for whom empty pots were common and the "middle class" a distant dream. Whatever Allende represented, whatever was happening in Chile under his rule, it could not have been accurately reported in generalities that meant one thing in the U.S. and quite another in Latin America.

Among the important missing perspectives in the coverage of Chile was the extraordinary record of what the United States Government was doing to the Allende regime. The assumption of Washington's official tolerance was an early and persistent theme in the journalism on Chile. Most often the subject of American policy was simply ignored. But some of the record, particularly the remarks of television commentators, makes quaint and embarrassing reading after recent revelations. "There has been and there will be no resistance by the U.S.," announced Smith on ABC as Allende was inaugurated. Eric Sevareid observed, in April, 1971, "Whatever the drift, what Washington can do about it is next to nothing."

As Smith spoke in October, 1970, the CIA was authorized to spend over a million dollars to defeat Allende. By the time Sevareid commented in the spring of 1971, the CIA reportedly began to spend another five million. The Nixon Administration's policy was scarcely "no resistance." Covertly *and* in the open, the U.S. applied extraordinary coercion to break the Allende government.

TOLERANCE AND INTERVENTION

In 1964, according to official sources, the CIA was spending $3 million to insure the defeat of Allende in Chile's 1964 Presidential elections. "No Communist [sic] had ever been elected," as one official explained the 1964 campaign spending, "and we pulled out all the stops."

The details of this and other covert CIA operations in Latin America were secret when Allende was elected. Yet some of the record was also public. Hearings of the Senate Foreign Relations Committee in 1969, for example, had strongly suggested the outline of CIA manipulation of labor unions in the Ecuadorian and Brazilian coups. The U.S. had brought obvious diplomatic pressure, including a suspension of economic aid, against the Goulart government. But among those who covered the Allende regime, avowedly more anti-American than either of the deposed governments in Ecuador or Brazil, there seemed little awareness of this background.

At the request of the White House, officials say, weekly intelligence reports on Chile and particularly the course of its Presidential campaign were sent to President Nixon from late 1969 through 1970. And, as early as June, 1970, policy was reportedly executed in two separate channels. The so-called Forty Committee, which approves clandestine operations abroad, authorized the CIA's covert intervention against Allende. Meanwhile, the other agencies of the foreign affairs bureaucracy, including the Department of State, Defense and Treasury, debated and carried out the policy of diplomatic and overt economic pressure.

Official sources indicate that the first major policy meeting on Chile was, appropriately enough, in the Forty Committee on June 27, 1970. "We can't let a country go Marxist," then Presidential assistant Henry Kissinger has been quoted as saying in that discussion, "just because its people are irresponsible."

The Forty Committee reportedly met again on September 18, two weeks after Allende's popular victory, and authorized some $500,000 in what official sources call "action funds" to bribe the Chilean Congress to elect Alessandri, the close second to Allende. The bribery plan was shortly abandoned as impractical, however. U.S. officials say the Committee subsequently approved $5 million to fund opposition to Allende in 1970-72, and then about $2.5 million more to support strikes and other dissident activities during 1973. These meetings in the West Wing of the White House were shrouded in the highest secrecy. But some results in Chile were not beyond the reach of investigative reporting. The "march of the empty pots" and other forms of protest against Allende, for instance, were similar to activities sponsored against Goulart in Brazil years earlier by organizations widely suspected of receiving CIA funds. Marlise Simons of the Washington *Post* went to Brazil and reported these similarities, including a comment by a Brazilian rightist that the Chileans had been "taught . . . how to use their women against the Marxists." Simons' story turned up no direct evidence of CIA involvement, though officials in Washington now confirm, as one put it, "Brazil shared our concern and did its part." But the Simons reporting, among the most enterprising from Latin America, came only after Allende's overthrow. From 1970 to 1973, millions of dollars passed in Chile to a number of organizations and individuals, issuing in dramatic actions, sometimes in the streets, without a trace in the coverage of a score of U.S. newsmen who ostensibly saw Chile as *the* story in the hemisphere.

If CIA funding was secret, the punitive diplomacy toward Allende was almost impossible to hide. As policies were reviewed, there apparently developed bureaucratic disputes over both the seriousness of the problems and how to deal with them. The State Department, according to a reliable source, was relatively "relaxed" about the forthcoming election, expecting Alessandri to win but believing "politics in Chile seem likely to polarize in any event." Among CIA analysts (not those in covert operations), sources report what one called "a rare division." "Some were openly biased toward Alessandri, some toward Allende," remembered a former official. Defense and Treasury reportedly recommended all-out opposition to Allende to protect economic and possible strategic interests.

"It was the 'who-lost-Chile' syndrome," said one former U.S. diplomat of the White House view of Allende. A source close to Kissinger added: "Henry thought Allende might lead an anti-U.S. move in Latin America more effectively than Castro, just because it *was* the democratic route to power."

Official sources insist, and the public record tends to bear out, that the determination to stop Allende went well beyond the stereotype influence of U.S. corporate interests in Chile. "Henry never gave a damn about the business community," said one authoritative source. "What really underlay his policy was ideology." Another witness describes an incident early in Allende's regime when the threatened copper companies proposed a deal to the Chileans in return for a favorable U.S. policy. The proposal seems to have involved a promise of U.S. economic aid to offset Chilean compensation to the corporations, a kind of foreign aid insurance payment on the nationalization. The plan reportedly won the support of Treasury Secretary John Connally and U.S. Ambassador to Chile Edward Korry. The former ambassador has said such an offer was made to Allende, but he improvidently declined it. Officials working with Kissinger remember his opposition to such concessions. "Our interests aren't necessarily the same," Kissinger is said to have told a corporate executive. "We have the larger national interest to think of." In this account of U.S. policy, corporate economic interests were secondary to political purposes, not the reverse, as has been charged and widely assumed. "Copper just gave us an opportunity to take the harder line we wanted to anyway," said one official. Perhaps *nothing* about the story of Allende would be as simple as it first seemed.

Whatever the precise motives, the course of U.S. policy toward Chile was clear from the outset. Once the highest per capita aid recipient in the hemisphere, Chile was cut off from development assistance throughout the Allende years. In August, 1971, the U.S. denied Chile any new loans from the Export-Import Bank. Also suspended were disbursements from direct loans previously negotiated and the guarantee and insurance program for commercial banks. The Export-Import Bank refused a $21 million credit to LAN-Chile airlines, a major source of Chile's foreign exchange earnings. In 1971, the U.S. brought pressure on the Interamerican Development Bank to refuse even emergency earthquake loans to Chile. Most visible of all, perhaps, was the U.S. opposition within the World Bank to any new loans to Chile from 1970 through 1973.

Meanwhile, the Pentagon cultivated the Chilean military. While the economic quarantine grew, arms aid during 1970-73 would total $47 million, including jet fighters for the Air Force that was to lead the September coup with bombing and strafing of the presidential palace.

There seems no sure way to estimate the exact impact of all these actions on Chile. The need for food imports, purchased only by the foreign exchange that vanished as copper production sagged, was obviously acute amid growing shortages in 1972-73. The U.S. cut both food aid and financial assistance at a moment when both were crucial to Allende's survival. According to U.S. Department of Commerce statistics, from 1969 to 1972 U.S. exports to Chile fell from $315 million to $186 million, imports from $151 million to $83 million. To the material economic effects, moreover, was added the political and psychological impact of ostracism.

Though discerning the clandestine efforts to wreck support for Allende may have required extraordinary journalistic digging, the economic warfare was carried on almost completely in the open, albeit in the remote and unglamorous offices of foreign policy. Literally all over Washington in the years 1970-73 were live sources, both U.S. and Latin, who knew what was happening to Chile. There were ample documentary records. There were those who disagreed with the policy —in State on the issue of Kissinger's hard line, in Treasury on the question of compensation for the copper companies, even in the White House, where Kissinger was anxious to combat State's softness.

In Santiago, too, the pressure could be seen with unusual clarity. Government foreign exchange figures, to take only one available index, charted a steady attrition—reduced, by 1972, to 10 percent of the pre-Allende level. In the U.S. Embassy sat Ambassador Korry, a former journalist who, by all accounts, was pungently outspoken in his opposition to Allende before the election and barely reconciled to the new regime afterward. It was, in short, a remarkable story with a singularly rich lode of potential sources. But it would be written only after the coup, and then, only in part when Laurence Stern traced the economic pressure in the Washington *Post*.

The unwritten, untelevised story of U.S. policy toward Allende's Chile was in part another casualty of the continuing failure of independent, inquiring reporting. In that sense, perhaps the failure is not irreparable. But the failures of journalism—in covering the policy made in Washington and the events on the scene—were also failures to understand and to report the reality of a very different culture.

During the waning days of Allende's government the coverage

from Chile changed little. When the coalition gained 44 percent in the March, 1973, congressional elections, indicating a swing of new support to Allende and even some "middle class" votes, the television networks were reluctant analysts. ". . . Has to be counted as a victory," said ABC.

On the day of the coup, Robert Schakne's wrap-up on the story for CBS was that "Allende *found himself* more and more isolated, and he was never able to bring about the socialism that he talked about" [emphasis added]. Reflecting on the coup on Sept. 13, Sevareid saw Chile as another example in Latin America of an "instability so chronic that the root causes have to lie in the nature and culture of the people. The policies of other nations, including this one, toward the southern hemisphere have to be minor and fleeting influences in comparison." Eleven days later, the United States recognized the junta, deploring that Chile's problems could not be solved by "the free interplay of political institutions."

As charges of Washington's complicity in the coup came from Chilean refugees and elsewhere in Latin America, the U.S. press seemed all the more certain of what had gone on in Chile. "On the known record, Washington had only the most peripheral responsibility in the downfall of Dr. Allende," editorialized the New York *Times* on the same day Stern's article on the economic "choke" appeared in the Washington *Post*. "To pretend otherwise," the *Times* concluded, "is simply to obscure the basic reasons for the Chilean tragedy." And for those who still doubted, there were Jack Anderson and Les Whitten who had, after all, uncovered the ITT scandal: "Our sources, who have access to the secret deliberations of the Forty Committee, assure us that no project was approved to depose Allende." It would be a fine distinction—whether millions of dollars for the opposition, millions that led to civil strife, were or were not approved to "depose" Allende.

Over the coverage of Chile remain puzzling, often unanswerable questions. How and why did journalists miss the complexity of what may well turn out to be one of the most significant stories in the development of Latin America, and its relations with the U.S.?

Journalists on the scene remember that few organizations, such as AP, UPI and the New York *Times*, maintained full-time resident bureaus in Chile during the Allende years. Other organizations gathered reports from correspondents based elsewhere. The duration of such visits usually ranged, depending on the reporters, from a few days to two weeks. But the number of such trips was greater than usual, particularly for the television networks whose correspondents gave more attention to Chile than they had given to any other Latin American country. Within the press corps covering Chile were some of the most experienced and respected foreign correspondents, including Juan de Onis of the *Times*, Lewis Diuguid of the *Post*, the *Monitor*'s James Nelson Goodsell, William Giandoni of Copley News Service, the

Miami *Herald's* William Nonotobano, as well as Robert Schakne of CBS, Tom Streithorst of NBC and Charles Murphy of ABC.

Several correspondents say that the U.S. Embassy was often a central source for reports out of Santiago. "They would come and ask what the [Allende] government is doing wrong, and just print that," said one former embassy officer, perhaps exaggerating a bit as he reflected on his wide contacts among U.S. correspondents. At least some officials who lived through the events are now highly critical of the media coverage in Chile. "The press coverage gave you the feeling that the Allende regime would fall any day," said a U.S. diplomat, "but you didn't have that feeling living in Santiago." "You never read anything about the good that Allende was doing," complained a former attaché.

Chile was also a revealing example of the sociology of knowledge among correspondents. If the anti-Allende U.S. Embassy was the first stop for many correspondents in Chile, it also seems clear that they relied heavily on one another, in this case only reinforcing the established tone and content of the Chile coverage. Many reporters going to Chile recall that they "briefed" themselves, for example, on past files of the wire services. Others reportedly followed the lead of colleagues on the scene. "The New York *Times* is like a meteor with a long tail," as one observer described this imitative effect. "Reporters necessarily cohabit," said an editor acknowledging the sameness of so many dispatches from Santiago. Recalling "the terrible herd instinct," one television correspondent remembered taking his crew to cover a "seizure" of land only to be rebuffed by the Chileans on the site. "They said that *Newsweek* was here last week," recalled the correspondent, "and they hadn't liked what was printed."

But all these factors, present in some way and to some degree in the coverage of any story, were only some of the limits to reports from Chile. There was also apparently a powerful urge from home offices to report the most radical side of the Allende story. The influence of "what sells" no doubt shaped something of the apocalyptic tenor of the accounts of Allende.

Still, there is no ready reason why sophisticated newsmen, who knew the Chile story was far more complex, did not resist editorial pressures to report 1970-73 in images that had proven "newsworthy" ten years before. Or did they know? There is little evidence that journalists covering Chile went beyond their familiar precincts, into the villages and urban slums where an important part of the story was unfolding without benefit of CIA money. "I can't say I interviewed many peasants," said one reporter, "and nobody else did either." The obstacles to such reporting, of course, are formidable. In much of rural or urban slum Latin America, the American reporter is a foreigner in several respects. Instantly separated by class as well as nationality and perhaps too by dialect (even if he speaks Harvard or Berlitz Spanish), he may

well face suspicion, hostility or sheer incomprehension. Yet it is there—
as well as in affluent neighborhoods and in street riots—that "newsworthy" events take place in Chile and elsewhere in Latin America.

More disturbing than whether journalists did not *try* to see such
realities, however, is the lingering question of whether they *wanted to.*
"I didn't 'interpret' the Allende regime as against the best interests of
the U.S. government. I *knew* it," said one, with somewhat unusual
conviction. "News in Latin America is a function of what interests the
U.S. government," said another," . . . [and] American interests in Chile
were business interests."

To the degree such views, conscious or not, molded the coverage
of Allende, newsmen confirmed the worst suspicions of American journalism in Latin America and through much of the rest of the developing world. It seems academic to argue that the press is *really*
independent of corporate or government bias if both its methods and
product show so little distinction. The habits of cliche and generaliza-
tion, the omission of stories through neglect or concern for what "sells,"
the lack of analysis or perspective in viewing complex events (like the
"march of the pots") that mean more than their surface appearance—
all this combined to produce not merely an impression of random
incompetence, but of general bias, whether intentional or not.

The Allende period begs so many questions. What is the proper
professional relationship between American correspondents and a U.S.
Embassy abroad? Were reporters in Chile captives of their limited
sources and mobility? What *were* "American interests" in Chile then,
or in Latin America today, and does a newsman report largely on the
basis of how *he* answers that question? Should not editors question
foreign correspondents, as the State Department should question em-
bassies, to avoid the distortions of a colony mentality that can overtake
Americans abroad—rather than assigning reporters to cover what other
reporters are covering? On the other hand, need foreign news coverage
be so hostage to editors' or producers' dated ideas of what titillates the
American public? As U.S. senators journey to Havana and the Ford
Administration gives its quiet blessing to the lifting of Cuba's diplomatic isolation, the journalistic obsession with the "red menace" in
Chile seems a sad anachronism. And the questions most journalists
ridicule with proud assertions of independence: how much are we
aware of the inevitable prejudices of culture and ideology, how much
has it cost us in informative coverage, how do we begin to cope with it?
Just as self-censorship may be a more potent restraint on the press than
official repression, unexamined views probably weigh more on foreign
correspondents than corporate or government pressure.

Vietnam and Watergate have unfrocked "national security" and
thrown it open to healthy public scrutiny as a pretext for policy. Foreign correspondents could shed the same cleansing light on equally

long accepted, and long abused, concepts of the "national interest" in countries such as Chile. When journalism abandons cliche for independent investigation abroad as well as at home, we may well learn that *our* interest is not necessarily what Kissinger, ITT, the Council on Foreign Relations, or even Cold War-scarred reporters have assumed it to be.

In a larger sense, the Allende story goes well beyond a single country or three-year episode. In my view, the man seems much more symptom than cause, a symptom of a swelling force for change that fits no neat ideological label, and grows beyond the control of Moscow, Washington *and* Havana. What happened in Chile was a tragedy not only for Allende and his country, but also for the rest of Latin America, where Allende's failure and the U.S. intervention fortifies the extremists of both right and left. In a world increasingly hungry for scarce resources, the failure of Allende may have implications beyond Latin America.

It is a tragedy for us too. Perhaps the task of reporting the Chiles is beyond the current capacities of American journalism. Allende is scarcely a hopeful precedent. Nor, for that matter, was Vietnam. There too we saw a world in cliches, and it turned out to be more complex. Remember Ngo Din Diem from the *Saturday Evening Post*—the "mandarin in the sharkskin suit who's upsetting the red timetable"? It is depressing to notice how little progress there is from Saigon in the 1950's to Santiago in 1970–73.

"In all truth, I don't know that anyone has all the necessary capacities," wrote C. Wright Mills in *Listen Yankee* nearly 15 years ago. "It is an extraordinarily difficult task for any member of an overdeveloped society to report what is going on in the hungry world today. . . ." Yet there was, and has been, no exit for us from that world.

Journalists, editors, and their audience can be certain of one lesson from the Allende story: on a continent where hundreds of children can die every day of malnutrition, where most governments still serve systems of economic privilege for the few, sooner or later we will have a chance to tell the story again.

FOR FURTHER READING

James Aronson. *The Press and the Cold War*. Indianapolis: Bobbs-Merrill, 1970.

Erik Barnouw. *The Image Empire: A History of Broadcasting*, Vol. III. New York: Oxford University Press, 1970.

Max Gordon. "A Case History of U.S. Subversion: Guatemala, 1954," *Science and Society*, XXXV (Summer 1971).

Gary MacEoin. *Revolution Next Door: Latin America in the Nineteen Seventies*. New York: Holt, Rinehart & Winston, 1971.

I. F. Stone. *Polemics and Prophecies, 1967–1970*. New York: Random House, 1970.

IV

BICENTENNIAL:
AN UNCERTAIN CELEBRATION

R ichard M. Nixon, chosen President in 1968 in an election notable for the low percentage of voters who went to the polls, proclaimed himself spokesman for a Middle America that supposedly treasured "law and order" above all else. His inauguration presaged a period of conservatism and repression of dissent. As if to confirm the gloomiest predictions of liberals, the President and his advisors chose to invade Cambodia, savagely bombed North Vietnam, and initiated criminal trials of war resisters while disregarding incidents in which police or National Guard forces had killed young demonstrators on college campuses. Yet this powerful administration could not fully carry out its designs. In several instances juries composed of what seemed to be Middle Americans refused to accept the flimsy evidence offered by the Justice Department against peace advocates. The resistance of Americans and Indo-Chinese people inexorably forced the President—a man who had founded his career on anti-Communism —to begin a retreat from Vietnam and to open the way to détente and recognition of Communist governments abroad.

A new issue claimed wide attention: the cause of the environment, or "ecology." For over a decade, concerned scientists and many others had been trying to arouse the public to the fact that America no longer possessed vast open spaces, clear air, and pure rivers. On the contrary, they insisted, its air and waters were polluted with sewage, noxious gases, and industrial waste; its wilderness was vanishing before the bulldozers; and its farmlands were being buried under concrete. In April, 1970, rising anxiety and anger found expression in the celebration of Earth Day. Young people especially, one organizer proclaimed, were saying "No" to all kinds of destruction, whether in America or in Indo-China—"we affirm life—a life in harmony with Nature." Some social activists feared that this preoccupation with the environment represented a mere fad or cop-out from more overtly political agitation; others, however, believed that the fight to save

the environment would lead to confrontations with the large corporations that would open people's eyes to the oligarchical structure of
American society.

Events in 1973 and 1974 shocked the country. Runaway inflation,
spurred by a supposed shortage of oil and tolerated by a government
in Washington that was almost paralyzed by the Watergate scandals,
threatened the standard of living of millions in prosperous America
as in other parts of the world. The American people learned that the
executive branch of their national government suffered from corruption
of an extent and degree that the most cynical could scarcely have
imagined. As one figure after another fell from high office, many of
them indicted for crimes, President Nixon fought a desperate battle to
save himself. Finally action of the Supreme Court and the House
Judiciary Committee undermined his position, and he was caught
with the "smoking gun" that convinced even his champions that
he, too, was guilty. With almost all of political Washington in favor
of his prompt departure, Nixon yielded and became the first President
of the United States to resign. The inauguration of Gerald R. Ford
was welcomed with a collective sigh of relief. The country congratulated itself on having an apparently honest and candid person as
President. But the advent of Ford did not presage startling changes.
Like Nixon, he was a political conservative who advocated large
armaments expenditures and opposed plans to use governmental
power to end inflation or to meet the desperate needs of the hungry,
the unemployed, and the dispossessed.

In the spring of 1975 Americans were beset with uncertainty
and bewilderment. As prices continued to rise, production slowed
down. Official reports—which always modify the facts—showed that
unemployment had reached a nationwide average of close to 9 per cent.
Not for more than thirty years had so large a percentage of the
work force been unemployed. Neither the Republican Administration
nor the Democratic Congress offered any clear remedy. Economists
of repute—professors, advisors to banks, official counselors to President
Ford—mouthed empty reassurances or, more frankly, confessed their
helplessness and ignorance in the face of what seemed to some an
oncoming depression. In foreign relations, even as the Provisional
Revolutionary Government at last took over in Saigon, Washington
authorities held fast against any thoroughgoing revision of American
policy in the world.

As the two hundredth anniversary of independence approached,
no group of present-day "founders" came forward to provide coherent
leadership to a nation afflicted with a general sense of malaise.
Perhaps, however, beneath the surface uncertainty, Americans, shaken
by the upheavals and disillusionments of the 1960's and early 1970's,

were taking time for reassessment. Certain signs suggested that they did not intend to suffer passively: here and there advocates of socialist alternatives found an audience and an outlet in the press; in some colleges students protested against economy measures that closed off opportunities for minorities; and in labor unions voices impatiently demanded action to assure employment for all. Out of this transitional, stage, organizations and coalitions might emerge that could articulate the issues and the ideas of late-twentieth-century America.

The articles in this chapter suggest some of the conditions that call for hard thought today. Paul Starr gives his impression of how former young rebels live in the aftermath of the campus upheavals of the sixties. James M. Naughton reports on a landmark event in the Congressional inquiry into the Watergate crimes. Sidney Lens seeks to account for the sudden shortages that have astonished inhabitants of supposedly affluent America.

REBELS AFTER THE CAUSE: LIVING WITH CONTRADICTIONS

PAUL STARR

Many of the students who came to maturity in the 1960's were in the forefront of activities that astonished and sometimes inspired their elders. Believing in democracy and freedom, members of the new generation dedicated themselves to turning their humanistic ideals into social realities. They worked for a variety of causes. The North Carolina sit-ins of 1960 called forth an outpouring of young people to demonstrate support in their own localities or to join the blacks in the South. Thousands joined the Peace Corps in their zeal to bring skills and organization to villagers in foreign lands, while other entered VISTA (Volunteers in Service to America), to aid the poor at home. By the middle of the decade the students, like many older people, were directing much of their energy to stopping the war in Vietnam. As they explored society beyond their middle-class milieu, they discovered more and more reasons to dedicate themselves to improving American society. As one student said, "To be a moral man, you had to try and change what was going on because it was bad."

Although many of the students sought merely to awaken social consciousness among those in positions of power, hoping to obtain legislation to alleviate poverty and discrimination, a vital minority thought along more radical lines. What they spoke of as "the movement," however, did not gather itself into a coherent organization or reach agreement on methods or theory. In 1962 a leading group, Students for a Democratic Society, set forth generous aims: "We would replace power rooted in possession, privilege, or circumstances by power and uniqueness rooted in love, reflectiveness, reason, and creativity." In light of subsequent harsh experience, some activists later came to regard that statement as vague and naive in its implications. Some turned to special causes or to guerrilla movements; others undertook more rigorous analysis of the structure in order to obtain the transformation they sought. Accomplishment of that task, they concluded, might take a long, long time.

Paul Starr, a student activist of the 1960's, reflects on what has become of some of his dedicated contemporaries. For the most part, he observes, they have made some adjustments; they live with the system, but not easily. They remain aware of inequities, but accept the benefits of privilege. Intelligent and well-educated, most have opted for careers that bring them the advantages and prestige of accomplished professionals. Some who once wanted to help the disadvantaged in direct ways find that the poor and their problems offer too little challenge and stimulation. Corporate law, experimental teaching in suburban schools, medical research in university hospitals provide ample physical resources, fascinating intellectual problems, and the companionship of stimulating coworkers; poverty law, authoritarian ghetto classrooms, and overcrowded community clinics offer exhausting and frustrating work and often provoke the hostility of professional establishments.

These one-time rebels, it seems, are weary of fighting the system and now seek to enrich their own lives with the traditional sustenance of status, income and children rather than continue to challenge the bastions of American society. Yet their experience in the sixties has marked them; they have not settled complacently into their careers. Perhaps at some later time they can exercise leadership in a nation more ready to listen to their call to build a free society.

□   □   □

T he sixties have almost receded far enough into the vaguely re-membered past to become the subject of nostalgia. The rush of new events—Watergate, the Middle East war, the energy crisis, infla-tion, the advent of a new President—seems to have pushed Vietnam and antiwar protest, the civil-rights movement, and the countercul-ture out of the national consciousness.

But among the people I know who came to political maturity then and who are now in their twenties and early thirties the effects of the Vietnam war years are still strong. They seem set aside by the experi-ence from people both younger and older—a great parenthesis in the succession of generations, their lives imprinted with the history of that period and its angers, hopes, faiths, and disappointments.

I don't mean only the few who belonged to "the movement"; it went further than that. The movement has come to an end—not crushed, but disintegrated; yet while its history has ended, its biographies are unfinished. The conflicts that no longer openly rend the society have been localized and turned inward, and now they quietly rend the lives of the people who carry within themselves the signature of the 1960's: social commitments and values, sometimes only the most cloudy ideas and unconscious assumptions, which place them outside the shared beliefs that ordinarily hold a society together.

It isn't my impression that many of them have turned conservative. They follow careers, it's true, but most seem to retain the cultural and political views they developed earlier. If it isn't always possible for them to act on those views, even if what they are doing now is totally inconsistent with them, they live (often uneasily) with the contradictions. Having come of age in the sixties, they absorbed a set of moral beliefs profoundly at odds with the prevailing institutions in America, and now they find themselves—young lawyers, doctors, school teachers, professors, social workers—caught between the implications of those beliefs and their own personal hopes and ambitions. Most of them want to do good but also to do well, and they find that it isn't easy to do either, much less both. Work that fully expresses their beliefs is hard to find, and even careers that potentially might provide such opportunities seem to have an inner logic that impels them to seek more prestigious but contradictory roles.

Like others before them, they take jobs, have families, and even assume positions of authority, but they don't really believe in the surrounding institutions and social arrangements. They do not share, to take an obvious but pertinent example, in the symbols and practices of what sociologist Robert Bellah calls the "civil religion" in America.

Carl is a young social-studies teacher in a suburban high school. He is conservative in manner and fairly traditional in his educational methods. He worries about his "objectivity" (even his use of the word identifies him as no radical) in presenting controversial issues like Watergate to his classes. A trip to the Soviet Union seems to have firmly persuaded him of the disadvantages of state socialism and the merits of an open society. And yet, like many other young teachers, he cannot bear to lead his students in the morning Pledge of Allegiance. "We couldn't bring ourselves to stand the kids up for it," he explains of himself and the other young teachers at his school. "It's symptomatic. We don't have a whole lot of freaky people, running through the halls and certainly not on the faculty, but the revulsion after hearing patriotism identified with slaughter for so long was so great that very few wanted to do it." Carl's wife, who teaches in an inner-city school, has had the same experience: "I find it hard to say and so I don't say it." (Her class sings "Little 'Liza Jane" in the morning instead of "The Star-Spangled Banner.")

And it is, as Carl says, symptomatic. In the aftermath of the sixties, there is a residual distrust of the society, a sunken current of disbelief in its institutions and apprehension about its future among many of those who took part in the politics or culture of dissent in the last decade. In earlier generations, there were also idealists as there have been in this one. But the disaffection left by the sixties is more extensive, especially in the upper middle class. If this generation, like previous ones, has made compromises and adjustments, it is not yet disposed to celebrate the virtues of America's way of life. Its members participate in the society, but without much respect for it. If it were threatened, many of them could not bring themselves to defend it, and if it collapsed, some might only congratulate themselves that they had always known it would. Formerly, members of the upper middle class who thought themselves progressive approved of the whole American society but were willing to criticize the parts. Today many of them are inclined to disapprove of the whole and accept the parts.

At least they accept the parts they play. Some are now diligent members of the crew and even officers on a ship they once hoped to sink. Doug studied Marxist philosophy at Berkeley and then went to law school, where he successfully avoided as much of the "straight" curriculum as he could, taking instead courses on Indians, drug use, social philosophy, and poverty law. After graduation he interviewed for a job at an Indian reservation. He contemplated his isolation in the community, the distance from all of his friends and especially his girl-friend, his utter lack of any real preparation for the responsibilities he would have as the only available lawyer, and then turned around and accepted a position with a well-regarded Midwestern law firm. There he now handles bankruptcies and insolvencies—still doing, he explains with a wry smile, "poverty law of a sort." He actually takes great pleasure in it.

"You learn," he explains to me one evening, "to really enjoy drafting a nice pleading or a tight memo or a succinct brief or a letter that has just the right edge to it to accomplish your purpose. You really begin to take satisfaction in being able not just to turn out pounds of paper, but to make those papers *move* the case and to get resolution—get the check from one person's hand to another."

But the satisfaction is purely professional. "All you're doing," he says later on, "is keeping honor among commercial thieves. You're not changing the concentration of wealth from one class to another. You're just making sure that the ruling class governs its affairs with a certain amount of order and keeps chaos from breaking out." Then a slight rationalization creeps in: "So, in a way, you may be helping a lot of smaller creditors from getting squeezed out, and I guess it does benefit the consumer because in the short run it keeps the cost of goods from being artificially inflated.

"But," he finishes, returning to the phrasing of undergraduate days, "it masks, I guess, the real split in power between workers and employers."

Doug has such a highly developed sense of irony about himself and his professional life that the contradictions between his work and his ideas don't seem to bother him very much. In any event, he says he may be leaving the firm in a few years.

Jobs can be switched, careers can be changed, but there are larger contradictions which people in the generation that said it would be different cannot easily escape. They know, for example, that America consumes more than her share of the world's resources—and they help consume it. They are aware that whites earn more than blacks in the United States—and most share in that collective advantage. They agree that wealth and comfort are unfairly distributed among rich and poor —and as professionals now, many of them benefit from that inequality.

Some have tried to be more fully consistent. Practitioners of a kind of radical social abstinence, they refuse to make any accommodation with the society. They remain outsiders, ideologically committed against working within capitalist institutions or just viscerally incapable of making the necessary compromises in speech, dress, and attitude. Usually supporting themselves with short-term jobs, they move continually from one project to another—a food cooperative this month, film-making the next, a radical therapy group a half year later. When old friends and acquaintances—insiders who have made adjustments and outsiders who have not—run into each other on the street, the silences grow longer and the distances greater. "There are incredible tensions now in the movement," says Herb Gintis, a radical economist now teaching at the University of Massachusetts after several years at Harvard, "between people who have gotten into the establishment like me and gotten jobs and people who are still pounding the streets and doing lots of good political work, but not pulling in the bread and having all the status."

Yet even the outsiders "pounding the streets" usually haven't made the break irreconcilable. Still young, often well-educated and articulate, they continue to hold a return ticket, negotiable at any time. Now and then you hear that, while X is still without a job, Y has finally decided to apply to law school, and Z has suddenly turned up in the pages of *The New Republic* after years of writing for underground papers and obscure radical publications. They were too talented, you say to yourself, to inflict on themselves a permanent and unnecessary exile. So they find positions in enclaves within established institutions or create what the radical writer Andrew Kopkind mischievously calls "sea-level" organizations (that is, midway between the underground and the aboveboard). Boston and San Francisco, in particular, offer an elaborate set of alternative institutions, making it possible to continue living in a community where almost everyone agrees with each other.

Beyond these fraternities of the disenchanted are the larger numbers who sympathized with one or another aspect of the counterculture. Very few ever really considered dropping out. With this generation, many middle-class families have reached a ceiling in their plausible social aspirations, so it was to be expected that their sons and daughters would search out new concepts of personal growth to replace older ones no longer meaningful. If your status can no longer be significantly raised, perhaps your consciousness can. This need for new cultural exploration may have combined with the special history of the sixties to produce an intensified concern for lives and careers that were not just secure but, as they say, relevant.

Sympathies and dispositions, however, are not easily translated into commitments, nor commitments into results. Those who set out on "relevant careers" could not anticipate that many of their own impulses, social and personal, were contradictory.

From the moment students with social concerns enter professional school, they learn that the most promising graduates do not go on to careers in public services or work with the poor. In medical school the brightest are encouraged to become specialists and researchers, while only the lower part of the class traditionally enters general practice. Graduate students in academic fields find that careers are made at élite universities; only the less successful will end up at state and community colleges, where the teaching loads are heaviest. Law students quickly learn that poverty law isn't "difficult enough" to warrant the attention of the more talented. Legal services for the poor involve mostly landlord-tenant problems, divorces, run-of-the-mill criminal cases. "You really want to spend your time working with these problems?" a professor will ask skeptically.

So the values that initially justified going to professional school aren't abandoned. They're put aside and replaced with more realistic and convenient professional values. Young doctors discover they cannot practice "good medicine" in a community clinic, at least not as well as in a research hospital. Young professors find they cannot teach theories of alienation to community-college students and that they need to do their work in universities where their colleagues share their interests. Young lawyers tell their friends that corporate law is more "intellectually challenging" than poverty or public-interest law, and tax law, in particular, has complexities which are "really fun" to disentangle (or entangle, if that's your job). Young teachers find that in inner-city schools they have to be rigid and authoritarian, while they can use experimental ideas with suburban children. Graduates of programs in administration begin to look askance at careers in public service; the expanding firms downtown are so much more "dynamic."

These professional values are not just alibis for desertion. They actually do reflect some of the realities of work. Community medical clinics, two-year colleges, inner-city schools, and public bureaucracies sometimes can be deadening places to work, an affront to anyone who has been trained to do his job well. The young professionals who choose "relevant careers" soon find, moreover, that it isn't only money and status they've sacrificed. They come home physically exhausted every day, worn out from working in overcrowded offices and classrooms with poor people whose desperate personal crises become part of their own lives.

Legal services for the poor offer a notable instance of these difficulties. Attorneys carry active caseloads, sometimes up to 100, that no law firm would conceivably permit. Office equipment and secretarial help are often unavailable, messages go undelivered, waiting rooms overflow with noisy clients, some of whom are as distrustful of legal-services attorneys as they are of the police.

"Everybody hates you; it's unbelievable," says Eva, a graduate of New York University Law School, who spent three years in legal services. "The judges yell. They hate us because all of a sudden they're forced to try cases that before had been settled [out of court] or had no representation on the other side. The other attorneys are insulting. The clients aren't particularly good sometimes. It's unpleasant from almost every angle. For a while you can take it because you win a case here and there. You're preventing someone from being evicted or making sure they get Social Security. So there's some kind of satisfaction that way, but it gets to a point where enough is enough."

Larry, a former director of a legal-services agency, recalls the same steady animosity from all directions. "You're constantly being attacked or criticized by the bar, which resents the intrusion into their turf of free legal services. And then being constantly attacked and harangued from Washington."

There are redeeming satisfactions. Willy Osborn returned to legal services this past year—he had first worked there as a VISTA lawyer—after doing an investigative report under Ralph Nader. We once worked out of the same office on different projects—he on the Maine paper industry ("the poop on pulp," he called it), I on the treatment of Vietnam veterans by the Veterans Administration. Over lunch in a neighborhood bar in the poor Italian section of town where he works now, he says he prefers the personal contact in legal services to shuffling papers in a downtown office building. People come in, he says, with "a kind of innocent moral strength." Out of a strong sense of propriety, they are reluctant to declare bankruptcy when it would be to their advantage, or they insist on paying bills that they don't legally owe. Much of the work turns out to be educational, explaining to poor people what their legal rights are against a landlord, the gas company, or a manufacturer.

"One of the most satisfying things," Willy says, "is to see a client who doesn't understand his rights awakened to see that he can have his rights enforced. Then it becomes a team effort—you and the client against the bastards."

Some of the clients are distrustful and uncooperative, but that too has to be put in context. "If you resent clients," Willy observes, "you're not being realistic. They've been through a lot of government agencies. Why should they trust you after being let down by so many other people? Your ego has to be in shape to handle that."

For Willy, there are still serious limitations to the work. "You get the feeling," he says, "that often you're dealing with the end results of the problems and that the source escapes you. Once in a while you get a case that involves a class action in which you can change the law for a lot of people. But most of the time, you're putting Band-Aids on the leaks in the pipe rather than turning it off."

Underfinanced and overworked—suffering, in Larry's words, from "the continuous, chronic problem of too many clients, too few resources"—most attorneys leave within a few years. A job in legal services is typically no more than a stopover at the beginning of a career. "I guess," Larry says, "I have lost my taste for the day-to-day stresses of litigating. I used to work on weekends, nights, mornings. I don't want to do that now. I've lost a lot of the drive I used to have when my work was the central thing in my life." Larry and his wife are looking forward to having children. "I'd like that to be of equal importance to my job," he says.

This feeling is hardly one that radicals, especially in the women's movement, could disapprove. The distinguishing idea of the "new consciousness' has been its rejection of compulsive work habits and bureaucratic styles. But, ironically, the places where the least "greening" into Consciousness III is possible are the institutions that serve the poor. They demand the very commitment to work long hours that some had thought they were rejecting in rejecting élite careers. So people like Larry often feel that their impulses toward social engagement and their belief in the priority of personal needs are contradictory.

There is a hidden convergence here. The intense subjectivity of the counterculture is not really so different from the materialism of the traditional culture it abhors. Both take men away from public into private concerns. The counterculture, like the dominant culture, has never had an ideal of self-denial. It has, in fact, had just the opposite: a Dionysian ethos that says, "Do it. Trust your impulses. Do your own thing. If it feels right, it is right." An ideology of this sort, like traditional individualism, can be used to justify the pursuit of pure self-interest. The counterculture, paradoxically, has contained the seeds of its own co-optation. "What do we sell out for?" a friend of mine ruminates on hearing what I am writing about. "A little sunshine in Vermont, a chance to spend more time with our friends? We think the things other people sell out for are crass, while the things we sell out for are natural. But are we refusing to bargain, or just asking another price?"

In one area—science—the rise of the counterculture in the late sixties coincided with changes in national policy to produce an acute crisis among young professionals. The counterculture challenged the meaning and value of scientific work and new technology just as the federal government was cutting back on funds for research and graduate study. Young scientists found their support collapsing underneath them both morally and financially. Many left their fields entirely, some for related professions like medicine. Others who stayed behind felt a sharp opposition between their work and the new denigration of science in American culture.

Medical students, usually a rather insulated group, were also affected by the new political and social currents. At Harvard, where psychiatrist Daniel Funkenstein has been measuring student opinion regularly since the 1950's, attitudes have shifted enormously. In 1959, only 8 percent of the student physicians favored group practice, only 4 percent wanted to abolish the fee-for-service payment system for doctors, and only 9 percent supported national health insurance. By 1971, however, 98 percent favored group practice, 61 percent were against fee-for-service, and 81 percent thought national health insurance a good idea.

There were also substantial changes in career intentions. Dr. Funkenstein divides medical students into two groups: the "bioscientific" students, who have high quantitative abilities and see medicine as a science, and the "biosocial" students, who have greater verbal skills and stronger interests in the social aspects of medical care. Around 1967, Dr. Funkenstein began seeing pronounced changes within each group. The plans of the "bioscientific" students, responding partly to the change in federal priorities, shifted from full-time academic and research careers toward more clinical roles. The "biosocial" students at Harvard began resisting the ethos of professionalism in a more unexpected way. In the early sixties, virtually all of them planned to be psychiatrists. From 1963 to 1966 Harvard did not graduate a single student who said he planned to be a family doctor. But by 1971, the proportion of entering "biosocial" students planning to be psychiatrists had fallen to under 10 percent, while the prospective family physicians had increased to nearly half. "They feel," Dr. Funkenstein has commented, "that most psychiatrists are not socially responsible, dealing as they do with only a small number of well-educated, financially affluent patients."

Jerry was such a medical student: Initially planning to go into psychiatry, he eventually decided to do social medicine instead. Like many others in the human services, he feels that his work as a doctor gives him an opportunity to act on his social values. "It is really a privilege," he says, "to be able to be of such use to people. It's a privilege that's based on a scarcity that is really appalling; but given that that scarcity exists, it puts the individual healer in a position to do an enormous amount of good."

This is, of course, what attracts the socially concerned to the professions. Professional occupations, the sociologists Richard Sennett and Jonathan Cobb have suggested, generally owe their status and desirability not merely to the high incomes they bring but to the opportunities for compassion and power they afford. The professional, they write, "appears to be able to express his care to others without fear of affront because they need that nurturance from him, and he has no need of any product or action in return to practice his art, save their submission to his will—a submission the patient in need of treatment, the client accused of a crime, the student in need of knowledge or a grade, does not refuse. This one-way street is freedom."

Jerry, however, is uneasy over this power, disturbed by the obsequiousness with which so many people treat him solely because of his professional status. "Maybe one of the worst things about medicine," he says, "is the way that the doctor has this role of magician and sacred person. There are healing aspects to it, but there are also a lot of abuses."

But at the start of his career, he isn't about to remake those relationships. "I just don't have time to sit down with patients and tell them my inadequacies. I'm afraid," he adds, laughing, "they'll learn about them on their own anyway."

Jerry's uneasiness about professional dominance in medicine is part of a widespread ambivalence toward social authority. Many young professionals, graduates of the New Left, believe that work, like politics, should be less hierarchical. Their desire to break down rigid relationships between teachers and students, doctors and patients, professionals and clients runs into serious obstacles. First, there are the institutional constraints that might be expected—the opposition of colleagues and fixed administrative rules. Even more important, the students, patients, and clients themselves are used to authority. "The kids have more respect for you," says one teacher, "if they think you're in control of the situation." Finally, as Jerry suggests, it's hard to spend time reconstructing the psychology of social institutions when you have immediate responsibilities, like caring for the seriously ill or teaching young children to read. In the end, these compelling needs are the strongest pressure forcing young professionals to accept the contradiction between professional roles and antiprofessional values.

In no field has the challenge to authority been more profound than in education, where new "open classroom" techniques, unstructured learning environments and doubts about schooling itself have attracted many young teachers. The classroom, however, can be a chastening experience. Marya has taught civics and ancient history for three years at a junior high school in a white working-class neighborhood. Now in her early thirties, she is a veteran of community organizing projects, Student for a Democratic Society (at its height she served on one of its regional councils) and the women's movement. Several years ago she went to Cuba with several other teachers to encourage adoption of "open classroom" methods, but today she finds herself less sure of their usefulness. "You get worn out," she says, after trying "open education" in a traditional school system. "It uses you up." While not turning her back on those ideas—if there were more support in the schools, she says, things might be different—she now recognizes that the more traditional approaches are valid alternatives. She favors giving students some choice in the curriculum, but opposes a completely unstructured environment. "Frankly, I know a lot more about history than they do. Their tendency at first would be anti-intellectual. I wouldn't give them the option of saying 'no' to some topics."

Like Marya, Phil entered teaching with a background in radical politics. He had come to M.I.T. in 1967 to study chemistry but soon became involved in the draft-resistance movement. Increasingly disturbed that his research was funded by the Defense Department, he left graduate study and turned to teaching. Science took on a totally different meaning at an inner-city junior high. "The kids have questions about everything," he says. "Teaching science at that point is teaching them about the world around them, which is a liberating education." Phil conceives of his role as helping students gain mastery over their world, and for that reason he wants to teach them "logic skills," to give them more homework ("They've been made to feel dumb. If they have homework and they can accomplish it, that reinforces self-respect") and to prepare them for standard aptitude and achievement tests. But other young teachers, more self-consciously radical than he is, oppose him on these issues. They see their role in the school not as preparing ghetto students to function well in the society but as preparing them to rebel against it. These teachers believe that all children have equal logical abilities, that homework is unnecessary, and that standard tests are so culturally biased that it is hopeless and reactionary to prepare black students to take them. "There's a point," says Phil, "at which that becomes a patronizing attitude and borders on racism."

This conflict, in one form or another, is endemic among radical professionals. The English teacher with minority children who speak a distinctive idiom can penalize them for "incorrect" grammar or accept their speech as a "legitimate" dialect. If the teacher regards their language as incorrect, they will suffer through lower grades. But if the teacher accepts their speech as legitimate, they will suffer later when they fail civil-service examinations and lose job opportunities because they cannot produce a standard English sentence.

Fluency in the dominant social forms involves more than language. It embraces social behavior in all its various aspects. The young teacher, lawyer, priest, psychiatrist, social worker and counselor can try to help the poor and distressed become fluent in the dominant forms of the society or to reject them and cultivate their own. The second course once seemed the very test of militancy (in revolutionary times it is), but under ordinary circumstances it has the inescapable effect of propelling the poor in a direction that will almost certainly bring them further pain and defeat. This no conscientious teacher or counselor, however radical, can readily accept, and so much like other professionals, they end up transmitting the dominant social forms, of some of which they disapprove. That, too, is a contradiction they must live with.

The young professionals who last in the institutions that serve the poor adjust to the limits and frustrations of the work. Most in this group, however, move on after a short time. There is probably no characteristic so common among them as this perpetual moving about, changing of jobs, experimenting with one possibility and then another. Some observers have celebrated these continual changes of direction as a perennial renewal of the personality, typical of a new "protean man." On the other hand, Jonathan Kozol, the free-school advocate, criticizes as thoughtless and harmful this endless shifting of commitments "from one moment of important dedication and of inert compassion to the next."

"There is a black child I know in Boston," Kozol writes, "who has now gone through four generations of white teachers, organizers, drifters, VISTA's, O.E.O.-supported revolutionaries and what he calls the hippie people, all in the course of six years. . . . They give him supper and they buy him shoes and take him out on hikes and sit down on the floor and play with him for one summer and one winter, and sometimes for one spring and one summer once again. Then they switch gears, and they are into a New Thing."

Virtually all of the institutions that serve the poor are afflicted by this transience. High turnover in the professional staff means little continuity of service or accumulation of experience. The young professionals who leave after a year or two never get to know the local gossip and the standing problems of the community. Even those who come with good intentions often end up using inner-city institutions as training opportunities, moving on to better jobs when they have accumulated enough experience to be able to open a practice or teach in a "good" school. In a sense, this, too, is a kind of exploitation of lower-income communities in which the capital of experience is continually being withdrawn.

The socially inclined professionals who leave the services of the inner city don't usually abandon the cause altogether. Often they move to some position where they can continue their work but don't have to deal with the poor on a daily basis. Larry, the former legal-services director, now does legal research in his own independent office for clients of his choice—often state agencies that need help implementing liberal programs he supports. Eva left legal services for a research center. These research and reform activities are quite common routes out of legal services. Both Eva and Larry legitimately claim they can accomplish more in their new roles, working as they are on bigger issues that affect larger numbers of people, not just individual clients.

This rationale is very similar to radical intellectuals' arguments for remaining at prestigious universities. Herb Gintis, the radical economist at the University of Massachusetts, would prefer not to teach at a junior college. "People," he says, referring to fellow members of the Union of Radical Political Economists, "who aren't teaching at élite places are usually alone. They don't have the kind of feedback they would need to do research; therefore, they can't do it. They also teach more, and they don't have time to write articles. So there's a split between an élite, most of whom work at least in pairs, usually more, and other people [who] just don't have the chance. If I went to a community college, I wouldn't have the chance either."

Herb recognizes that his own satisfaction in his work is somewhat inconsistent with his politics. "Why should I be a radical economist at all?" he asks. "Right now I'm perfectly happy. I have a nice house, I have time to do sports, play music, share in taking care of the baby"— little Hucky, in fact, is crawling over him this moment—"doing everything I want. Why should I be [a radical]? Well, I have to be. I couldn't live without being that. It's a contradiction, but I'm not willing to give it up."

Nor are many other people I know. They want the best of both worlds, the élite and the anti-élitist. The contrast between their relative comfort and their radicalism makes them eminently vulnerable to satire, custom-made targets for Tom Wolfe or William Buckley. They practice what might be called socialism at a distance or, what would seem more incongruous if it weren't so fashionable, populism from the top. I would probably find it all rather funny myself if I weren't at least partially guilty of it too.

Yet I know what bitter resentment this privileged radicalism invites. Last spring, on a trip to the University of Illinois, I met a graduate student in education who asked persistently about the sociologist Christopher Jencks, a professor in my former department at Harvard and principal author of the controversial book "Inequality." Like many others, the student had misunderstood Jencks's work as saying that "education doesn't matter." Genuinely upset, he responded (in so many words): "You people at Harvard may not know how much education counts since you've got all the advantages, but down here we know better." The same message underlies all the resentment against the new radicalism of the well-educated and the well-off: "You people may not understand the value of American society because you've had all the advantages, but down here we know better, even if we've had only a few."

It seems to them a profound injustice that some people should receive so much from a society and believe so little in it. To the radicals at the top, on the other hand, it seems a profound enigma that so many people should receive so little from a society and believe so deeply in it. A good portion of the intellectual energies of the left goes toward explaining why the working class in America has been so unreceptive to socialist ideas.

There is, I think, an inner contradiction that is at least partly responsible for both the political failures of privileged radicalism and the personal quandaries of so many socially concerned young professionals. I would explain it in terms of a shift from a Christian to a social ethic. When St. Augustine said to God, "Thou hast counseled a better course than Thou hast permitted," he was saying that there were certain necessary contradictions in the Christian universe between being a man of God and a man. In a more secular age, we have decided that many of the traditional Christian contradictions are unnecessary. We no longer proscribe and conceal inner biological urges but, instead, our inner drives for power and status. They can never be mentioned or acknowledged without shame or embarrassment. In replacing a Christian with a secular democratic ethic, we have exchanged old contradictions for new ones between our belief in social equality and our desire for self-validation through achievement and esteem. Just as the Christian prohibitions were the source of innumerable hypocrisies about sex and individual conduct, so our new ethic gives rise to endless hypocrisies in politics and social life.

The generation of the sixties, drawn to a vision of a society of equals more radical than our historical democratic ethic, represents only a new form in which this contradiction has been encountered. To be sure, there have also been external limits on their activity, including the immediate needs of school children and the sick, as I indicated earlier. The secret of a stable social order is that even the people at the bottom usually insist that the rules be followed out of the well-grounded fear that in the short run they may be even worse off without them. So out of necessity the radical professionals end up following the rules, too, and the contradictions they feel within themselves now lie dormant.

Whether those contradictions will fade with age, burst or continue to fester depends on the larger history unfolding before us. The only precedent we have—and it isn't really a precedent for middle-class radicalism at all—is the radical generation of the Depression. It first suffered severe shocks in the mid- and late thirties with the Moscow trials and the Hitler-Stalin pact, events that cost it many members. It lost still more during World War II, which forced a suspension of all radical activity and ended the Depression itself. And it suffered its final agonies in the ordeal of McCarthyism, which turned the generation against itself and destroyed whatever self-confidence remained.

Perhaps the generation of the sixties will be reduced to a similar fate. Twenty years from now, its only gesture to its youth may be to turn out for fund-raising meetings for the last six deserters in Sweden, as the old left today still turns out for its martyred heroes, the Rosenbergs. They too may have stories improved over the years, not of union meetings but of Selma or the Peace Corps, the Pentagon march in '67 or the day they "took" the administration building back in '69. Perhaps tears will come to their eyes too as they watch old news film, and wonder to themselves where all their anger and indignation went.

But things could turn out to be less sentimental. At some point, there probably will be a national crisis and a demand for loyalty, and those who have taken part in the society without believing in it will be forced to a decision. The *détente* at home, which now permits an abscess of disbelief in the nation's heart, is only a reflection of *détente* abroad. If the international one breaks down, I suspect the domestic might follow. An economic crisis might provide the same impetus. At that point, all the dormant contradictions could come throbbing to the surface. Those who had preserved a balance of per-

254 ■ BICENTENNIAL: AN UNCERTAIN CELEBRATION

sonal commitments would be forced to make the kind of painful choice of loyalties that made the sixties so difficult an experience. If the past 60 years of our history offer any indication—two world wars, a world Depression, two wars in Asia—such crises will come soon enough.

FOR FURTHER READING

* Paul Jacobs and Saul Landau. *The New Radicals: A Report with Documents.* New York: Random House, 1966.

Paul Lauter and Florence Howe. *The Conspiracy of the Young.* New York: World, 1970.

Priscilla Long, ed. *The New Left: A Collection of Essays.* Boston: Porter Sargent, 1969.

Kirkpatrick Sale. *S.D.S.* New York: Random House, 1973.

WATERGATE:
THE HOUSE JUDICIARY COMMITTEE
DECIDES TO RECOMMEND
THE IMPEACHMENT OF
PRESIDENT RICHARD M. NIXON

AND OTHERS

"What, indeed, is Watergate all about?" the *New York Times*
asked rhetorically in July, 1974, and then proceeded to answer its own
question:

> Watergate is about a President of the United States who has repeatedly
> shown contempt for Congress and the courts; who has established a new
> and imperial doctrine of "executive privilege"; who has subverted the
> Constitution by his disregard of powers reserved to the Congress; who
> has flouted the constitutional injuction to "take care that the laws be
> faithfully executed" and who is deeply suspect of obstruction of justice as
> well; whose minions dared to trifle both with the electoral process and also
> with some of the most sensitive agencies of the United States Government;
> whose close associates and subordinates—for whose actions he is ultimately
> responsible—have been convicted of crimes against the people of the
> United States; who himself has already been named as a co-conspirator;
> who has connived in misuse of campaign funds; who has cut corners on
> his own income tax returns; whose careful excision of relevant material in
> supplying transcripts to the public suggests a sense of ethics more fitting
> to a slippery political fixer than to the President of the United States.

Early in the morning on June 17, 1972, police summoned by an
alert watchman captured five men illegally searching the offices of the
Democratic National Committee in the "Watergate" complex in
Washington, D.C. Routine investigation at once uncovered the fact

© 1974 by The New York Times Company. Reprinted by permission. This article,
written by James M. Naughton, is based on reporting by him, R. W. Apple Jr., Diane
Henry, Marjorie Hunter, and David E. Rosenbaum, all of the *New York Times*. It
originally appeared in the August 5, 1974, issue of the *Times* under the title "How a
Fragile Centrist Bloc Emerged as House Panel Weighed Impeachment."

that these burglars were in some way connected with the Committee to Re-elect the President, which was headed by prominent allies of President Nixon. Further inquiries by the FBI, journalists, prosecutors, and judges, and by Congressional committees revealed a pattern of skulduggery and invasion of personal liberties and, step by step, traced responsibility up to the President himself. During the two-year period between the summers of 1972 and 1974, some thirty members of Nixon's administration, including his first Attorney-General, John Mitchell, and his two chief aides, H. R. Haldeman and John D. Ehrlichman, were indicted, and some of them convicted, for their roles in the sordid and criminal activities known collectively as "Watergate." At last, on August 9, 1974, in order to avoid impeachment and removal from office, Nixon resigned.

Strangely enough, the Watergate incident had remained in the background during the Republican campaign to re-elect Nixon in the fall of 1972. With a few exceptions—notably, the *Washington Post*—the media showed little desire to explore the implications of what many referred to as the Watergate "caper." Nor could Democratic candidate McGovern stir much indignation among citizens who regarded the burglary as merely a foolish action committed by a few overzealous subordinates. Nixon was retained by a tremendous electoral vote.

But in the winter and spring the small cloud grew to a storm that burst over the White House. As the original burglars were tried and convicted, certain participants added their confessions to mounting evidence that assistants and intimates of the President himself had planned the break-in and had subsequently conspired to cover up its origins. That crime, moreover, constituted only one instance in a line of conduct that embraced wiretapping of journalists and officials, burglary of a psychiatrist's office, solicitation and acceptance of secret and illegal campaign contributions, compilation of an "enemies" list, and attempts to use the Internal Revenue Service and the CIA to harass critics and suppress FBI inquiries.

Courts and press brought to light facts so discreditable and so suggestive of further ramifications that in May, 1973, Nixon was forced to authorize his new Attorney-General, Elliot Richardson, to appoint a special prosecutor to investigate the entire Watergate matter. In that position Archibald Cox, a Harvard professor of law, pursued the inquiry so thoroughly as to embarrass the President. In the summer a special Senate Committee on Campaign Expenditures—the "Watergate Committee"—held televised hearings that introduced to millions of viewers a succession of witnesses many of whom, like Mitchell, Haldeman, Ehrlichman, and John Dean, had been Presidential counselors until discredited by the spreading scandal. Dean, admitting his own part in the cover-up, maintained that the

President had participated also. Yet perhaps the most fateful revelation occurred when a White House aide, in the course of explaining routine procedures, mentioned that the President had secretly installed electronic equipment to record his own conversations and discussions with his advisors. Special prosecutor Cox sought to obtain the tape recordings for use in his investigations.

On a Saturday afternoon in October, five months after he had appointed Cox, Nixon ordered Attorney-General Richardson to fire the special prosecutor; Richardson refused to do so and resigned. Immediately thereafter, the Deputy Attorney-General, William Ruckelshaus, was asked to perform the same task. He too refused. Before Ruckelshaus could submit his resignation he was fired. Nixon elevated a more compliant subordinate that very evening, and he proceeded to oust Cox.

The "Saturday Night Massacre" provoked cries of outrage from all over the country. Among a public recently startled by the enforced departure of Vice-President Spiro Agnew, the President's popularity sank to a point where, according to a Gallup poll, fewer than 30 per cent approved of the way he was handling his job. Congress began to take seriously proposals already made to impeach Nixon, and in February, 1974, the House instructed its Committee on the Judiciary to consider the impeachment of the President. Nixon, who was obviously surprised at the public reaction to his dismissal of Cox, appointed another special prosecutor, this time Leon Jaworski of the Texas bar, who picked up where Cox had left off. Once more, the prosecutor, who was preparing a case against Mitchell and six others for obstruction of justice, sought access to certain documents and sixty-four tape recordings. When the President refused, Jaworski obtained subpoenas—court orders—for the material. Appealing to the U.S. Supreme Court, Nixon insisted that an absolute "executive privilege" exempted him from compliance. But on July 24, 1974, Chief Justice Burger, speaking for a unanimous Court, explained that the President must obey the orders: "The allowance of the privilege to withhold evidence that is demonstrably relevant in a criminal trial would cut deeply into the guarantee of due process of law and gravely impair the basic function of the courts."

During these proceedings, the legal staff of the House Judiciary Committee, though unsuccessful in its own efforts to obtain tape recordings from the White House, had amassed and presented to the Committee's members a great deal of evidence. In a few days of open debate early in August, Committee majorities recommended that the whole House impeach the President on three charges: obstruction of justice, abuse of power, defiance of subpoenas calling for material the Judiciary Committee needed to carry out its constitutional function in regard to impeachment. The Supreme Court decision actually precipitated the final crisis: Nixon now had to yield up to the special prosecutor tapes that proved, in contradiction of his pleas of innocence and ignorance, that only six days after the Watergate burglary he and Haldeman had laid plans to block further investigation. In a public statement, he confessed to having done wrong, yet gave the impression that he hoped to be absolved for his good intentions. But he had provided his own *coup de grâce*. Most of his defenders, including all of those on the Judiciary Committee, quickly repudiated him. "I feel betrayed," said one. Republican leaders told their standard-bearer—now an intolerable burden on their party—that after impeachment the Senate would surely convict him. Nixon avoided that fate by announcing his resignation.

The events of Watergate suggest numerous reflections and questions. Analysts may differ on its significance for American democracy, as observers who, seeing a glass that contains a certain amount of water, may describe it as either half-*full* or half-*empty*. Did the two-year process prove that the political system "works" or that it does not? Why did the Judiciary Committee majority refuse to recommend impeachment for the secret bombing of Cambodia? How well did the free press fulfill its functions—to seek the truth and to inform the people?

The following article tells a story of political strategy, persuasion, and soul-searching among the members of the Judiciary Committee. It suggests questions as to sources: How did these reporters obtain their information? How might a historian check their sources? Assuming that the narrative is substantially accurate, what does it show about the "center" in American politics?

□ □ □

The verdict of the House Judiciary Committee came, in the end, from the President's own men. Seven Republicans, three conservative Democrats. In all, ten natural allies of President Nixon whose votes, shaped in anguish and cast in sorrow, were the critical mass of an explosive moment in history. That moment came to pass, visibly, stunningly, in the televised decision of the Judiciary Committee to lodge the first formal charges against a President in more than a century. Yet the real drama of impeachment, the test of wits and struggles of conscience that produced the decisive votes, occurred largely in private.

It was a drama at once constitutional, political, and personal. It involved the reluctant conclusion months ago by the committee chairman, Representative Peter W. Rodino Jr., that the White House tapes and other evidence traced a pattern of misconduct by the President whose signed portrait graced the chairman's office wall. It turned on a strategy designed to provide time for John M. Doar, the special counsel, to assemble the evidence that might convince key Republicans and Southern Democrats—the crucial, uncommitted center of the divided committee—that a vote for impeachment was worth the peril to their own political careers.

It concluded a massive, procedural sleight of hand through which Mr. Doar was able to lay before the committee, without objection from the President's lawyers or . . . defenders on the committee, the central elements of evidence on which the judgment would ultimately be based.

And the climax was caused in part by an uncharacteristic attempt by the senior Republican, Representative Edward Hutchinson of Michigan, to put pressure on the committee minority to make a united defense of the President. The gambit backfired, driving four Republicans into a bipartisan caucus—called, self-effacingly, "the Unholy Alliance"—where the first two articles of impeachment were drafted.

The alliance of the center in favor of impeachment almost collapsed twice, over a procedural disagreement and a tactical lapse, in the closing days of the committee deliberations. But when the inquiry ended, . . . only ten bitter-end Republicans out of the thirty-eight committee members had opposed adoption of the resolution that urged, in the stark language of parliamentary law, "that Richard M. Nixon, President of the United States, is impeached for high crimes and misdemeanors." And the votes of the ten critical men at the center echoed fatefully through Congress.

Walter Flowers, Democrat of Alabama: "Aye." James R. Mann, Democrat of South Carolina: "Aye." Ray Thornton, Democrat of Arkansas: "Aye." Robert McClory, Republican of Illinois: "Aye." Tom Railsback, Republican of Illinois: "Aye." Hamilton Fish, Jr., Republican of New York: "Aye." Lawrence J. Hogan, Republican of Maryland: "Aye." M. Caldwell Butler, Republican of Virginia: "Aye." William S. Cohen, Republican of Maine: "Aye." Harold V. Froehlich, Republican of Wisconsin: "Aye."

How the ten came to their separate judgments to enact two or more articles of impeachment and then coalesced to shape the wording of the indictment formed the central act of the drama. Based on interviews with each of them—and with other committee members and aides, some on condition that they not be identified—here is how it happened:

THE SEARCH

Representative Rodino vacillated. He was overwhelmed. In his first year as chairman of the House Judiciary Committee, the Democrat from Newark—an amateur poet, an immigrant's son, an unknown quantity up from the Congressional back benches—suddenly was thrust in the path of onrushing history by two White House calamities.

On October 10, 1973, Spiro T. Agnew resigned from the Vice-Presidency in disgrace. The President nominated Gerald R. Ford to be Mr. Agnew's successor and the Judiciary Committee was preparing for the first Vice-Presidential confirmation hearings in history. But on October 20, President Nixon ordered the dismissal of Archibald Cox, the special Watergate prosecutor, and within three days, amid a firestorm of public and Congressional outrage, Mr. Rodino was directed to begin an inquiry into the impeachment of the President as well.

At the urging of senior House Democrats, Mr. Rodino searched for a special counsel on impeachment, someone with unusual credentials: a lawyer of national repute, old enough to be mature but young enough to withstand a rigorous schedule, familiar with Washington and, above all, a Republican—to reassure Congress and the nation that the inquiry would be even-handed.

Names cascaded into the chairman's office from friends, law school deans, members of Congress. There were persistent references, often without the easily forgotten name, to "a guy in Justice in the sixties."

In November, Mr. Rodino summoned the "guy in Justice" from Brooklyn, where he directed the Bedford-Stuyvesant Development and Services Corporation, for a three-hour interview on Capitol Hill. John M. Doar was just what the chairman wanted. He had joined the Civil Rights Division of the Justice Department under President Eisenhower and risen, in the Kennedy and Johnson administrations, to the leadership of the assault on racial discrimination.

He was almost sleepily placid; he knew little about Watergate and nothing about impeachment; he was fifty-two years old; he professed no animosity toward Mr. Nixon, and he was, nominally, a Republican.

But Mr. Doar was the first candidate to be interviewed, and Mr. Rodino temporized and searched. He wavered, now wondering about the president of a sectarian university, now leaning toward a federal prosecutor appointed by Mr. Nixon, and even fastening for a time, in an irony that would later haunt Republican opponents of impeachment, on Albert E. Jenner, Jr. Eventually the committee's Republican minority, anxious to obtain their own counsel of national stature, would hire Mr. Jenner, a Chicago trial lawyer and fixture in the American Bar Association hierarchy, without knowing how close he had come to being the

Democrats' counsel—and Mr. Jenner, a devoted civil libertarian, would join in advocating impeachment.

On December 17, when Mr. Doar's name appeared in the *New York Times* as a leading prospect—planted, it turned out, with four other names by a Rodino associate who hoped to prod the chairman into some decision—Mr. Rodino summoned Mr. Doar again: This time he got the job. . . . The selection of John Doar, a Rodino confidant said, "was the most important decision of the whole inquiry."

THE EVIDENCE

Two days after Christmas, Mr. Doar arrived at his new office on the second floor of the rickety old Congressional Hotel, now a House office annex, and could not enter. He had no key. He sat on the floor until someone arrived to let him in. He would, in time, have all the locks changed and many more added in an effort to keep secret the evidence that accumulated on the conduct of the President, so much evidence, trivial or urgent, that the architect of the Capitol would install bracing beams to prevent the second floor from sagging.

Mr. Doar plodded. He insisted, to the dismay of impatient pro-impeachment Democrats, on personally examining every scrap of evidence: Watergate grand jury testimony, thousands of pages of Senate Watergate committee files, and the nineteen recorded White House conversations that the President initially surrendered to the courts in an unavailing effort to stem the tide of public opinion.

Why Mr. Nixon surrendered the first tapes, then refused to yield more, then issued edited transcripts, then defied court and Congressional subpoenas, and finally risked the order of the Supreme Court that said he must comply with the Watergate prosecutor's tape demands remains a mystery to both his defenders and accusers in Congress. "The White House has erred in dribbling out its story over the months and, frankly, having it pulled from them," [said] Representative Charles E. Wiggins, the California Republican who marshaled the defense of the President on the committee. . . . Each time he urged Mr. Nixon's defense lawyers to take one step or another in support of the President, Mr. Wiggins added, the answer was the same: "Well, we don't make decisions on this question. It's a Presidential judgment."

Whatever the explanation for the erratic White House defense strategy, it apparently affected Mr. Doar, and later the committee majority, in two central ways.

First, in succumbing to public pressure to yield the first tapes . . . , Mr. Nixon provided material that Mr. Doar and others saw as clues to a broad pattern of alleged misconduct. "The release of those tapes was a major mistake," according to Representative Don Edwards, Democrat of California, a one-time agent of the Federal Bureau of Investigation. "The hardest kind of case to make is one of conspiracy. We never could have done it in the Watergate case without those tapes."

Second, in defying committee subpoenas for 147 more taped conversations and in publishing expurgated transcripts of some discussions that could be, and were, compared unfavorably with the full content of the few tapes the committee had, Mr. Nixon apparently abetted growing suspicion that he was withholding the evidence that might destroy him. "I just think he's hurting himself," Mr. Railsback kept saying of the President's attitude toward the tapes. Mr. McClory pleaded privately with the White House to cooperate and, spurned, eventually drafted Article III of the bill of impeachment, accusing Mr. Nixon of trying to impede the constitutional inquiry into his conduct.

By late March, Mr. Doar concluded that there was evidence enough to build a case, largely circumstantial but in his view no less persuasive, for the impeachment of the President. He briefed Mr. Rodino on the evidence in long evening chats in the chairman's office. He took Mr. Rodino to the inquiry offices, clamped earphones on the chairman's head, and played the tapes. "Oh, my God," Mr. Rodino would say in his raspy voice as he listened to the recordings.

THE STRATEGY

Once Mr. Rodino became convinced—and dismayed, according to those around him—that impeachment should go forward, the question was how. He talked at length with Mr. Doar about the natural reluctance of members of Congress to use the awesome power of impeachment and of the need for a broad-based, bipartisan recommendation from the committee if the full House were to agree to a Senate trial of the President and [if] a trial were to be conclusive and not lead, as happened with Andrew Johnson 106 years earlier, to a narrow acquittal that crippled the President but left him in place. "The decision," Mr. Rodino kept telling Mr. Doar, "has to come out of the middle of the committee."

There were two elements to the strategy that emerged—one political, one evidentiary—but . . . both aimed at the same objective, to buy time for Mr. Doar to construct and present a case that would . . . be clear and convincing to the conservative Democrats and the Republicans on whose judgment the outcome would hinge.

The political phase of the strategy was brutally simple. It was to preserve a bipartisan approach and . . . an image of fairness by holding in check those in the committee's majority who were prepared . . . to presume the worst about Mr. Nixon's conduct. At closed party caucuses, Mr. Rodino kept warning the Democrats that the proceedings must be fair—that the committee's decision was one that the public in turn would judge and that the nation at large might not accept the verdict if Democrats were seen to have jumped to a partisan finding.

The Democrats were, for the most part, remarkably passive, though some resented Mr. Rodino's exhortations. Representative John Conyers, Jr., Democrat of Michigan, objected bitterly, in a series of . . . news conferences, that Mr. Doar seemed to be too deliberate, too slow, . . . too reliant on the investigations of others. Another Democrat groused privately that the chairman seemed overly willing to "carry these guys" —the conservative Southerners—"on a velvet pillow."

The fruits of Mr. Rodino's part in the strategy may have been described best, however, by Mr. Railsback, a senior member of the Republican social hierarchy in the House. "Rodino deserves a lot of credit for 'keeping the lid on,'" he said, smiling to acknowledge his adoption of a phrase from the White House transcripts. "He could have blown it all if he hadn't suggested restraint by certain Democrats."

The second element of the leadership strategy, the one left to Mr. Doar to devise, was far more complicated. It centered on the nature of the case.

Mr. Doar and Mr. Jenner, along with most members of the committee, had reached agreement early in the inquiry that a President might be impeached and removed from office on proof of serious wrongdoing that was damaging to the nation or to the Presidency, even if the misconduct was not, in the strict sense of the law, criminal.

Moreover, the committee lawyers believed that, while many of the items of evidence seemed inconclusive if examined singly and without reference to other elements of the case, taken together and viewed with a broad perspective they formed a cumulative pattern of misconduct.

But James D. St. Clair, the President's chief defense lawyer, and a number of the committee Republicans contended that Mr. Nixon was liable to impeachment only on hard, direct, incontrovertible proof that the President had personally committed severe violations of criminal law.

At first, Mr. Doar tried to convince Mr. Rodino that the White House had no more right to take part in impeachment hearings than a suspect under investigation by a regular grand jury.

The suggestion that Mr. St. Clair be barred from the inquiry met with stiff opposition from the committee centrists and from Democratic liberals such as Representative Robert W. Kastenmeier of Wisconsin and Mr. Edwards of California, who argued that the public would never understand or tolerate what would seem to be a breach of elementary fairness. Mr. Rodino agreed. He overruled Mr. Doar and admitted Mr. St. Clair.

How, then, was Mr. Doar, without betraying . . . his . . . promise to be evenhanded, to introduce the evidence that might show a pattern of wrongdoing? Would not a constant stream of objections to . . . Mr. Doar's emerging case come from Mr. St. Clair or some panel members— those members who, as one minority staff member described them, were "predisposed to consider one fact in isolation, to say, 'That doesn't prove anything' "?

The answer was mass, simplicity, and balance. Mr. Doar and his staff merely presented to the committee virtually every piece of evidence they had—thirty-eight thick looseleaf volumes. 7,200 pages in all—and reduced each item to a sparse, unargumentative statement of information. The approach had the added virtue of impartiality. It was, an associate of Mr. Doar's said later, "ingenious."

THE CASE

It took Mr. Doar until May 9 to collate the material. . . . Never quite satisfied with the briefing books, he kept producing them barely a step ahead of the hearings.

"We begin at the beginning," he told the committee—and Mr. St. Clair, at a nearby counsel table—that first day of the closed hearings. And he did, with a background paper that started, "On January 20, 1969, Richard Nixon was inaugurated as the 37th President of the United States."

As the hearings went on, Tuesday through Thursday for ten weeks, one after another of the members said that, had the sessions been open and televised, the nation would have been bored to death. All day the inquiry staff read the "statements of information" and cited the attached evidence, much of it by then public knowledge, from which the factual findings were drawn. When Mr. Doar read the material his monotone drove some on the panel to distraction, they said, and once, on May 21, Mr. St. Clair dozed off briefly.

Only when the committee listened to a White House tape and the members emerged to recount varying, sometimes conflicting, versions of its contents was there much excitement. Some Democrats expressed disappointment that there were no new "bombshells." Some Republicans, hoping for a decisive single piece of evidence to ease the burden of judgment, kept noting the absence of a "smoking gun."

But the rudiments of the case apparently were there, like pieces of popcorn that form a decorative Christmas tree chain only when someone strings a thread through them.

When the Watergate material had all been presented, the standard assessment was that it had been inconclusive. Mr. Wiggins dismissed even the Watergate tapes, saying that there had been nothing "implicating the President in spitting on the street, even." Only a few members saw a pattern as it emerged. "This building they've been constructing, a brick at a time, is completed," said Representative William L. Hungate, Democrat of Missouri, "and it's not a cathedral."

Mr. Cohen took his volumes of evidence home, read and reread them, cross-referenced them to Senate Watergate committee volumes and even to some segments of *All the President's Men*, the Watergate book by Bob Woodward and Carl Bernstein of the *Washington Post*.

Representative Paul S. Sarbanes, Democrat of Maryland, kept track of the activities of close White House and 1972 campaign associates of Mr. Nixon's who had been convicted of, or indicted [for,] crimes, and developed this simile: "You go into a grocery store and see a whole section of nice-looking tomatoes. You pick one up and it's rotten on the bottom. You figure, all right, it's possible to have one rotten tomato. You pick up another tomato and it's rotten. After eight or ten rotten tomatoes you wonder about the whole grocery store."

But the key group at the center, while displeased with what it had seen of Mr. Nixon's conduct, was uncertain by the end of June whether there was anything to warrant impeachment.

In early July, Mr. Doar ran a thread through the popcorn.

THE ADVOCATE

By late June, the committee Democrats were restive, exhausted, and alarmed. Some of them felt awash in a sea of evidence without a rudder. They complained at a party caucus that someone would have to pull the relevant facts together because, as a senior Democrat put it, Mr. Doar and his staff were too "neutral." Mr. Doar assured the Democrats that he would be prepared to become an advocate "at the appropriate time," but some doubted that he could succeed.

They began bickering in caucuses and, to Mr. Rodino's alarm, questioning the chairman's judgment by voting with the Republicans on some procedural questions.

On June 26, after Democrats [had] divided on three procedural votes in succession at a meeting to determine who would be summoned to the hearings as witnesses, Mr. Rodino recessed the meeting and took the Democrats into a nearby office. "I want to know who's with me and who's against me," he said, glaring at his colleagues. "I want to know now, before we go out there." When the Democrats returned to the meeting they stuck with the chairman.

On July 6, when committee members returned from a quick Independence Day respite, . . . Mr. Doar's senior assistants—Richard L. Cates, Bernard W. Nussbaum, Evan A. Davis, Richard H. Gill—began conducting "seminars" for Democrats to suggest various theories of evidence that could be drawn from the voluminous material. What emerged from the seminars was the alleged pattern of misconduct that Mr. Doar outlined in a 306-page "Summary of Information" he presented to the full committee, along with four suggested articles of impeachment, on July 19—the day he became an advocate. In brief, the case that Mr. Doar constructed was as follows:

• Mr. Nixon "made it his policy" to cover up the roots of the Watergate burglary and thus obstructed justice.
• Agents of the President, including the White House "plumbers" unit, committed and planned burglaries and unlawful eavesdropping as part of a "pattern of massive and persistent abuse of power for political purposes."
• In defying Judiciary Committee subpoenas, Mr. Nixon engaged in contempt of Congress and, more significant, "justified" an assumption that if the White House tapes and other withheld evidence had been favorable to Mr. Nixon they would have been produced.
• By underpaying Federal income taxes during his first four years in the White House, Mr. Nixon committed "willful" tax evasion and failed to adhere to an oath to uphold the nation's laws.

On that day, just before Mr. Doar was to begin his final summation to the committee, Mr. Rodino pulled the special counsel into a small . . . office . . . a few paces away from the . . . hearing room. The chairman wanted a fiery advocate and Mr. Doar was more like a dormant volcano.

Mr. Rodino set about antagonizing his counsel deliberately. He told Mr. Doar the 306-page document was "not good enough," that the committee did not need just another summary of the evidence but needed to be told why it was important and why the case was documentable. Finally, as Mr. Doar's face reddened and his temper rose, Mr. Rodino, feigning disgust, walked out. Boiling, Mr. Doar followed into the hearing room. One Republican member said . . . that . . . Doar had "a gritting set to his jaw" and his change of demeanor was "dramatic."

. . . Doar said he had "not the slightest bias" about Mr. Nixon but that he could not be indifferent to an attempt by any President to play "a central part in the planning and executing of this terrible deed of subverting the Constitution." For ninety minutes, he talked extemporaneously about laws and Presidential obligations and about the impeachment evidence. Of course some inferences must be drawn, he said, because of the nature of the Watergate cover-up:

> You find yourself down in the labyrinth of the White House, in that Byzantine empire where yes meant no and go was stop and maybe meant certainly, and it is confusing, perplexing and puzzling and difficult for any group of people to sort out. But that is just the very nature of the crime—that in executing the means everything will be done to confuse and to fool, to misconstrue, so that the purpose of the decision is concealed.

He ticked off items of direct evidence too. And he told the panel he had arrived at his conclusions by this standard: "You don't go forward in serious matters unless you are satisfied in your mind and heart and judgment that, legally and factually, reasonable men acting reasonably would find the accused guilty of the crime as charged."

THE CENTER

Armed with Mr. Doar's analysis of the evidence and [with] notes they themselves had made during the hearings, the members in the middle—the group Mr. Rodino had said must make the committee's decision—began coming to grips with what they referred to constantly as their awesome responsibility.

Representative Cohen had seemed for weeks on the edge of a vote to impeach. Alone among the Republicans he was asking biting questions of the impeachment witnesses. Then, on July 11, at a caucus of the Republicans, their normally taciturn senior member, Representative Hutchinson, seemed to try to isolate Mr. Cohen as the only potential outcast. The last witness had been heard earlier that day, all the evidence was in, and only the deliberations lay ahead. What Mr. Hutchinson said took on exaggerated meaning.

"Republicans cannot vote for impeachment," he declared. Then he asked—ominously, it seemed to some of those present—for a show of hands of Republicans who might vote for impeachment.

Representative Railsback objected with unusual vigor, that he for one was uncertain what he might do. And Representative Wiggins, presumably sensing that the incident could have a counterproductive effect, stepped in to cut off the discussion.

It was, nonetheless, a turning point of the deliberations. Mr. Railsback, Mr. Cohen, and Mr. Fish talked after the caucus about the "disturbing implications" of Mr. Hutchinson's attitude. Representative Butler, who had missed the caucus, joined [these] three Republicans for lunch. . . . It was the beginning of what some later would call . . . the "Unholy Alliance," others "the Terrible Seven," and one member, in an allusion to a film in which disparate gunslingers teamed up to save a Mexican town, . . . "the Magnificent Seven."

Four days later, on July 15, Mr. Railsback . . . told Mr. Cohen . . . that he too was disturbed by evidence that suggested Mr. Nixon had obstructed the Watergate investigation and had sought to use the Internal Revenue Service to political advantage.

On Sunday, July 21, Mr. Cates went to Mr. Cohen's home . . . to brief Mr. Cohen and Mr. Fish, for nearly five hours, on his interpretation of the Watergate evidence. That same day . . . Mr. Railsback went over and over Mr. Doar's 306-page summary, underlining, his wife . . . said later, "statements that seemed to go against the President." From [this] analysis, Mr. Railsback said, . . . "for the first time I got a full picture of the events, and of the President's participation in them."

Simultaneously, it turned out, other key centrists were coming to similar conclusions.

Mr. Fish talked with his family about "what impeachment meant to the country, to the Presidency" and, by indirection, whether to join in it.

Representative Hogan was driving home late Saturday night, July 20, from a speaking engagement and tried to sort out why he had been "disconcerted" during the speech. "I realized," he recalled, "I had been a victim of the Wiggins trap. I was focusing only on one leaf, not the whole forest. What difference did it make whether [the President] approved hush money? He certainly didn't reject it. It was the whole pattern, and I didn't see it until that night in the car."

On the Democratic side, Representative Thornton of Arkansas . . . the night of July 22 . . . drafted "a list of offenses that seemed to me to be of the kind that could support impeachment charges." Representative Flowers [of Alabama] and Representative Mann . . . from South Carolina, discovered in conversation that their views on the evidence were the same, and that Mr. Thornton agreed with them.

On July 22, Mr. Flowers approached Mr. Railsback and said, "Why don't you get your guys, and I'll get my guys, and we'll get together?" Mr. Railsback agreed.

THE DRAFTERS

At 8:30 A.M. on July 23, the Unholy Alliance—Republicans Railsback, Cohen, Butler, and Fish, Democrats Flowers, Mann, and Thornton— gathered, for the first of many times during the week of the impeachment debate, around a conference table in Mr. Railsback's office. . . .

"It was a terrible butterfly-in-the-stomach day," Mr. Fish later recalled. "I would have questioned my judgment if everybody else had decided against impeachment."

The group discussed those issues they could agree were not grist for impeachment—secret bombing in Cambodia, Mr. Nixon's political donations from corporations and industries—and then agreed they all could support two articles of impeachment, if [they were] phrased . . . carefully, without political hyperbole. Mr. Railsback agreed to draft Article I, alleging obstruction of justice in the Watergate case. Mr. Mann said he would try his hand at Article II, accusing Mr. Nixon of persistent abuse of power.

The political risks were clear. Mr. Flowers leaned toward Mr. Butler at one point, and noting how near the old capital of the Confederacy was to Washington, he drawled, "You better be careful, Caldwell. Every pick-up in Richmond could be here by nightfall."

Democrats who had been assigned by Mr. Rodino to draft impeachment articles gladly consented to Mr. Mann's suggestion that the draft come instead from the coalition of centrist Republicans and Democrats. The morning of July 24, the day the first formal Presidential impeachment deliberations in 106 years were to begin, the Unholy Alliance met again in Mr. Railsback's office. At 7 P.M., barely forty-five minutes before the debate began, they finished a rough, and not totally satisfactory, draft. It was introduced that night by Representative Harold D. Donohue, Democrat of Massachusetts, who had been a fellow Navy officer with Mr. Nixon at a small base in Iowa during World War II.

Throughout the week-long debate, the coalition revised the drafts of Articles I and . . . II, and Mr. Mann shuttled with the various versions between the coalition group and the liberal Democrats working under Representative Jack Brooks of Texas. The two clusters agreed on a substitute Article I. Friday, July 26, it was introduced by Mr. Sarbanes. They agreed on a substitute Article II. Monday, July 27, it was offered by Representative Hungate.

They helped to shape, but did not all sanction, an eventual Article III—Mr. McClory's charge based on the President's defiance of committee subpoenas—and when the week was over it would be the President's men who had drafted the indictment of Mr. Nixon.

THE FRAGILITY

The alliance of the centrists and the more liberal Democrats was, as Mr. Railsback warned when some Democrats pushed unsuccessfully . . . for a fourth and a fifth article, a "fragile coalition." Twice, in fact, it had seemed on the edge of cracking.

The procedure the committee would use to decide whether to adopt articles of impeachment proved to be one of the few bitterly contested issues. Mr. Rodino and the liberal Democrats wanted to obtain maximum impact by debating Article I and then voting on it—thus casting the die for the rest of the debate—before proceeding to deliberate over Article II. But Mr. Mann told a Democratic caucus at the beginning of the week of deliberations that he had promised his group of conservatives and Republicans there would be only one set of votes, at the end of the entire debate. "If I have to vote on an article of impeachment on Friday night on prime-time television, vote on an article of impeachment on Saturday night, and then vote on an article of impeachment on Monday night," Mr. Flowers told the caucus, "by Monday there'll be trainloads of my constituents up here."

Grudgingly, Mr. Rodino agreed at the caucus to go along with the Southern Democrats and Republicans. But it did not turn out that way.

Representative Kastenmeier fumed at the approach. When the committee met late on July 23 to adopt a procedural resolution setting the form of the debate, he introduced an amendment. It proposed what the

Unholy Alliance did not want—debate and then an immediate vote on each article in turn. Mr. Rodino was alarmed. But Mr. Kastenmeier, joined by ten other liberal Democrats, was adamant. He whispered angrily to the others that conservatives and Republicans were having their way on the shape of the articles and that enough was enough.

Mr. Flowers was furious when the committee voted 21 to 16 for the Kastenmeier plan. "I thought we had lost him for good," Mr. Edwards said.

The second crisis of the fragile coalition came on Friday, during the debate on Article I. Republican opponents of impeachment complained ... that the article was unfair because it did not specify the details of the obstruction-of-justice charge, the dates, names, and events on which it was based. None of the proponents was prepared to answer the challenge.

"We were flabbergasted," Mr. Cohen recalled. He said Mr. Wiggins and the other opponents of the article "chewed us up" all day Friday, before a nationwide television audience. At a dinner recess, the Unholy Alliance gathered at the Capitol Hill Club, and some members were said to be ready to buckle unless the case could be defended fast. That night, Mr. Railsback stepped in and rattled off a string of supporting items of evidence. The next day, Mr. Doar had a long list of evidentiary citations on the desks of the Article I proponents.

On Saturday, July 27, the fourth day of debate, the President's defenders switched tactics. No longer insisting on specificity, they abandoned a set of motions to strike each of the nine sections of Article I. Mr. Flowers, determined that his constituents [should] know why he had decided to favor impeachment, took up the motions to strike his own language. The parliamentary gambit enabled Mr. Flowers and the other proponents of Article I to give a day-long recitation of the evidence they had lacked so visibly on Friday.

THE VOTE

Finally, at 7:03 P.M. that Saturday, the committee's nine-month-long anguish reached a climax. Garner J. Cline, the associate general counsel, called the roll. One after another the seven members of the Unholy Alliance voted to impeach. So, as was expected, did Mr. Hogan. And in a mild surprise, Mr. Froehlich, who had wavered all week, voted to impeach, too. Two days later, on Monday, Mr. McClory would join the centrists in voting for Article II and, on Tuesday, for Article III. The fragile coalition had held.

It was the first vote, on Saturday night, that released the pent-up agony. When the roll-call ended, at 7:05, and Article I had been adopted in a 27-to-11 vote, some on the committee sat at their places, drained.

Others went into the cloistered committee offices behind the hearing room and sobbed. . . .

In that historic moment, Kenneth R. Harding, the House sergeant-at-arms, rushed up to Mr. Rodino and said, breathlessly, "A plane has just left National Airport. . . . We had a call . . . that it's a Kamikaze flight that's going to crash into the Rayburn Building." Mr. Rodino ordered the Judiciary Committee's now-historic hearing room cleared and, in a bizarre epilogue, went to his cubbyhole office to look out the window for the Kamikaze plane.

No plane appeared. Mr. Rodino sat, as if at the wake of a friend, speaking of inconsequential things with Mr. Doar. Suddenly he rose without a word and walked from the office. And cried.

FOR FURTHER READING

Carl Bernstein and Bob Woodward. *All The President's Men.* New York: Simon & Schuster, 1974.

* *The Fall of a President* by the staff of the *Washington Post.* New York: Dell, 1974.

* *The Impeachment Report.* New York: New American Library, 1974.

Jeb Stuart Magruder. *An American Life: One Man's Road to Watergate.* New York: Atheneum, 1974.

* *The White House Transcripts.* Introduction by R. W. Apple, Jr. New York: Bantam Books, 1974.

RUNNING OUT OF EVERYTHING

SIDNEY LENS

Americans, who have traditionally enjoyed a high material standard of living, have long taken for granted a supply of goods of uncountable number and indescribable variety. During World War II they got along without new cars or washing machines and accepted rationing of butter, meat, and gasoline, but after this interruption they eagerly turned once again to buying the necessities and conveniences produced by an industrial establishment more energetic than ever before. Growth, said the economists, was the key to never-ending prosperity; in happy agreement, advertisers urged good citizens to consume to the utmost. With good conscience, therefore, Americans bought automobiles that were increasingly wasteful of gasoline, well-marbled beefsteaks, electric can-openers and similarly unessential gadgets, and air-conditioning units that they would need for only two or three months of the year. Although poor people could not readily obtain such marvels, their problem seemed to be not scarcity of goods but lack of money, and "easy" credit terms enabled many of them to join the majority of heavy consumers. Grown-ups wandered wide-eyed through shopping centers like children living a fantasy of magic and ice cream.

Few of the people thus captivated by physical objects asked where all these things came from, worried about the exhaustion of America's raw materials, or its prodigal consumption of a disproportionable share of the world's resources, or inquired into the ultimate efficiency of the corporate machine that spewed forth such abundance.

Political and intellectual developments of the 1960's and 1970's have forced Americans to consider the sources of their riches and to question the equity of the distribution system and the value of ever-expanding production. Many young members of the counterculture have explored simple communal living, and environmentalists have reminded consumers that we live in a finite and fragile ecosystem. In the 1970's Americans suddenly experienced scarcity—not voluntarily chosen, not vicariously observed in Africa or Asia, but directly. In the supermarket, such taken-for-granted items of diet as onions and raisins, for example, suddenly disappeared from the shelves. People lined up at dawn for gasoline, while utility companies raised their rates and warned that energy supplies might soon run out.

Why the shortages? Some analysts pointed to the rapidly growing world population, others to the fact, obvious but long ignored, that oil and coal reserves are limited; some denounced the countries that produced raw materials and that recently banded together to exact higher prices from industrial nations; and some, like Sidney Lens, singled out the quasi-monopolies that control much of the world economy and, echoing some little-heeded proposals of the early 1930's, called for some system of rational planning. In this article, Lens explains why we need to plan, but he leaves to the reader the question of who will do the planning, and for what ends.

□ □ □

Comedian Frank Darling says, "The way to get prices up is to tell you there's a shortage. There's a shortage of gas, a shortage of wheat, a shortage of paper—and the greatest shortage of all is the shortage of truth." One can hardly argue with this reflective observation.

The National Association of Manufacturers, not celebrated for its sense of humor, last year distributed a poster that read: "Yes, we have no bananas, steaks, eggs, blue jeans, candles, gas, tennis balls, freezers, wheat, leather, air conditioners, fuel oil, pyjamas, floor covering, sardines, chicken, paper, hot water bottles. . . ." The poster added a touch of whimsy to an increasingly unfunny problem.

The men who did Richard Nixon's economic thinking—Herbert Stein, Earl Butz, William Simon—were telling us a year ago that if we would let prices find their true higher level on the free market, we would soon have an abundant supply of everything. The dreams of these economic sages have now been partially fulfilled; prices are rising about 12 percent a year—a steeper rate than at any time since 1947. But the shortage problem is still with us. The "abundant economy" has turned, perceptibly and insistently, into a "shortage economy," though the full import of this change has not yet impressed itself on the national consciousness.

A Congressional survey of 258 major industries this August showed that 245 of them confronted shortages of at least one commodity vital to their business. Honeywell, Bell & Howell, Stokely-Van Camp, and Utah International said they were short of almost everything they needed; 108 firms were unable to get a sufficient supply of petrochemicals, 106 were buying steel on a catch-as-catch-can basis, 94 were hit by shortages in nonpetroleum chemicals, 74 could not find enough aluminum on the market, 62 lacked an adequate supply of copper. All told, the 245 corporations listed a "shortfall," to use William Simon's overworked term, of 64 commodities.

Large companies. *Business Week reported* on August 10, 1974, are "seeking alternatives for practically everything—General Foods needs a sugar substitute. Clorox has to find a replacement for soda ash in bleach and so on." Aluminum Company of America is so squeezed for raw materials that it has decided to abandon one of its most popular items, household aluminum foil, on December 31. Housewives clamor in vain for jars and tin lids to can peaches, pears, and berries; they are not available because there is a scarcity of soda ash and tin plate. Del Monte Corp., unable to purchase enough glass for jars, fiberboard for boxes, and tin plate for cans, has decided "not to get very far away from what we are doing now"—to stick to the old products, in other words, and introduce no new ones.

The most visible form of scarcity has been petroleum, because it reached most consumers, and we gradually became accustomed to long queues at the gas pumps and the melodic pleas of William Simon to conserve gasoline. But scores of other shortages disable the economy. "There isn't anything *not* in short supply," complained Inland Steel's purchasing agent recently.

The list of scarcities for part or all of this year includes paper, plastics, steel, toilets, freezers, cotton, copper wire, lumber, onions, raisins, chicken, beef, gasoline, fertilizer, propane, nylon, acetate yarns, salmon, penicillin, cortisone, cement, aluminum, vinyl, tin cans, antifreeze, paints, sporting goods, plastic lamps, and many other products. "We're experiencing something out of all dimensions to what we experienced in the past," said a senior vice president of Manufacturers Hanover Trust, "a supply slowdown." In the construction industry earlier this year the "supply slowdown"—pipe, sheet metal, plastics, reinforcing rods, paints, ceramics, and plumbing, electronic, and electrical items—cost 100,000 jobs, in addition to those lost because of the slowdown in housing purchases resulting from high interest rates and the lack of mortgage money. Every shortage led to others, affecting prices and production in mysterious ways we have never experienced before.

An obvious effect of shortages, either at the producer's or consumer's level, is that prices rise. In our peculiar form of "free market," prices seldom fall when demand is "weak," but they *always* rise when demand outpaces supply. Gasoline and every product that uses petroleum, such as plastics, went up astronomically earlier this year in cadence with a contrived shortage. The domino effect is inexorable. Soybeans, in short supply, cause a boost in soybean oil prices from thirteen cents to forty-three cents a pound, and mayonnaise, salad dressing, and many other products that use soybean oil rise accordingly. When such instances are multiplied by thousands, they account for much of our raging inflation.

The full significance of the shortage economy, however, extends far beyond its effect on prices. It is a fever chart of the basic economic and political ailments of the 1970's. It is a manifestation of a crisis—more properly, a blend of a half dozen crises—qualitatively different from anything we have ever experienced. The half dozen recessions since 1945 may have been, as the economists said, "adjustments" to rectify secondary imbalances. The current shortage-inflation-recession syndrome, on the other hand, reflects a breakdown—a breakdown of the Bretton Woods money system, the disarray of the dollar on the world market, the shattering of the *Pax Americana*. In sum, the shortage economy is a symptom of the *decline of American power*. The United States can no longer organize the world in its image, and can no longer impose the necessary *discipline* on its allies, on its satellites (such as Iran), or on its own national and multinational monopolies.

This crisis in power manifests itself in different forms at varying times—a supply slowdown, price-gouging and inflation, semi-panic on Wall Street, a credit crunch, economic pressure on Washington's allies, and above all a drop in the living standards of the American people. From the third quarter of 1972 through the second quarter of 1974 the real wages of 52 million workers in private industry fell by 8 percent—the worst decline in living standards since the Great Depression. And it is going to fall further.

The First National Bank of Chicago, which is more candid about such things than are politicians, shows how the petroleum crisis alone must lead to a drop in living standards. The oil producing nations, it says, will be exacting $60 billion a year more from oil importing nations this year than last. Since the weak economies of such producers as Saudi Arabia, Iran, Libya, and Venezuela can, at most, absorb additional purchases from the United States, Western Europe, and Japan of $10 billion or $15 billion a year, that leaves a deficit for the West of $45 or $50 billion.

"This means," said the First National Bank in its August 1974 report, "that the importing country has to expand its export of goods and services to pay for the more expensive imports. To accomplish this, some resources that would have been used to produce goods for domestic consumption will have to be channeled into the production of goods for foreign consumption (exports). This means that *consumers' real incomes must decline because there is less real output available for the domestic population.*" (Emphasis added.) The hope, of course, is that the West can borrow back that money from the oil countries, or can lure that money into the purchase of western real estate and stocks. But additional debts draw interest and must be repaid in due course, so the long-term prospect is for even worse balance of payments deficits. When the oil problem is compounded by the dollar-gold problem, the copper, bauxite, coffee, sugar, and many other similar problems, living standards in the West must fall, and the specter of depression—not recession—becomes real.

How did this situation originate? Why has a country with such monumental resources—the envy of every nation on earth—become a "land of shortage"? How did three decades of unparalleled U.S. "prosperity" come to such an abrupt halt?

The answer lies in the peculiar circumstances of that prosperity: It was built on the quicksand of militarism, and the United States now cannot survive without militarism and cannot survive with it. During World War II, national income in the United States more than doubled and the capital equipment industry, in the words of the National Planning Association, was "nearly twice the size which would be needed domestically under the most fortuitous conditions. . . ." "Free enterprise" America required a vast new market to dispose of this surplus—or face depression. But the rest of the postwar world—friend and foe alike—was in economic chaos and not far from revolution.

Washington "solved" the problem in brilliant fashion. Any nation willing to join the "American system" was given aid (some $150 billion in economic and military assistance), as well as the protection of America's military power, against internal revolution and Soviet pressure.

To prevent "disorder"—that is, revolution—the United States built the world's greatest navy, acquired 2,500 minor and major military bases abroad, stationed about a million troops overseas, and was prepared to intervene at a moment's notice against any government or force that threatened to secede from the "American system"—as it did in Korea, Vietnam, the Dominican Republic, Lebanon, the Congo, and other "trouble spots." In return for this military protection and economic aid, those who accepted the American arrangement had to pledge an "open door" for U.S. private trade and investment (as well as that of America's allies) and adherence to the Bretton Woods money system which made the dollar the international unit of exchange.

For a quarter of a century this *Pax Americana* worked tolerably well. The CIA and Pentagon intervened in dozens of countries to assure "stability," to overthrow governments it did not like, or to install right-wing forces it approved. But the cost was a shattering $1.4 trillion spent on militarism since 1945, causing budget deficits for all but three years since 1952, some of them as high as $25 billion, and an astronomical increase in the national debt. Every year but two (when there were small surpluses) America also suffered multi-billion dollar balance-of-payments deficits. Two-thirds of the U.S. gold hoard fled the country, and as of 1972 about $82 billion were floating around the world, accepted by other nations because they were allegedly as "good as gold," though they were actually much depreciated in value. Finally, in August 1971, a staggering deficit of about $25 billion loomed on the horizon. Uncle Sam's credit was no longer sound, the dollar was shaky, and the nation needed to increase exports and decrease imports to keep its ship from foundering. In this circumstance President Nixon took the drastic step of devaluing the dollar—to make U.S. goods cheaper abroad, and foreign goods more expensive here— and he instituted wage controls in an effort to hold down costs for U.S. entrepreneurs so they could remain competitive on the world market.

It seemed like a simple and decent solution—except that other nations took countermeasures, and eventually the dollar, the economic pivot of American power, had to be devalued further, then abandoned to float at whatever price it could command. Today the international money system is in chaos, with currencies rising and falling 10 or 15 percent against each other, and exporters and importers hedging sales and purchases by speculating on the currency market.

Domestically, the system of controls was a fiasco, like plugging a broken dam with a cork. The lifting of controls was just as bad. Controls led to shortages, which then accelerated inflation, and both problems survived. Neither controls nor the "free market" can cure our present sickness, for what is happening is that the tide of debt has reached our chins, and we are faced with an old mortgage to pay. We mortgaged our future to support militarism—so that we could exact discipline for the *Pax Americana*; now we must pay the mortgage by lowering our standard of living.

Thus, by a long and circuitous road, we have arrived at the shortage economy, intractable inflation, and a looming depression.

Consider these examples of how our weakened world position exacerbates the problems of supply and price:

Last year there was a shortage of many kinds of paper, including cardboard boxes, cartons for TV dinners, and, most notably, newsprint. Two large newsprint firms, Crown Zellerbach and Powell River, cut sales to their regular customers by 7 to 12 percent. Salt Lake City dailies reduced circulation by 7 percent to conserve the precious product; *The Boston Globe* cut down its comic section from twelve pages to ten; the Marshall Field papers in Chicago cut newsprint use by 10 percent, and *The New York Times* reported difficulties in obtaining paper for its magazine and book review sections. The drop in supply was coupled, as usual, with a jump in price: from 1970 to January 1974, the price of newsprint spiraled from $152 a ton to $213.50.

The paper shortage, like so many others, is mystifying to the average citizen. In 1973 it might have been attributed to the paperworkers' strike in Canada, but the strike was long over. According to the industry's trade journal, *Pulp and Paper*, there was not only a sizable rise in production in the United States, but in imports from Canada and Europe as well. Some theorists traced the problem to unconscionable "hoarding"; if true, however, that only indicates there was apprehension that supplies would run out. Why should buyers worry when production and imports were on the rise?

Their worries were justified by two circumstances, one going back to the beginning of the Cold War in 1945, the other to devaluation of the dollar and the imposition of price controls in 1971. As a result of the *Pax Americana*, industry burgeoned and capital became so concentrated, through merger and other devices, that today only 500 industrial firms account for three-quarters of industrial employment and two-thirds of sales. Under the New Capitalism our main industries—steel, rubber, autos, paper, certain foods, aluminum, electrical appliances, and others—are dominated by two to four companies each. Those companies, often interlocked with the same banking interests, conspire to *administer* prices. The Federal Trade Commission estimates that if the highly concentrated industries were broken up by antitrust action, prices in those industries (the heart of the economy) would fall by at least 25 percent. Collusion sometimes goes further. Oil companies collude to win drilling rights at low cost, or collude to drive independents from the scene, or collude to cause a shortage in order to exact concessions—such as the Alaska pipeline and relaxation of environmental standards—from the federal government.

That seems to be the case with the paper companies as well. They not only administered prices but contrived a "shortage" to exert pressure for additional cutting rights in such national forests as Tongass and Chugach in Alaska. In 1973, however, the pressure for concessions from government—perennial under the New Capitalism—was complicated by the existence of domestic price controls. International sales were not subject to controls, and the paper moguls took full advantage of this fact. In the first half of 1973, export of chips and pulp to Japan increased by 49.2 percent, reducing to that extent the stockpile at home—hence, a paper "shortage." And what was so attractive about selling to Japan? A representative of the American Paper Institute put it candidly: "other countries seem to be paying a higher price due to the Cost of Living Council's freeze on price increases."

Another perplexing group of shortages has been that of foodstuffs. Something is rotten in the wheat bins when the nation whose farmers produce two and a half times as much wheat as is consumed at home came within a whisker this year of bread shortages and bread lines similar to those in gasoline. And though that specter has momentarily receded, the long-term prospect both in bread and food generally is that deficits in supplies will come and go. The Administration, says the Community Nutrition Institute of Washington, "sooner but probably reluctantly later, will be forced to ration food."

The international balance of payments pinch dictates that we must sell more food abroad each year. What will happen, then, if we have a serious drought? If Washington, in those circumstances, reduces exports to feed the home population, America's balance of payments position will worsen and we will be unable to import such items as bauxite and copper; if, on the other hand, Washington insists that export commitments must be met, we will have dire shortages —and perhaps hunger—at home.

A new factor has been added to the equation, for the food industry, contrary to conventional wisdom, is also dominated by monopolies. According to the Federal Trade Commission staff, seventeen food and food-related industries are so concentrated that they are "producing an overcharge to consumers of more than $2.5 billion." Government studies indicate that three companies sell two-thirds of processed dairy products; four firms dominate 70 percent of the cracker and biscuit market; four firms take care of three-quarters of bread and processed flour sales; three firms handle 85 percent of breakfast cereals; six firms have 90 percent of the grain sales overseas, and one firm has 90 percent of the soups.

Moreover, a quarter of all food production is "vertically integrated" —big companies control production from the farm to the retail market, and are able to manipulate supply and the cost to consumers almost at will. And the food industry is falling under the aegis of conglomerates which have invaded it for tax shelter and other reasons. As William Robbins reveals in *The American Food Scandal*, the turkey for your Thanksgiving dinner may be produced by Greyhound, your ham by ITT, lettuce by Dow Chemical, potatoes by Boeing, fruits and vegetables by Tenneco, and fruit juice by Coca-Cola. If new price controls were imposed, as they might have to be to check inflation, the conglomerates which tower over the industry would not hesitate to boost their exports—at higher foreign prices—even while Americans went hungry.

Then there is the bewildering situation in the meat markets. By December 1973 hamburger was selling at about a dollar a pound, a whopping 28 percent more than in January. The reason, according to the Department of Agriculture, was that farmers brought two million fewer cattle to market than the previous year—lower supply, higher price. But that explanation begged the question: Why did the cattlemen reduce their herds? The answer lies in the realm of foreign relations and international trade. For both political and economic reasons, the United States sold a vast amount of grain to the Russians, causing an imbalance in the supply of feed grain at home, hence a boost in feed grain prices, hence a boost in the cost of producing a pound of beef, hence the withdrawal of marginal producers unable to earn an adequate return.

Concurrently there was the collapse of the dollar and devaluation. The dollar became cheap currency for Japanese, Swiss, and German buyers—the same number of yen, francs, and marks brought considerably more dollars and therefore considerably more grain or cattle. As foreign importers rushed to buy American foodstuffs—U.S. exports went up from $8 billion annually to $20 billion within two years—the end result was shortages and higher prices at home.

The most insidious shortage of the whole shortage economy, of course, is the one in energy, and particularly in petroleum. Here all the dilemmas of American capitalism coalesce: We need a safe supply of oil not only for our economy but for our vast military machine. Under the profit maximization system, our Government is unwilling or unable to check the greed of the seven oil corporations, five of them American, which constitute a tight world cartel. But as the Seven Sisters contrive shortages and inflate prices, all the economies of the western world, dependent on the Seven Sisters for their fuel, totter. Each country seeks to repair its balance of payments difficulties at the expense of the others—through devaluations, floating of currency, trade restrictions, unilateral deals with the Russians, Chinese, and Arabs, and other makeshift devices. The fabric of the *Pax Americana*, already severely strained, shreds further.

In this state of weakness and confusion, the "terms of trade" between the advanced nations and the weak oil-producing countries have been totally reversed. Who would have predicted eighteen months ago that a barrel of oil that costs eleven cents to produce in Saudi Arabia would be selling on the world market for $10 to $12, three or four times its previous price, or that the oil-producing nations would be *draining away* from the big western powers an additional $60 billion each year? Twenty years ago, under these circumstances, the United States (or Britain) would have occupied Saudi Arabia and Iran. Indeed, twenty years ago the U.S. Central Intelligence Agency organized a coup d'etat against the Mossadegh government in Iran because it had nationalized the oil industry, against London's and Washington's wishes. Now the United States would have to run over the Soviet navy or face endless guerrilla warfare, as in Vietnam, if it chose to take such action. In light of these realities, more and more weak nations can be expected to assert control over their own resources and do what the great powers have done for centuries—charge whatever the market will bear.

By now everyone is acquainted with the raw facts of the energy crisis. The United States consumes 6.5 billion barrels of oil and 22 trillion cubic feet of natural gas a year—monstrous quantities that will eventually exhaust the subsoil. But that time is still remote, for according to the U.S. Geological Survey there are proven and suspected (but as yet undiscovered) reserves of 500 billion barrels of oil and 2,400 trillion cubic feet of natural gas, enough for many decades. The energy is there, but it is not being properly tapped and, in the case of oil, not being refined in sufficient quantities in the United States.

In 1973 not a single major refinery was built in this country, and in the previous five years only enough to refine 1.9 million more barrels a day, though demand swelled by three million. Why is there a "refinery gap"? M. A. Wright, chief executive officer of Exxon, was disarmingly frank before a Congressional committee: "It is a problem of how much people want to pay for it [oil]. If they want to pay enough for it to make the market profitable in Europe, sure, we will sell it there. We are in business. . . ." From 1963 to 1972, the five largest companies increased crude oil production in the United States by 45 percent, but outside the United States—where it was more profitable—by 97 percent. The shift in refining was even more drastic, going up only 34 percent in the Western Hemisphere and 176 percent in the Eastern Hemisphere.

Such manipulation of the oil market, and through the oil market of national economies, is possible only because the U.S. Government helped the Seven Sisters become the largest cartel in history. For "national security" reasons—where have we heard that rationale before?—the State Department has since 1950 openly encouraged the five American firms and their British and Dutch partners to function as a tight cartel—aided, abetted, and protected by U.S. diplomacy and military power. Without that power American firms would never have gained their original oil concessions in Latin America and Canada; other foreign companies could enter this hemisphere only on sufferance of the State Department. Subsequently, State performed the same service for the U.S. firms in the Persian Gulf states, Africa, and Asia— in tune with U.S. economic and military aid. Nations that granted concessions received economic aid and military protection; those that did not were fortunate if the CIA refrained from overthrowing their governments.

The vise in which the Great Powers now find themselves, euphemistically called the "energy crisis," thus began with the formation of a Washington-sponsored world monopoly. It was tightened before and after the Yom Kippur war in the Middle East last year, when the oil producing nations suddenly realized their bargaining strength and doubled and redoubled the price of their product. Moreover, while the Seven Sisters were also exacting their pound of flesh, the oil nations took advantage of the Middle East war forcibly to buy up some of the foreign company holdings on their soil.

Thus a schism developed among the three actors in the drama— the United States and its allies (the consumer states), the Seven Sisters, and the producing nations. The producer states gained substantially. The Seven Sisters were hurt minimally—they lost some control over the extractive end of the industry, but remain a multinational monopoly in shipping, refining, and marketing; they will recover the extra royalties and taxes they must pay the producing nations—and more—from reductions in their U.S. taxes. According to Stanley H. Ruttenberg, a former assistant Secretary of Labor, the jump in oil from $1.90 to $8.30 a barrel increased tax credits for the American corporations at home from $1.13 to $5.56 a barrel, a "hardship" Exxon, Texaco, and the others can live with.

Only the consumer states lost heavily—though the United States lost least of all because more than two-thirds of its oil comes from domestic sources. The western world (including Japan) is now weighted down with a balance of payments problem that is not amenable to solution without slashing standards of living. The Nixon-Ford proposal to achieve energy "independence" by 1980 is a pipe dream. Thornton Bradshaw, president of Atlantic Richfield, points out that the United States can, at best, reduce its dependence on foreign oil by 1980 from 18 percent to 15 percent of its needs, but even that only through the huge expenditure of $50 billion a year for the next decade.

In effect, the "energy crisis" is a manifestation of a world-wide change in political fortunes: The socialist countries are growing stronger, and they can offer the Third World increasing diplomatic, economic, and military support; the Third World is beginning to feel a sense of growing control over its own destiny, and the Great Powers are in obvious decline.

A chart of the rise and fall of American power, which the shortage economy now punctuates, would look something like this:

1. From 1945 to 1965, steady growth; American foreign investments doubling, redoubling, and then redoubling again; living standards rising dramatically.

2. From 1965 to 1971, coincident with the Vietnam war and other crises, the gradual appearance of the credit crunch and all the problems associated with balance of payments deficits.

3. From August 1971 to the 1973 Yom Kippur war, the first clear evidence of a turnabout in international political power, and the consequent turnabout in economic fortune.

4. From the Yom Kippur war to the present, a "free world" in traumatic decline that can only end either in a "managed" reduction of living standards in the West or in a dreadful, unmanaged depression. Italy and Britain are already only a few steps from such a depression, and are thinking in terms of the kind of "austerity"—lower consumption levels—they were forced to adopt during World War II.

In this state of political decline, a capitalist America (and its allies) cannot avoid further economic pressure. What the economists call "terms of trade" are turning against the United States not only in oil, but in many other commodities. In the era of imperialism, the terms of trade were a means by which the advanced countries robbed the underdeveloped ones. While Colombian coffee, for instance, was going down from eighty cents to forty-five cents a pound in the late 1950s and early 1960s, the price of a Chevrolet was going up—it took much more coffee in Bogota to buy a Chevy from Detroit. A tractor made by Ford, the Major, could be bought by a Uruguayan national in 1954 for the equivalent of twenty-two young bulls; in 1963 it cost the equivalent of forty-two young bulls. The underdeveloped countries were in constant hock to the developed ones, forced to borrow more and more to keep afloat.

Now this process is being reversed. "Oil," said *The New York Times* on January 27, 1974, "is just the beginning, for three reasons. First, the lesson of this startling reversal of power seems obvious for other countries with key primary products: Band together and your revenues can rise dramatically. Second, higher oil prices force the other primary producers to increase their own export earnings to pay for their oil needs. Third, OPEC [Organization of Petroleum Exporting Countries] itself appears ready to support the formation of other cartels, as the one way to avoid opprobrium for bankrupting the "developing countries."

The danger is that the four countries that control the supply of copper (Chile, Peru, Zaire, and Zambia), now joined together, will be doing the same things as the petroleum producing nations. The price of copper went up from 53 cents a pound in July 1973 to $1 in December. Five bauxite countries (Australia, Guinea, Guyana, Jamaica, Surinam), four nations that control natural rubber, and four that account for virtually all the tin exports may raise prices and create synthetic shortages in the near future. U.S. pressures may prevent concerted action here and there, but in the long run it will take place anyway, both because American power is limited and on the wane, and because, as the price of gold increases (it is now four times what it was in 1972), the inflationary pull becomes irresistible.

The economists of the Nixon and Ford Administrations are reacting to the shortage economy and inflation as if they were traditional problems, requiring only "adjustments" such as those that adjusted our six postwar "recessions"—monetary manipulation, fiscal changes, tax incentives, and the like. According to one of Nixon's former economic advisers, Paul W. McCracken, the cause of our troubles is that "we obviously have run out of plant capacity before we have run out of employable labor." Thus if we can "cool down" the economy, so that demand drops and steel companies can again operate at, say, 85 percent of capacity instead of 95 percent, all will be well again. Inflation will abate, and shortages will disappear as people buy less. If there is unemployment, the Government can provide a few hundred thousand public service jobs and increase jobless compensation. Such prescriptions have already proven themselves naive, for the economy *has* "cooled down"—we are in a recession—yet inflation shows little sign of slackening, nor are the shortages disappearing. And if the economy cools down much further, we may check inflation only to find a steep rise in unemployment.

President Ford, whose geniality temporarily obscures his Nixonite philosophy, is preparing to perform the feat of the century. He tells us he will reduce inflation without attacking its two major causes—military spending, which contributes nothing to the consumer economy and withdraws many billions of dollars, and monopoly, which incessantly fuels the inflationary fire. This is the kind of "Band-Aid" economics and diplomacy that brought us to our present despair.

The shortage economy tells us that Keynesian capitalism, which patched up the planless economy through deficit spending for forty years, has exhausted its potential and its usefulness. The *Pax Americana*, which organized the planet around the goals of the American military-industrial complex, is similarly passing into oblivion. We cannot live endlessly by going deeper into debt or by exploiting the peoples of other nations. We must learn to live by our own labor and ingenuity.

The shortage economy tells us that capitalism is in decline as a viable economic system, that it can only plunge us into depressions, international trade wars, monetary conflicts, and military confrontations. Not only radicals, but many populists and liberals as well, now recognize what Charles Beard and John Dewey told us in the 1930s— that our only salvation lies in a planned economy. Dean Acheson hinted at that back in November 1944, when he said that under another system—that is, socialism—the United States could adjust without being concerned with foreign markets, but that under our present capitalist system it could not have "full employment and prosperity" unless it found some way to dispose of its giant surpluses. The internal market of the nation can be controlled and shaped by the Government, which has political and police power to enforce its will; but the international market is something else again—here 150 or so sovereignties clash with one another, and there are no means to control them short of war, the threat of war, or the *Pax Americana* discipline the United States was able to exact for a quarter of a century.

Under a planned economy, by contrast with the so-called free economy, the Government could plan the allocation of resources to meet the needs of our people. It could begin by calculating a realistic balance of trade and money accounts around the world, and then determine how our $1.4 trillion gross national product should be apportioned after allowance is made for the outward flow.

An American planned economy in which the resources were put at the people's command would not be nearly so dependent on monetary and trade gyrations abroad. It could reorder its priorities to meet human needs rather than the greeds of private monopoly. Having determined that it requires so much for exports and can expect so much from imports and so much from its money accounts, the Government could proceed to set the level for minimum and maximum living standards. By controlling foreign trade through a state monopoly it could free itself from decisive dependence on such trade. Its surpluses could be channeled inward to improve living standards, and its factories could be redirected to meet the actual needs of people rather than the artificial demands induced to enhance private profits.

By slashing the $90 billion-a-year war budget and the 2,500 military bases it maintains abroad, the nation could attain a degree of prosperity and stability never known before. Instead of the tail (foreign trade, private monopoly) wagging the dog, the dog could finally wag its own tail. The shortage economy is a warning that we disregard at our peril, and it is an opportunity that must be seized.

FOR FURTHER READING

A. J. Culyer, ed. *Economic Policies and Social Goals: Aspects of Public Choice.* New York: St. Martin's, 1975.

Irving S. Friedman. *Inflation—A World-Wide Disaster.* Garden City, N.Y.: Doubleday, 1975.

Peter Hill and Roger Vielvoye. *Energy In Crisis.* New York: Drake, 1975.

Seymour Melman. *American Capitalism in Decline: The Cost of a Permanent War Economy.* New York: Simon & Schuster, 1974.

Louis Turner. *Multinational Corporations and the Third World.* New York: Hill & Wang, 1975.